GOLDA

OTHER BOOKS BY RALPH G. MARTIN

A Hero for Our Time: An Intimate Story of the Kennedy Years

*Jennie: The Life of Lady Randolph Churchill—
The Romantic Years: 1854–1895*

*Jennie: The Life of Lady Randolph Churchill—
The Dramatic Years: 1895–1921*

Cissy

The Woman He Loved: The Story of the Duke and Duchess of Windsor

Skin Deep—A Novel

Boy from Nebraska

The Best Is None Too Good

The Bosses

Ballots and Bandwagons

*World War II: A Photographic Record of the War in the Pacific from
Pearl Harbor to V-J Day*

The Wizard of Wall Street

The G.I. War

A Man for All People

Lincoln Center for the Performing Arts

President from Missouri—A Juvenile

Charles and Diana

WITH ED PLAUT:
Front Runner, Dark Horse

WITH MORTON D. STONE:
Money, Money, Money

WITH RICHARD HARRITY:
Eleanor Roosevelt: Her Life in Pictures
The Human Side of FDR
Man of the Century: Winston Churchill
Man of Destiny: Charles De Gaulle
The Three Lives of Helen Keller
*World War II: A Photographic Record of the War in Europe from
D-Day to V-E Day*

G O L D A

Golda Meir:
The Romantic Years

Ralph G. Martin

CHARLES SCRIBNER'S SONS

New York

The author gratefully acknowledges permission from the following sources to reprint material in their control:

Adler & Adler for material from *Memoirs of a Fortunate Jew* by Dan Vittorio Segre, copyright © 1985 by Gruppo Editoriale Fabbri, Bompiani Sonzogono, Etas Sp.A. English-language translation copyright © 1987 by Dan Vittorio Segre.

Judy Bauman for material from *Zichronot*, written by Shana Korngold, published 1968 by Idpress, Tel Aviv.

Harper & Row, Publishers, for material from *Exile and Return* by Martin Gilbert, copyright © 1976 by Martin Gilbert.

Midstream and *Pioneer Woman* for material from "My First Days in Kibbutz Merhavia" by Golda Meir.

The Putnam Publishing Group for material from *My Life* by Golda Meir, copyright © 1975 by Golda Meir.

Reconstructionist Press for material from *White Fire: The Life and Works of Jessie Sampter* by Bertha Badt-Strauss, copyright © 1956 by The Jewish Reconstructionist Foundation, Inc.

Shikmona Publishing Co., Jerusalem, for material from *Pillar of Fire* by Yigal Lossin, copyright © 1983 by Keter Publishing House, Jerusalem.

Charles Scribner's Sons
Macmillan Publishing Company
866 Third Avenue, New York, NY 10022
Collier Macmillan Canada, Inc.

Library of Congress Cataloging-in-Publication Data
Martin, Ralph G., date.
Golda / Ralph G. Martin.
p. cm.
Bibliography: p.
Includes index.
ISBN 0-684-19017-6
1. Meir, Golda, 1898–1978. 2. Prime ministers—Israel—Biography.
3. Zionists—Biography. I. Title.
DS126.6.M42M32   1988
956.94'053'0924—dc19   88-17004   CIP   [B]

Macmillan books are available at special discounts for bulk purchases for sales promotions, premiums, fund-raising, or educational use. For details, contact:
Special Sales Director
Macmillan Publishing Company
866 Third Avenue
New York, NY 10022

10 9 8 7 6 5 4 3 2 1
Designed by Nancy Sugihara
Printed in the United States of America

*This book is dedicated to my dear daughter Tina
who made herself a part of it from the very beginning
with her superb research and her shared excitement*

Preface

It all began when I was a young reporter aboard a rickety Greek ship going from Naples to Haifa with a cargo of refugees from all over the world. They had been shunted from camp to camp, from country to country, but they still talked more about tomorrow's hope than yesterday's horror. All they wanted was to stop running. All they wanted was a home in their homeland. You could see them every morning packed in the bow of the boat, straining for first sight of "Eretz Yisroel," the Land of Israel. And then, tears, cheers, hysterical laughter, rhythmic clapping of hands, spontaneous singing, forming a circle to whirl round and round, faster and faster, in the traditional ecstatic dance of the hora.

The hard reality ashore was a state not yet a year old offering them short rations and cold tents and the phrase "In Israel, the person who does not believe in miracles is not a realist."

"Don't worry," people told me with a warm glow in their eyes. "Our Golda will take care of these refugees."

What piqued me then, what stayed with me, was the wonder: who was this "our Golda" (Golda *shelanu*), who could stir such feelings in people?

All I vaguely knew was that she had been a Milwaukee schoolteacher, caught by a cause, who had come here as a young woman to work the earth with her hands. She was soon running the country. When the

British had imprisoned most Jewish leaders in Palestine several years before, it was Golda who became the effective leader of the Yishuv, the entire Jewish community. She made all major decisions of life and death. She was then still in her forties. That's when she became "our Golda."

In the course of years, I watched her grow into greatness. She had remarkable poise, dignity, without awe of anyone, presidents or popes. When she spoke as the voice of her people, she used short words and simple sentences, but they had a way of pulling at your emotions. I was not surprised when polls picked her as the most important woman in the world, one of the outstanding women of our century.

What surprised me, flabbergasted me, was that there had never been a full biography of this woman, not even in Hebrew. Her autobiography had been ghostwritten—Golda too busy even to read the manuscript. There had been a memoir by a friend, another by her son, some books for teenagers, several pictorial biographies, and little else.

That's when I decided to write this book. It was not easy. In this small country of Israel, where gossip is almost as basic as groceries, Golda somehow had managed to keep her private life so private that even her family and closest friends knew only fragments.

To be a biographer, someone said, one must be both a detective and a dramatist. That's true. The way I work is to start with archives—letters, papers, speeches, documents, diaries, oral history, passports, book references, government reports, memos, recorded interviews, pertinent articles, everything. My archival material for this book concerned not only Golda but those closest to her. I also had to understand what Kiev was like when she was born there, what kind of fun she had in her Milwaukee neighborhood, the scene in Palestine when she first arrived. Besides the many invaluable archival sources in Israel, there were similar treasure troves in New York, Washington, D.C., Milwaukee, Chicago, Denver, California, Baltimore, Bridgeport, London, Cairo, and many other places. Supplementing them were private files of scrapbooks, photographs, videotapes. They filled four of my filing cabinets.

Once I read everything, I felt qualified to interview people in depth. I began with those at the rim of her life, edging toward those who knew her best. This included hundreds of people and took several years. What gratified me was not only that so many were still alive, but that they were so eager to talk. A friend's daughter who had witnessed Golda's courtship in Chicago; a young man who had shared her apartment for years while he went to school; the president of Israel who had served as her intelligence chief during the siege of Jerusalem; a woman who had prepared Golda's Arab costume for her secret meeting with King Abdullah; a confidante privy to Golda's serious thoughts about suicide; and Golda's last lover.

The great gold came from people at the hub of her life: her most intimate friend, who had spent more time inside Golda's soul than anyone; her daughter, who had gone with her to Moscow, but confided that she and her mother never had a single, long, intimate conversation; the son of Golda's first and primary lover, who had marvelous memories and incredible love letters; her closest companion, who traveled with her everywhere and had a tape-recorder mind; her oldest friend, who helped her run away from home when she was fourteen, and remembered everything vividly as if it were yesterday.

There is something magical in researching her childhood, knowing that this was a child of destiny. You search for the first signs of evolving character and personality. Anger and rebellion when forced to work in her mother's grocery store. Compassion and determination, when she was still a child, organizing a recital to raise money to buy books for poor schoolchildren. The brassy kind of courage, real *chutzpah*, of a teenager planning a parade into downtown Milwaukee to protest pogroms in Europe. Feisty independence at sixteen, leaving her sister's home in Denver to find her own room and job—because her sister had berated her for having too many late dates.

By this time, Golda had become so alive to me that she could have walked into my room and I would know what she might be wearing, what she would probably say, and even what she was thinking. How can I make anyone come alive to anybody else if she is not alive to me?

I once spent seven years of my life writing *Jennie*, a biography of Winston Churchill's mother. The night after writing about Jennie's death, we had dinner with friends. That night I felt ill, presuming it was something in the food. The next day, in my barn, polishing the chapter about her death, I felt ill again, then realized what it was. I had spent seven years of my life with Jennie, and I didn't want her to die!

I felt the same way about Golda. Take the face on the book jacket. I found it in a group family photograph, and it haunted me. The determined thrust of her chin, the challenging look in her eyes, and her loveliness.

That was the single great surprise for me in this book—Golda's beauty as a young woman. That full firm figure, the long lustrous hair, the magnetic sparkle, the way she threw her head back when she laughed. One could quickly understand why so many men chased her and wanted her. History has created the myth that Golda was tough, purely pragmatic. David Ben-Gurion had called her "the only man in my cabinet." She had the steel when it was wanted. But beneath the steel was poetry, music, romance. Her letters to her lover—after her marriage had disintegrated—were the greatest revelation of all to me. They were letters of such tenderness, passion, longing, loneliness—a side of Golda almost nobody knew.

The men she fell in love with were men of power, the pioneering giants of her time. They had opened doors for her, pushed her career, but she still had to prove herself, again and again. And she did. In this tight society, managed by men, she was the only woman, the only American, to break into their inner circle.

Of her private life, Golda once admitted, "I was no nun." She was also no saint. Her critics were many and there were black holes in her life. But this was a woman who lived in a state of emergency, paid her dues, earned her greatness.

Out of her strength, she helped create a nation; out of her spirit, she helped mold a people. If Israel had a voice in the world, it was the voice of Golda.

When Golda was dying, her final firm words were "The truth must be told."

And that is the challenge of my book.

1

Stretching from the Black Sea to the Baltic, the Pale of Settlement contained most of czarist Russia's five million Jews. Most of them lived in tiny villages called *shtetls* or in carefully controlled ghettos in towns. At the turn of this century, Pinsk was an improbable place. It was improbable not only because it was one of those rare towns with an overwhelming majority of Jews, but because it was full of creative ferment—writers, scholars, political firebrands. A grocer impressed a visitor by reciting "by heart" a poem by Schiller. A touring rabbi expressed amazement that some Pinskers could present, with equal fervor, the case of the religious Jew and "the licentious freethinker." "A wise man hears one word," said the Pinsk proverb, "and understands two."

Pinsk, just before 1900, was a ramshackle town of rickety wooden houses on narrow, twisted streets sitting at the edge of a swamp near two rivers, the Pina and the Pripet. In an ancient age, it had belonged to the prince of Kiev. The first flow of Jews had arrived from Lithuania about the time Christopher Columbus discovered America.

It was a prosperous place, a marketing center near the Baltic ports. Jews had built schools, synagogues, factories. At Jewish factories, whistles blew early Friday afternoon to permit workers to hurry home and prepare for the Sabbath. The 21,965 Jews then made up three-fourths of the population, but the Russians still ruled.

Menachem Naiditch shared in the prosperity. A man of energy and enterprise, he owned a two-story tavern, part of a long row of inns lining the road to the Dnieper River. Of his six children, Bluma was the most willful. At a time when almost all marriages were arranged by a *shadchen*, a matchmaker, pretty, redheaded Bluma made her own choice. Sighting a tall, handsome stranger on the street, she promptly found out who he was, breathlessly told her parents that this was the man she wanted to marry.

His name was Moshe Yitzhak Mabovitch, fresh from army service, a former yeshiva student at Slonim, less than 100 miles from Pinsk. Most yeshiva students were poor, migrating from home to home, fed by charitable families, occasionally sleeping on school benches. A song about such students noted how "they swallowed tears." Respect for such scholars was deep, and families often sent sons to study the Talmud at the tender age of three. A touch of honey was put on the first page of the first Talmud lesson to sweeten the long, almost savage learning process. In making a suitable marriage, many families considered brains more important than money. Piety was another badge of honor. It was a family fact of distinction that Moshe's father served thirteen years in the Russian army and never ate any cooked meat, because it wasn't kosher. So pious was he that after his army discharge he slept on a synagogue bench with a stone for a pillow to atone for any unwitting sins he might have committed. He died young.

Pious men, lost in the spiritual mazes, needed earthy, practical women to keep their world going. Moshe's mother, Tzipka, was such a woman, best known for her neatness and her tendency to take charge.

Bluma's grandmother Buba Golda, was also such a woman, described then as "the man in the family." The Russian word *buba* means "grandmother." A tall, thin, stubborn, bossy woman, she told everyone exactly what to do. She was decisive in the family's acceptance of Moshe as Bluma's bridegroom. "What matters most of all," she said, "is whether or not he's a *mensch*, a person of integrity."

Moshe was not only a *mensch* but a skilled carpenter. He was, however, "innocent and confiding," and needed Bluma, who was "more enterprising" and also had "a man's head." Both were "born optimists . . . very sociable."

As part of the traditional dowry, Moshe could eat free at his in-laws' for two years. That house was already so overflowing that beds were laid out in a T-formation, even in the kitchen, with several people in a bed. Nobody went hungry, but the usual food was bread and onions dipped in salt, beans mixed with potatoes, and perhaps a little meat or fish on the Sabbath.

Moshe and Bluma lived in a small, smoky room until their first child, Shana, was born. They then decided to move to Kiev, where there was a greater need for carpenters. Since Kiev was outside the Pale of Settlement, Jews needed a special permit to live there. This meant a government exam to prove a needed skill. Moshe proved it by making an exquisite chess table.

Tourists called Kiev "a doll of a city." It perched like a jewel on hilly bluffs overlooking the majestic Dnieper River, close to the Carpathian Mountains. Kiev had broad boulevards and magnificent mansions, but Moshe and Bluma and Shana Mabovitch lived in a dark, damp room on the city's fringe. No Russian city had a greater history of hateful anti-Semitism. Kiev Jews lived with fear in their bones. For hundreds of years, again and again, Kiev Jews were attacked, massacred, expelled. In the early seventeenth century, King Sigismund III had declared that "holy Kiev" with its 400 churches was "profaned by the presence of Jews." Even much later, Jewish traders were allowed in the city for a single day in the year, but only if they stayed at an assigned inn.

Despite the double taxation and tight control, highly skilled Jews eventually prospered. Kiev Jews had built a beautiful synagogue, a famous hospital specializing in surgery and eye diseases, and even a Jewish theater. A prominent Jew refused to open a bank when told that all his directors must be Christian. A petition circulated at the time to expel all special-permit Jews. The governor of Kiev, General Levashoff, explained his reluctance: ". . . their expulsion would not only lead to an enhancement of prices of many products and articles, but it would not be possible to obtain them at all."

Moshe and Bluma had five other children in the next nine years, a girl and four boys. All of them died. When their second child, Sarele, had smallpox, the Polish doctor told Bluma to go to the cemetery and light candles. When an infant son had a bad cold, the treatment involved rubbing hard with turpentine and grease, then wrapping him tightly in an old sheet. The fumes asphyxiated him.

"Don't worry," consoled Buba Golda. "God gave and God took. God will give you another son."

There were three other sons and they all died in their early years, two of typhoid fever within a month of each other.

When Bluma felt most bitter, she would say of her children, "God took all the good ones and look what he left me!"

Just before Buba Golda died at the age of ninety-four, she gave final orders: wash her body, put her in a clean dress, say the proper prayer. According to an ancient custom, the family took the dead great-grandmother's hand and put it on Shana's body to give her long life.

Soon afterward, on May 3, 1898, Bluma gave birth to another daughter, Golda, the namesake of her bossy great-grandmother.

With all the deaths of their children, Bluma was suddenly highly conscious of sanitation. At Golda's birth, Bluma and Moshe felt they could finally afford the help of a white-robed midwife. Bluma even washed Golda three times a week. Moshe's mother, Buba Tzipka, moved in with them; her fanatical neatness was to prompt Bluma to greater cleanliness.

Shana recalled that Goldie—which everyone called her—"was a very pretty baby but very stubborn and very noisy." Bluma prepared a pacifier for her by chewing on a piece of white bread with a little sugar, folding it into a piece of fabric, and letting Goldie suck on it.

This was the year of the Dreyfus case.* The noted author Émile Zola was then jailed for writing "J'Accuse," a pamphlet denouncing the French army command for anti-Semitism, for forging documents that would betray a Captain Dreyfus. They had accused him of being a spy, stripped him of his military rank in a humiliating public ceremony. In reporting the story, a Paris correspondent of a Vienna newspaper, a bushy-bearded, intense, handsome Hungarian named Theodor Herzl, wrote of the French crowds yelling "Death to the Jews!"

A Jew himself, Herzl had always believed that Jews could and should be assimilated into their different nations. The Dreyfus case changed his mind. It did not matter that Dreyfus was later reinstated with full honors. The cry "Death to the Jews!" had convinced Herzl that Jews needed their own homeland. "We are one people," Herzl wrote. "Our

---

*Alfred Dreyfus (1859–1935) was the only Jew on the French General Staff, in his time. Accused and convicted of being a traitor, he was later completely exonerated and reinstated in the army.

enemies have made us one. . . . Distress binds us together." This became his dream of Zionism.

Goldie had two sharp memories of her first five years in Kiev: hunger and fear. The hunger in their home was sour and deep. Moshe built beautiful ornamental furniture and one of the first iceboxes in Kiev. He then borrowed money to make a wagonload of samples in a bid to make school furniture. They liked his work, but not his Jewish name, and they kept his samples without payment. He was afraid to demand his money because they might revoke his special permit.

From what she remembered and what she was told, Goldie recalled "how desperately" her father looked for work. "He would be out all day and much of the night, and when he came home in the bitter dark of a Russian winter, there was rarely enough food in the house to make him a meal. . . . If there was salt herring on the table, that was a red-letter day." It was a feast when Bluma made potato pancakes. The usual meal was bread and potatoes.

There was no meal without the potato, and no limit to its use and versatility. Women considered it a gift and a challenge. "For each meal, they looked different and tasted different. Sliced, browned, and cooked, it was there. The main flavor was onion, but once in a great while there was an added spoonful of chicken fat."

"From my older sister's stories," said Golda years later, "I knew how often she went to school without eating—she would faint from hunger in school.

"One picture is engraved in my memory. When my younger sister, Tzipka, four years my junior, was still a baby, six months or less, my mother was cooking porridge, a great luxury for us in those days. My mother gave me a little and the rest to my baby sister. She finished eating before me; then mother took a little porridge away from me to give to her. I remember the shock at being deprived of this rare porridge. Even now I can still summon up, almost intact, the picture of myself sitting in tears in the kitchen."

Reflecting on it, Golda added, "I was always a little too cold outside and a little too empty inside."

The great Jewish storyteller Sholem Aleichem, who also came from Kiev, wrote about a very holy, very poor man who died and went to heaven. He had been so saintly in his life that the angels told him he could have anything he wanted. He hesitated. They pressed him to name something, anything, and he finally said quietly, "I would like a warm roll and butter."

"In the world there is a czar without pity," wrote the poet Mekrossov. "Hunger is his name."

Then there was the fear.

Czarist Russia recorded 5,063,000 Jews in the census of 1897. In expelling Jews from Moscow in 1891, the czar set the anti-Semitic tone for the country: "We must not forget that it was the Jews who crucified our Lord and spilled his priceless blood." Russian anti-Semitism wasn't simply a national heritage. It was part of the political need for a scapegoat to divert the public mind from their poverty.

The propaganda tool was the so-called blood libel. This was the horrendous lie that Jews used the blood of Christian children during Passover. There is no blood in the Passover service. But a typical quatrain that inspired pogroms was:

The Jew sells the child to the devil
And gives the devil his soul
The devil pays in gold
The child he will later devour.

The depth of this ingrained belief is difficult to imagine. It has been absorbed, accepted, repeated in world history. No amount of denial could ever utterly wipe it out. Printed handbills even granted permission to inflict "bloody punishment on the Jews."

The word "pogrom" technically meant "storm." To Jews, though, it meant mobs, looting, rape, murder, and organized massacre. A memorandum from Minister of Police Von Plehve to the governor of Bessarabia in 1881 advised, "Let our boys have some fun with the Jews."

Part of the fun included attacking the caravans of peasants and their wagons, and carrying away the loot. Drunken hordes found more sadistic fun in breaking into synagogues and tearing to shreds the sacred Torah scrolls.

The pogrom prelude in Kiev was the *oblavy*, an official manhunt for Jews without a permit. It was often done in the middle of the night, house to house, with violence and looting. To twist the knife, Jews were taxed double to pay for the expense of the *oblavy*. Some compared it to the convict forced to buy the rope that would hang him. In another

Sholem Aleichem story, the landlady warns Jewish tenants of a coming *oblavy* "so that we have a chance to melt away like salt on the water."

Golda's most dreaded memory that she retold again and again happened when she was four years old:

"We lived then on the first floor of a small house, and I can still recall distinctly hearing about a pogrom that was to descend on us. I didn't know then, of course, what a pogrom was, but I knew it had something to do with being Jewish and with the rabble that used to surge through town, brandishing knives and huge sticks, screaming 'Christ-killers' as they looked for Jews, and who now were going to do terrible things to me and my family."

One little girl told of her Christian friend's advice to paint a cross on her door to divert the crowd. Another told of a family putting liquor on a table in front of their house so the mob would get drunk and leave them alone. A woman wanted to bury all the knives and scissors so the mob could not use them for weapons. In pogroms where Jews tried to protect themselves, soldiers dispersed them "at the point of the bayonet . . . driving them indoors to await the drunk-crazed rioters."

Goldie watched the panic and listened to the wailing of the grown women. In the frightened face of her father, all she saw was helplessness. What she didn't understand, she later said, "was what a futile effort my father was making to keep people out of the house who were bent on killing Jews. . . .

"It was characteristic of my father that he made no attempt to hide his family. There were stairs in the entry, leading to a neighbor on the second floor. I can remember how I stood on the stairs together with a neighbor's daughter of about my own age, holding hands, watching our fathers trying to barricade the entrance by nailing boards across the door. I can hear the sound of that hammer now, and I can see the children standing in the streets wide-eyed, not making a sound, watching the nails being driven in." She later added, "I remember how scared I was, and how angry."

That pogrom never happened, but Goldie never forgot her fear and her anger. It was a fear and an anger that helped shape her life.

Later she would say, "If there is any logical explanation . . . for the direction which my life has taken . . . [it is] the desire and determination to save Jewish children . . . from a similar experience." Discussing Russian pogroms in those early years, she added that pogroms were possible anywhere. "It doesn't matter where it will be—it is the same story, the same story." She would often say, "I have a pogrom complex—I have to plead guilty."

In the two years before 1903 there were some 690 reported pogroms. Only occasionally was any Russian ever arrested for anti-Jewish activity. One such Ukrainian peasant protested in court, "They told us we had permission to beat the Jews. Now it appears it is all a lie!"

The family moved often to make "a new beginning," but, as Shana put it, "actually there wasn't any difference between one wretched flat and the next and more often than not we had to uproot our belongings from one dark hole only to set them down in a worse one."

In one move, Shana recalled that "our new neighbor in the common corridor was the wife of an officer in the czarist army. I never saw the officer himself—we were so frightened of the police that whenever I heard the sound of spurred boots, I would flee at once to our room."

Goldie's life at the time largely moved in a different orbit. When she was four, Shana was a mature thirteen, going to school. Orthodox Jews had no formal educational programs for daughters. Young women growing up in these narrow, confined circumstances, with a hunger to learn, had to fight for the right to do it. Shana did. When her mother wanted to send her to a school to learn dressmaking, she cried and rebelled until they finally placed her in a school for poor Jewish children. It was most uncommon to find a girl there. Shana protested when Goldie trailed after her, but their mother said, "It's okay . . . what's the difference . . ." When Goldie tore a page out of Shana's notebook, Shana wanted to hit her, but Bluma got angry at Shana. Goldie was her prize and her beauty and could do no wrong. Shana resented this bitterly. She recalled how Goldie "loved to look at herself in the mirror when Mother combed her hair." Shana also remembered her small sister dictating long imaginative letters to their cousin about make-believe things "and doing it very seriously." Goldie was four when her younger sister was born. She remembered it vividly because they named her Tzipka (later Americanized to "Clara") after their grandmother, who was buried that same day.

Goldie's father had a life of misery and crisis. Once he even had his own carpentry shop, with a partner, but it didn't last long. When he couldn't find work as a carpenter, he became a watchman. Another later child died in infancy. Bluma, still full of mother's milk, became a wet-nurse for a rich family. The family gave her food to take home, so her family finally had enough food to eat. Her daughters sometimes accompanied her, and for the first time in their lives they saw a doll.

The time came when they only had dried fish and bread for a holiday dinner, and Moshe said, "I can't stand this anymore; I'm going to America." The hunger and fear persuaded him that it was no longer any "great privilege" to live outside the Pale. As a Jew in Russia, he felt himself "a stranger of whom the only thing known is that he has no home." He then brought his family back to Pinsk to live with Bluma's father while he sold his tools and furniture to pay for a steerage ticket to "the *goldena medina*," the golden land.

In the *goldena medina* of America, the report was "all work is done by machine, and even the dead are taken to graves by electrically drawn carriages. Jews could live in any part of the country and own land anywhere. A democratic government permitted everybody to get ahead in life, everybody who was willing to work hard. Anybody who saw the President could shake hands with him, and even speak to him. And they didn't cook in earthenware, but in porcelain or tin pots." Furthermore, in America "people there eat white bread in the middle of the week and not just on the Sabbath—and one might eat meat every day just like the millionaires."

More than two million Jews left Russia between 1881 and 1914, most of them for the United States. "Yesterday, 200 families passed Kovno en route to the U.S.," recorded a diarist. Hurriedly emigrating after a pogrom, a man said, "I don't want to own anything. I want my family alive."

"Go. Go to America. Get out of here while there's time. Everything will burn here, not just the forest."

And from the *goldena medina*, the word came in letters: "Jews can walk in America with their heads held high."

Two U.S. commissioners, sent to Russia to assess the growing migration, reported: "The Jews are expressing awareness and anxiety, begging for the opportunity to begin life *somewhere*. Where, they do not know or care."

But leaving Russia was a difficult business. "If you tried to get your visa, they would put you in the army or tax you or beat you. The less

Jews had to do with the authorities, the better." The ambivalent Russians didn't want the Jews—at the same time they didn't want to admit this officially, and let them go.

The mild but stubborn Moshe had made up his mind. What Moshe told his family was that he would go to America for several years, make a fortune, then return to Pinsk where they could then live like human beings. Men like Moshe saw America as a kind of bank where you went to pick up the dollars scattered on the sidewalks and came back with your pockets full. Wives worried when their husbands went alone, wondering whether America "would gobble them up."

Crossing the ocean in steerage in 1903 meant sharing an unventilated cargo hull with as many as 2,000 men, women, and children, sleeping in tiers of narrow metal bunks, the men and women often separated by no more than a few blankets draped over a line in the center of the room. There were often fewer than two dozen toilets for a thousand people, and the air was foul. In the close quarters where people could neither stretch nor walk, they bickered constantly. As Lee Salk, whose brother later helped discover the polio vaccine, recalled, "The crew would open the hatch from above and the first-class passengers would look down as if these people were animals and throw bread and scraps of food to them."

Ellis Island was the "Island of Tears."

"Tears, everybody had tears. There was not a smile on anybody's face. They thought, 'Maybe my child won't get through . . .' " Immigrants were poked, prodded, probed to determine whether they could stay or must be sent back home. And then they were accordingly tagged.

Fearful immigrants saw every uniformed guard as an enemy soldier, every iron railing as prison bars, detention areas as wired cages. And many immigrants remembered how many fat rats were running on the island boardwalk.

An immigrant wrote on the wall: "Why should I fear the fires of hell. I have been through Ellis Island."

Yet there was also much kindness. Women wearing white celluloid cuffs to keep their sleeves clean circulated among the people distributing free food. Many people had never seen a banana before, and some tried to eat it unpeeled. Immigrants with minor ailments who had failed the physical were often permitted to stay for treatment and take another physical. One small boy, Israel Baline—with a childhood memory of a mob burning his home—later became known as Irving Berlin and had good reason to write the song "God Bless America."

Moshe wrote little of all this to his family. He did write that he got a job in New York for three dollars a week and would soon start sending them money.

In Pinsk, Goldie was no longer hungry. At her grandfather's tavern, there was always enough food. She watched her mother and aunts slicing, chopping, cooking in big pots on the old coal-black stove, everywhere the smells of simmering onions and drying peppers and browning bread.

Friday night's Sabbath was Goldie's lingering memory, a tradition she continued throughout her life. Men scurrying to the synagogue in their patched-up frock coats, old women in their ginger-colored wigs, wives sweeping and scrubbing their houses, washing the woodwork, preparing all the traditional foods: the braided white bread called the *challeh*; the chopped, rolled *gefilte* fish; the homemade noodles; the chicken soup; a *tsimmes* of carrots and sweet potatoes; noodle pudding with raisins; roast chicken—or whatever part of all this they could afford.

At the solemn lighting of candles on the dinner table, the women covered their heads to *bentsh licht*, the evening prayer. The dinner feast was a time for sipping wine, retelling family stories, welcoming all visitors, singing and laughing.

Recalling the scene, a house full of uncles, aunts, and cousins, Golda added softly that none of them had survived the Holocaust.

At five, Goldie was feisty, independent, spirited. According to her aunts, Goldie not only often refused to listen to reason, but often defied a direct order. Nor would a spanking change her mind—if she was stubbornly set on something. "There's a *dybbuk* [little devil] in her," one of them said.

Goldie loved the tavern: the sound of customers singing and arguing as they drank their schnapps in the big room of smoky oil lamps. And just outside the kitchen, there were always the geese waiting to be fed. She had her own dog then. But she hated cats. She once tried to separate two fighting cats with her foot, and one had slashed her skin.

Enterprising Bluma had been successful in making and selling cakes and bread, collecting regular customers by going door to door. She did well enough to move her daughters into two rooms of a small house near the police station. Shana was her problem child. Nearing fifteen,

Shana was a redheaded young woman of high spirits and bristling ideas. She had joined a youth organization called New Winds, a group of ten boys and girls who met in the home of Chaya Weizmann Lichtenstein (the sister of the future president of Israel). There she learned history, economics, politics, and Zionism, and read underground newspapers.

Russia, then, was in a traumatic time. Revolution was brewing in small cells all over the country. Shana was part of one such cell. This group felt that their only hope for real freedom, for Jews, too, was the overthrow of the czar. Coupled with this, Shana believed in the Zionist dream of eventually creating a Jewish home in Palestine.

Shana and her friends distributed pamphlets by a young man named Shamai Korngold. The grandson of a noted scholar, Shamai had sacrificed his mathematical aptitude for his revolutionary ideals. A handsome young man with long hair down to his shoulders, Shamai had the code name of Copernicus, and constantly wore disguises because he was wanted by the police. At first sight, the highly verbal Shana was "stunned into silence and fell in love."

"Shana was a fabulous person, . . . with a lot of guts," said Tzipka. "She had a tremendous amount of determination. She was a wonderful human being but she was a real danger to our family. She used to distribute revolutionary material. If the Cossacks caught you doing that then it was the end of you and the end of your family. So my poor mother . . ."

While Bluma could not and would not discourage Shana from her "great and beautiful cause," she still could hear the screams of young captured revolutionaries being brutally beaten by the police next door. Years later, Golda said how vividly she still recalled those screams.

In those days, and afterward, Shana was an austere, severe taskmaster, a perfectionist "relentless about the things that really mattered to her." "She was an idealist, and strong!" Golda said. "Shana wouldn't budge left or right from her ideals." In those days, too, Shana and Goldie grew closer together as sisters, Goldie trying to become as much like Shana as she could. It was Shana who gave Goldie her first lessons in reading and writing "and even a little arithmetic." Bluma bought Goldie a notebook in which she copied Hebrew letters from the prayer book. She was in the middle of this once when her mother called her. When she didn't come, her angry mother stormed in, grabbed the notebook, and tore it up. "When I call you, you come." Goldie yelled, cried, sulked for days until her mother agreed to buy her a new notebook if she promised to come quickly when called. Goldie thought the request unfair, and refused. It was the mother who finally surrendered and bought the notebook anyway.

Shana, Shamai, and their small group held their secret meetings in various places, in the woods, in different houses. One of their ploys was to get a police permit for a wedding, then hire a band, post a guard, and meet in the back room. When police were sighted, the meeting stopped and the band played. At one meeting, Shana barely escaped by jumping off a roof.

Bluma meanwhile had moved again, to a small one-room house of their own near the swamp, and Shana held one of their meetings there while her mother was at the synagogue. They held it in the kitchen where Goldie and Tzipka shared a bed. The kitchen had a big black iron stove built into the wall with a warming shelf on the top. The shelf was a favorite private place for Goldie when she wanted to be alone.

Goldie was stretched out on her hideaway shelf one day when Shana assembled a meeting, and Goldie heard it all. As she later told her sister, she didn't understand everything they were saying, "but she listened and she was fascinated."

When the group discovered her and ordered her out, she threatened to tell the police if they made her leave.

"If you do," Shana told her quietly, "I'll be sent to Siberia and I'll never return."

In tears, Goldie promised never to tell anybody.

"For me, Shana was perhaps the greatest influence on my life," Golda said afterward, ". . . a shining example, my dearest friend and my mentor. . . . Shana was the one person whose praise and approval—when I won them, which was not easy—meant the most to me."

While there were no pogroms in Pinsk, they were nearby and everywhere else, particularly after Kishinev. In Kishinev, near the Romanian border, in April 1903, there once again circulated the infamous "blood libel" that a Jew had murdered his Christian servant and used her blood for the Passover service. The later-revealed fact was that the young woman had committed suicide and her Jewish family had desperately tried to save her.

What made the Kishinev pogrom worse than the others, and more memorable, was the intensity of its horror. A witness afterward described it to Shamai and Shana:

"... Some Jews had nails driven into their heads. Some had their eyes put out. Children were thrown from garret windows, dashed to pieces on the street below. Women were raped, after which their stomachs were ripped open, their breasts cut off. Still the police did nothing. Nor did the city officials. Or the so-called intelligentsia. Students. Doctors. Lawyers. Priests. They walked leisurely along the streets watching the show."

It lasted three days. A garrison of more than 5,000 czarist troops stood by idly. A hundred were injured and forty-nine killed, more than 2,000 families left homeless, some 1,300 homes and stores looted and destroyed.

Chaim Nachman Bialik wrote a poem about it:

Arise and go to the city of the killing and you will
        come to the courtyards,
and with your eyes you will see and with your hands you will feel
        on the fences and on the trees and on the stones
    and on the plaster
        the congealed blood and the battered brains of the slain.

In the United States, Secretary of State John Hay deplored the atrocity but added, "We should not be justified in assuming that this enlightened sovereign [the czar] is not doing all that lies in his power to put a stop to it." He also noted, "No civilized nation has yet taken official action."

None would.

All over Russia, Jews had their own memorial for Kishinev—they fasted for a day. Goldie insisted on fasting, too, even though she was not yet six—and nobody could dissuade her. Bluma had told her that only grown-ups fast and she had answered, "You fast for the grown-ups; I will fast for the little children." A dozen years later, almost on Goldie's wedding day, the new Russian regime in Kishinev officially apologized to the Jews for what had happened.

While the Pinsk Jewish majority overwhelmed their town, they did not control it. Nor were Pinsk Jews free from fear. Mothers still dressed their teenage sons as girls when Russian army recruiters arrived. A new anti-Semitic organization, the Union of the Russian People, had organized secret fighting units known as the Black Hundreds, who traveled from town to town inciting hatred and violence against the Jews.

In October 1904, there was a celebration in "the big street" of Pinsk because of the rumor that the czar no longer forbade political meetings. Instead, Cossacks came charging down the street with their whips and sabers, wounding many, arresting more. Shana barely escaped by putting her pamphlets under a basket of onions.

Several months later, on Passover, Pinhas Dashewski crossed over the narrow Pinsk bridge with his friend Moshe Weizmann. "You Jews get off the bridge," yelled the chief of police. Pinhas slapped him on the face, raced away. Again, more arrests, more beatings.

Shortly before, on Red Sunday, a group of laborers and farmers, led by a priest, walked to the czar's Winter Palace to ask him to better the lives of peasants. The Cossack answer was to shoot into the crowd, killing hundreds.

Afterward, Cossacks were sent everywhere in Russia to quell disturbances. A brigade came to Pinsk. "They would gallop through the town on their horses not caring on whom they trampled, and would brutally beat any suspected young men and women they might find. They would wave their sabers, shout their anti-Semitic slogans, and laugh."

Goldie remembered a cold night when she was playing with Tzipka and a friend in the middle of a muddy street. Suddenly a group of hard-riding Cossacks raced directly at them, their horses jumping right over them, so close she could see the flashing of their hooves. She came home splattered with their mud, still shaking from the fear of it. Nor would she ever forget the drunken peasant grabbing her and her little friend, banging their heads together and yelling, "That's what we'll do to the Jews. We'll knock their heads together and we'll be through with them."

At that point, Bluma made a decision. They would no longer wait for her husband to return. It had been three years. She and her three children now would join him.

"It doesn't matter if you've saved enough money or not," she wrote him. "Believe me, we must come. Now!"

Moshe was then in Milwaukee. He had made the move at the urging of HIAS (Hebrew Immigrant Aid Society), which was trying to disperse immigrant Jews around the country. Moshe was working as a carpenter on the railway, riding back and forth on the wooden trains in case something needed fixing.

He didn't have enough money for official government exit permits for his family, but he did have enough for faked passports, train tickets, a small cabin on a ship that would take them to Canada, then to Milwaukee by train.

For Bluma it was a time of mixed feelings—leaving her father and sisters and brothers and friends whom she might never see again, going to a strange land with a strange language. But it did mean reunion with her husband, safety for her daughters.

For Shana, it was even more difficult. She was in love with Shamai, imbued with her cause. Shamai urged her to go, indicated he might follow.

For Goldie and Tzipka it was a time of excitement and adventure. "Going to America then was almost like going to the moon," Golda said afterward. Goldie was then almost eight.

Jewish neighbors came to Bluma with advice, with envy, with packages for relatives in America.

There were all kinds of stories that caused concern: these illegal conductors who arranged the trip would sometimes leave their immigrants stranded in the middle of nowhere; white slavers reportedly kidnapped young Jewish girls, selling them into brothels as far away as South America and the Orient; an immigrant woman was shot and killed by a soldier at the Polish border while she was carrying her child through the swamp; at every border all immigrants reportedly were disinfected with kerosene; and many immigrants finally reached America only to be shipped back because they weren't healthy enough.

Goldie admitted that she "felt scared" at the time of going. At the marketplace, Goldie heard Pinsk women read aloud letters from their relatives in America, and the opulent descriptions seemed to surpass *The Arabian Nights*.

Abraham Cahan visualized America as a country of tall, beardless young men in gray spring overcoats, speaking an English that sounded like "the language of birds," living on a landscape so flimsy that "a good European rainstorm could wipe it all off as a wet sponge would a colored picture made with colored chalk on a blackboard."

Immigrants all brought tea kettles, books, towels, bedding, blankets, perhaps a small wheel of cheese, a giant round loaf of bread, an oversize salami, as well as private treasures with which they could not part. A woman brought a Caucasian rug with an image of a life-size tiger. Another brought books. And one man even brought a goose-down pillow that contained the caul in which he was born.

The antiquated Russian wooden train coaches looked like American boxcars, dingy, creaking, lit by a few kerosene lamps. Those who wanted to read brought along their own supply of thick candles. Those who could read would read aloud from their newspapers to those who could only listen.

"My father had helped a friend reach America by taking that man's wife and daughters with him on his papers and pretending that they were members of his family," Golda later said. "So when our turn came to leave, we also had to pretend to be other people."

Their journey, in the spring of 1906, would cross the border at Galicia, on to Vienna, and Antwerp, where they would board their ship to Quebec, Canada, then a train to Milwaukee. Forty-year-old Bluma had the passport of a twenty-year-old girl; seventeen-year-old Shana kept her hair loose, trying to look twelve; Goldie was supposed to be five instead of eight. And four-year-old Tzipka had to cross the border with a total stranger whom she was told to call "Mama."

Somebody told the story of a young bride who had to pretend to be the wife of an old man, while her husband acted as one of his sons. She burst into tears until she was finally persuaded that she would be reunited with her husband aboard ship. The story caused a good laugh.

At Galicia, on the Russian-Polish border, they were supposed to cross by train. The man paid to make arrangements, however, said that the soldiers had been alerted for faked passports and it was too dangerous. They would have to cross by wagon. Bluma refused, accused the man of trying to cheat her and pocket the money for the train tickets. The wagon would be more dangerous, she said. She would return to Pinsk and tell everyone that he was a cheat.

The cowed man decided he could arrange the train crossing after all. "Our actual crossing was effected by bribing the police with money Mother had somehow managed to raise," Golda recorded.

Arriving in Galicia on an icy spring morning, they stayed in an unheated shack for two days, waiting for their train to Antwerp. They slept on the floor and Golda remembered how much Tzipka cried. At another border crossing where the immigrants walked, a bribed soldier told a mother with a crying child, "If you don't keep that baby quiet, I'll have to kill you both or else everybody else will be killed."

In the confusion of the border crossing, their luggage was lost or stolen. It was a two-day train trip and they sat up all the way, but their excitement had heightened.

Antwerp was an old city with many ancient buildings and beautiful trees, a spired cathedral at its center, old men feeding gulls or fishing. You could smell the ocean of this bustling port. It was also a city of bars and brothels and waiting immigrants of all colors and races from all over the world, of rich women in wide satin skirts, of men with ebony canes and gold watches. But the bulk were the masses of poor Jews and their ragged children.

Bluma and her family were taken to an immigration center for paper processing and a disinfecting hot bath. Bluma had sewn some surplus money into their clothes, and had used it to buy some underwear and sweaters for her daughters. The exact date of departure was always uncertain, since the owners wanted to pack the ships to capacity to make the most profit. Bluma was fortunate; the wait was only forty-eight hours. On boarding their ship, tickets were stamped or punched at every step, pieces torn off them. Goldie was warned not to let loose of her small sister's hand. She later recalled that their ship looked more like a Bowery flophouse than an ocean liner.

"There were sailors dragging and hauling bundles and boxes from the small boat onto the large ship, shouting and thundering as they worked. There were officers giving out orders in loud voices, like trumpets. There were children crying, mothers clutching them, fathers questioning the officers on where they should go. And there seemed to be everything under heaven that had any noise in it come to swell the confusion of sound."

All immigrants were ordered below. "It was dark there and we didn't like it."

It was a fourteen-day trip in a dark cabin stuffed with four other people, bunks without sheets and standing in line for ladled-out food "as though we were cattle." Still, it was a considerable upgrading over the ordinary steerage in which their father had traveled. He had been determined that his own family would not travel as he had.

But nobody could control the sea. The boat "danced on the water like a ballerina," bending and rocking like a crib. The waves of water looked like high hills. The creaking boat seemed ready to break.

"So many people remember their voyages in terms of herring and seasickness." Herring was the prime food, rumored to cure seasickness, but few were well enough to eat it.

"When the bell rang, we all stood by our cabins with a cup and a little plate," said Shana. "One of the crew would dole out a little unpalatable food. All got seasick. The only one who felt good was Goldie."

"I can remember staring at the sea for hours," said Golda. Her favorite place was the bow of the ship, where one could watch the moon gradually disappearing and the beginning of the dawn and the slow rising sun.

". . . The sea shall not affright thee. . . ."

It did not affright Golda, who loved standing in the fierce wind, eating all the herring they gave her, "making up unbelievable stories of the unimaginable riches of America."

When they finally sighted land, so many people stood on one side of the ship that they were told to move elsewhere or the ship might tip over. "Like a hand held toward us, America was waving. Everybody was waving back. Hello, hello, here we are . . ."

2

For Goldie, it was all magic and miracle. First there was the train trip from Quebec filled with restless expectation as she stared out of the windows. Then, arriving in Milwaukee, the strange sight of all these beardless men, including her father, whom she scarcely remembered. Shana had thought he looked "astonishingly handsome in a black suit, and without his beard." Afterward, they all squeezed into an automobile for the first time, "a wagon without horses," driving past five-story buildings that seemed to scrape the sky.

Then, suddenly, she felt back home again. Familiar stores with familiar signs, people speaking a language she understood, women even wearing babushkas. They were in Milwaukee's lower west side, packed with the bulk of the city's 8,000 Jews.

Milwaukee's first officially recorded Jew was a fur trader in 1794. It was almost fifty years later before Milwaukee had a *minyan*—it takes ten Jews to make a *minyan*, the minimum needed for a religious service. Three years later, when Milwaukee incorporated as a city with 20,000 people, it had a hundred Jews. When Goldie and her family arrived in 1906, Milwaukee was a clean, young industrial city of some 300,000 and the popular jingle was:

21

Milwaukee, you're a fine little town,
Your girls are so blond and your beer so brown ... .

Walnut Street was the city's Jewish spine, cutting through ten square blocks of ghetto. Moshe's family of five moved into his rented room in an apartment of Polish Jews named Badner. Golda remembered that the Badners warmly welcomed them with their first full meal in months. Most of all, Golda recalled the hot rolls. "I don't think anything ever tasted so good after that."

There were other miracles. No more water from a well. You simply turned a handle in the sink. You pushed another handle to flush a toilet. Instead of straw-covered ice in a hole in the ground to keep food cool, there was now ice in a box.

Her father had Americanized much in those three years. Moshe Yitzhak was now "Morris." A skilled carpenter, he was now working part-time at the railroad roundhouse repairing wooden train cars, the proud member of a trade union. He not only belonged to a synagogue, but occasionally substituted for the cantor because "he had a beautiful voice and loved singing." Neighbors described him as a believer in people, "a lovely person." He was a tall man with a quiet soul and a core of stubbornness.

One of the first things he did after they arrived was to shepherd his flock of "greenhorns" to Shuster's Department Store for new American clothes. Only seventeen-year-old Shana resisted. She was still wearing black, in mourning for Zionist leader Theodor Herzl, who had died two years before. When her father bought her a straw hat covered with flowers, she refused to wear it. She was a socialist and a worker, she insisted, and she would not wear anything like that. Her mild-mannered father became angry. "This is what we wear in America!" he said. That made Shana feel he "was ashamed of us ... was a stranger to her."

Goldie had no such qualms. She loved the bright colors of her clothes, her billowing hair ribbons. She loved everything she saw. To her, the store was a wonderland and she never wanted to leave. "I spent the first days in Milwaukee in a kind of trance."

Not Bluma. Bluma bustled. She wanted more space, more money. "Bluma was an ambitious bundle of energy. She was short, kind of wide, a plumpish figure with red hair pinned in a knot in back. I think she had a good mind and I never saw anybody with so much pep. At home, she was the hub, the force, the tough one with the drive, the enterprise, the practical mind. Neighbors knew her as a Tartar, flaming hair to match her flaming temper. When a person annoyed her, she snapped, 'If I don't like someone, they don't have to live in this world.' "

The *Milwaukee City Directory* of 1907 notes that the Mabowehz family then lived at 615 Walnut Street. What was interesting was the evolution of their family name. In Russia and afterward, the family referred to itself, among themselves, as "Mabovitch." Golda used that spelling in her autobiography. But in the census and city-directory records, on Moshe's naturalization papers, and in all of Goldie's school records, the name is spelled "Mabowehz."

The change might well have been made by customs or immigration officials, who often spelled names the way they sounded. There is, however, a family story that Bluma had asked a sign painter to put their name on their first store—and that's the way he had spelled it and that's the way they had kept it. "And so we spelled it that way, too."

Goldie's younger sister, Tzipka, later complained that she had so much trouble in school getting everyone to spell it that way that "I always swore that the first man who proposed to me with a one-syllable name, I'd marry—and I did."

Nearby, at 623 Walnut, Bluma had found an empty store and converted it into a *kreml*, a grocery store. She knew nothing about the business but insisted, "It's in my blood." When she was a little girl, her father had had a store and she had helped him.

The family all opposed the idea but she brushed them aside. It was a small, dark store, but she soon filled it with bags of lima beans, rice, coffee, selling most of it in small scoops. She quickly expanded into "barrels of sauerkraut, pickles, raw herring, sausages, butter, candy, bread, and rolls . . . with a fruit stand outside." She learned a few necessary phrases in English, but most of her customers spoke Yiddish. "Women would order an eighth of a pound of butter, a cup of sugar in a paper bag." Moshe built some shelves, and sometimes helped, but hated it. "When some women touched the rolls, he would get angry and tell them to go to the competitor across the street."

"Mother hoped Shana would be her right hand in the store," recalled Tripka, "but Shana said, 'This is why I came to America? To argue over the price of apples?' " She compared a shopkeeper to a social parasite.

"I want to work," she said, "but on my own." She found a job making buttonholes in a tailor shop.

Bluma had to trudge to the wholesale market very early every morning to buy her supplies on credit, and somebody had to stay in the store. That meant Goldie, not quite nine, who was so small that she had to stand on a box behind the counter to serve the customers. Like her father, she hated it. What she hated most of all was that it made her late for school. For her, this was "awful, and I used to cry all the way to school." Bluma dismissed her tearful complaints. *"Vest zein a rebbitzen mit a tag shpeter."* ("So you'll be a smart woman a day later.")

It took an imperious truant officer with a black mustache to warn Bluma that she was breaking the law. Every child under fourteen had to go to school regularly, and on time. This cowed even Bluma, and she got up an hour earlier to go to the market, freeing Goldie.

"Goldie's mother? A loving mother?" Golda's friend Regina reflected. "I'll tell you the truth. I really don't think so."

In her younger years, Goldie spoke critically of her mother, often mocking her. She mocked the fact that her mother was so nostalgic for Pinsk in the early days, that nothing in America seemed as good as it had been in Russia, "even the fruit." At this point, Goldie laughed and asked, "Who ate fruit in Pinsk?"

But, in her later years, Golda's attitude toward her mother changed somewhat. She described her as "beautiful, shrewd, clever," but she never ever really liked her. Later she had a grudging respect for this woman, marveled at her *chutzpah* in starting the store, making it work, bringing the family together. And she remembered, too, that her mother also had a love of singing and that there was often "laughter in her."

Goldie had her mother's force and laughter, her father's stubbornness, and their shared love of singing.

"Goldie was so full of energy that it was exciting to be with her," reminisced Regina Hamburger Medzini, then a tall, thin girl, a year younger, who walked to school with her every day and shared the same classes.

The newly built stone and brick Fourth Street Elementary School seemed a magnificent place to Goldie. She had never ever been to any school. Everything she had learned before, she had learned from Shana. "Goldie loved school," said Tzipka. "She was conscientious and good in every subject. I remember she did her homework on the kitchen table." Fourth Street School records do show exceptionally high marks for Goldie in reading, spelling, arithmetic, and German. Milwaukee, with its large German population, required the German language in school. Ironically the young Goldie now learned to sing "Deutschland über Alles."

Returning to Fourth Street School many years later as an adult, she told the students, "Here I found freedom, kindness and cleanliness. . . . It was here I first experienced a lack of prejudice." She later added, "In America, I lost my terror of Pinsk and Kiev."

Goldie integrated quickly. She had an innate charm plus a real curiosity about people and made friends easily. It would always be that way. She had this special eagerness that quickly caught others. Her mind would always carry the impact of her early Russian nightmares, but now they were softened by the chatter of young girls all eating a remarkable concoction called ice cream and a fizzy drink known as "soda pop."

Young Tzipka was marred by fewer memories to forget. But some of them remained still sharp. When the family went downtown to see their proud father marching in a Labor Day parade, some mounted police moved in to contain the crowd. One horse reared up unexpectedly, and suddenly Tzipka was reminded of the Cossacks in Pinsk jumping over her and Goldie in the street.

"And I yelled out, 'Cossacks! Cossacks!' and I went into convulsions."

"We had to take her away," Golda remembered, "and she stayed in bed for days with a high fever." Reflecting on the incident, Golda added, "So look, the America I knew was a place where men on horseback protect a parade of workers; the Russia I knew was a place where men on horseback massacre the Jews . . ."

This was an isolated incident for Tzipka. Still, unlike Goldie, she didn't like school. Her mother had sent her to kindergarten to get her out of the way while she tended store. At home she was Tzipka, or "Tzip," but the Irish principal renamed her "Clara."

A bright, peppy little girl of five, Clara found kindergarten boring, "everything so formal and organized." Her teacher made them sit in silence between lessons, their hands folded on the table. When they did their coloring books, they all had to use the same colors in the same places. Goldie, who was in second grade, assured her that school would improve, that second grade was "wonderful." But Clara much preferred playing with Goldie, creating kites out of newspapers, sewing rag dolls, acting in skits.

Nine-year-old Goldie, however, was trying to move closer to Shana. Shana was having a difficult time. She seemed unable to blend easily into America. The one thing Shana wanted was her independence, and the price was high. The price was work instead of school, drudgery at pitiful pay. It delayed her learning the language and there was no time to make friends. What she had was constant confrontation with her parents. She was even jealous of Goldie "because she was so beautiful and everyone spoiled her."

Bluma had moved the family to another store, with rooms behind it. There was one big room with a window, two small rooms, and a tiny kitchen and corridor. Compared to Kiev and Pinsk, they all still regarded it "like Paradise."

They now had an inside toilet, a black kitchen coal stove, and a tin bathtub on the back porch. For extra water to wash hair, they still put out buckets to catch the rain. The parents had one room, Shana the other, and Goldie and Clara slept on the daybed in the living room.

"My mother used to laugh because Goldie and I were so polite to each other in bed," said Clara. "Everytime one of us turned, we would say, 'Excuse my back.' "

There were also occasional guests. Her friend Regina sometimes slept there overnight, with them on the daybed, "talking the night away, jabbering of this and that." Crowded conditions were so common then that the subject was put into a poem:

Mother, is it true that when you die
That you are at least buried in a coffin alone,
You do not sleep with everybody,
With your hands and feet
Wound round each other?

"These people did not look like desirable acquisitions when they first arrived," reported the *Milwaukee Sentinel* on the immigrant Jews. "The racial desire for self-betterment is not snuffed out by the filthy environment into which their poverty forces them. . . . It is safe to say that the younger generation of them will turn out some valued citizens."

Most of the immigrants had pride. The Hebrew Relief Society reported in 1905 that "only two percent of Jewish immigrants who land on our shores ever ask for aid." Those who did "never remain on the poor list longer than absolutely necessary. . . . We have many poor, but no paupers."

Immigrants on Walnut Street even resented a mission of prosperous German-Jewish women who came "to teach immigrant children the art of cleanliness." Among Milwaukee Jews then, there was a traditional distance and suspicion, and even dislike, between these successful, staid Jews and the immigrant Russian-Polish. The immigrants loudly proclaimed that their children would learn cleanliness by family example, "not by a mission of female German Jews."

"Forget the old country and what you did over there," immigrants were advised. "Throw it out of the window."

Many of them did. At the Mabowehz home, though, they still celebrated the Shabbat on Friday night. The Shabbat was the weekly time of prayer for the religious. For the secular Jew, it was the time for family and friends, a respite from the backbreaking week, a reaffirmation of who they were and where they came from. "We had hardwood floors," Clara remembered. "Father used to scrub the floors for Mother before Sabbath. Then we wore dresses which were so starched that we could stand them up." While Goldie quickly lost any deep religious beliefs, she never lost her sense of tradition, her need for roots.

Goldie loved to wander on Walnut Street. It throbbed. Everybody seemed to walk there to meet everybody else. The heart of the street was Boris Schoenkerman's drugstore.

In Pinsk, her playground was the middle of a muddy street; here it was a world of busy shops and rushing people. Nothing was more exciting for Goldie than to walk up and down the street with a gaggle of her newfound little girlfriends, *ooh*ing and *aah*ing, pointing, giggling, staring, skipping, running. Nor were their mothers ever concerned for their safety on this street. It was like a warm, comfortable cocoon.

When a marriage was in trouble, the young couple considered Boris's a family court. When someone had an ailment or a rebellious son or simply a need to talk, Boris was always there to listen. A Russian intellectual with a large fund of common sense and a great sense of humor, Boris was the neighborhood's oracle, their final word.

Young lawyers also lingered in the drugstore "because you never knew who would walk in with a legal problem." They called these "bread-and-butter cases without very much bread or butter." On the other hand, if someone wanted specific free advice on how to become a citizen, they would go to the anteroom of Nathan Sand. Sand, who later became a good friend of Goldie's, would also help them book passage for any immigrating relatives.

If the congested ghetto had a little lung of open, breathing space, it was Lapham Park with its pavilion for concerts, shows, and a hall for a dancing school that was also rented for weddings. In those early years, Goldie was more interested in the great hill where she and her friends could go sledding in the winter—if they could borrow a sled. More likely they simply waited for the snow to turn to ice and then Goldie and her friends would just slide down on their bottoms.

The nearby Settlement House, later renamed for Abraham Lincoln, was a homemaker haven. It had a Happy Hour Club for making hammocks, a Rosebud Club for crocheting slippers, a Sunshine Club for knitting shawls. It also had choral groups, literary groups, military drill groups, as well as regular evening entertainment where mothers danced and children "spoke pieces."

The need for free entertainment was urgent at a time when children used cardboard inside their shoes to cover the holes because new shoes cost thirty-nine cents a pair.

A special salvation—and Goldie later loved it—was the *shvitzbud* (steambath). The adjacent Schlitz Brewery provided free hot water for the steam. The hours were separate for women and men, and they all relished it as a refuge for the weary, as their single precious chance to forget the family and chores and sit in thick clouds of steam, draped in heavy towels, drinking tea and sharing gossip.

A Settlement House annual report noted that "15,567 persons have good-naturedly or otherwise submitted to all kinds of inconveniences in their desire to get a bath. Income: $413.95."

For the more affluent, and sometimes for Goldie, there was "the nickel show." The Rose Theater (named after the owner's daughter) had fifty unpainted chairs and featured movies plus a variety of traveling vaudevillians. These early movies had neither sound nor titles and needed a storyteller to translate the action into Yiddish. In the midst of the frenzy, mothers in the audience might nurse their babies, fathers felt free to boo or applaud on inclination, and children raced up and down the aisles.

Shana seemed outside of all this. She hoarded her money to finance a future escape. Family friction had intensified. Shana had intercepted a letter her mother had written to an American-born relative of a friend in Pinsk, saying she hoped he and Shana might marry. Shana tore up the letter, "which also tore the relationship between Shana and her parents."

Long afterward, Bluma complained to friends that she had three daughters, "and none of them married a doctor."

Soon after that, Shana took a job in Chicago in a men's clothing factory. Restless, she moved to another job as a seamstress. An infected finger swelled her hand, making her unable to work. Reluctantly, she returned to Milwaukee. Her mother welcomed her with the words, "When it hurts, everyone runs home."

Clara later defended her parents against the charge that "they were kind of strict and a pain in the neck." Clara's defense was that "they had a problem with two kids who weren't easy to raise. My father was a wonderful person but he was never a breadwinner. My mother knew what it was not to have money and she wanted her daughters to have an easier life. She wasn't looking for anything for herself; she was trying to find a way to make it easier for them. Maybe she didn't use the best judgment. Maybe she didn't size up the daughters she had to do business with. But she was a typical Jewish mother, and worried about them."

"We were different, but also alike," said Shana of herself and her sisters. She and Goldie were stubborn and strong-willed, she noted, "Goldie even more so. She didn't like to admit she was wrong. If she retreated, she was very mad at herself. Tzipka (Clara) was different, always wanted peace in the house, willing to give up an argument for the sake of peace. She was innocent, easily fooled, and paid a heavy price for it." Clara then seemed more like her father, Shana and Golda more like the mother they so much disliked.

Clara called Shana "one of the kindest, most generous people," and she adored Goldie; but the two paid little attention to her. "They were both very mature for their years, and I wasn't," Clara admitted.

"Shana carried the brunt of being the oldest child. When you're nine and there are eight kids after you, that's a different kind of nine. You're an old woman at nine. That's why Shana was like a second mother to Goldie."

She was not, however, a second mother to Clara. The gap between them was more a difference of interest than age.

Part of the gap was that Clara was her mother's "*goldena kint*" ("golden child") because she was then so obedient. Clara withdrew into herself, her imaginary world, to retreat from the conflict. She was perfectly content to play by herself in a corner. She would play grocery store and pretend the sand was sugar. Her mother even let her keep a stray dog which followed her home. When the dog died, Clara accused her mother of crying "more over that dog than you would if I died."

Goldie was more concerned with Shana, now listless and depressed. Goldie combed her hair, helped her dress, gave her love and attention. For the two, it was a bonding time.

Goldie still visualized her big sister in heroic terms. To Goldie, Shana was the fiery revolutionary in Russia doing all those brave and wonderful things. She saw Shana now as the young woman strong enough to stand up against their mother and fight for her independence. There was too much that nine-year-old Goldie did not understand about her sister, but what she felt was a kind of star-struck admiration.

As for Shana, little Goldie was her only support in the family, her only listening post. To no one else could she unburden herself. In a large sense, she needed Goldie more than Goldie needed her. Perhaps this also forced Goldie to grow up faster.

And then things suddenly changed for Shana. A letter from an aunt in Pinsk informed her that Shamai had been arrested, escaped, and was now heading for New York. She enclosed his New York address.

Shana was exultant. She excitedly wrote Shamai and invited him to Milwaukee. Yes, he wrote, he would come. Goldie went with Shana to the railroad station to meet him. She saw them embrace. Shana shyly confided to her afterward that it had been their first kiss.

Bluma was incensed at Shamai's arrival. She felt he was a starry-eyed radical who would never amount to anything. She was convinced of this when his wealthy grandfather offered to give Shamai his full inheritance if he would go to Palestine and promise to pray in the synagogue. Shamai's reply then was that he didn't want to go to Palestine and he wouldn't pray in the synagogue. Shana was proud of him for it but Bluma was aghast. Years later, when a changed Shamai did go to

Palestine, his grandfather no longer had a fortune—the Russians had appropriated it.

"As little as Goldie was at the time, she felt that something wasn't right about our parents' dislike for Shamai," Shana later recalled. Goldie, however, was "very friendly to Shamai and I liked her for it. For these two [Shamai and Goldie] to put up with me at that time, one had to be an angel. . . . I was convinced that Shamai would leave me, and he would be right."

What distressed Shana was the bleakness of their future, their dependence on her parents, and her health. She started spitting blood. It was tuberculosis, "the White Plague." Some 154,000 people were dying of it each year, with ten times as many affected. The Hebrew Relief Association pointed out "the prevalence of tuberculosis among our people." There was no known cure. The only treatment was fresh air, nutritious food, and rest. A National Jewish Hospital for Consumptives had been built in Denver with the motto "None may enter who can pay. None may pay to enter." Statistics were not encouraging: only half of the patients were fully cured. For 25 percent the treatment came too late.

Shana went there full of foreboding. Shamai promised to join her as soon as he earned some more money, but she wondered if she would ever see him again.

Many Denverites claimed their city had become a TB dumping ground. They claimed that almost half of the city's 6,000 Jews had come to care for the other half who were sick. Some of the sick hemorrhaged in the street and slept in parks. A *Jewish Outlook* headline read COUNTY COM-MISSIONERS THREATEN TO DEPORT PAUPER HEALTH SEEKERS.

Shana called it "foolish pride on both sides," but she and her parents never wrote each other. "I felt that if a daughter goes away to a sanitarium without a penny in her pockets, they can write first and also send a few dollars."

Shana wrote to Goldie, routing her letters through Regina. She wrote of the round, two-story hospital which looked like a hotel; it was clean and light-colored, with as much milk as you wanted and tables covered with white cloths. At night, the well-wrapped patients moved onto the balconies to sleep in the fresh air, "even on the coldest nights."

"Then the concert of coughing began. We could tell the condition of the patient by the cough."

Most of the patients were young, many in their teens. Shana was only eighteen. She told Goldie that mail call "was like an electrical storm, exciting everyone."

"I am very good in school," wrote Goldie in 1908, at the age of ten. "I am now in third high and in June I am going to pass into fourth low. I haven't got what to write. If you write me a letter, I will write you more. Truly yours, your lovingly sister."

Her early letters, like this one, were simplistic, often badly misspelled, her grammar poor. It was a reminder that she had been in this country for only two years.

One piece of Goldie's news concerned the Chinese laundryman next door. Goldie had run some errands for him and he promised her some handkerchiefs from China. She and her sister laughed: what kind of handkerchiefs could they have in China? "The ones he gave her," said Clara, "were so beautifully embroidered that we used them as doilies."

In another letter, Goldie added, "I can tell you that Pa does not work yet and the store is not very busy and I am very glad that you are out of bed."

In some letters, Goldie enclosed a few dollars.

"The money in the letter was very useful to me," Shana said afterward. "I was literally without a *pruta* [cent]. But where is Goldie getting this money? I was worried about it. I received a letter that I shouldn't worry, she wasn't taking it from the box. She saves this from change that mother gives her for school money." Goldie, however, later admitted, "Once or twice I borrowed the stamp money from Mother's till."

Goldie was a dutiful daughter, and whatever she did, she did well, however grudgingly. She was not, however, a devoted daughter. Still, she and her mother were much alike. Both had an inexhaustible supply of energy and determination. Both were feisty. Bluma called Goldie a *kochleffl*, a stirring spoon, because she was always stirring up things.

She proved this with her campaign for schoolbooks. School was free but books were not. To get free books, children had to plead poverty. "Goldie felt it was such a very humiliating thing for a child to admit she was too poor to pay for books."

"I was indignant!" Goldie later said.

But what could an eleven-year-old girl do about it, even if she was an indignant *kochleffl*? What Goldie did was to appoint herself chairman of a group of collected friends she called American Young Sisters Society. They needed a meeting place, so Goldie somehow persuaded the owner of Packen Hall to donate it for a night. She and her Young Sisters then painted posters, knocked on doors, asked parents to come to their meeting, even promising free entertainment.

"Nothing in life happens," she later said. "It isn't enough to believe in something. You have to have the stamina to meet obstacles and overcome them. . . . What you do is what you are."

There seemed little fear in her when she stood up in front of that hall, speaking "clear and forcefully." Her mother failed to persuade her to write that speech "because it made more sense to me to say what was in my heart." What she simply said was: we need money to buy books for poor children because all children need schoolbooks. It was her debut of more than a thousand speeches to come, almost all of them unwritten, saying "what was in my heart."

Next on the program, the Young Sisters "spoke pieces." Goldie recited two poems, "The Tailor" and "The Two Sacrifices." Clara, then six, regarded by the family as its dramatic actress, also recited a poem, "Eight Souls and Only Two Beds." "But I couldn't remember the second verse," she admitted.

And her listening parents? What a long road they had come in such a short time. Not so long ago they were fearful that Shana might be caught and tortured in a Pinsk police station; now they were in this American hall, listening to cheers for their children.

A Milwaukee newspaper reported:

"A score of little children gave their playtime and scant pennies to charity, a charity organized by their own initiative too. . . . And it is worthy of comment that this charity is itself a loud comment on the fact that little children may go to public schools without proper possession of books. Think what that means . . ."

It *was* impressive. An eleven-year-old girl conceiving, planning, organizing, making it happen. Here was a preview of how Golda would perform all her life, throwing herself into causes without reserve. Shana once had noted that Goldie's most positive physical feature was the curvature of her mouth "that reflected willpower and independent judgment."

Goldie had written Shana about the fund-raiser, calling it "the greatest success . . . and the entertainment was grand."

Shana was improving. She wrote Goldie that she had stopped coughing, gained weight, and was soon scheduled for discharge. She also confided the source of her constant torment: would Shamai still want to marry her, a tubercular? A young woman in her room already had received a note from a young man "who had left her."

Goldie reported the family news: they had moved again, this time to nearby Tenth Street, behind another store. This one was a delicatessen called "Miller and Mabowehz," and their father had gone to work there as a butcher. "It looked more like a drugstore than a butcher shop because he'd be constantly washing the scale and counter after each purchase . . . he was so immaculate."

Goldie's neatness came from her father, not her mother. Part of Goldie's job, every Sunday morning, with Clara's help, was to clean Papa's clothes, as well as their dresses, in the backyard, using naphtha, a highly inflammable liquid. Her own private chore, which lasted her lifetime, was to wash and press her skirt and blouse each evening to have it fresh for the next day.

Goldie didn't write Shana about everything, usually trying to emphasize the positive to her sick sister. Once she sent Shana a photo of herself in a folk dance costume. Shana dismissed it as frivolous.

"You wrote that you don't like my picture. I am glad because I see how dearly you love me. But don't take it so hard. . . . I am still the same old Goldie that you left nearly three years ago. . . . As far as I can see, I don't see any harm in it."

Her mother had another miscarriage. When she was strong enough to start a store again, Goldie escaped by getting a summer job with Regina at Gimbel's.

"We'd walk from Tenth Street to Gimbel's downtown, quite a walk, about three-quarters of an hour, to save the nickel carfare," said Regina. "We were messenger girls. In those days you had girls running down the aisles bringing change and handing out parcels, for which we got three dollars a week. We always handed this money over to our mothers. One department in the store had candy and nuts and we *craved* the salted peanuts—we both ached for it—but it was five cents a bag. We swore to each other that when we had any extra money, we'd buy a bag of peanuts *every day*!

"We also taught English to Polish and Romanian Jews at ten cents an hour." This money they kept.

It took a lot of ten-cent lessons to pay for a winter coat, "but that was the first thing I ever bought with my own earnings," said Goldie.

Goldie and Regina once got free tickets for the play *Uncle Tom's Cabin*. For Goldie, it was peak excitement. She literally lived every dramatic part of that play, jumping to her feet and shouting her outrage when Simon Legree was so cruel to little Eva.

Sometimes Goldie did more than shout her outrage. One of her girlfriends told about a classmate who threw a penny at her, saying, "Pick it up!" When she did, he pushed her away, saying sneeringly, "A dirty Jew will pick up every penny." Then he ran away with his friends.

"That evening Goldie organized a demonstration in front of that boy's house protesting his anti-Semitism. When it came to anti-Semitism, Goldie never lowered her head!"

She had come to the United States with the bitter certainty that Jews everywhere were oppressed. Many years later, when asked whether—in her growing up—she was more aware of being a woman or a Jew, she replied, "Oh! Being a Jew, without any doubt!"

But more than ever now, she was also learning about being a woman. From Shana came the most romantic news.

The person she loved most was now consummating her own love. A letter from Shana: "Shamai is mine!" Shamai had arrived in Denver, pledging his love. Her doctor had advised her not to get married, but Shamai had said, "Where is it written that you have to have a long life? We'll live a shorter one, but together."

The fiery revolutionary with the long hair once known by the code name of Copernicus was now a man named Sam, washing dishes in a sanitarium during the day and pressing clothes in a tailor shop at night. In his free time, he studied English, bookkeeping, and typing. Despite this metamorphosis, Sam was still a young man with stars in his eyes who wanted the moon. His stars and his moon were not simply the American success story but the big words like world peace and equality for all, and Zionism.

"Sam was a very gentle person," Clara remembered, "but also determined. And wise enough to know when to take a stand. And Shana was wise enough to know when to back off. So he'd let her get away with all the little things, whatever she wanted. But if there was something important to him, he'd take a stand."

After her hospital discharge, Shana, once even known as "Jennie," worked in a private tubercular sanitarium, serving in the dining room, helping in the bakery, and shoveling snow when necessary. "One day I felt a deep pain in my chest," she wrote. Her mouth seemed filled with a salty liquid. "I spat and saw red spots on the snow."

There were so many TB cases in Denver—some forced to live in tents because fearful landlords evicted them from boardinghouses— that there was now a Jewish Consumptive Relief Society providing more hospital beds. Their creed came from the Talmud: "He who saves a life is considered as if he had preserved the whole world." Shana spent four more months there before being discharged as presumably cured.

She found some work in a barber shop, but Sam now sometimes had no work at all. A letter from Goldie tried to be reassuring: "I am not sorry because Sam did not buy me a present because he does not work. I am very obliged for the ribbon and it is enough for me."

When Shana wrote despairingly that she could not write often because she did not have two cents for a stamp, Goldie sent her some stamps, adding unhappily, "Pa isn't working."

Moshe had started his own contracting business but didn't do well "because he never charged much. . . . He was too honest to succeed."

"He generally trusted a man until he had been proved wrong," said Golda later. "This resulted in many disappointments for him, but he was unfailingly warm-hearted, always ready to do things for others and see the good in everyone."

The family story was that their trusting father went to buy some apples, but never looked at the bottom of the barrel. "They'd give him a few nice apples on top," said Golda, "but they'd put the rotten ones at the bottom of the bag. The juice of the rotten apples made a trail behind him."

Goldie was the first to learn a year later that Shana's daughter had been born. But Shana added that she was so fearful of her past TB that "I couldn't bring myself to kiss the child."

The Federal Census of 1910 listed Morris Mabowehz as forty-six, his wife, Bella, forty-three, then identified as "Keeper/grocery store." It reported, too, that Louis Sabelinsky, aged twenty-eight, also a brother of Morris, was then living with them. In the Jewish tradition, newly arrived immigrants moved in on their *landsmen* (relatives or former neighbors) and usually slept on the couch, if there was one.

If Bluma was "Bella" in the census, she was still "Bluma" at home, just as Morris was "Moshe." But Goldie was still "Goldie" on all her school records. She was soon smart enough to be skipped from the second half of the seventh grade to the eighth grade, but a note on her file indicated that she was "talkative." Her class picture in 1911 showed a strong-featured, handsome girl in a high-necked blouse. She was then thirteen, restless, and unhappy.

"My mother didn't want me to have an education," she said. "She thought it was for men only." The planned future of young Milwaukee Jewish girls was to quit school, clerk in a downtown store, and then "marry, marry, marry, while quite young."

Bluma had more miscarriages, forcing her to bed for several weeks, giving Goldie the brunt of the work. "So I cooked and scrubbed, hung laundry and minded the store, choking back tears of rage all the time because I was forced to miss even more school." Describing that time, Goldie said, "Life was very intense."

She was the class valedictorian in a white dress at her elementary school graduation, her grades excellent, her teachers all predicting a bright future.

Grade school graduation was more than a stepping-stone for Goldie and her peers. It was like crossing a mountain range and climbing to a peak, wondering what next.

No one in her family had ever reached that peak, and few of her peers wanted much more. But Goldie, even then, wanted *much*, much more. She now wanted to go to high school and then become a teacher. Becoming a teacher then seemed to be the *only* option available to an educated woman.

"Do you want to be an old maid?" asked her mother.

Bluma knew the state law forbidding female teachers to marry. Even Goldie's mild-mannered father agreed that men didn't like their wives to be too smart. Her mother suggested an alternative: secretarial school, "like all good girls."

"I don't know why . . . I never can explain to myself why I had such a horror of working in an office," said Golda later. "I suppose that's why I was punished and worked in an office in my grown-up life. Anyway, then I wouldn't hear of it. That's where the big clash came."

Stressing the need for security, her mother warned, "A clever girl you'll never be!" If secretarial school was good enough for her friend Regina, why wasn't it good enough for her?

Goldie argued, cried, despaired, then defiantly enrolled at North Division High School in the fall of 1912. Nor would she take any more money from her parents. She worked afternoons and weekends at a variety of jobs, still teaching English to immigrants at ten cents an hour.

In the *Jewish Courier*, an editorial asked, "Is there anyone who does not see the estrangement that is developing between Jewish parents and their children?"

This gap was hardly unique. It was common to almost every ethnic group, no matter what its history.

There is little question that Bluma loved Goldie, and even once had favored her. Her pride in Goldie was always obvious. But Bluma had been brought up with a fixed concept of the woman's role, a role unchanging for generations. Men studied the Torah and women studied the kitchen. A woman managed the home, raised her children, helped her husband—even managed a little store, as she was doing—but never, never had a woman in their family attempted higher education for a separate career. A woman might be the quiet boss in her family, but never a real boss in the outside world.

Goldie, now fourteen years old, saw herself as a new woman in a new world.

To cap the crisis, Bluma found a potential husband for Goldie. Mr. Goodstein was a pleasant man in his early thirties. He was in real estate and "quite well-to-do and really in love with Goldie," said Clara. "When he first asked Mother, she said, 'But she's so young!' Goldie was still only fourteen. And he said, 'I'll be willing to wait a few more years.' "

Bluma urged him on Goldie, stressing the wonderful future he would provide, but Goldie was incredulous. To her Goodstein was "an old man . . . twice my age."

In retaliation, Bluma flatly demanded that Goldie quit school. Goldie wrote of her despair to Shana and Sam on November 15, 1912.

"No, you shouldn't stop school. You are too young to work; you have good chances to become something . . . ," wrote Sam. Spurred by a wife and child, Sam now operated his own tailor shop during the day, working as a janitor at night. "You should get ready to come to us. We are not rich either, but you will have good chances here to study and we will do all we can for you."

Shana added a footnote: "You must come to us immediately."

Goldie remembered her mother's favorite axiom: "When you say no, you never regret it." She knew how her mother felt about Sam: "another lunatic with grand ideas and not a cent in his pocket." And she knew how bitter Bluma was about Shana. Goldie decided then that it was useless asking for parental permission. She must run away.

She checked the train schedules, the fare, and made her plans, confiding only to her dear friend Regina, whose help she needed.

Shana sent Goldie part of the money for a train ticket with the following advice: "The main thing is never to be excited. Always be calm and act coolly. This way of action will always bring you good results. Be brave."

It was advice that Goldie never forgot, repeating it and repeating it as long as she lived.

Besides some small savings of her own, Goldie borrowed the rest from an older friend, Sara Feder.

The final plan was simple, but dramatic.

"She lowered her small suitcase out of the window at ten o'clock at night," said Regina. "I took it home and hid it in the bushes. Then in the morning, she called on me to go to school as always, but we picked up her suitcase and took the trolley to Union Station. Years later, I sent her a picture of Union Station, just to remind her."

In her farewell note to her parents, which she left on her pillow, Goldie simply wrote that she was going to live with Shana, "so that I can study." Goldie later recalled looking at her sleeping sister Clara, "whom I didn't really know very well ... but that night I stroked her face and kissed her."

Goldie was still at the station waiting for a delayed train when her parents found her note. Clara described the scene, her mother sobbing, saying, "She's so young!"

"They loved Goldie very much," said Clara. "They were hurt. They couldn't understand."

In the resulting confusion, nobody checked for her at the railroad station. When they finally did, the train had just gone.

Clara bitterly resented Goldie's leaving. "I wrote her one of my so-called poems in which I said she preferred eating pig with my sister instead of being with our family in Milwaukee."

Bluma meanwhile stormed over to Regina's mother. "When I got home from school," said Regina, "my mother made me admit that I knew Goldie had taken the train. I had to tell them, but I didn't give too many details. Then she gave me a few good slaps—I never let Goldie forget that."

Regina afterward added an enigmatic note: "I hope I won't hurt your feelings, but everyone thought you had eloped with an Italian. How they got that idea, I can't get at ..."

3

Goldie stepped off the train at Denver's Union Station, "a little confused from the trip, from a night without sleeping." Not quite fifteen, Goldie had the full-formed body of a beautiful young woman, her firm jaw softened by the crinkling of her deep blue-gray eyes when she smiled. "Her face was wise and rich in expression, her eyes piercing, but a little sadness in them. She looked older than her age. Her mouth often had a stubborn set, showing the self-confidence and sense of direction." Tall, with long chestnut hair, Goldie wore the inevitable ankle-length black skirt and a high-necked white blouse, and carried her embroidered purse and a small suitcase.

Shivering on the platform were Shana, now almost twenty-four, Sam, and their two-year-old daughter, Judy. Shana looked at her younger sister, "blessed with a lot of good attributes, also faults worth watching," and it made her remember "my own childish girlhood years." The sense that stayed with Shana was that here was "a girl who stood good on her own feet."

On that wintry day in February 1913, the small family group boarded the yellow streetcar that crossed the trestle bridging the South Platte River, past the Denver city limits. The small group trudged up a hill to a small, tidy brick bungalow at the edge of the ghetto, on Julian Street. The ridge overlooked the river, was beautified by trees and wildflowers.

On a wet day, though, you still needed wooden planks to cross the nearby muddy streets.

The neighborhood had a feeling of a separate small town, almost a country air. The place next to Shana even had a cow and chickens. Shana baked her own bread, and sometimes put an extra loaf on a pulley in her kitchen that took it to her neighbor. Most of her neighbors were too tired after work to go anywhere. Instead, they sat on their front porches to watch the passing people. A friend recalls her father commenting on one of Shana's late meetings or Goldie's late dates: "A young lady shouldn't be walking on the streets at ten o'clock at night."

That year of 1913, Woodrow Wilson was inaugurated as the twenty-eighth President of the United States, and Richard Nixon was born. The most popular novel was *Pollyanna*, by Eleanor Porter, urging everybody to be more positive in order to succeed, no matter what the odds. That was also the year New York City's Grand Central Terminal opened, a biochemist isolated vitamin A, Henry Ford started his automobile assembly line, and zippers became popular. World War I was still a year away.

An exuberant travel writer had described mile-high Denver, nestled near the Rocky Mountains, as a city of optimism, buoyancy, and extravagance, an American Paris. It was not Paris. The big local news that year was the merging of the *Denver Post*–owned circus with Buffalo Bill's Wild West Show. The city directory then listed more than 150 mining companies, sixty-three blacksmiths, thirteen carriage- and wagon-makers, twenty-nine horseshoers, and twenty-five cigar manufacturers. Surprisingly, Denver also boasted the largest collection of Chinese pheasants in the country and an electrically operated fountain featuring endless patterns in artistically created colored water, the reflection shimmering among the small boats.

The Denver winter, too, made Milwaukee seem mild to Goldie, giant drifts of snow enveloping everything. It was magnificent, made the fresh air brisk and emanated a kind of clean white hope. Goldie loved it. And she laughed at the enterprising small boys with wooden carts hitched to dogs, doing the shopping for the homebound people.

In the gold rush of 1859, it was "Pike's Peak or bust," and Jews came to Colorado along with everyone else. They came mostly as traders, but some of them went into cattle ranching, while others pioneered three (unsuccessful) agricultural communities.

The early Jews were largely Orthodox, and included a *mohel*, who specialized in circumcising newborn male Jews. The Sabbath for these Orthodox Jews was not simply ritual, it was "a holiday laid on the street," something you could "feel." Simhat Torah was such a joyous holiday that they literally danced through the street on the way to the synagogue. And Tashlich, the annual time of purification, meant a parade of people, dressed in their best, heading for the Platte River to cast their sins into it.

Denver was a city of 225,000 with 6,000 Jews when Goldie came there. Most Jews settled in an area of four square blocks of West Colfax, under the viaduct, on the city's west side. The majority had come with "lung trouble" and were "chasing the cure." Many came on stretchers, completely ravaged, soon destined to die. More came penniless, and often were found dead in doorways.

Similar to Milwaukee's Walnut Street, large families packed into small tenements, "but we were happy. We didn't know any better. We were just like a big family where nobody had any money."

Sometimes little girls even went to school wearing bloomers made out of flour sacks. Such was the fraternalism that most people could name every family on the block. "It was so close-knit that when somebody sneezed, your next-door neighbor said, '*Gezundheit.*'"

Shana sensed Goldie's concern about worrying her parents. "Goldie, however, doesn't have regrets," she recorded. "When she makes up her mind, she carries out her decisions."

Shana's often-repeated motto fit Goldie then:

"A person is weaker than a fly and stronger than iron."

There was more fly than iron in Goldie in those days. She was tired, overwhelmed. She had, after all, done an enormous thing. For a girl, not quite fifteen, in that era, it was a monumental move. Few of her peers ever even dreamed of it. To cut the umbilical cord of a highly possessive Jewish mother was like cutting steel.

Shana had done it, but then Shana was older. Goldie knew Shana was now proud of her, and that pride meant more to Goldie than her mother's hurt. Shana was her model. Without thinking about it, she loved Shana more than she loved her mother. She did not feel like an outcast; she felt she was home.

"I prepared a delicious dinner for her," Shana said. "Little by little, she recovered."

A new world opened when she enrolled at North Side High School. Newly built and twenty blocks away, North Side High was made up mostly of "rich Gentiles," Italians, and very few Jews. This was a strange world, the first time she had mixed with such totally different young people, the American Americans. Her initial adjustment was not easy. Yearbooks stressed "the value of football" and accented the social hour, "the laughter and gossip of pupils ... and music loud and sweet." It must have boggled Goldie's mind to know that the dance rage was the Turkey Trot and the latest fashion was the hobble skirt. And can anyone imagine Goldie's reaction to the class yell: "Boom a laika, boom a laika, WOW! WOW! WOW!"

Goldie had little time to sample any of this. There is also no record that she dated any boys wearing Prince Albert coats and knickers, going to the class picnic at Clear Creek. Straight from school every day, Goldie hurried to the trolley, paid her nickel fare, got off in the heart of town near the famous Brown Hotel. There her brother-in-law Samuel Korngold was listed in the city directory as "Prop. Wisconsin Cleaning and Pressing Works." Goldie pressed clothes, waited on customers, and shut shop at seven while Sam hurried over to the Mountain Telephone Company, where he worked as night janitor. Afterward, Goldie went home to help Shana prepare supper and do the dishes. The kitchen table cleared, she could then use it to do her homework.

Golda was an "A" student. She got the top grades in English, algebra, Latin, ancient history, music, and German. She got her only "C" in a required course called mechanical drawing, which she never could describe. As for physical culture, her lasting memory was the uniform, the middy blouses with voluminous black bloomers that met the black stockings below the knee.

As much as school stretched her mind, it didn't create the dynamism that made her what she was. The ideas that seeded and nurtured her all happened night after night at her sister's house.

The home of Sam and Shana was a haven for all the *catootnicks* (nonconformists) in town. These were the poets, philosophers, rebels, writers, radicals from various political fringes who came almost nightly for tea and talk. Mostly they were lung-sick, lonely young bachelors anxious to divert themselves with hot arguments on how to solve the problems of the world. Shana tried to shoo Goldie to bed before the discussions began, but "I managed to stay up most nights by volunteering to disinfect the cups afterward—an offer which was rarely turned down."

As the youngest one there, Goldie mostly listened, absolutely fascinated by the sparkling conversation. Admittedly, most of the heady talk "was way over my head." She knew absolutely nothing about such philosophers as Kant and Kropotkin. Nor did she understand anything about all the political splinters that made up Zionism.

What did sink deep into her soul was the basic talk of Zionism itself, the need for a new national home in Palestine, Eretz Yisroel. "That made the most sense to me," she said. It made more than sense. It became such a beacon, and she saw it so clearly, so sharply, so emotionally that it seemed to shape her life into an arrow, with one direction. She was no longer a young girl wondering where to, what next. She now knew.

"The Jews are one people, because our enemies have made us one," pronounced Theodor Herzl at the first Zionist Congress in Switzerland, the year before Goldie was born. "We might perhaps be able to merge ourselves entirely into the surrounding races, if these people were able to leave us in peace for the space of two generations. But they will not leave us in peace."

The dictum of this Zionist Congress began with a blunt declaration: "The task of Zionism is to secure for the Jewish people in Palestine a publicly recognized, legally secured homeland."

"At Basel, I founded the Jewish state," Herzl recorded in his diary. "If I said this out loud today, I would be answered by universal laughter. Perhaps in five years, and certainly in fifty, everyone will know it."

Goldie knew it at the age of fifteen.

No Turkey Trot, no hobble skirts, no "Boom a laika, boom a laika, WOW! WOW! WOW!" Instead, a remote place she could hardly visualize called Palestine. It was then part of the Turkish Ottoman Empire, but a thin flow of Jews continually migrated there, regarding it as part of their 2,000-year-old heritage, a land given to them by God.

Many disagreed. "A delusion and a snare . . . so absurd it borders on insanity. . . . the assimilation of Jews among his fellow men is not only a possibility but a necessity. . . . In the United States, and only here, will the Jew finally find his Zion."

More sharply, a Denver rabbi said Palestine was sterile and only fit for Jews to die in.

But Goldie, urged even more by Shana, had been caught by the Zionist dream personified by Herzl. Goldie never forgot that it was Shana who had worn mourning clothes for Herzl for two years after his death. The Hebrew origin of the word "zion" was "rock" or "stronghold," but became synonymous with Jerusalem.

The difference in their commitment was that Shana had paid her dues by the daily danger she had faced in Russia, while Goldie was a fresh convert who still saw everything mainly in terms of adventure and challenge.

In analyzing all of her life, "challenge" was a key word. And, perhaps, here in Denver, that word took on its greatest strength. Palestine was a challenge. Zionism was a challenge. And now, more than ever, the future was a challenge.

"I suppose you meet high intellectual people who always talk about books and dry subjects," Regina wrote sixteen-year-old Goldie.

She had a more social life, too. As her friend Minnie Willens—who walked to school with her—later recalled, "Goldie was vivid," and the male members of the nightly group soon courted her. They began taking her to lectures, concerts, walks in the park. It was all very heady for radiant, romantic Goldie. Some declared their love, a few even proposed marriage, and Goldie found herself coming home at night later and later. Her energy was inexhaustible, and her frenetic social life did not seem to interfere with her school grades or her outside work.

One would have expected Shana the revolutionary to be permissive about Goldie's social life. She wasn't. She was now a respectable wife and a responsible mother, with all kinds of community obligations. She organized a bazaar: "HELP VICTIMS OF THE WHITE PLAGUE. Admission 25 cents. One free chance with each ticket for a solid 14-karat-gold watch." Shana now kept her Zionist beliefs carefully compartmentalized while she lived this more conventional life. Just as she maintained the tradition of the family Shabbat, she similarly kept a tight, critical watch over Goldie. Goldie felt she was being treated more like another child than a younger sister. More often and more loudly, Shana complained about Goldie's late nights with young men.

At first sight, Shana looked tiny and fragile with the delicate fine-boned face of a little bird, a little shadow of a woman, her hair pulled back tightly into a little bun. But the real Shana was dynamic and hot-tempered.

"Shana thought that what she said was direct from God," remembered Regina. "She was always driving people to do things according to her precise standards, constantly criticizing. She could be a very hard person, dogmatic and domineering, often very difficult and very selfish like her mother. She was not a warm person. I know somebody who once called her a lemon."

Surely, some of Shana's bitter trials may have soured her. Living on the thin economic edge may have drained some of her warmth. Was there any jealousy of a much prettier younger sister being buzzed around by so many young men? Or did the worried, harried Shana envy Goldie's lack of responsibility? Or was it simply that she didn't have time to be too considerate?

She unquestionably bore down on Goldie, much like their mother might have done. Goldie's awe of her dramatically lessened. As intensely as Goldie still admired and respected Shana, she now resented her "bossiness," her frequent nagging, "watching me like a hawk." Goldie wondered whether she "might just as well have stayed in Milwaukee."

Finally, the explosion came. The small house was no longer big enough for a willful teenager and a strong-minded woman. Goldie bolted. "I marched out of the house in the black skirt and white blouse I had been wearing all day, taking nothing else with me."

Her deed was unexpectedly daring, even more daring than the first time she left home. The first time, she knew where she was going. Now she didn't. Suddenly Goldie had no job, no home, no money. Going back to her parents would admit utter defeat, and this was something she could never ever do. She never knew what it was to be shamefaced, cowed, or beaten. It seemed inconceivable, though, that she would stay away long. After all, Shana was not only the greatest influence in her life, but her absolute model, the one she adored most in the world.

What Goldie wanted was something much more. She wanted to prove that she was her own person. She wanted to show Shana, and everybody else, that she had her own independent spirit, her own stubborn pride, and would fight for it. She didn't know how, but she did know why. In the chronology of her life, this moment was critical. It was a prologue of the woman to come. "When she makes up her mind," Shana said of her, "she carries out her decision."

Where could she live? Who would take her without money? Her only hope was a young couple she had met, both seriously ill with tuberculosis. They had a small room with a foyer. Yes, she could sleep in the foyer until she found a job, and another room. The couple went to bed early, coughed most of the night. "The man was in the last stages." If Goldie wanted to read late, the only possible place was the bathroom.

More critical and more painful was her next decision. What about school? She loved school. She had run away from home to continue it. But she needed a full-time job to pay for room and board. This, then, was the price of her independence: find a job and quit school. Or else surrender, go back to Shana, apologize. Surrender was not an option for Goldie. She quit school. In her young life, this was the low point, her most mature decision, her first real defeat. She once had dreamed of college. Her school yearbook that term defined college as "a castle in the air." How she must have grimaced at that. She was suddenly, dramatically, bitterly in the real world now.

Her father had once told her, "When you chop wood, you get splinters."

The only job Goldie could find was in a laundry, stretching curtains. The stretcher nails made her hands bleed, but the work paid six dollars a week, more with overtime. She didn't know then that men workers who did the same job made twice as much.

So now she had her independence, a tiny room of her own, but the price was steep. The price was the awareness that she was "almost as lonely as independent." She never before had been really lonely. She was always a people person with friends easy and everywhere. Never was it more true with all the young men at Shana's house. This rift with Shana had its own impact on those young men. Coming to Shana's house at night was their needed ritual. Most of them now felt it would be imprudent to visit Goldie now and maybe anger Shana. Goldie now faced a painful reality: dull work, pitiful wage, bitter independence, and a lonely, empty room. If she didn't cry then, when would she cry? And if she did cry then, she would never ever admit it.

As long as she lived, she would always hate being alone. Perhaps it all began here.

Never before had she been so vulnerable.

And then came Morris.
Morris Meyerson was a shy, gentle man who loved books and music.

He was not as flashy as his other young friends at Shana's, nor as verbal, and among the youngest—he was not quite twenty-one. Neither tall nor handsome, he wore steel-rimmed spectacles and his hair had started to thin. His had been a life squeezed by circumstance. He was only twelve when his family had come to Philadelphia from Lithuania, and his father died soon afterward. Morris worked during the day, went to school at night, but never stopped studying, never stopped reading, never stopped listening to music. Basically, Morris was a highly private man. Shana's daughter, Judy, remembered, "He didn't like a lot of people around. He liked his family, but everybody else, 'Stay away . . .' "

His life changed when his sister Sarah got tuberculosis. The whole family, his mother and three sisters, moved with him to Denver, where Sarah became Shana's hospital roommate and her good friend. The two were discharged nearly together. Listed in the city directory as a "sign painter," Morris found the work sporadic and the pay poor. He never could afford a blue serge suit at the May Company Store, a suit that cost $11.50. They paid twelve dollars a month for an apartment on Galapagos Street, near a Lithuanian synagogue, at the edge of an Irish neighborhood.

Morris and Goldie needed each other. Goldie was at the edge of adulthood, a confusing, frightening time. She needed a rudder, a family, love. Morris was also searching. Meeting Goldie was as if somebody suddenly had ripped apart his careful cocoon of books and music. He had never ever met anyone like her before. She had a life force he had never known. She had zest and joy and a quickness of spirit. She had a marvelous laugh that left him tingling.

Goldie willingly let Morris envelop her. He was not only her suitor, but her substitute family and her substitute school. Music had been a magic mystery to her, and he seemed to know all its secrets. Poetry had appeared an impractical flower in her hard, realistic world. He seemed to pull poems out of the air, and he made books come wonderfully alive.

Morris became her rudder. Golda would later say, "Denver was a turning point because my real education began. In Denver, life really opened up for me." She could have substituted "Morris" for "Denver."

Morris's interest in politics was almost nonexistent: he had no concern for Zionism. But his concentration on Goldie was complete. He persuaded her to find another job, this one taking measurements of skirt linings. And, when she finished work, he was almost always there, waiting.

Without money, their entertainment had to be mainly free. Denver prided itself on having more free concerts in city parks than almost any other city in America. Most concerts were a musical mélange such as tenor solos from "Moonlight Bay," Strauss's "Blue Danube," scenes from *Il Trovatore*, Liszt's Second Hungarian Rhapsody, "Gems from Stephen Foster," the overture to *Tannhäuser*, the "Swedish Wedding March," a marching song called "Boost Denver," and even the Jewish prayer music, "Kol Nidre."

Almost every park had a band. In Washington Park, the Denver Letter Carriers' Band noted that "popular encores will be played after each number." Introductory words were kept to a minimum. One program advertised "one short speech by one short man short of time."

Nor were Denver citizens modest about their music. They trumpeted the quality of their fifty-piece municipal band, called their new bandstand "the best equipped and most perfectly arranged in the West, rivaled only by the ones in Philadelphia and Chicago." For a memorable concert that June, they even removed the "Keep off the grass" signs.

Goldie described the music "that floated out over the thin Rocky Mountain air," and added, "To this day, I associate certain pieces of music with the clear dry air of Denver and the wonderful parks in which Morris and I walked in the spring and summer of 1914."

That summer the United States Marines had occupied Vera Cruz because the Mexican president had refused a twenty-one-gun salute to the American flag. Marines boasted of a weapon that "can shoot 400 Mexicans a minute and never get hot." But the incident ended when the Mexican president resigned. World War I had begun in Europe but we were not yet in it—the Germans were trying to cut through the Russian lines. In Chicago, 6,000 suffragettes had marched demanding the vote. In Denver, the first-prize winner in a dandelion-picking contest got three dollars. A careful count showed that 63,256 dandelions had been picked from Broadway to Cherokee Street.

Morris gave Goldie an intense introduction to his home away from home, Dickinson Library. Here the two became part of lectures, meetings, discussions, story hours, with time out for tea. "We read books together," said Golda. "Byron, I remember especially, and the Book of Job." Morris also made reading lists for her which "were always terrifyingly long." The really serious lectures were at the Workmen's Circle on subjects scientific, economic, philosophical, psychological, or historical, "which develops morals and clears the mind of the dust of the factory. . . ." The other young people they met there were more concerned with the world than with themselves.

Other things cost money. It cost a quarter for admission to the public dances where the number of women a man could bring "is not limited." It cost another quarter to see traveling Jewish actors playing in *The Price of Love*, or *The Woman of Today*. More often, Morris and Goldie went rowing at Sloan's Lake, shared an occasional soda at Weiner's Drugstore, and went on long walks where they held hands, recited poetry, and fell in love.

> Instants may come when the magic seems broken,
> My vision is blinded, my compass untrue.
> Suddenly awakens my jubilant singing,
> Turns once again its lodestar to you.

Goldie was becoming a woman, and this poem epitomized her emerging tender feelings, although in later years, a friend once said of Golda, "She was never soft or clinging."

She was then.

Surrounded and smothered by three sisters and a mother, Morris still knew remarkably little about women. Romance to him was the poetry of Byron or the overture to *Romeo and Juliet*. The physical part of love was still an unknown adventure. Hand-holding was a tremulous experience and a good-night kiss was an event. He was too shy to express his love and Goldie was not yet bold enough to take the initiative, and so "for a long time we said nothing to each other about the way we felt."

"I had a postcard from Goldie in which she rhapsodized about Morris," said Regina, "how she met him, how much she was in love with him, how she couldn't wait for me to meet him." In it, Goldie admitted that Morris wasn't very handsome "but he has a beautiful soul."

What was equally important to Goldie was that Morris seemed even more interested in *her* soul, much more so than all the other young men she had met at Shana's with their freethinking concepts of love and sex. She felt the depth of Morris's love; he had made it glow like a literary romance, which made him so absolutely different from the others. All this is why she settled so exclusively on this shy young man. He stretched her mind and her soul at the same time.

Morris gave her flowers he had picked in the park, the only ones he could afford. Occasionally he found an art reproduction in a magazine that he cut out and framed himself, giving it to her as a special gift. She made much of all of it.

Trying to please him, Goldie paid fresh attention to her clothes, something she was never before concerned with because she couldn't afford anything new. She would wash her only blouse every night "so I'd be spick-and-span." And one day she splurged on a new red straw hat which cost her ten cents at Woolworth's. The salesgirl had warned her that any rain would make the color run down on her head. From then on, she was increasingly nervous about the weather at their outdoor concerts.

Goldie had time to think of all this at the *shvitz*, the steam bath at Cook's where "everything is spotlessly clean and perfectly sanitary." Wrapped in a thick towel, soaking in the steam and sipping tea, Goldie would consider her various options.

"I can't even imagine why a teenager would want to go to a *shvitz*," said the daughter of one of Goldie's close friends. "I once went with my mother and it was no fun. It was embarrassing." This same woman found a note in her mother's papers recording that a man named Max Sunshine acted as Goldie's escort when she went to the *shvitz*. Who was Max Sunshine? An admirer? An older man protecting a teenager in an unlikely neighborhood? There is no other record.

There is also no record of what she thought in that *shvitz*, but we know what she felt. She missed Shana and she knew, more than ever, that she now needed the counsel of an older sister, particularly an older *married* sister. It had been six months since they had even talked to each other, and she now decided to bend her pride and make peace, but on more independent terms. If she did now go back to Shana, she also could return to school. Maybe college would no longer be "a castle in the air"? Maybe teaching was still a viable future? Morris had so intensified her need for learning.

Morris? She was still too young to marry, only seventeen, although she knew some who had married even earlier. She loved Morris, truly loved him, but was he ready for marriage? He was still the prime support for his mother and three sisters, one of them a chronic tubercular. She also knew how unpredictable was his part-time sign-painter pay. The romantic present did not seem to correlate with the practical future.

She made her peace with Shana, but the rest of her future now suddenly shaped itself. A letter came from her father. She and her parents had not written to each other since she had left. Whatever home news she got came from Regina. Looking at her letter, she expected the worst. Who had died? Her mother? Her sister? Some crippling financial disaster?

She knew how much pride her father had to swallow to write to her. It was simple, almost stark: if she valued her mother's life, she should come home at once.

What should she do? Did she suspect that her parents had somehow discovered that she had left Shana, left school, was living alone, that they now wanted to save her "from a fate worse than death"? She loved Morris but she did not love her job. She wanted to go back to school. She missed her friends in Milwaukee. She missed her father.

Morris understood all that Goldie felt. He also knew that she was too young for marriage and he was not yet ready.

Go home, said Morris firmly. He promised to follow as soon as his sister was cured.

"One night before I left," said Golda, "Morris told me shyly that he was in love with me and wanted to marry me."

Both must have wondered if this was the end or the beginning. Shortly before leaving, Goldie received a letter from Regina congratulating her on her "blissful happiness," a letter which was badly timed.

4

Milwaukee hadn't changed much in three years, but Goldie had. She now had a supreme self-confidence. She had defied her parents and her dogmatic sister, and had proved her independence. She had lived on her own, supporting herself. And she had been desired, courted, fallen in love. The world was her oyster and she was not yet eighteen.

"Goldie was fearless," recalled her friend Sadie Ottenstein, who lived across the alley and now walked with her to school every morning. "There was nothing giggly about her even then. She was a firebrand with very strong convictions. For her, everything was either right or wrong, with no middle way. We always ran to her with our troubles." Reflecting on this, her best friend Regina Hamburger added, "Goldie changed the whole course of my life. I don't know what would have happened to me if I hadn't met her."

Her parents also now knew Goldie for what she was, a young woman with her own determined mind, who seemed head and shoulders above them. Relations particularly with her mother now improved. There were no more quarrels about how much schooling she should get, or whether she should become a teacher. It was Goldie's decision.

High school senior Goldie became even more serious than ever about her studies. "Goldie was always head of our class," noted Regina, "and I limped after her as second-best pupil." The greater difference in Goldie was that her goal was now sharper. Thanks to Morris and her intellectual Denver friends, she had become "a voracious reader." "We went to the public library several times a week," said Regina, "and took out all kinds of books: Dostoevsky, Tolstoy, Chekhov, Gogol, de Maupassant, Anatole France, Victor Hugo, Arnold Bennett, Galsworthy, H. G. Wells. And many a tear we shed over Dickens's *Tale of Two Cities*, *David Copperfield*, and *Oliver Twist*. And the American writers, of course: Hawthorne, Mark Twain, you name it. And the thing to remember is that we had no TV or radio to distract us." Goldie also tried playing the piano but gave it up because "I decided I would rather spend my time reading books."

"The first opera I ever saw was *Aida* with Goldie and we sat way up in the topmost gallery, but it was wonderful. And Goldie and I often went to the theater, at ten cents a ticket. Very good Yiddish plays came to Milwaukee . . . mostly on sad themes and we had a good cry. . . . Four out of every five boys at school fell in love with her . . . she was so vibrant and attractive."

There were even girls who developed crushes on her. A letter from one of them said: "I do need a friend in whom I can confide all my longings and desires, and I am sure I have found it in you. . . . Yet it is probably true that you do not need me. You have many true friends who really admire you for your true worth; you have various organizations and doings to keep you busy; and best of all, you have the courage of your convictions. You see, all qualities which I lack."

Horror stories of the World War started coming out at that time. Jews were the certain victims. When the Russians retreated, they massacred Jews, calling them German sympathizers. When the Germans retreated, they slaughtered the Jews, calling them Russian sympathizers.

Goldie and her friends always reached for poetry to fill their feelings. This was a favorite:

There must be a huge cup in Heaven
And as the Jewish tears fall,
That cup will be filled.
And when it will overflow
Then, maybe, the Jewish people will be helped.

Equally poignant was this plea she received:

"Dear friend, must we not pay with something that we are in America and not with the massacred downtrodden Jews of the Ukraine.... Will you be able to escape from your conscience?"

Goldie was a woman whose conscience was never quiet. "Goldie and her hard-working father did a tremendous amount of work raising money for the Jewish Relief Society for clothes and food. I think Goldie felt, too, that it was the kind of thing Shana would have done, and she was following in her footsteps," said Regina.

Father and daughter went from door to door raising money, and this became the new base of a growing bond between them, a deeper relationship. Moshe could do this thing now because he felt more secure and assimilated, financially and emotionally. Being involved in this cause for a common good also gave him a greater sense of personal worth and satisfaction, made him better able to stand up against the demanding force of his wife.

Golda's fund-raising technique differed from her father's. Faced with a reluctant giver, she simply stared at him and said, "I wasn't born among royalty either." She usually got the donation.

Comparing herself then to Goldie and Shana, Clara said, "If there was something they felt they had to do, they did it.... I always felt left out.... Goldie was so much more serious-minded. She never went in for the kind of nonsense I did. I went in for baseball and all that stuff. I was really the only American in the family."

Clara tried to fight her own fight. She organized a group of teenagers, boys and girls, who called themselves the Tenth Street Gang. Their purpose was to confront a roving anti-Semitic gang from a nearby neighborhood known as the Totemic Indians. But when the Indians challenged Clara's group to a fight, "I was so scared, I hid under the grocery counter." Yet she was proud of her father's encounter with the Indians. Noticing a crowd gathered outside a local store, he was told, "They're beating up the grocer, a Jew."

"Well, what are you standing out here for?" he said, and went in and started fighting the Indians. "Others followed him when Father chased them down the street. They never came back to our section."

Goldie's father crossed the bridge between the two worlds, but Clara never really did. She stayed on the American side.

"I even joined the Campfire Girls. My family couldn't quite make me out. I remember the first time I put powder on my face . . . they were sure I was going to be a streetwalker. Why should a respectable girl put powder on her face?"

The deeper reason for Clara fighting her own fight was that she needed desperately to get out of her sister's shadow, develop her own confidence, be her own person.

"If I didn't love Goldie so much, I could hate her." Clara, then not quite a teenager, had lived in peace with her parents, still their "golden child." "Goldie was such an excellent student. The story of my life was that when I stood up in class in front of one of Goldie's old teachers, the teacher would always tell me, 'You're not like your sister Goldie . . .' I've heard that all my life, 'You're not like your sister Goldie . . .'"

One of Clara's reasons for simmering anger against Goldie was that she felt Goldie could do anything she wanted, Goldie could even run away "while I was stuck with the store."

"You know, Goldie never in her life as much as powdered her nose!" said Sadie Ottenstein, another girlhood friend. "Never! She told me that young women are like flowers. Nothing has to be added to them to make them more beautiful. I finally powdered my nose, Goldie or no Goldie. But I was thirty-five before I dared to put on lipstick."

With their improved finances and a better apartment, Moshe expanded his Zionist involvement, and Bluma happily went along. Bluma saw it as lending social excitement, and some local status, to provide "an open sofa" in her living room for the incoming flow of prominent speakers. Goldie's return also meant a continuous open house for young Zionists, as well as a regular stream of letters from Morris. Who was this Morris? Goldie simply smiled and said cryptically, "Oh, just somebody." Bluma promptly tagged him "Mr. Somebody."

"Golda was quite secretive about the whole thing," said Clara. "She felt this was her affair. She confided in Regina, but not me."

When Bluma's curiosity grew too great, she steamed open one of Morris's letters. Since her English was too poor to read it, she asked Clara to translate it into Yiddish. Yiddish was still the spoken language at home and the children were all fluent in it. Clara at first refused to translate. "I was heartbroken. I didn't want to do it. I was horrified. I was a Campfire Girl, honor bright." But Bluma was adamant. As a mother, she said, she had a right to know.

Clara read part of the letter. In English, it said:

"Are you still worrying about me and the meaning of the strain of sadness you discern in my letters? My sadness is . . . only part of that universal sadness that is bound to permeate every person endowed with the least bit of sensibility and clarity of vision. Can any thinking person be altogether happy and satisfied? Therefore, don't worry. Be the same happy, smiling Goldie you were heretofore."

Satisfied, Bluma resealed the letter. Nothing was said to Goldie until Clara's guilty feelings forced her to confess to her sister what had happened. She insisted that she had not read "the more personal bits." Goldie was furious. For a long time, she would not talk to either her mother or Clara. From that time on, all letters from Morris were mailed to Goldie at Regina's house.

Morris's influence was apparent when Goldie joined a literary society after school, a group that discussed Yiddish classics and brought in speakers from Chicago to conduct seminars. Admission was twenty-five cents and she later smilingly recalled a man refusing to pay, insisting that he had not come for the lecture "but to ask questions."

Attending one of these lectures, about Jewish dramatists, was Isadore Tuchman, a young, ardent Zionist. A blond man with heavy glasses, he came to Milwaukee by way of Poland and Dubuque, Iowa—where he started as a cigarmaker, then prospered as head of a paper company. Golda later credited him with being a paramount influence on her. He was impressed with her from the first.

"I noticed this striking girl on the platform surrounded by old women. I thought what on earth is this young girl doing with all these old women? She doesn't belong at all!" What further impressed Tuchman was Goldie's fluency in Yiddish, her personal ease and control as chairman. "So I got in touch with her and asked if she'd join our movement."

His movement was the Poale Zion.

Poale Zion was a Zionist political splinter group that sprang up sporadically in the 1890s in Switzerland, Germany, and Russia. It synthesized socialists and Zionists, called them "two branches of the same trunk." Other twigs included ethics, utopianism, ideals of biblical prophecy, dialectical materialism, and the vision of a better world for mankind. For these Jews, all this could only happen in a homeland of their own in Palestine.

Goldie saw it as another challenge, another excitement. New horizons, a new door to a new world. She felt both flattered and aroused. More and more now, she was emerging from Shana's shadow and was being recognized for herself.

As flattered as she was, Goldie did not jump at joining. As she said repeatedly, "I will not be a parlor Zionist." Joining Poale to her meant a commitment to go to Palestine. She was not yet ready to make that commitment. "That made no sense to me whatsoever, to be a Zionist and just stay in America. It just made no sense." But she was ready and anxious to attend meetings, soak in as much as she could.

The persuasive Tuchman then talked Goldie into teaching at the Poale Zion Folkshule. The unique Folkshule concentrated on teaching children some of their heritage, the songs, the stories, the poetry, all in Yiddish.* The particular appeal to Goldie was that it combined the cause with the language she knew so well.

It was open on Saturday afternoon, Sunday morning, and one more day during the week. Everybody there was a volunteer, receiving no salary, and this was the only time Goldie was ever a teacher. "I liked to teach," she said. "I never had any problems with discipline or anything like that. I wanted to be a teacher ever since I was eight."

"I always thought I was her one failure," said a former student. "She tried to teach me Yiddish and failed."

"Politics, politics, politics," said Mrs. Tuchman, describing their frequent evenings at Goldie's house. It came on Sabbath nights after the lighting of candles, the prayer over the wine, and the delicious chicken soup with noodles.

In these discussions, Goldie was no longer the eager, curious girl she had been in Denver, sitting and listening on the sidelines. Now she was an ardent center of conversations, made more noticeable because there were so few other women.

"After the politics," said Tuchman, "we joked and sang." Goldie later added, "I always sang at the drop of a hat."

---

*Yiddish is a thousand-year-old language combining German, Slavonic, and Hebrew vocabulary with a Hebrew alphabet. Originally the language of Ashkenazi Jews in Europe, it spread all over the world and was once used as the mother tongue of more than eleven million Jews. There has been a recent movement to introduce Yiddish into the curricula of universities.

"Goldie's house was a kind of headquarters for the young people, at all hours," said Sadie Ottenstein. "It never bothered her mother. She always made us feel welcome, no matter what time we came. I don't know how she managed. Sometimes the boys would help out and bring some corned beef, bread, and pickles. But Bluma always made tea or coffee. And there was this barrel of wine that never seemed to get empty. We used to joke that they would put in more water and out would come more wine."

"My father used to go to Goldie's house for meetings," said Sadie Ottenstein's daughter Aviva. "These were people who really had nothing. None of them. But they'd play practical jokes on one another. He once told me of somebody putting some silverware into somebody's pocket just before he left the house, saying, 'You know, I think something's missing,' and then pulling the silverware from his pocket. Big joke! But they were a very tight, close group."

Sadie recalled that most of the young men were in their twenties, and the only other young woman besides Goldie was Sarah Feder, who was also a teacher.

"They were a pioneer group, all idealistic with a capital 'I,' " Sadie continued. "They worked six days a week and then spent Sunday morning teaching children at the Folkshule."

Another Poale haven was the home of a Hebrew poet. His private library became a clubroom for many of the Poale Zion bachelors, especially those who had to board with other people. They would discuss books and issues and read poetry aloud. One of their favored poets, whom Goldie considered her "voice," was Rachel of Kinneret.*

Somebody described Rachel the poet to Goldie as "slim and erect in a long white dress, her long fair hair in a braid down her back, her blue eyes full of light and gaiety."

Rachel had written of her dream to work the land in Palestine:

No deeds of high courage
No columns of flame,

*Rachel Bluwstein (1890–1931), one of the first modern Hebrew poets, even though she didn't know any Hebrew when she first went to Palestine in 1905 from Russia. Many of her poems have been set to music and are still sung in Israel. Worked on a new settlement near the Sea of Galilee. Died of tuberculosis when she was forty.

I bring you,
My country,
To add to your fame.

She had left a home of wealth and culture to go to Palestine, to learn the language so she could write her lyrics in Hebrew about the rebirth of Palestine. She wrote about the hard life with poetic joy "in a spirit of exultation."

With all her energy, even Goldie often found it difficult to cope with all her new activities. "One of Mother's greatest problems with Goldie used to be trying to get her to go to bed at night—and then trying to get her up in the morning," said Clara.

Although Bluma viewed her Goldie with a new respect, she still would argue with her, and tease her. In a discussion about God, Goldie tried to explain that everything ultimately comes from nature. Bluma's reply was simple: "*Nu*, Goldala, let's see you make the rain come."

More and more, Goldie was edging closer to joining Poale Zion. The big push came from one of the visiting celebrities, Nachman Syrkin, one of Poale's founders. Man wasn't simply an economic animal, said Syrkin, he was an individual force with the power to shape history. Syrkin preached with a passionate fire, urging all Jews to put their lives on the line, make an *aliyah*, a migration to Eretz Yisroel (Palestine). He even urged Poale Zion members to walk on the sunny side of the street to get used to the blazing sun that they would find there.

"I found myself dreaming of joining the pioneers in Palestine," Golda said.

Poale Zion was highly selective about new members. The minimum age was eighteen. Goldie was a few months younger, but she was well known for her work, and they waived the rule. Poale Zion had an anthem, in the form of an oath, solemnly sung with clenched raised fist. Part of it was:

We swear it, we swear it,
Our oath mixed with blood and tears . . .
Brothers and sisters, we've suffered enough now;

Enough, enough, in exile to stay!
Take courage, take courage, to battle for freedom;
With courage, with courage, go forth to the fray.

Hearing the news, Morris Meyerson was not pleased. His interest was poetry, not politics. In a letter dated August 1915 he wrote:

I do not know whether to say that I am glad or sorry that you have joined the Zionist Party, and that you seem to be so enthusiastic a nationalist. I am altogether passive in the matter, though I give you full credit for your activity, as I do to all others engaged in doing something toward helping a distressed nation. . . . The idea of Palestine or any other territory for the Jews is, to me, ridiculous. . . . The other day I received a notice to attend one of the meetings . . . but since I do not care particularly as to whether the Jews are going to suffer in Russia or the Holy Land, I did not go. . . .

A majority of American Jews agreed with Morris. Zionism was a distant gleam of a remote dream for intellectual, idealistic, middle-class Jews. The *Jewish Daily Chronicle* editorialized, "Here in America lies the destiny of the Jew. . . . Every condition is right here for the accommodation of the conditions of modern life to the demands of the old faith." Rabbi Samuel Hirshberg sermonized to his Milwaukee congregation that there was no need to teach Yiddish to their children. "A religion can never make a man a foreigner; a language and foreign habits of thought can and must." There was no nobler, no grander tongue than English, he said, and he urged all Jews to develop "an all-pervading Americanism."

This same kind of ferment pervaded most Jewish communities in most large cities. Traveling speakers heightened it. Of those favoring Zionism, one of the most respected was the lofty voice of Louis D. Brandeis, soon to be an eminent member of the United States Supreme Court. "Palestine holds out a hope to the Jews," he told a Milwaukee audience. "It is to give them more liberty, not less. It is to give them what every race has, the privilege of dwelling in the land of their fathers. . . . Let us have a nation among the nations of the world."

One must keep remembering that Goldie was still not quite eighteen years old, still only a high school student. When she and Regina would go to a Poale Zion meeting, their mothers still asked them, "Where are you going? When are you coming home?" And when they answered, "After ten," the mothers' reply invariably was "How much after ten?"

With one exception, all Poale Zion members were unmarried, most of them poor, most of them working in shops. "I was the only one going to school," said Golda.

She and Sadie would walk to school in the morning, walk home for lunch, back again to school and back again home at three-thirty. Her grades still remained excellent: algebra, 89; plane geometry, 90; music, 86; rhetoric and composition, 88; American classics, 90; American literature, 90; English literature, 92; general history, 88; physiology, 90; physiography, 89; zoology, 90; Latin, 90. Her lowest grade was in drawing, 73.

Goldie was still in high school when they put her on the Poale Zion Executive Committee. Tuchman soon assigned Goldie to head the Gewerkshaffen, the annual fund-raising drive to help Jewish workers in Palestine. It was highly successful. They asked her to form an English-speaking branch of Poale Zion and she refused, saying that Poale Zion members "should know Yiddish at least."

Yossel Kopelov, Denver's philosopher-barber, had come to Milwaukee to join Goldie's group. He soon reported to Morris:

> This race of humanity, I mean girls, are already perfect ladies when we think they are only children. . . . They embody the life principle, they are the riddle of the universe, and that is why we are craving to solve them. And as for care and tenderness, don't worry, plenty of it. Always know that if a girl is loved by one, she is cared for tenderly by others too. . . .
>
> She is primordially good and she cannot be stuffed with base matter. She has a natural inclination toward the good and noble. . . .
>
> Meanwhile may I tell you that I am very glad of my stay in Milwaukee. I am very happy if I can contribute something to her mental store. She is real, young, energetic and studious and, from a nonpartisan point of view, she is not only a treasure but a kingdom. . . . I am reading Job with Goldie."

"Those about her, from her, shall read the perfect ways of honor." That's what it said about her in *The Tattler*, her high school yearbook, when Goldie graduated in 1916. It also mentioned her membership in the Lincoln Society, the Science Club, and the Pageant. At graduation, the girls wore white dresses, the boys blue-serge trousers. Some reports indicate she was the valedictorian, but a classmate insists, "I was the valedictorian, not Goldie, and I think that nettled her. I was no special favorite of hers, nor she of mine, but she was always an independent thinker ... always had her cause in mind—helping the underdog." Emphasizing this serious purpose, *The Tattler* also offered this further advice on Goldie: "Should not try to let her philosophy get the best of her enjoyment of life."

What next? A new phase of her life, but what phase? Morris was still in Denver writing her romantic letters. Palestine was still her goal, but one needed money and a plan to get to Palestine, and she had neither yet. Teaching offered security, vacations, a feeling of usefulness, a well-ordered life. She enjoyed teaching at the Folkshule, and her children enjoyed her. Enrolling at Milwaukee Normal School for Teachers therefore seemed a natural thing to do. But was it getting "the best of her enjoyment of life"?

"I remember Golda well because we both started Normal School together in the middle of a semester," said Louise G. Born, who became a teacher. "This meant we each had to do all the work in half the time. But we got through. She was a dominant girl who even at that age thought she carried the world on her shoulders. She always talked about *that* being wrong and *this* being wrong. So one day, I said, 'Goldie, if everything's wrong, why don't you start your own country?' And she said, 'I might just do that.' "

Soon after she started at Normal, she knew it was not enough. Teaching meant security and some satisfaction, but she now wanted a greater fulfillment, a greater excitement, a greater adventure.

The first time Goldie was scheduled for a Poale soapbox speech outdoors, her father was horrified. She would do no such thing, he insisted. If she did, he would pull her off her box by her braids. Goldie nevertheless made her speech to a large crowd. She saw her father among them, but he disappeared. When Goldie got home that night, her mother was waiting. She told Goldie that her father had come home shaking his head, saying quietly over and over again, "God knows what this girl may be able to do ... I don't know where she gets it from ... what a tongue!"

Long afterward, telling about it, and smiling, Golda said she still regarded that "speech on the crate" as "the best I ever made in my life."

Her scope was broadening—her first soapbox speech, her first outdoor rally. More and more thresholds.

Tuchman was always in the audience, and she turned to him to help provide the substance for her speeches.

Labor unionist Louis Perchonok recalled, "Even then Goldie's innate talent had begun to reveal itself—free of stage fright, courageous, possessing a reservoir of energy." Ottenstein added, "She'd look at a group and know immediately what to say and how to say it." "She had the ability to say the right word at the right occasion," Regina said, "and she was much better when she spoke spontaneously than when she read something. . . . Charisma is a tired word, but she had a lot of it."

Her giant leaps in self-confidence in her public life contrasted sharply with her growing questions about her private life. Throughout her life, this contrast and this conflict would always be unsatisfactorily unresolved. Her great worry at that time was her long-distance relationship with Morris. Did he still love her? Was she beautiful enough for him?

"I have repeatedly asked you not to contradict me on the question of your beauty," Morris wrote her. "You pop up every now and then with these same timid and self-deprecating remarks which I cannot bear."

Besides beauty, she had dynamism, and the combination dazzled most of the seventy young bachelors in her Poale chapter.

"Lincoln Park was our hangout," said Sadie Ottenstein. "It was almost three miles north of our neighborhood and seemed to be in the wilderness. It was a long walk after the end of the bus line. All the invited young women packed lunches which were auctioned off to the men, proceeds going to the Folkshule. We sat in a big circle singing songs. We had the grandest time. It was so beautiful, so inspiring. I don't think any group in the city, in the state, in the world ever had a more wonderful time than we did. When I think of it, I would like to live it all over again."

For Poale Zion, "our religion was Eretz Yisroel, the Palestine homeland." They celebrated Jewish holidays, not with prayer but with singing. As one of the members said, "When we sang, we sang with a holy feeling." "Did we sing!" said Ottenstein. "We sang so much! I don't know when Goldie was there when she wasn't singing!" Bringing a new song to a Poale audience was considered better than the best speech. Goldie sang her Yiddish in a warm contralto voice. One of her favorite songs was about a man in a small town selling salted fish. It is winter and it is cold and it is raining, and there are no customers. He sits there alone and starts to daydream, and it is a wonderful dream. He dreams there is a Jewish state in Palestine and everyone there is an angel. While he's daydreaming, a customer enters his store. She wants to buy a small amount of fish. There are several stores selling fish in that area, but this woman has come into *his* store. Business has been so bad that this storekeeper has barely been able to feed his family. But instead of jumping up to serve her, he is angry at her because she has interrupted his wonderful daydream.

The folksong ends with the thought that it is this illogical mystical daydream that has saved the Jewish people throughout time and history.

Goldie's Poale Zion primarily focused on Palestine. In Russia, the Zionists had split into the Reds and the Blues—the Reds who cooperated with the Bolshevik Revolution, the Blues who didn't. Goldie's Poale Zion were the Blues. In Milwaukee, which had elected a socialist mayor and a socialist congressman, and had a socialist daily newspaper, Poale Zion members were forbidden by their philosophy to join the Socialist Party. Poale Zion members were supposed to be strictly Poale Zion, with no other political loyalty. It would take Hitler to blend all Zionist splinters into a single solidarity.

Goldie's understanding of herself had matured by 1917. It came out of the complex growth of her intellect and experience and it crystallized the direction of her life. She decided that what she really wanted, more than anything else, was to pioneer on a kibbutz in Palestine. A kibbutz then was a small agricultural cooperative settlement usually set in the middle of nowhere equipped with almost nothing and dedicated to the goal of making the desert bloom. Where could she find a greater challenge? The Normal School yearbook that term had an article, "Responsibility," which emphasized that "a responsibility once assumed is just as binding as any obligation can be . . . for man's thought must end as it begins, in faith."

This was her responsibility, this was her faith. She would not be a teacher. She would be a pioneer. She quit the Normal School.

Goldie got news of a fresh outbreak of pogroms in Poland and the Ukraine. The personal shock came when she heard that forty Jews in Pinsk "were lined up near the wall of the church and shot."

"I remember my grandfather's house . . . facing the church. So whenever I think of it, I think of these men." She worried about her grandfather and other relatives, and later discovered that some very close neighbors were among those shot.

The stark reality of the new pogroms galvanized her into quick action.

Goldie decided to stage a protest parade in downtown Milwaukee, a public protest against these pogroms.

Hearing about it, the owner of one of Milwaukee's biggest department stores warned her: "You'll make a laughingstock of the Jews. They won't even be able to march straight down the street."

"I don't worry about that," said Goldie.

"You are going to embarrass me so much that I am going to move out of town," he told her.

"That's your privilege," Goldie replied.

What she strongly felt was that "we would earn the respect and sympathy of the rest of the city" by showing how they felt about the murder of these Jews.

Goldie was right. Many non-Jews joined the thousands of Jews, representing fifty organizations, in the parade to the Municipal Auditorium. Men, women, and children marched four abreast, followed by a band and a color guard of army veterans, bearing the Zionist colors of sky blue and white alongside the Stars and Stripes. Those were the days when such protest parades were few, and this event got national publicity.

What a heady coup for a teenager, what an emotional victory! An extubercular bookkeeper in Denver, Solomon Bloomgarden, better known as "Yehoash, the Yiddish bard of the Rockies," wrote a poem that fit the event:

When forward to the fate you sally
And must your warriors assess
'Tis not your arms you should tally
But rather hearts you must stress.

Her debate with Morris continued. Goldie tried to transmit some of her own excitement about Palestine to him and got this response:

"Have you ever stopped to think whether your Morris has the one attribute without which all other refinements are worthless, namely 'the indomitable will'?"

To support herself, Goldie worked in the Lapham Park Library. "We were both in the same library training group," said Ruth Shapiro. "Goldie never had any idea about being a librarian. This was just a job, a place to work." Ruth remembers her vividly as the beautiful girl in simple clothes who talked to a staff meeting about her childhood in Russia "and held everybody's attention."

Her library file included this comment: "She is a good person to have for library work and I am glad to have her."

Her library pay was only twenty cents an hour. It would take a long, long time to save enough money out of that to pay for passage to Palestine. Palestine seemed even farther away.

Her world pivoted on Poale Zion. Palestine needed people. It needed engineers, doctors, truck drivers, farmers, carpenters, clerical workers to volunteer for the fifty settlements there. The hope was that the volunteers might settle there permanently. Zionism needed more members—there were then only 130,000 throughout the world. And its immediate urgency was food and clothes for its Palestine pioneers.

Poale Zion featured fund-raising dinners. "We'd do our own cooking, shopping, serving, dishwashing. We'd go to the butcher and get ten pounds of chuck steak at ten cents a pound, and maybe two pounds of noodles and charge a dollar a dinner."

A Zionist executive estimated that "three cents' worth of bread a day (a loaf) will keep an individual alive in Palestine."

The picture of Palestine for Goldie was not simply that of an impoverished place that needed everything. It was a place of excitement where things were birthing, sprouting, growing, happening. It was adventure and conflict and challenge. Most of all, it was challenge. Something new in the world was happening there.

The news from Palestine brought an overflow of Jewish concern at this time. Published letters told of the roads "lined with starving persons, selling all their possessions for the price of bread." Retreating Turkish soldiers raped and robbed and massacred while the land was still theirs.

A Jewish legion had been organized to fight alongside the Royal Fusiliers in the British army to free Palestine from the Turks. "We Jews didn't want Palestine handed to us on a platter," said Harry Chemarow, one of the 10,000 volunteers. "We wanted to earn it." Morris Strezin, a North Division High schoolmate of Goldie's, later killed in an Arab raid, wrote home: "Jews have died for all other countries. It is good to die for our Palestine."

"I wanted to go, of course," said Golda, "but they wouldn't take any women. . . . I was heartbroken." She was also too young.

Most of the Milwaukee volunteers met at Goldie's house. Goldie's mother gave each volunteer a little bag containing a prayer shawl and homemade cookies.

Goldie finally got the news that she was waiting for: Morris was coming. His sister was well enough to return to Philadelphia with his mother and other sisters. He would come directly to Milwaukee, straight to her. Would she please find him a room? Goldie not only found him a room, but she rented a separate one for herself, on the same street.

Their relationship had changed since Denver. Morris was the same Morris, but Goldie was no longer the same Goldie. No longer was Goldie the impressionistic, romantic teenager, soaking in everything he said as being all-knowing and all-wise. The love was there, still deep. Morris's constant, sensitive, soul-searching letters had kept the flame kindled. He was, after all, her first real love. The large variety of young men Goldie had known in Milwaukee and Denver had never stirred her as Morris had. Morris had moved her mind with beauty and imagination, giving her a dimension she had never known, giving her an awareness of herself she had never had.

Goldie now had more answers than questions. Palestine was an answer, firm and sharp in her mind. Marriage with Morris was an answer, but it would have to include Palestine. If Morris wanted to marry her, he would have to marry Palestine.

"Morris was a wonderful fellow," said Mrs. Isadore Tuchman, "a fairly quiet, lovable person, nice looking, a bland, round face, not too tall—I think Goldie was taller. He never talked. He just went where Goldie went."

"He was a little, inoffensive guy," claimed a former classmate of Goldie's. "She was the power behind the throne—you could tell that right away." Ottenstein added, "Whatever Morris did was because he loved Goldie so much."

"It was a mutual love," Golda later insisted. "I was in love with Morris."

Their courting continued. Milwaukee didn't have as many free concerts as Denver, but Bradford Beach was marvelous on a hot summer Sunday. Under her dress, a woman wore her bathing suit, usually down to her ankles and buttoned up to the neck—otherwise she could be arrested for indecency. Also required were a swim cap and flat rubber shoes with stockings. For a basket-lunch picnic at Lake Park, you needed two transfers on the trolley line to get there. For the price of a single beer, you could also enjoy the free lunch counter at Jacob's Beer Hall, and a quarter got you a gallery seat at the Davidson Theater.

"We read books together," said Golda. "He gave me every capacity I have for enjoying what you probably call culture—poetry, music, philosophy. Of all the single, identifiable influences in my life, this has been the most personal and the most lasting."

"Morris opened a whole new life for all of us," said Sadie Ottenstein. "At that time we all had phonographs, but our records were mostly popular music. But then here comes Morris with opera, opening our ears to really beautiful music for the first time. When the Metropolitan Opera came to Milwaukee, it was Morris who got us all seats for a quarter apiece, and then explained the story of the opera to all of us. I got to love opera. I remember when I bought my first opera album."

Among the steady stream of Zionist speakers came David Ben-Gurion and Yitzhak Ben-Zvi, one of the Poale founders in Palestine. "The two Bens," as they were soon called, would one day father a country, but then they were just two young men, banished from Turkey, still wearing their Turkish red tarbooshes when they landed in New York. Ben-Zvi was tall, almost gawky and approachable; Ben-Gurion was short, intense, with fiery eyes, and less approachable.

Their arrival received minimal attention. The mass of American Zionists considered their back-to-the-soil concept as alien and uncouth. Ben-Gurion had written, "A homeland is not given or received as a gift; it is not possessed by gold or conquered by the power of the fist; it is built by the sweat of the brow. We shall receive our land not from a peace conference ... but from the Jewish workers who shall come to strike roots in the country, revive it, and live in it."

The hard fact was that after months of touring thirty cities in the United States and Canada, lecturing, pleading, persuading, the two Bens had convinced only about a hundred pioneers to return with them. Most of them were working-class Poale Zion, first-generation immigrants.

The numbers seemed few, considering the fact that three times a day in prayer the Orthodox Jew asks God to return him to the Land of Israel. He drinks a glass of wine with the blessing "Next year in Jerusalem!"

What infuriated "the two Bens" and Goldie were the many people who still suggested other alternative homelands in Uganda and South America. The Poale answer was "We don't want just any country! We are Zionists! We want to return to our ancient ancestral land!"

Goldie was in awe of Ben-Gurion. He was scheduled for a Saturday night speech in Milwaukee, and a lunch the next day at Goldie's house. Goldie wanted desperately to hear his speech, but the Chicago Philharmonic came to Milwaukee twice a month, and Morris had bought their tickets long in advance. She had had so many meetings that month, disappointing Morris, "that I just didn't have the courage to say that I would not go to the concert."

The next morning, when she went to the Folkshule to teach, a *chavera* (comrade) told her that Ben-Gurion would not lunch at her house that day, because "somebody who could not come to listen to him speak is not deserving to have him as a guest."

Goldie accepted the rebuke as just.

She was still busy trying to persuade Morris about Palestine. Despite his quiet, mild manner, Morris had a stubborn mind. He was more interested in world peace and justice.

"You get your new Jewish state," he said. "So there'll be another country in the world. So what?"

Goldie's reply was, "But internationalism doesn't mean the end of individual nations. Orchestras don't mean the end of violins."

Goldie also quoted the sage Hillel in the Poale Zion brochure:

"If I am not for myself, who will be for me? But if I am for myself only, what am I? And if not now, when?"

In her time apart from Morris, in her increasing involvement with Poale Zion, Goldie found herself an exhilarated member of a new family. She was so completely committed to this group, so absolutely identified with its cause, that she would never again function as an individual in the same way. Not only did this sense of identification suit her perfectly, but she was excited at this feeling of belonging to something so much larger than herself.

Morris was repelled by this. He didn't believe in movements or groups or causes. He believed only in the individual spirit. The difference between them then seemed unbridgeable.

Goldie declared no ultimatums; instead she simply said, "I beg you to come with me." But he would not budge.

Just about that time, Ben Shapiro told his family that he was going to Milwaukee to try to persuade this *meshuggina* young girl to come back with him to Chicago "to stir things up." *Meshugge* means "wild and crazy," but Shapiro meant it as a compliment for her enthusiasm. He felt Chicago's sleepy Poale Zion needed someone like her. His fellow Poale leader, Baruch Zuckerman, agreed. The two men, who would emerge as future giants in Zionism, made their pilgrimage to Milwaukee. At the same time, Goldie heard from Regina, who had moved to Chicago to work for a chemical firm. The philosopher-barber Yossel Kopelov had joined her there, and the two planned to marry soon. Regina added her persuasion. "I am sure if you came, Chicago would wake from its deep sleep. You are a good motor." Yossel, however, as a concerned friend worried aloud for Goldie about her "overactivities."

"They were fascinated by her," said Shapiro's daughter Judy. "My father said she was wasted in the small town of Milwaukee."

Goldie found the offer flattering. The two men had made the need sound urgent. What made it even more attractive was that it gave her breathing space away from the increasingly painful discussions with Morris.

"I loved him very much and he loved me very much," Golda explained later, "but there was a clash of two wills ... I also had a will of my own!"

Yossel Kopelov counseled her about Morris before she came to Chicago.

"You ask me if hearts are made to be broken. With our minds, why it should be that way. In reality it is so, and the greater the heart, the more it breaks, the more it suffers."

5

"We went to this place in Michigan every summer and Papa used to come for the weekends," said Ben Shapiro's daughter Judy. "Well, one Saturday afternoon, he got off the train as usual and just behind him there was a young woman. He didn't have a chance to introduce her because my mother went right up to her and said, 'You're Goldie.' Then we all walked along the lake, and the way my mother and Goldie talked, you'd think they'd known each other all their lives. And I heard my mother use the familiar '*du*' in Yiddish and I took her aside and said, 'Mama, you've just met her. How can you address her in this familiar way?' And she just laughed. But that relationship between Mama and Goldie continued until Golda's dying day.

"We went on hayrides and she taught us all kinds of folksongs in Yiddish. She used to sing beautifully. I was only seven and I remember we used to play jacks on the tile floor with her. And she used to tell us all kinds of stories. We used to call her 'the good fairy.'"

The so-called kosher core of Chicago, Roosevelt Road, was a *tummel* place, an action place. It made Walnut in Milwaukee and West Colfax in Denver seem small-scale. It suited Goldie perfectly. She especially needed it now because, as Regina recalled, Goldie was very moody and unhappy because of the break with Morris.

Goldie moved in with the Shapiros at 1306 Lawndale Road, a quiet

75

residential street a block away from Roosevelt Road. It was the kind of street where Goldie heard fiddlers playing Jewish melodies in the street and waiting for nostalgic housewives to throw them some coins wrapped in newspaper.

The Shapiros had a four-room apartment in a three-story building, and Goldie slept in a converted storeroom in the hall. Ben had a liquor store and his wife was a corsetiere. For the Shapiros, open house was always. "We had a huge kitchen where everything happened," said Judy, "people coming and going constantly. I remember the stormy meetings, the stormy arguments. The phrase I remember most was 'I'm perfectly against it.' "

When she had too much talk, Goldie could always go to the noisy life of Roosevelt Road, the mile-long stretch from Kedzie to Crawford, where you could see and find almost anything you wanted, from women plucking chickens on the sidewalk to a bathtub in a vegetable market made green by the spinach they washed. You could see a horseradish-grinding machine working overtime, women trying on shoes from a pushcart, hoping to find two that matched and fit, a hot dog with all the trimmings for a nickel at Flukey's.

Goldie felt part of the Shapiro family. "My father didn't have a car," said Judy, "so he'd pack the whole family and Goldie into a taxi and we'd all go down to the lake and take a walk." On a gusty day, a walk along Lake Michigan for Goldie was a challenge and an event, and it could blow everything out of her mind. Shana helped, too. She and her family lived only a block away from the Shapiros. Sam then worked for a local Jewish newspaper.

The Korngolds had come to Chicago in 1916 and moved in with the Zackler family, who had a single-family house with a big backyard. "My mother came from Denver," said Esther Zackler, "and she knew Sam from there. We had the kind of household like the one in *The Man Who Came to Dinner*. Sam and Shana arrived one day and stayed with us for about six months."

Zackler's daughter remembered how lovely the big backyard of the house looked in winter, filled with heavy snow. "I also remember the rats running around. That's so vivid in my mind."

Goldie saw them often, of course. Shana would always listen when Goldie needed to talk, and when Shana answered, Goldie listened hard. Surprisingly, Shana had mellowed. Her serious illness had caused her to reevaluate the basic values of her life. Her marriage to Sam had been wonderfully happy, and she was delighted with her children. The ardent revolutionary Zionist had replaced the word "cause" with "contentment." She tried to pass some of this on to Goldie, suggesting that perhaps her priorities were wrong, that Morris should come first.

Goldie didn't have too much time to brood. She had her job and she had Poale Zion. Her job was at a local branch of the Chicago Public Library as "junior library assistant, appointed temp., Sept. 27, 1917, $480 per year."

"It was an afternoon job, because she had all those meetings at Poale Zion," said Judy. "She would come home very late—those meetings would last until 4:00 A.M. sometimes. Then she would take medication before going to sleep because she was afraid she would wake up with a migraine headache. Those headaches were awful, just awful. I remember she loved to sleep."

As soon as she was free, she went to Poale Zion. Its headquarters were at 3222 Douglas Boulevard, near Douglas Park, above Glicksman's Yiddish Theater. Glicksman's great success was a Yiddish adaptation of *Hamlet* with a Kaddish, a prayer for the dead, in the final act.

Douglas Park served as another tonic for Goldie. An expanse of lagoons, flower beds, and woodlands, it was a peaceful oasis in a frenzied area. Before Goldie had come, the neighborhood was tough and crowded with Dutch, German, and Irish, who fought the young Jews "for territorial rights in the park." Teenagers put gum in the beards of elderly Orthodox Jews. Store signs read "We want no Jews." By the time Goldie arrived, though, the area was almost all Jewish with 51,000 people per square mile, twice the city average.

There were more shades of opinion among them "than there are political parties in central Europe," editorialized a local paper. Even the synagogues—and there were forty-nine of them—were often divided into occupational groups: the laundrymen's synagogue, the carpenter's synagogue, and even a synagogue for politicians. Small splinter groups, so intensely jealous of their own dignity and importance, became supersensitive to any real or fancied slight. Any peacemaker "required a character of steel—one with the wisdom of King Solomon, the eloquence of Demosthenes, and the statesmanship and tact of Lord Chesterfield." Golda herself later quoted, "True, we are a very small people, but remarkably hard to take."

Moving into this political mix with speeches and seminars, trying to smooth it into some kind of unity, Goldie was in perfect training for the battleground of her future. In Palestine, there were even more political splinters "speaking the tongues of Babel."

Out of this neighborhood came such notables as Benny Goodman, Admiral Hyman Rickover, and future Supreme Court Justice Arthur Goldberg, whose father was then a fruit peddler. Golda would later meet Goldberg, and they would become fast friends.

"We almost hated Goldie after a while," said a younger contemporary of her's, "because our parents always held her up to us as an example all the time of the kind of young Zionist we should be."

A Poale Zion member recalled coming home from a meeting and telling his wife about this young woman Goldie whom he had met that night. She was someone, he thought, whom his wife "might like for a friend."

The World War went into high gear when the United States declared war on Germany. Some Jews proposed a separate Jewish Legion within the American army, but Rabbi Tobias Schamasaizer protested.

It would be a mistake, he said, to separate Jews from the rest of the citizens of this land "when it comes to a matter of fighting for our country. Our flag is the Stars and Stripes. We place the shield of David in our temples, not on the fields of battle. America wants no separate residents."

The *Jewish Daily Courier* brought up the age-old query, "Who is the Jew?" The answer: "He speaks all languages, yet not one is his own. He is a stranger unto himself. . . . According to natural law, he should have vanished long ago. But look at him, always young, always old. He still dreams of the new youth."

In her own imagination, Goldie had already left America. In her own inner being, she was already working the land in some Palestine desert. Although she still had a shadowy concept of the place, she never saw it then as a faraway land of stone and thorns, a poor place with narrow horizons. What she knew she saw in newspapers, magazines, pamphlets: heroic-looking bronzed young men stripped to the waist, smiling behind hand-held plows; red-cheeked young women with colorful bandannas, peeling potatoes, also smiling. Everybody smiling. Or singing. So picturesque, patriotic, colorful, inspiring. In the heart of her soul, Goldie was with them.

Goldie *was* in love. In hindsight, many have pooh-poohed her romance with Morris. They claim it was more a mixture of admiration, loyalty, and pity on Goldie's part, that Morris was a mild nothing compared to Goldie's life force. Even some of Goldie's closest friends insist that Goldie and Morris were too odd a couple for real love.

The truth seems otherwise. Morris was Goldie's counterpoint, yes; but in his own right he was a highly intelligent, ardent, sensitive young man with a tough character and principle. And at this time in his life, Morris had only one main influence: Goldie. He found it impossible to stay away from her, and soon came to Chicago.

"I remember being a little girl in Chicago when Morris came courting Goldie," said Shapiro's daughter Judy. "They were in the living room; we were in the bedroom and the door was open. We were sort of eavesdropping. We were making up stories on what was happening. We were very much intrigued about what was going on."

When they were not acting like lovers, they were still trying to persuade each other about Palestine. The picture Goldie painted came more from her romantic imagination than from reality. She described more flowers than sand, more songs than malaria, more love than murder.

"The truth is that I didn't have exact information, but I knew very clearly what I wanted," said Golda later. "My mind is not so complicated. Once I accepted that there is no other solution for the Jewish problem but a home for the people, I decided to go there."

Morris, the bookish dreamer, tried to insist that she was painting a fantasy. But suddenly the fantasy seemed closer to the fact. On November 2, 1917, British Foreign Secretary Arthur James Balfour declared:

> His Majesty's Government view with favor the establishment in Palestine of a national home for the Jewish people, and will use their best endeavors to facilitate the achievement of this object.

It seemed unbelievable to Goldie.

"I felt there is indeed a God, there is justice! . . . And the world will change for the good . . . How can you describe happiness?"

What had happened was a mix of timing and chemistry. The chemistry was a vital synthetic explosive which the British army desperately needed. A former Pinsker neighbor of Goldie's, Chaim Weizmann, had created it. A grateful Balfour reportedly told him, "You know, I believe that when the guns stop firing, you may get your Jerusalem." The timing was right because the British had the added incentive of attracting German Jews to the British side in the war.

At age ten, Chaim Weizmann had written: "Let us carry our banner to Zion.... For why should we look to the Kings of Europe for compassion that they should take pity upon us and give us a resting place? In vain! All have decided: The Jew must die, but England will nevertheless have mercy upon us. In conclusion, to Zion!—Jews—to Zion! Let us go!"

Discussing Uganda as a possible alternative to Palestine, Weizmann had asked Balfour, "Suppose I were to offer you Paris instead of London, would you take it?"

"But Dr. Weizmann, London is already ours."

"This is true," Weizmann replied, "but Jerusalem was in our hands when London was just a swamp."

Weizmann earlier had insisted, "Palestine should become as Jewish as England is English or America is American!

"The Jews will go to Palestine anyhow, whether you want it or not. There is no power on earth that can stop the Jews from getting to Palestine. You gentlemen can make it easy for them; you can make it difficult.... Help us and it will help you."

Morris's case against a homeland had crumbled. Goldie was ecstatic. The Palestine romance was real. The dream was coming true. And Morris must be hers now.

The truth was that Morris had always been hers. If there had been no Balfour Declaration as a trigger, he still would have made his move. "I told him that if he wanted me, he had to come to Palestine.... To be perfectly honest, if he could have had me without Palestine, he would have been happier. But he couldn't, so he came."

He agreed to go with her to Palestine "as a wedding present." Now that he finally, reluctantly, told her that he would go with her to Palestine, would she marry him right away? Oh, yes, she said, oh, yes!

Perhaps neither of them knew the ancient saying: "Forty days before a man is born, God tells him who he'll marry. Then you search. Sometimes you find, and sometimes you don't find."

In Milwaukee, the two decided on the simplest civil ceremony. Goldie's mother was almost apoplectic. Such a wedding without a religious service would be a family shame she could not endure. If they did this, she insisted, the family would be forced to leave Milwaukee.

"Finally, after arguing a lot about it," said Golda, "I thought to myself: how selfish can a person be? After all, to me, what does it mean standing ten or fifteen minutes under the *chuppa* [bridal canopy], so what?"

"I went with Goldie to the dressmaker to buy her wedding dress," said Sadie Ottenstein. "It was a light crepe de chine—we didn't know from chiffon then. It was the plainest of the plain."

In all Milwaukee, the most important rabbi of all was Solomon Schein-feld. He didn't look important; he was short and plump. But he had fierce eyes and a long beard and a great dignity. He and Goldie had worked together on many Zionist committees, and he agreed to officiate at the wedding. For Bluma and Moshe, there was no greater honor. The day would come when a wing of the library at Hebrew University in Jerusalem would have a plaque with his name.

Scheinfeld seldom strayed from the traditional text at any wedding, but this time he made an emotional speech about the dignity and dedication of this nineteen-year-old bride.

The traditional Jewish wedding has great gaiety, as well as drama. It does not come simply from standing under a *chuppa*. After putting the ring on the bride's finger and pronouncing the nine words of betrothal, the bridegroom is given a glass which he stomps on and smashes. The sound of broken glass is a reminder of the destruction of the Temple in Jerusalem. It expresses the yearning for their lost nationhood.

That drama was done, but the gaiety was minimal. There was none of the traditional gathering of family in the wild, circling dance called the hora, with bride and groom seated in their chairs lifted high above the dancers. No bridesmaids, not much wine, and little laughter. Despite the years of love and longing, this was a wedding of two pragmatic people who accepted the minimum of traditions only out of respect for their parents. It was almost as if they had to prove how modern they were.

"Who came to Goldie's wedding?" recalled Sadie Ottenstein. "My husband, myself, Joe Dubinsky and his brother Meyer, Yossel Kopelov, Arthur Spiegel, Dorothy Weingrod, a very small group. It was in the Mabovitch dining room. Of course there were no bridesmaids then. Food? I think we had boiled potatoes and herring after the ceremony. Dancing? The guys didn't know their left foot from their right foot."

The rabbi, who never ate or drank anything after the service, had eaten a piece of Bluma's sponge cake, and liked it. Bluma was consoled, and she never let Milwaukee forget this honor to her.

The certificate of marriage listed Morris as twenty-four, his occupation "sign painter." Goldie didn't list any occupation. She no longer wanted to be a teacher, and certainly not a librarian. Nor could she ever imagine herself simply as a housewife.

They were married on December 24, 1917, and the British army gave them a wedding present by liberating Jerusalem, after four centuries of Turkish rule, on Hanukkah, the joyous Jewish holiday of the Feast of Lights.

A less unexpected wedding present was an eleventh-edition set of the *Encyclopaedia Britannica*. Morris and his friend Yossel had bought it a year before and agreed that it would belong to the one who married first.

Years later an intimate asked Golda why she married Morris. However charming, cultured, and gentle he was, his personality was so utterly different from hers—why did she marry him? Golda answered softly, "Because I loved him."

At the end of her life, asked to name the most formative forces that shaped her, she answered:

"Childhood in Russia, which means poverty, pogroms, and political repression. Parents and elder sister—trade unionism from my parents, socialism from my sister. My husband, which means everything I have learned to enjoy in the world of culture: poetry, music, books, ideas."

She repeated often to close friends that Morris had been one of the two most important men in her life.

Until the day she died, Golda kept a framed drawing of Dante and Beatrice in her bedroom. Beatrice was the symbol of divine revelation through faith that guided Dante through Paradise. Morris kept an identical copy of that drawing on his bedroom wall, too. Golda also kept an early picture of herself and Morris on the night table next to her bed. An intimate friend insisted that there was an interval when Golda put that photograph elsewhere, but it was there in the last years before she died.

"Ours was a great love," Golda once said. "It lasted from the day we first met till the day he died."

* * *

Goldie and Morris rented a three-room apartment at 1311 Chestnut. As Goldie put it, "I worked and kept house." Morris now listed himself in the city directory as a sign writer for Aultman on Jefferson Street. "He and Goldie never had much money," said Clara. "From a financial standpoint, I guess he was a very impractical man." Part of their money, however little there was, was put into Goldie's private *pishke*, her savings account to pay for passage to Palestine.

Now came a family drama that indicated better than anything else the future course of Goldie's life.

Poale Zion had a weekly paper struggling to stay alive. A crisis meeting of its leaders met to decide its fate. Should they try to keep it going or shut it down? Their solution? Start a *daily* paper. "A crazy thing to do then," Golda later admitted.

The dramatic moment came when they asked Goldie to travel the country and Canada to help raise money for the paper.

"My father was furious," Golda recalled. "A few minutes after the wedding, you are leaving your husband and going? Who leaves a new husband and goes on the road?"

It was a good question. What young woman, barely nineteen, truly in love with her brand-new husband, would dream of leaving him like this?

Golda's answer was simple: "At Poale Zion, whatever I was asked to do, I did. The party said I have to go, so I went." Her friend Sadie made it even more explicit: "She would walk on all fours if they told her to."

All their friends understood that Goldie belonged to Poale Zion and Morris belonged to Goldie. Nobody understood this better than Morris.

Goldie found this mission of traveling the country alone, meeting new people, a constant adventure. The longer her travels lasted, the more confident she became. Friends say that the growth of her personality at this critical time was almost palpable. She seemed exhilarated.

The gnawing thing was her guilt. Guilt would flaw her life and perhaps this is where it all began. A few close friends questioned the depth of her guilt about Morris. Did she express it then because she was expected to express it since it was more womanly? Was she simply conforming to social rules?

Goldie seldom conformed for the sake of conforming. Guilt was simply part of the price she was prepared to pay. And she was so powerfully inner-directed that it was highly uncharacteristic of her to express it often. She was never more certain of her political beliefs and her role. Her path was clear, a path she would follow the rest of her life. It was not an uncommon attitude of men and women in the Movement. The priority of the party was absolute, priority over husband, children, friends, lovers, everything.

For her work, Goldie was paid fifteen dollars a week, plus expenses. Expenses included a coach seat on the train, and meals—without desserts. "If I had an ice cream, that was my expense," she said, "because the party is not supposed to give me ice cream. I didn't smoke at that time, thank God." Nor did expenses include hotels. "The idea of staying in a hotel, you might just as well stay on the moon. I slept at the homes of party members, sometimes together in one bed with the woman of the house." Poale Zion was like an extended tribe. Years later many an unremembered woman would remind her, "We slept in the same bed."

Traveling in Canada presented a problem. Wives then became U.S. citizens only if their husbands were, and Morris had not yet become one. Her father refused to loan her his passport, and was indignant about it. "Oh, no, if that's what you need in order to go, then you don't go."

"Canadians were very stiff about allowing Russian-born to come in," Golda later explained. "Besides that, I came from Milwaukee, a socialist city, for a Jewish daily paper." When she still tried to get through Canadian customs without a passport, they grabbed her. They allowed her to call an important Canadian Zionist. She had a vague idea that he was a member of Parliament and so expected this Very Important Person to arrive in his glory and sweep her into safety. "It was a snowy blizzard and who comes toward me—a little man in a leather jacket on his way to work."

The little man, however, persuaded customs to let Goldie enter. The Canadians she met reacted strongly:

"We beheld her at this time as a phenomenon ... perfectly Jewish background, spoke flawless English, unique charm, young, slender, she won all our hearts and this without having to resort to oratory."

Fund-raising involved selling shares in this future newspaper. One sale bothered her. "I have on my conscience that poor man in Minneapolis ... what a terrible thing it was. But I did it in good faith. I don't remember his name but he was a tailor."

She sold him by saying, "We must have a daily paper—we are saving the world. Whatever you have, you must give to this paper." The man admitted that he had three hundred dollars saved to pay for passage to bring his wife and children from Europe. Goldie, the twenty-year-old idealogue, was insistent: "How can you doubt? How can you question? Give the money *now*! The paper will flourish and you will get the money back to send for your family a few months later."

"When he came to the station to see me off, he asked, 'Look, are you sure the money is safe?' I was so indignant that he was doubting the word of the party—which was sacrilegious to me—that I wouldn't shake hands with him."

Die Zeit (*The Times*) struggled for a year, then died, none of the loans repaid. Years later, Golda told her friend Marie Syrkin, "I still have that *chaver* on my conscience."

Morris pricked her conscience much more. She was doing so well that Poale Zion extended her travel to months at a time. Her letters were often hurried but they all had wifely warnings: eat enough, rest enough, don't worry about lack of work or money. "Only take care of your health." Almost each letter ended with "I long for you."

"Morris was a *wonderful* person," insisted Clara. "He was like a big brother when I needed a big brother. I was a teenager with all the emotional trauma of teenagers. And he was very kind, very intelligent.

"I remember when Goldie came back from one of her speaking tours, he would always have fresh flowers on the table. The trouble was that Goldie loved to be with people, loved to be surrounded by people. She had to do things. And Morris was a very private kind of person."

When Morris had married Goldie, he married the Movement. Some of their friends, the unkind ones, mentioned with a slight smirk that it seemed at the time that Goldie was the husband and Morris the wife. The truth was that the frequently unemployed Morris shopped, cooked, and cleaned the house while Goldie busied herself with a dozen groups, even when she was in Milwaukee. Since Goldie had neither the time nor interest in shopping, Morris even bought her clothes. "And whatever Morris bought was okay with her," Sadie Ottenstein explained.

"We had seven couples in our original group," said Sadie. "We were always together Monday, Tuesday, Wednesday, Thursday. We took the streetcar about seven-thirty to go to the Poale meetings, walked two long blocks on wooden sidewalks, and came home about midnight. Friday night we'd hold a Shabbat. Then if the Poale Zion didn't have anything happening on Saturday or Sunday, we were free to visit each other's houses for dinner. And all the time we'd talk. We'd talk, talk, talk. We didn't always agree with each other, but we were always very loyal to each other and we remained friends for fifty years."

Campaigning for her cause, Goldie was refused the right to talk inside the synagogue. "Listen to me," she told Louis Perchonok, "someone bring me a bench. When they leave the synagogue, I'll speak to them outside."

Some of the congregation complained that "it was a *chutzpah* on the part of youngsters to detain a crowd on a holiday outside the synagogue." Goldie apologized for detaining them. "It's not our fault—it's the fault of your leaders—the president and trustees who closed the door to our people." And then someone in the crowd yelled, "Speak as long as you wish!"

Chaim Weizmann, then president of the World Zionist Organization, had uttered his plaintive plea about *aliyah*, "Jewish people, where are you?"

Writer I. B. Singer explained a popular view: "If you take a people that lived in the country for 800 years . . . and suddenly tell them, 'Leave your country and go to live somewhere else,' you cannot expect the masses of people to do so. It is a wonder that even small numbers of people heard the message and did it. . . . We have wives, apartments, children, relatives—no human being is ready suddenly to leave all this because Professor Weizmann or some other leader told them to do so."

"I remember well," Golda said later, "that leading *chaverim* of the Movement saw something irregular in our *aliyah*; almost a sin toward the Movement." Perhaps it was a mixture of guilt and envy.

Poale Zion, fragmented as always, continued to face varied threats to its survival. Beyond that, the World War created assorted particular problems for Jews ranging from relief to refugees, as well as the persistent crises in Palestine. Philadelphia became the scene of two national conventions, one after the other in 1918. The first was a Poale Zion group of delegates; the second was the historic first meeting of the

Golda's grandparents in Russia.

She lived with them in Pinsk at the turn of the century.

The Mabovitch family before leaving for America: (from left) Golda, her father Moshe, sister Shana, mother Bluma, and younger sister Clara.

A new American immigrant: Golda, age eight.

They settled in Milwaukee, Wisconsin. Gimbels, the store at left, front, was where Golda later worked.

Golda (seated, extreme right) in elementary school

…and in high school (seated in front in striped dress).

At age fourteen, Golda ran away to Denver to stay with her sister Shana, the one person most important to her

...and she worked in her brother-in-law's shop.

When she returned to
Milwaukee two years later,
she knew what she wanted.

She wanted to go to Palestine as a pioneer with the man she loved. Golda is
in center of photo, Morris Meyerson on her right.

Her dear friends lasted her
lifetime: Sadie Ottenstein

...Raziel Shapiro.

American Jewish Congress, organized to help Jews in Europe and to form a postwar program for Jewish people all over the world.

Goldie was elected as a delegate to both of them. "She had this natural flair for getting along with people," said the other Milwaukee delegate, Isadore Tuchman. "I tell you her mouth was gold. Everytime Goldie opened her mouth, it had impact somewhere. When she appeared among delegates, talking about issues, everybody saw that she was more than the average girl."

She was in her element. She was with people who believed as she believed, and with the same intensity. They all shared the language of enthusiasm. One of them was Ben Shapiro, her Chicago friend. They had more than mere hope in the future; they had certainty. "Few speakers were more moving than Goldie," insisted Rose Kader, who was at the Congress with her. "She could move people to tears. And herself as well. We used to stand offstage with huge man-sized handkerchiefs." Another member described Goldie as "an outstanding example of the American-bred Labor Zionist, a unique woman leader." Incredibly enough, this impressive young woman was then only twenty years old.

"This is the life for me!" Goldie wrote her friend Regina. And to Morris, she added, "I tell you that some moments reached such heights that after them one could have died happy."

Goldie never forgot the excitement of that week in Philadelphia, and the pleasure. "We had two or three other young girls in the party and we had a very jolly group. We went on picnics and there was a lot of singing. We had a really good time."

Morris now had second thoughts about his agreed *aliyah*. Now he had an intense taste of what it meant to be second on Goldie's priority list. Their time alone together became more minimal: her hurried exits for endless meetings, late nights away from home, the long trips lasting months. Then, when she was home, their apartment was always crowded with her political people. Where was their privacy? He wanted her so much and he was getting so little. It was not difficult for him to imagine how much worse it would be in Palestine.

Shana sensed what was happening and counseled compromise to Goldie:

"I don't want to shatter your dreams. I know what it means, but, Goldie, don't you think there is a middle field for idealism right here on the spot? Oh, my! Oh, my! How much work there is to be done by those who believe. And as far as personal happiness is concerned, grasp it, Goldie, and hold it tight. There are not many who can speak about happiness. You behold happiness without much effort and don't grasp the real value of it. . . . The only thing I heartily wish you is that you should not try to be what you *ought* to be but what you are. If everybody would only be what they are, we would have a much finer world . . . find your own self."

Goldie had found herself a long time ago. She didn't want to be what she was, but what she *ought* to be. She never quite believed that only out of the past could you make the future. Nor even that you must accept "the richness of the mixture" to make the most of yourself. What she did believe was that a person was the sum total of the acts that make up her life—no more, no less.

"All of us in our crowd dreamed of going to Eretz Yisroel," recalled Sadie Ottenstein, "but Goldie was the one who picked herself up and went, and that was the difference."

What would she have done if Morris had decided not to go with her to Palestine?

"I would have gone alone, but heartbroken."

And why was she sacrificing the comforts of the United States for the hazards of Palestine?

"I went for selfish reasons. I wasn't going to let them build everything alone and I'd be out of it. I just couldn't *imagine* letting them build it alone!"

6

The four friends arrived in New York City in September 1920, some of them slightly frightened. For Goldie and Regina, this was the culmination of a dream. They had shared so many years of teenage visions about this great adventure in this romantic pioneer place called Palestine. The two were like sisters, coming together. Their lives had diverged only after high school when Regina went to Beaver State Business College to study shorthand and typing, then got a job with the *Milwaukee Leader*, and afterward with a Chicago chemical company. Both Regina and Goldie were known to their mocking friends as "Zionuts." If Zionism had blinded them to much else, it was now their strongest bond.

The two men were different. They were both gentle, philosophical friends, who saw at least two sides, and often more, to every question. Morris was the more reluctant convert to Palestine, Yossel the more excited, even though he still had his doubts.

The four had come to New York primarily because wages were higher here, and they needed money to pay for passage.

"We found a six-room apartment on the second floor in Morningside Heights for seventy-five dollars a month, three bedrooms, a sitting room, and a kitchen." Joining them to help share the rent was a Canadian couple named Manson whom Goldie described as "very nice people." They were also planning to go to Palestine.

Morningside Heights was "a kind of island in a restless sea." The Heights rose sharply on three sides, and gradually on the south, to a height of 150 feet above the Hudson River, the highest area in Manhattan. On the west was Riverside Park, and on the east black Harlem, sweeping up to a stony cliff. Goldie's street on this islandlike height was a neighborhood of frame houses flanked by a wooded area called Morningside Park, with Columbia University nearby. "You could see it from there," said Regina. Nearby was Grant's Tomb, whose design was described as "the final horror of the Civil War."

Everyone soon found work: Morris painted signs, Yossel became a barber, Regina got a job as secretary at the *Menorah Journal*. At a nearby branch library, Goldie once again became a librarian. When she had left her Milwaukee library job, her superior had reported, "What a waste! She might have finished as head librarian." A friend noted, "Goldie acquired quite a taste for tea at the library. She guzzled it by the quart."

Poale Zion was headquartered at 266 Grand Street, in the heart of New York City's Lower East Side, where two square miles of squalid tenements housed a half million people, a majority of them immigrant "greenhorn" Jews. It was said that the beds in East Side tenements were never cold. When one shift got out, another shift got in. Some also said then that the Jews had the independence and freedom here as if they were in Palestine. The Jews were concentrated between Division and Houston streets, and from the Bowery to the East River, with the Williamsburg Bridge running through the heart of it over to Brooklyn.

The first day Goldie arrived at Poale Zion headquarters, bright and eager to volunteer for anything, Pinhas Caruso "remembered the despair on her face when he gave her a broom and asked her to clean up the floor." But she did a good job.

Nearby was the Orchard Street pushcart market where Goldie could buy everything from *knishes* (boiled buckwheat groats or mashed potatoes, wrapped in a skin of dough and baked) to hot *arbes* (boiled chick peas). Besides an enormous variety of ethnic food, there was every size, kind, quality, and price range of clothes that even Goldie could afford. Elsewhere, for observation only, were small shops with ornate Victorian lamps or ancient gold candlesticks. Most stores had their own *shleppers* who tried to entice potential customers into the store.

Walking through the neighborhood, Goldie would see old people sitting on the stoops in front of their tenements, children cooling themselves in streams from illegally opened fire hydrants, young boys playing stickball in the street, some people even snoozing on their fire escapes.

Scattered throughout the area were the small restaurants where immigrant intellectuals gathered to discuss Tolstoy or the editorial in the *Forward* or current theater and art. Ibsen's *Ghosts* was unsuccessful on Broadway, but a great hit here. Published Yiddish poets sold more books than poets who wrote in English. Out of this area came a variety of entertainers such as Al Jolson, Milton Berle, and the Marx Brothers; a future Democratic candidate for President, Alfred E. Smith; musicians named Irving Berlin and George Gershwin. Gershwin was the same age as Goldie. To put everything in perspective, there was a small Jewish cemetery nearby, bought in 1682 by some Jews who had fled here from Spain.

Poale Zion had had a national convention in Pittsburgh the year before, announcing a total membership of 7,000. The daily Poale Zion newspaper, *Der Zeit*, for which she had helped raise funds, was now finally being published. The editor, Jacob "Moshe" Goodman, and his wife, Fanny, became Goldie's lifelong friends. Afterward she never came to New York without visiting them. Moshe had run a neighborhood restaurant, a gathering place for writers and musicians, but many said business was bad because Moshe gave away so many free meals to his impoverished friends.

"The Goodmans were all heart." Both were very short, almost swarthy, Moshe with a thick flowing mustache and a hot temper; Fanny, plump and motherly, who described herself as a simple, plain woman. Said their daughter, "My father was very quiet, reserved, a very bright man with a wonderful sense of very dry humor. My mother was a very vivacious person, always interested in everybody's business, and always talking." They lived in the Flatbush section of Brooklyn; Goldie and Morris went there often for Shabbat dinner.

Before the restaurant, Moshe had been one of the founders of Poale Zion in New York. "He was a man of integrity," said Jacob Katzman, "the conscience of the Movement. When there was a question of principle being debated at a meeting, he could always wax hot under the collar."

Moshe complained to Goldie that the local newsstands refused to handle *Der Zeit* because the competing papers threatened to withdraw from the stands if they did. "Nobody asked me to do it," said Goldie, "but I and Nina Zuckerman and Regina would go and stand on the corners and sell newspapers."

Nina and Baruch Zuckerman were two more of Goldie's *chaverim*, again lifetime comrades. Baruch was a great big man, and very heavy; Nina was a registered nurse with a great sense of humor, and very beautiful. "My life has been intertwined with this family," Golda later said.

"I think I was eight or nine when my sister took me to a meeting," Golda recalled, "and for the first time I was part of an audience and I heard a man speak from the stage. I cannot claim to have understood everything or that I even remember what Baruch said on that occasion. But the picture of Baruch standing on that stage as I sat next to my sister, intent and involved in what was happening—that I cannot forget."

Baruch had come to America at the age of seventeen and immediately became integrated into Zionist organizational work. When he married Nina, she put him through preparatory school to be a dentist. It didn't work. "He went through his theoretical studies with flying colors," said his daughter Nomi, "but when it came to seeing a little blood in the mouth! . . . That was it! Finished!"

Moshe told the story of Zuckerman coming to his restaurant for dinner. Nina had put him on a strict weight-loss diet, "and he was hungry, poor guy. So he came before she did, had a nice *big* meal, had the dishes cleared away and waited for Nina. Then, with her, he would order a salad and cottage cheese. And she never could understand why Baruch didn't lose weight on her marvelous diet."

The Zuckermans and the Goodmans lived in the same building in the Bronx. The whole feeling among Paole members resembled that of an extended family. Goldie felt part of it; Morris never really did.

Goldie was particularly close to Baruch Zuckerman ever since they had traveled together, raising funds and organizing for Poale Zion. "They lived together, practically," observed Baruch's daughter Nomi. Goldie not only regarded Baruch as a great orator, a quintessential explainer, and a very warm human being but as "one of the giants of Poale." "We saw each other often. He was like an older brother who guided me, explained and helped me understand many things that appeared very involved and complicated."

Goldie and Morris had their private time mostly on weekends. They liked the long walks at sunset on Riverside Drive along the Hudson River, the concert recitals at the Institute of Musical Art. True, they were squirreling away their money to pay for passage, but they still occasionally went to the theater and the opera, sitting in the cheapest seats.

Morris did not go to many Poale Zion meetings with Goldie, but she never missed one—and there were many. If Goldie was still having trouble exciting Morris about Palestine, she had no trouble convincing her friend Raziel Shapiro, with whom she had boarded in Chicago, that she should join the *aliyah*. Raziel had written Goldie that she and her husband had decided on a divorce, and she now wanted a new life.

"My mother, sister, and I were supposed to go with Goldie," Raziel's daughter Judy remembered. "Everything was packed including our furniture. But then, at the last minute, we didn't go. I don't know why my mother changed her mind."

Mind-changing on *aliyah* is not difficult to understand. Uprooting a total life for an unknown future is the kind of monumental decision that few people can face. That's why the Poale Zion members looked at Goldie and her group with such awe and envy. Even for a dedicated Zionist, the permanent jump to Jerusalem, forsaking family and friends, took a special courage. The Mansons, who shared Goldie's apartment, soon also changed their minds about going.

Morris, too, hoped hard that Goldie might reconsider, but it was a dead hope. During her whole stay in New York, Goldie was on an infectious high.

"We used to walk through Central Park at midnight," said Regina, "and nobody ever bothered us. There was no fear of walking out at night anywhere. There was still the El [elevated trains] on Third Avenue, and another El on Eighth. I had an interesting job at the *Journal*. I met all these literary lights." One of Regina's new friends at the *Journal* "was a compulsive talker" and whenever she was due to visit Regina at the apartment, "the others used to run." "In the evenings, Goldie would cook and I'd wash dishes. I'm no cook at all. Sometimes Mrs. Manson cooked. We all chipped in for everything. We didn't have many friends in the neighborhood; we didn't have time."

The one who had the most time was Morris, because he got very little work as a sign painter. He was able to explore not only the cultural mecca of Columbia University but neighboring areas. Morris became a walker in the city, fascinated by the way the different foreign sections seemed to live in proximity to one another as they did on the map of Europe. The Spanish lived near the French, the Russians near the Hungarians, the Greeks close to the Italians, and the Germans adjoining the Austrians. What other city newsstand had papers in two dozen languages? It was a city of a thousand marketplaces. He had already felt the cruel indifference of the city, as well as its magnanimity. Perhaps more than anything else, he felt invisible here.

Here in New York, which anti-Semites elsewhere jeeringly called "Jew York," Goldie felt relaxed and secure, even to selling a Jewish socialist newspaper on the streets. The New York State Assembly had passed a bill permitting persons who observed the Saturday Sabbath to work on Sundays. The bill passed 126 to 13. In addition, the New York State Senate adopted a resolution favoring the establishment in Palestine of a national home for the Jewish people. But Golda was well aware of intolerance elsewhere in the United States. The success of the Russian Revolution had stirred American radicals. Strikes increased and were often bloody. Shortly after Goldie's arrival in New York, a bomb had exploded in front of the House of Morgan on Wall Street, killing thirty people and injuring hundreds. The street literally ran red with blood.

Attorney General A. Mitchell Palmer, the "Fighting Quaker," headed up the Big Red Scare, rounding up "the Bolshies." The white-hooded Ku Klux Klan went into full gear with a hate campaign against Reds, Blacks, Catholics, and Jews. The New York State Assembly expelled five of its members on the ground that they were "little Lenins" in our midst.

Once again the Jew became a natural scapegoat. Henry Ford circulated the "Protocols of the Elders of Zion" (created in a novel written in 1868),* passing the fiction as fact, accusing Jews "of plotting the sub-

*The prime fictional source for "Protocols of the Elders of Zion" was the novel *Biarritz*, written under the pen name of Sir John Ratcliffe. (Prof. Jeffrey L. Simmons, Yale University, in *The New York Times*, July 26, 1987.) Part of it came from an earlier novel, *Un Dialogue aux Enfers Entre Machiavelli et Montesquieu dans XIXème Siècle*, published in Brussels in 1864 by Maurice Joly. (Prof. Mervin B. Freedman, San Francisco State College.) The forgers of the Protocols were later revealed as agents of the Russian Secret Police in Paris.

jugation of the whole world and being the source of almost every American affliction including high rents, the shortage of farm labor, jazz, gambling, drunkenness, loose morals, and even short skirts."

Goldie read about the quota system against Jews in many colleges, the refusal of numerous landlords to rent to Jewish tenants, the scandal in Annapolis over the hazing of a Jewish boy. Goldie could have rationalized her upcoming departure, but she needed no excuse, no rationalizations. Her course was always positive and clear.

By the spring of 1921, the group had enough money to buy tickets on the S.S. *Pocahontas*. It was easy to say good-bye to the impersonal world of New York, but it was not going to be so easy to say good-bye to Shana, and to their parents.

Leaving Shana would hurt the most. Leaving her would be like leaving a large part of herself. Even when she and Shana were not together, Goldie always knew her "second mother" was not too far away, always available for advice and judgment. Now Shana truly would be too far away. It would not hurt much to leave her mother. The tension with her mother was still strong. Her father? Yes. They were close now, especially with their common work for Poale Zion. There was a new bonding. Clara? She still hardly knew her. Her friends, and there were many, yes, yes, yes, she would miss them a great deal. They were part of happiness at school, her happiness in the neighborhood, the excitement of her growing-up years. Those years had never been too giggly, but they had been warm and memorable.

Philadelphia was the first stop for her and Morris. They saw his mother and three sisters, Sarah, Bertha, and Rae. Sarah was the tubercular. "She was married to an expert in Semitic languages who taught at a university in Philadelphia." His sister Bertha "was not close to the family," and Rae was "a very simple woman."

Morris's mother spoke little if any English. "She was small and punctual. If she had to go somewhere, she'd always leave three hours early. She had married twice and both her husbands had died, causing her to rebel against God."

None of them had much approved of Morris's marriage to Goldie. It is perhaps doubtful they would have approved of his marriage to anyone. He had been their major support.

There is no record of what Morris thought on leaving them. He had been close to his surviving family, had gone with them to Denver, had corresponded regularly with them after he had left. Since he was as skeptical about the future in Palestine as were they, it must have made the good-byes a little more querulous, as if he might well have suspected that they would all one day say, "I told you so . . ." But the gravitational pull of Goldie was stronger than all of them, stronger than any of his doubts.

The Milwaukee farewell was more tearful. Goldie's parents promised they would join her in Palestine as soon as she was settled. But Goldie wondered if she would ever really see them again. She was most moved when she looked at her father and saw "tears rolling down his cheeks." Her ebullient mother now "looked so small and withdrawn" and her effervescent sister, now a teenager at the University of Wisconsin, "looked strangely somber." It was more of an emotional wrench than she had expected. When she had run away to Denver, the break was clean and quick. Now looking at her older parents, despite the zigzag of their relationship, she felt a devotion that was still strong. Maybe they really would join her in Palestine. But not Clara. Her young sister was now an American American.

Just before they left Milwaukee, there was a wedding for one of Goldie's old Poale Zion friends. "There were a couple dozen of us, dancing together, having a good time," said Sadie Ottenstein. "When we parted after the party and said good-bye, we didn't expect ever to see each other again."

Goldie dreaded going to Chicago. There would be no tears with Shana. Shana was a stoic. Her emotions were there, but deep. Shana would keep the talk on a practical level, want to know all the plans, all the details. She would have very specific comments and criticism. And then their good-byes would be brief, almost curt, but with dignity. Deep, deep down each would feel the void. But no tears, never any tears between them.

The scenario almost went according to expectation. Shana predictably asked her questions, made her comments. During a moment's quiet, Sam asked Shana, jokingly, "Maybe you'd like to go, too?"

"Yes, I would," Shana replied quickly.

Everyone stared at her in shock. Her face was absolutely serious, almost grim with resolve.

Sam now suddenly realized he had asked the wrong question of the wrong person at the wrong time. Shana later said, "Sam was sorry but it was too late."

Every person in that room knew that once Shana had made up her mind, there was no changing it. But why had she made up her mind? And when? Had she been brooding about this ever since Goldie made her decision to go, or was it really a sudden, almost impulsive move?

The idea probably had been simmering within her for some time. After all, she had been the original Zionist zealot, the one who endangered her life in a Russian revolutionary group. She was the one who had put Zionist principles above all else. And she was the one who instilled in Goldie most of her Zionist spirit.

She made it clear she had been thinking about this because she immediately spelled out her practical plan: she would go to Palestine with their two children—Judy, ten, and Chaim, three—but only if Sam would stay behind and send them money, and follow later.

The dramatic moment became tender when Sam accepted the inevitable with a warm supportive feeling.

Looking at them all now, without exultation but almost defiantly, Shana said simply, "I am going."

That moment changed many lives.

Goldie was absolutely exultant. Aside from Morris, the one person she loved most, admired most would now share this great adventure with her.

Violent Arab attacks against Palestine settlers later that month resulted in the murder and mutilation of some forty Jews. This impelled Sam to plead with Shana to postpone her trip until the violence ended. Then, he said, they could all leave together as a family. Consider the danger, he warned.

"Then I *must* go," she said simply.

Shana and Goldie were both fighters. Danger was never a warning to them, only a challenge. Now mingled with a cause, the danger only added a fillip of extra excitement.

At Poale Zion headquarters in New York City, a set of small offices that moved often, the Goldie group began to assemble from various parts of the country. This was a time when the flow of Americans to Palestine was still small, and so this gave Goldie and friends a special aura. They were practicing what the others preached. At Milwaukee, when she left, Poale Zion *chaverim* had insisted, "There wasn't really anybody in those days to take her place."

"We had several meetings before we left," said Regina. The recent Arab riots were on the minds of many and they had been told, "You're crazy, you won't be able to get into Palestine, there's no more immigration." Somebody again raised the question of postponement.

"But I was very stubborn," said Golda. "I said, 'Look, if we go back each one of us settles down again.' This was it. I don't know whether we will ever decide again to go."

Later Golda would admit, "Looking back now this was probably the craziest thing that anybody could do."

She had some mix in her happiness, claiming "a permanent nostalgia for the great beauty of the American countryside. I loved America."

"I owed America much," she later observed. "I arrived a frightened little girl. When I left, I was a self-confident young woman. I was not fleeing from oppression and insecurity; I was leaving of my own accord a good, generous people. I was born under a tyranny, but brought up in a democracy. It was a country which had fought for its independence, and had written its own constitution. It was a pioneer's country. It had a dream, the American dream. It still believes in tomorrow. I took what I valued with me. So I had no regrets about leaving anything behind. I was leaving to participate in the setting up of independence and security for my own people."

A philosopher named John Berger has said that to emigrate is always to dismantle the center of the world and move into a lost world of fragments. But Goldie saw this emigration as a means of redemption for the Jews.

Whatever nostalgia and lingering sadness the group had was now overcome by the almost suffocating thrill of approaching fulfillment, their overwhelming tremendous dream of being pioneers. Goldie did some last-minute shopping, buying ten blankets.

"Why so many, Goldie?" a friend asked.

"If I have to sleep on the ground, I want to be prepared for it."

"I expected nothing," said Goldie. "Before we had left, we sold everything." She got rid of what she called "civilized matters."

"We sold the curtains because who needs curtains in Palestine? We expected to live in tents. No electrical equipment, no electric iron, but I remember among us we had a hair dryer. For two years in a row I didn't buy myself a winter coat; who needs a winter coat in Palestine? So I had a suit with a little fur collar and that was that. I even took the fur off. The only thing we took with us was a gramophone, and we had very good records. We felt you could have that in a tent, too, because it didn't need electricity ... and, oh, we took several boxes of books, half fiction, half nonfiction.... I didn't even bring any silk stockings because our conception was that we were going into the desert or the wilderness."

Shana and her children arrived in New York just before the ship was to sail. "We stayed at the Zuckermans' and had to remain a few days extra because there was a strike on the ship." It was a strike over low wages.

"Our friends at Poale Zion gave us a going-away party. Many were jealous."

After the party, eighteen of them slept at the Zuckerman three-room apartment on Vyse Street in the Bronx. Most of them slept on the floor, side by side, and they talked late into the night before turning out the lights. Nomi Zuckerman recalled her mother telling the group, "I'm going to put ribbons on your toes so that when you wake up in the morning, you'll remember whose feet are whose."

The next morning they sailed on the *Pocahontas*.

It seemed peaceful enough at the start, a pleasant day, May 23, 1921. Even the decrepit ship, the S.S. *Pocahontas*, seemed romantic as well as exciting.

The excitement quickly heightened, the romance disappeared.

As soon as the ship set out to sea, the crew mutinied. They were striking, they said, because the ship was absolutely unseaworthy. To help prove it, they sabotaged the engines, mixed seawater with the fresh water, and sprinkled salt on the food. In an open fight among themselves, one sailor shouted at the passengers, "Your ship will sink in midocean."

Shana's daughter, Judy, who was ten at the time, noted, "It was a terrible, horrible trip but I had a good time. There was a boy my age who was studying dancing in New York. We had a great time!"

"Four of us shared a cabin," said Regina, "Goldie and I and our husbands. My husband, Yossel, was a very friendly man, an intellectual, much older than me. Morris was a quiet fellow, somewhat older, not much. And between me and Goldie, why should there be friction? What would we fight about?"

Of the several hundred passengers, Goldie's group consisted of twenty-two, most of them in their early twenties, several past thirty, three with small children, and one visibly pregnant. The pregnant woman was Dina Kaplan, whose husband, Abe, had been Goldie's teacher in high school. Golda later described all of them: "We were a small group, young, full of hope and zeal, ready for anything."

They were all young enough to regard the wild events with some humor, and strong-willed enough to survive the inconveniences.

"I think Goldie and I were among the younger people aboard," said Regina. "I'll tell you this, I had no influence on Goldie. Look, she used to confide in me, but she was always the leader. There was a young man named Gold in our group who took hold of Goldie, sat her down and taught her Hebrew. They spent a lot of time together.

"Most of the people on that boat were going to Italy on holiday. We met some of them, but mostly we stayed together as a group. Except for Morris, we were all excited about going. We knew it wouldn't be all rosy. My old aunt said, 'You're going into the wilderness.' But we all saw it as a great adventure. Look, at that age you're romantic."

"I say again, we didn't expect anything," recalled Golda. "You couldn't know the life there. It wouldn't be true to say that any of us had a real picture of what it would be. I don't think we even talked about it, but nobody was expected to have prepared anything for us."

The ship took a full week to reach Boston. News of the traumatic trip reached Chicago and Sam pleaded with Shana to come home, but again she refused.

The *Pocahontas* docked in Boston harbor for eight days while the captain fired most of the ship engineers, changed some of the crew, and fixed the broken pumps. Poale Zion party members had journeyed from New York with food and speeches, urging them on, treating them as heroes simply for not giving up. Isaac Hamlin was one of those Poale Zion people who organized the entertainment for their departing friends. The mood was described as "festive." "It was my privilege," he said afterward, "to have Goldie as my honored guest on the canoe rides on the Charles River. When we bid farewell to the group, some felt like joining them."

"An old couple left the group and went home," said Shana. "And so did a young bride." Sam again telegraphed them to come home, but, again, as Goldie said, "When she decides something, that's it . . . she wouldn't budge."

"We got off the boat during the day," said Regina, "but always slept on the boat at night. We had no money for hotels. Every day our *chaverim* came to say good-bye to us and the next day we were still there."

Once again at sea, the *Pocahontas* again ran into multiple problems. The pumps collapsed, the boilers burst, fires broke out in two bunkers, and the engine room started to flood, causing the ship to list. Sabotage continued. Unknown to the passengers, three sailors were put in irons, including two in charge of the dynamo. The situation became plainer to the passengers when the refrigerators mysteriously broke down, spoiling much of the food, which had to be thrown overboard.

Goldie and her group, as well as the other passengers, learned about most of these disasters in dribbles of rumors, usually long after the fact. It was not as if they could do anything about it anyway, and they were still sailing in the right direction. The food was a problem, but they shared what they had. They kept intact as a tight group and forgot some of their misery in laughter and singing. Goldie well remembered her father's favorite philosophical sayings: "As long as you're healthy . . ." and "It could always be worse."

"During all this, when all of them were downhearted, it was Goldie who raised their spirits," Regina remembered. "We used to sing folk songs, things like that. Goldie was never in better singing voice."

Nightmare turned into paradise at Ponta Delgada in the Azores. The place seemed idyllic, and beautiful. They would be there for extensive repairs, said the captain, for at least a week. These nineteen young people were anxious to flee the ship for a while, wondering what to do. Their answer came in the shape of a delegation of bearded Sephardic Jews from the island who spoke only Portuguese.

"These Portuguese Jews heard that some idiots were aboard this ship," said Regina, "and that we were stranded for a while so they hunted us up, used sign language, took us away with them, then showed us a good time."

It turned out that there were thirty Jews on this island, and they were so Orthodox that they had foresworn eating meat since the death of their rabbi.

Ponta Delgada was an important port on Sao Miguel Island, the largest city on the largest island in the Azores. Morris soon learned some of its history, that it was the site of naval battles between the English and the Spanish. For Goldie and Morris it was a lovely time for long walks in the lush scenery with the backdrop of volcanic mountains. There were all kinds of delicious fruits from apricots to pineapples, and vineyards were everywhere. After the horror of the shipboard meals, the food here, with its vast variety of fish, was an incredible luxury.

"I remember when four of us went to a restaurant and the bill came to 15,000 escudos and we were panic-stricken because we only had ten dollars among us. But then we discovered that this bill translated to about two dollars."

All seemed serene again as they boarded ship, waving good-bye to their new Sephardic friends, en route to Naples. Then, gradually, horror unfolded. Again, it all came to them in whispered rumors, all of them unbelievable, all of them true. The captain had put four engineers in irons because they were overheard saying they would sink the ship before it reached Naples. While the ship had been in port, the captain, it seems, had foiled another plot to burn the ship so it could never leave. Another engineer had been listed as a suicide, even though he was discovered dead with his hands tied behind his back. The captain had a brother aboard, and he had to be chained in his cabin because he had gone raving mad. The sea was so rough that one woman broke her leg. One of the passengers had died, and had to be dumped over-board because the refrigeration again had broken down. The meat was ruined, and passengers found themselves eating rice with salty tea. Finally, after thirty-four days, as the ship limped into Naples, word came that the captain reportedly had killed himself in despair—although many later claimed he had been murdered.

"See Naples and die," said all the travel posters, and they felt they almost had. Built at the base of the volcanic hills, with Mt. Vesuvius as the backdrop, the city rose from the shore like an amphitheater, a jewel of a city with the slopes as a diadem. It was spectacular enough for them all to forget for a moment what they had been through.

It was a city of palaces and churches, and museums and music.

For Morris and Goldie, the music was most important. The San Carlo Opera House was one of the largest in Europe. But first they found rooms at the waterfront in the Imperial Hotel for $1.50 a night. No restaurants—they made their own meals.

"When we went into the hotel we used to hide the food under our coats because we weren't supposed to bring food in," said Regina. "Mostly bread and cheese, things like that."

Shana described that whole time in Naples to Sam as "a chaos and a mishmash."

The reality of Naples, behind the beautiful façade from the sea, was a noisy, dirty place blurred by the friendly gaiety of the people. Wherever Morris and Goldie walked, they seemed to find burgeoning festivals in the side streets.

Goldie and her friends stocked up on oil lamps, mosquito netting, toilet paper, and food.

"The strangest thing is that milk is fresh straight from a cow," Shana wrote Sam. "I mean that literally. You go out in the street and see a woman with a cow and a calf. You stop her and she milks a pitcher full for you right on the spot."

Stranded in Naples, the small group of nineteen now needed another ship to Palestine, where, they learned, there had been new riots. Since Palestine had no adequate harbor, ship passengers disembarked at sea and were rowed ashore by Arabs. With the riots at their peak, Arabs now publicly refused to row ashore any Jewish passengers.

"It seems we can't go any farther," Shana wrote Sam. "We got a funny answer from the companies, really something to laugh at. Christians and Moslems can go to Palestine, but they can't sell tickets to Jews. They do this for our own sakes because the Arabs throw the Jews into the sea. So here you have a sad joke—no Jew can enter Eretz Yisroel."

The group finally found a ship leaving in six days from Brindisi, on the east coast of Italy, for Alexandria, Egypt. Arriving in Brindisi, the nineteen discovered a new problem—all their baggage had mysteriously disappeared. The ship was leaving in a few hours. The steamship company assured them their baggage would follow on the next ship. The group wavered in indecision whether to leave or wait.

"You can wait for baggage; I won't," said Goldie.

Her decision decided the others and they all boarded the ship.

Once aboard, Shana recorded her doubts to Sam. Their children looked so thin and hungry, she wrote. "God, what am I doing to them? To whom and to what do I lead them?"

They were not the only Zionists aboard. There was a small group of Lithuanians whom Yossel described as "young people with hard muscles who can sleep on hard decks, who eat hard bread made of bran, and who speak Hebrew with the hard Sephardic accent. Real Hercules types, who are ready to build a land on just foundations with their backs."

"They obviously regarded themselves, not without reason, as superior to us," Golda later added. "They made it quite clear that we were soft, spoiled immigrants . . . who would probably run away from Palestine after a few weeks." Admitting her envy, Golda continued, "I could hardly take my eyes off them; they were everything I wanted and hoped to be myself—dedicated, austere, and determined."

Goldie was determined to befriend them, but the Lithuanians "wanted nothing to do with us." Among other things, the Lithuanians sneered because the "soft Americans" had cabins while they slept on the deck.

To prove that they, too, were tough pioneers, Goldie proposed to her group that they sacrifice their cabins and also sleep on the deck— after providing sleeping space for their children. Goldie's proposal was not enthusiastically received. For one thing, the group pointed out that those who slept on the deck did not get any hot meals. Pressing her point, Goldie suggested they could organize their own kitchen. Gradually, reluctantly, Goldie persuaded her group. Just as gradually and just as reluctantly, the barriers between them and the Lithuanians finally broke down. Toward the end of the trip, all of them were singing together, Hebrew and Jewish songs, and dancing the traditional hora.

Everybody on board had to check in with Mindel. He was the immigration official on the ship representing the British Mandatory Authorities in Palestine, and he was also Jewish. Examining Goldie's passport, he mockingly asked her how she expected to make a living in Palestine. Years later, Mindel would work for Goldie, "and was forever apologizing for having sneered at us abroad ship."

"The ship goes swiftly," Yossel wrote Sam. "We are approaching Egypt. I have strange feelings of excitement and uncertainty."

Landing at Alexandria, they again found themselves between two worlds, with all the restless tension of being on the last leg of their chaotic journey. The time it had taken was so much more than they had expected, an interminable time, yet full of adventure. The city's seawall provided a magnificent promenade along the shore for several miles, and some short streets took them into the Grand Square, a tree-lined oblong open space with handsome, Italian-style buildings and a large statue of Alexander on a horse.

Goldie saw her first Moslem mosques, the slender minarets and the curved domes, the veiled Egyptian women, her first camels, the Europeans in their stylish carriages. She also saw the naked children covered with sores, eyes veiled by trachoma, and the rotting garbage in many streets.

Goldie's vivid memory of Alexandria was the fear of finding herself surrounded by beggars covered with flies. She had conjured up the childhood terror in Pinsk, when she first found herself facing hordes of beggars. "I knew that if one of them actually touched me, I would scream—pioneer or not!"

Even this anxiety faded fast as they entrained for the overnight trip to Palestine. Despite their heightened expectancy, most of them still harped on the unspeakable dirt, unspeakable heat, and the lack of water. Goldie was less concerned with the hard reality than with her fantasy of the future. Most of their information about Palestine was mixed with rumors and visions. And Goldie's vision was a clear and shining thing that made her transition into action so much easier. She seemed to think what she wanted to think, dream what she wanted to dream, and her dreams were dramatic. That's why it was so much more natural for her to be able to stir the rest of the group that night to sing "Return to Zion," which they sang "quite rousingly."

"It was hot in July," recalled Golda. "The windows were closed but that didn't help much—the sand, we were just covered with sand, the eyes, everything. Poor children, not a drop of water on the train, of course."

It was the middle of the night when they saw the long, slender shadows of the palm trees on the Egyptian border at El Quantara. They had to wait until midnight when somebody showed up at the passport office. There was a problem at customs about the pregnant Dina Kaplan—they didn't want to let her through. Immigration officials there seemed unusually obtuse and difficult, and Goldie lost her temper with one of them "to very little avail." Moving in to help them resolve their problems was "a very nice English policeman." This surprised them, as they had heard that the British "didn't want to help them into Palestine." This one not only traveled to Tel Aviv with them, "but many years later, he attended a *Pocahontas* reunion."

It was dawn when their train moved across the Sinai peninsula through a blinding sandstorm. Many of the people on this train to Tel Aviv were Arabs with their families. "Most of them looked at us with eyes of hate and suspicion. We would hear them yelling at each other. At every stop, the beggars swarmed aboard and some suitcases were stolen. The children slept in the hot, heavy air." As they finally arrived in Tel Aviv, one of Shana's children was asleep in Goldie's arms.

The real *aliyah*, the real adventure, had now begun.

As they stared in wonder, one of them said, "It's like coming to another planet!"

7

This is a country no bigger than a house.
My roots are here.
I have to live now.
There is no time to wait for more suitable times.

They seemed so forlorn, this small cluster of nineteen, standing at this wooden shack of a Tel Aviv railroad station on that noon of the four-teenth of July 1921. Exhausted from their two months of travel, they stared at the sand, sand, sand, and flies, masses of flies, all this in a sun so scorching nobody could stand in it. White stucco houses in the distance seemed deserted, and the only life they saw anywhere was a slow-moving camel caravan near some faraway dunes.

This was the Promised Land? This was their glorious moment?

As they stood there, stunned into silence, Yossel finally said, "Well, Goldie, you wanted to come to Eretz Yisroel. Here we are. Now we can go back—it's enough."

Nobody smiled.

"Somebody said, 'This is it!' and I died," said Shana's daughter, Judy. "I started crying because I wanted to go back home."

A poll of the group, taken at that moment, would have found all of them ready to go back—all but Golda.* Her mood then, as always, was the mood of Zionist pioneer Rachel Ben-Zvi, wife of Yitzhak, a founder and leader of Zionist socialism. Before she left for Palestine from a

---

*Author's note: From now on, I will refer to her as Golda, except in a direct quotation when someone refers to her as Goldie. She officially changed her name to Golda Meir in 1956.

Russian prison camp in 1908, she was asked, "But what will you *do* in Palestine?"

"I will *live!*"

One of the few things Golda saw alive near that railroad station was a single tree, somehow growing out of that sand. If that tree could live here, if Rachel Ben-Zvi could live here, she could.

Shana saw the lone tree "as a symbol of the Jewish people sitting in a sea of hate and suspicion of its neighbors."

All that desolate sand made the name Tel Aviv seem like a dry joke, because the name, in Hebrew, meant "hill of spring." It also seemed a little grand to call it the first all-Jewish city in the world. Founded a dozen years earlier by sixty families, it was planned as a suburb of small homes for Jews working in adjoining Jaffa.

The ancient Arab city of Jaffa, with its stinking, twisting streets, loomed on a giant rock overlooking the sea and the Jews. Just two months before Golda's arrival, Jaffa Arabs had gone on a pogrom, killing forty-seven Jews—almost as many as the Kishinev pogrom—and wounding hundreds more. This did not fit the concept of the Jewish-born British prime minister Benjamin Disraeli that "Arabs are only Jews on horse-back."

British High Commissioner Herbert Samuel afterward gave Tel Aviv the status of a "town council" with the right to rule its people with its own municipal court, fire brigade, and police force. The pogrom gave the few police an outsize importance. A dozen of them were promptly hired and proudly uniformed—even though they had no jail—with Jews still fleeing from Jaffa. Tel Aviv also had a mayor who always rode a white horse. Asked about its population, the mayor replied that it was impossible to say, because "by the afternoon or the next morning, there would be a hundred or two hundred more." Americans called it "a 'Jack and the Beanstalk' city."

Tel Aviv had no power station to supply electricity, but it did have a high school, the tallest building in town. There was a hotel, a ram-shackle single story named Barash, after the owner. It was Barash who scooped them up at the station and gave them a place to sleep and bathe.

Shana went shopping for food and returned horrified at the flies that covered everything. "The bread was lying on the dirty blanket, dust-covered. The food was exposed to the flies and sun, and the meat wasn't fresh." She wondered, "How can we raise our children in such filth!" This was the first time Goldie had ever heard Shana complain. But then she and Regina were similarly horrified to discover colonies of bedbugs in their rooms. Morris, whose possessions were few, was not exultant when his razor disappeared on their first day in Palestine. He was not a man to say, "I told you so," but his unhappiness was evident; his brooding contrasted sharply with Golda's excitement.

As if to cap their discouragement, they had dinner with the Hadaris, the only Americans they knew in town. The Hadaris served them hamburgers on which they all almost choked. It turned out "that a piece of soap must have fallen in by accident." The Hadaris informed them that they were returning to the United States in a few days. They couldn't take it, because "of all the horrors," including the destruction of their carpentry shop in Jaffa during the Arab attack.

And so it began.

The group split and scattered. Golda and Shana found a two-room apartment on Lillienblum Street with an outside kitchen, and a toilet in the yard shared by forty or fifty people. Shana and her family slept in the front room near the door. When Golda and Morris came home late, and didn't want to disturb the children by opening the front door, "we used to crawl in the window of our room."

Golda's hopes of getting into a kibbutz quickly disappeared. The main reason they had applied to a kibbutz called Merhavia was because they knew an American who had gone there. The reply from the kibbutz was curt: their application would be considered in September.

Something that made them laugh was one greeting they got: "Thank God you millionaires have come to us from America; now everything will be all right here." In order to eat, the "millionaire Americans" had to find jobs. Morris found work as a bookkeeper with a British installation in Lydda. He worked from seven-thirty until two, earned three and a half pounds sterling* a week, and came back to Tel Aviv on weekends. Yossel became a barber again. Regina was a secretary in a brick factory and made the most money because she knew shorthand. Golda was forced to do what she had done in Milwaukee—give private English lessons to immigrants.

*The British pound sterling was then worth about five dollars.

"Ah, that is what you came here for," a friend commented, "to spread English culture."

"I came home and cried," said Golda.

Shana also cried. "Is this the welcome we receive in the land of the Jews?" she asked Golda. Her son had contracted glaucoma and her daughter suffered a painful case of boils. They had no money for doctors, so she went to the hospital pleading for a job to pay for their medical care. There were no jobs. That's when she burst into tears, the only time Golda had ever seen her cry. Ultimately, Shana worked in a hospital for several months without pay until they finally gave her a job, accepted her children as patients, and cured them.

Despite so many disappointments, Golda maintained her high spirits and wrote to Shana's husband, Sam:

> Those who talk of returning are recent arrivals. An old worker is full of inspiration and faith. I say that as long as those who created the little that is here are here, I cannot leave, and you must come. I would not say this if I did not know that you are ready to work hard. True, even hard work is hard to find, but I have no doubt that you will find something. . . . There may even be pogroms again, but if one wants one's own land, and if one wants it with one's whole heart, one must be ready for this. When you come, I am sure we will be able to plan. Perhaps you will come with us to Merhavia. Get ready. There is nothing to wait for.

Golda never forgot the austere young man who had refused to lunch at her family home in Milwaukee—because she had not come to hear him speak the night before. She later learned his earlier story. He had come to Palestine from Poland at the age of twenty with a knapsack on his back, walked across the sand dunes that became Tel Aviv, stayed at a small Jewish colony called Petach Tikva ("Gate of Hope"), and wrote: "I did not sleep. I was among the rich smell of corn. I heard the braying of donkeys and the rustling of leaves in the orchards. Above were the massed clusters of stars . . . my heart overflowed with happiness . . . I am in Eretz Yisroel . . . in a Hebrew village."

He had come, he said, to be born anew. He had come as David Green, but later Hebraized his name to David Ben-Gurion.

Golda learned that this legendary Ben-Gurion lived on the second floor of a nearby building, that he had just returned from a mission to Russia. She remembered being part of a small awed group gathering in his room on a Saturday afternoon "sitting on the floor, listening to his report."

Ben-Gurion had been part of the Second Aliyah—the word *aliyah* meant "going up" in Hebrew. That was the wave of 35,000 Jews who had come after the turn of the century and before the First World War. Most of them worked as laborers in the cities. An estimated 25,000 had come in the First Aliyah, 1882–1903, mostly from Eastern Europe. Golda and her group had come at the tail end of the Third Aliyah, 1919–23.

Trying to vivify those in her immigrant wave, Golda said, "Look, the Third Aliyah people were girls and boys in their teens. They had nobody to care for, they carried no responsibility for anybody except themselves, most of them burned their bridges saying, 'This is it. There is no going back.' They came mostly from Eastern Europe, really with an enthusiasm, on a mission, a historic mission, although they never said it. And they had no complaints."

"This is a poor country, but it is my home," wrote one young man. And another added, "There is such a spirit here that you can feel it in the wind. Not just for Jews, but for Christians and for all the people who have come here from all over the world."

The Third Aliyah would total some 35,000, who wanted primarily to work the land. The number of Americans among them was proportionately small. Their Palestinian peers had a contempt for them because they didn't surrender their passports on arrival. Morris didn't, but Golda did, "so she wouldn't have a foot in each country." When Golda registered in Jaffa as an immigrant on July 27, she was Certificate Number 2083.

They had come to rebuild a country and be rebuilt by it, Golda had said. Golda and her *aliyah* saw everything as a "spiritual bouquet," a revolt against yesterday. "It didn't matter what kind of home you grew up in. You didn't at all want what had been there yesterday, but rather something entirely different—to build things up by yourself."

"Life here is bitter, bitter," an immigrant wrote home, then added, "I could not live anywhere else than in this beloved, blessed land of mine."

Part of the bitterness was that there was no money for anything, not even enough to help resettle those in the Jewish Legion of the British Army who wanted to stay in Palestine.

"Anybody who wanted to come could come, but there was nothing for them to do when they arrived here. There was no work because there was no building. There was no land to be farmed except the bits that had already been bought by the Jewish National Fund. So the pioneers were in camps without tents, with nothing to do."

"What? No bread? . . . I'm not hungry . . . No shoes? Never mind . . . I like walking barefoot . . ."

"There is no comfort to be had in this country. It is a place that makes you have dreams you do not want, and that makes you acknowledge things in yourself you would rather not know."

Even the most optimistic Zionist leaders felt that this tiny country, this desolate place of rock and sand, could never hope to sustain even a small percentage of the 15 million Jews of the world.

When Weizmann came to Palestine after the Balfour Declaration to collect contributions to buy land, "Whoever had a gold ring threw it into the hat. Whoever had earrings threw them in as well. A watch? That, too. . . . At the time we thought we already had a state. We thought we were already free."

"Of course we want Zionists to come into Palestine," Emir Faisal told a British delegate at the Paris Peace Conference in 1919. Faisal, who would later be crowned king of Greater Syria, added, "We know what will happen—they will bring vast sums of American and other capital from abroad. They will bring in the greatest scientists in the world: all the greatest scientists are Jewish. And the territory of Palestine—now so arid and so much of it a desert—will be transformed: it will become a garden: it will blossom like a rose. We shall borrow their experts; we shall work together. We shall do the same in all the countries which we Arabs turned into deserts. We shall make them flourish again as they used to in the past."

Faisal had hoped to be king of all the Arabs in the Ottoman Empire, but never lived long enough to fulfill his ambition, or to see what happened to the Jews.* Faisal was a supporter of the British, who had received a League of Nations mandate to administer the area of Palestine after their defeat of the Turks. The British were pledged by the Balfour Declaration to foster a homeland for the 80,000 Jews in Palestine, who made up about 11 percent of the population. The British high

*Faisal died in 1933.

commissioner, Sir Herbert Samuel, arrived in 1920, a year before Golda. Samuel found his military predecessor at Government House, also known as "Occupied Enemy Territory Administration South." The general asked Samuel to sign a receipt for Palestine, which read, "Received from Major General Sir Louis J. Bols, K.C.B., one Palestine complete." Samuel signed. "Palestine complete" was then roughly 240 miles long, twenty-three miles wide in the north, and about seventy-five miles wide in the south.

Samuel later reported to his king the buildup of Arab hatred and tension, but also noted how the Jews had changed the landscape. "When I first saw it in 1920," he wrote of the valley of Askalon, "it was desolation, not a house, not a tree." Now, he said, they were building villages, a university, an opera house. He also noted that there had been only one motor car in all of Palestine in 1914—by 1922 there were almost a thousand.

In the year 1921, Golda was one of 9,140 immigrants. Immigrants generally steered clear of Arabs, particularly in the wake of recent riots. Jews generally regarded Arabs then as unfriendly and mysterious, and the British soldiers as "tall, slim figures expressing a stiff aloofness . . . always ready to cut short their work and play games." Added to this, they felt the British were generally arrogant and "seemed more at home with the Arab landowners."

Two weeks after Golda was settled, she and Morris journeyed to Jerusalem for the first time. "We went directly to the Old City, to the Wailing Wall.* Although I knew what the Wall was, and what it represented, I cannot honestly say that on my way to the Wailing Wall I was very emotional. I suppose I pictured it more or less as a monument. Until I got there. Then everything changed. And then everything made sense. I had heard, of course, that men and women—old people primarily—put little pieces of paper with wishes on them in the cracks of the Wall. I can't say that it had made much sense to me. All of a sudden it made sense . . . this was the symbol of our struggle, of having

---

*When the Romans destroyed the Second Temple, Jews continued to pray at that surviving retaining wall, lamenting the desolation of their people. A synagogue was built there shortly before the Crusader period and the wall became the holiest shrine of Judaism. The Wailing Wall was renamed the Western Wall after the time of statehood.

been driven out from this country. But this remained, the Wall was there as a fortress of guarantee that the land will be there when the Jews come back. To me it was everything. It is almost something alive. And if it's alive, then you talk to it, you have contact with it."

What did she write on the piece of paper that she put in the Wall? "I wrote then that this country should be rebuilt."

Golda's situation lightened. Thirty-three trunks had been lost and sidetracked to Syria. The Syrians not only had kept them, but wanted to charge duty on everything. Golda and Morris went to Jerusalem to plead with the American consul and the British high commissioner to argue their case. "And finally, with God's help," Shana wrote Sam, "the baggage came."

They now had pots, pans, tablecloths, bedspreads. Morris converted two trunks into a sofa, two more trunks into a dresser, framed pictures for the walls. His real disaster was to discover that his books had arrived waterlogged and torn. His cultural lifeline still was his phonograph and his records. Everywhere they found a multitude of new friends, all hungry for music.

"For years afterward I used to meet people whom I did not recognize and they would say, 'Oh, I used to come to listen to your phonograph records.' Everybody brought somebody else. Anybody that knew us would bring along people and we served tea and they listened to records." Even Golda's grandson, Gideon, told in later years of meeting someone who said, "Your grandfather lent me stacks of his records."

Something else impressed Golda: the way these people looked and walked. The Orthodox bearded ones no longer had the shuffling gait of the old ghetto. Now they had a sprightly prance, an eager attitude. Most of all, Golda glowed when she looked at her peers, the young people in khaki shorts, tanned and vigorous, all talking Hebrew. It was difficult to believe that this was a city of 15,000 people built on dust and that the jackals were howling only a few miles away.

"Imagine taking Latin from the cloister . . . and making it the vernacular!" said an American traveler admiringly. "Yet this is exactly what the Jews have done with Hebrew. They have brought Hebrew from the synagogue and made it the language of housewives, chauffeurs, shopkeepers." He marveled most at youngsters yelling in Hebrew while they played football.

However fluent Golda became in Hebrew, fluent enough to make speeches, she would always be mocked for her American Hebrew. "I thought I would never understand Hebrew."

Hebrew caused a problem with their mail. They had had their early mail sent in care of the Labor Party, "so we used to come for our letters and the man in charge would not answer us in Yiddish." Their Hebrew improved, but the mail did not. When they moved into a house, the mail was supposed to be delivered to them. "For some time we didn't get any letters. The letter carrier lived across the street, so we asked his wife. 'Oh, yes, I did see the children playing with some letters the other day . . .' " These were some of the primitive things that irked even Golda.

Golda and Morris and Shana did what they could to create a semblance of home in Tel Aviv. The failure of their fantasies meant pulling at their strength and imagination to cope. Shana's daily concern was milk for her children. She and Golda grimaced at the memory of their mother in Milwaukee using leftover milk to wash the leaves of rubber plants. Their neighbors mocked them when they put up screens to keep out flies, calling it American *narrishkeit* (nonsense) and adding, "You're bigger than a fly!"

The brash new Tel Aviv did not have the holiness of Jerusalem, the exoticism of Tiberias, the mysticism of Safad, but it was a Mediterranean city lapping at the sea. There was a small theatrical group performing in a tent, a water tower where young people met and argued and sang, and Shabbat was still Shabbat with its prayerful quiet and its traditional food and flowers on the table. To remind them of the Arabs, they could see the minaret of a mosque at the city's outskirts.

Still, for Golda, Tel Aviv was temporary, a transition. As she put it, "I came here to work, not to teach English."

And then they heard from the kibbutz.

8

In the summer they burn and in winter they freeze.
Then why do they come, and why do they stay?
Don't you long for Fifth Avenue, pine for Broadway?
Don't you long for a bath in a white porcelain room?
Can they stand these discomforts, this pricking and sticking?
Just camping at night, and just working by day?
Then why do they come, and why do they stay?
                                                    —*Jessie Sampter*

The region known as the Emek includes the Jezreel Valley spread out like a green and golden carpet extending beyond the River Kishon to the north, almost to the edge of the Lebanon Mountains. To the east, it merges with the Jordan Valley, south to the plateau of Judea, and west within sight of the Mediterranean.

Part of the Emek, the Merhavia kibbutz, originally was a malarial swamp, then a temporary camp for German pilots in World War I, and finally a failed cooperative filled with members of the Jewish Legion. In Hebrew, *merhavia* means "God's wide spirit."

The spirit had stayed, and so had some former members of the Jewish Legion, when Golda and Morris applied for membership in 1921. In September, the kibbutz voted against the application of Golda and Morris. Of the two votes they got, one was from their American friend. They applied a second time, and again were turned down. "Not only because we were Americans, but because we were a married couple. The thirty-two men were all bachelors and they wanted single girls."

The eight single women at Merhavia also objected to Golda because "they had heard all about American girls." All of the eight had come from Eastern Europe; most of them had been in Palestine for at least eight years. They pointed to the fact that almost a third of American immigrants returned to the United States. American women particularly were too soft for tough physical work, they said, and wouldn't last long. Golda loudly protested, applied a third time, demanding a probationary period to prove themselves. The kibbutz finally agreed to a one-month trial period.

The kibbutz represented Golda's vision of a new life in a new old land. She quoted the poet Rachel, "making music with the hoe, and to draw upon the earth," and A. D. Gordon* and his "religion of labor" in which "man becomes one with himself, society, and nature."

"The Second Aliyah had accepted the notion that we were all going to be the owners of orange groves, stores, and factories, and others would do the work for us," Golda observed. "I'm convinced that we would not have been justified in owning a country that someone else had built for us and did the work for us.

"There are things that have to be done with your hands. You have to soil your hands somewhere. And so I wouldn't like to see all of us with university degrees and have somebody else do the dirty work for us. That would hurt our society in a very dangerous way. That is not Zionism."

In Golda's Zionist vision, the spreading kibbutzim would form the spiritual core of the homeland. The idea was that kibbutzim would help their people grow into a nation living on their own soil as of right and not on sufferance, living in houses they had built, eating food they had grown. "Nobody should do things for them," insisted Golda.

She then told about her friend Sophie Heller, making her *aliyah* to Palestine, saying good-bye to a friend who had just returned from fighting with the Jewish Legion. "Now it's a pleasure to hold your hand," the man had said, "when you go to Palestine and you work—it will be an honor."

The first kibbutz, Degania Aleph, grew out of an argument between a group of workers and their farm manager about visiting sick fellow workers. The group borrowed money and started their own cooperative farm, making their own rules, and so the kibbutz was born in 1911. A visitor described the "primitive and innocent youngsters, wildly talking,

*Aharon David Gordon (1856–1922), spiritual guide of that part of Zionism that emphasized settlement of the land by Jews "by their sweat." His teaching was a mix of Zionism, mysticism, socialism, and agrarianism.

singing, and dancing as they gathered in a large room with a table in the center and long benches."

The concept came from a German sociologist named Franz Oppenheimer, who believed that equality would eliminate social conflict. Everybody shared all work, responsibility, and profits. Everything was collective, including child-rearing.

Shana theoretically agreed with the concept of the kibbutz, but she decided against going with Golda because she knew that her husband didn't want to go. Shana also knew that few kibbutzim were likely to accept a woman with children whose husband was elsewhere. Beyond all that, the kibbutz rules went against Shana's grain. The idea of hard work didn't faze her, but everything else did. She didn't like the idea of not being able to own anything, of going to a laundry place once a week for her weekly clothes, which might or might not fit. She was a neat, organized, possessive person. Regina also had planned to go with Golda, but she, too, changed her mind. Her husband also didn't want to go. Suddenly, too, she found herself in great demand as a skilled English-speaking secretary. Her salary was far above what most people earned.

Golda was still not certain what to expect. She knew the kibbutz would not conform with the sugary portrait British High Commissioner Samuel had painted of a place bordered by small, single-storied white houses, well spaced out along wide roads, "houses with porches and little gardens of flowers, smiling groups of men and women in working clothes under a cloudless sky."

What Golda and Morris found at Merhavia in September 1921 was depressing: a few shacks, a few trees, mostly mud and rocks. The settlement was surrounded by a cement fence and gate with openings for guns. In the distance were several Arab villages, "and they used to take potshots at us from time to time." Far away was the imposing Mount Tabor, singled out for its beauty in the Psalms, and still regarded by many as a holy mountain.

Merhavia's mission was to drain the swamp, clear the rocks, plant trees, and create an economic future in grain, vegetables, and dairy products. The big crop seemed to be tomatoes. Within the compound were a few cattle and chickens, several horses, and recalcitrant mules. The mules carted the kibbutz milk to the train every morning for the Haifa market. Kibbutzniks laughed when a mule broke free of his harness and returned to the stable, leaving the driver to carry back all the gear. Another stubborn mule received this ultimatum from his rider: "Either you or I—the two of us can't stay in Merhavia."

Inside the fence, on one side was the kitchen and dining room, the storeroom, and the laundry. Nearby were the living quarters, with a few separate rooms for expected couples, the others sleeping in barracks. "The whole thing might have been a block square."

"I well remember my first day's work," said Golda. "It was the threshing season and they told me to 'sit' on the board of the threshing machine that revolved in the barn and threshed the grain." After that came picking almonds until her hands were yellow. "But the terrible backbreaking work was to try to dig a hole below the rocks with a pick to get some soil to put seedlings in."

Kibbutzniks elsewhere echoed what she felt:

"The hoe came up against a pile of stones. The blade sank into a kind of marsh, and I could not pull it out. I used all my strength, and was drenched in sweat. My hands were covered with blisters, which soon burst open. My skin peeled off and blood oozed from the wounds.... I worked with all my strength, and strained my muscles until my hands and feet shivered, as though from malaria. After a day's work came a sleepless night, pains in the back and loins. And there was the troubling thought—will my physical strength and determination suffice to stand the test?"

"It was dead soil. You had to have deep conviction to attempt revitalizing such soil."

"We had no idea that it would be that hard, but if one wants to live for an ideal, he can overcome hardship."

"One does not work for a living, but for life itself." "... Because success in becoming one with it was the essence of such an elated experience...." "Our hunger for work in the soil after thousands of years of exile overwhelmed us." "By the sweat of thy brow shalt thou eat bread."

"I looked at my hands, thumbs scorched, fingernails hardened. And I would not trade this world for yours, never, not for the best of all possible worlds."

And Golda? She was so exhausted that day that "the weight of a fork seemed a ton. I forced myself to eat, even though it was hard to look at, let alone swallow." The bitterness in the food came from olive oil sold by Arabs from goatskin bags.

Did she ever think of going back to the United States then?

"No. Never. Never, not even for one minute because when I left, I left with the idea that this was it. It was not a question of try it. There was nothing to try. I wasn't disappointed in anything. Nothing was *too* hard. I expected it to be hard here. I did not come to Palestine after anybody had prepared anything. Nobody owed me anything."

Arabs had called this part of their valley Death Swamp, and referred to the water source as the "well of poison." Golda and Morris soon discovered that everybody either had had malaria or was getting it. To battle this, they were served quinine at each meal. The one thing that depressed Golda most was the single toilet, "about a half kilometer away." "It was a horror at night to go out in the mud, really a horror. Especially in the winter, especially if you had a fever."

Most toilets consisted of four holes, without partition, at the edge of a settlement. "Comrades always went there in pairs, so that when one of them crouched, the other stood guard . . . because of the snipers."

For Morris, the personal deprivation was that he couldn't boil some tea in his room. In a kibbutz there was no such thing as a private teapot or a private anything. Private property caused hours of argument and tension.

Golda always felt that the toilets and the tea were the two discouraging drawbacks, the symbolic keys that stymied the growth of the kibbutz movement.

They had to want tea very much to cross "quite a big yard" to the kitchen on a winter night. "We used to pour tea straight from the hot-water heater but we hardly ever had the patience to wait for the water to boil so we drank it hot but unboiled," Golda said. "I used to go because I liked the company to sit around with."

It was a company of people "who, because they were uprooted, were now busily engaged in building a world in which to forget their past." It was a company from which she could not expect pity or kindness but on whose human solidarity she would always be able to rely. "It was the type of solidarity that shied away from privacy and individualism.

Necessity and ideology privileged a group rather than the individual."
For this reason it was wise to adhere to the group as quickly as possible.
Those who remained aloof suffered.

Morris suffered; Golda thrived.

The probationary period passed, and the Meyersons were accepted.
"I still believe that the scales were tipped in our favor by the phonograph," Golda later commented. "It was the first phonograph in the
country without the horn—and many good records came with it. Of
course, they would have been happy to accept the phonograph as a
dowry without the bride who owned it, but we wouldn't agree to that."

Everybody got their same clean clothes from the same communal
shelves. "Neither my shirt nor my underclothes were my own. I wore
them but they were not my property. . . . Tomorrow someone else might
wear them." Everybody ate in the same communal dining room, even
shared the same communal shower. The shower was a social rite after
the day's work to share gossip, exchange information, solve problems.
Men and women showering together fostered a sense of equality and
natural relationship.

"We sometimes used to go into the communal shower all covered
with dust, open the tap, and no water came out," Golda remembered.
"When the water stopped, someone had to climb up the tower to make
some adjustment. I didn't understand why we needed a man to fix it;
and when I climbed up the ladder for the first time, it was a shock for
the girls, and the boys, too."

Water was gold. One kibbutz had to take four cans on a donkey for
a half hour to get their daily water supply. Another kibbutz brought a
barrel of water to the middle of the fields. The sun was so ferocious
that some insisted the water practically boiled.

There were two dozen kibbutzim in 1921. Their original purpose
was agriculture and colonization; later they evolved into military out-
posts. The world got an ominous warning that year when Hitler's storm
troopers in Germany began to terrorize political opponents. That was
also the year when Winston Churchill became Britain's colonial secretary, Warren G. Harding was inaugurated President of the United
States, and the first radio broadcast of a baseball game was made from
the Polo Grounds in New York.

Morris was not much interested in the news of the world. At Merhavia
he seemed caught by the beauty of the place, particularly at sunset. In

the spring, too, there was a rush of wildflowers in a panorama of startling color everywhere. Even his physical work seemed to give Morris some satisfaction. In writing all this to his mother, he sadly noted his frustration at not finding anybody else to share his love of music, art, or books. For Morris, the worst was the utter lack of privacy. As a married couple, Golda and Morris did have their own room with two cots. Morris made furniture, some cupboards out of orange crates. To the mocking laughter of the others, he even put some flower decoration on a strip against the wall of their room. Depressing him completely was that kibbutz committees ran everybody's life to the smallest detail. He had hoped that sharing this new adventure with Goldie would mean spending more time together. The opposite was true. The kibbutz had no regard for family relationships either in work assignments or days off. They even discouraged the constant joint appearance of a couple in public. "The husband and wife who stuck together and were seen often in each other's company were viewed with scorn." The brooding Morris became increasingly isolated.

Golda had great enthusiasm for the challenge of the kibbutz and loved it:

"Look, to me the kibbutz is an ideal form of human society. I don't say everybody in a kibbutz is an angel, and I don't say they don't have difficulties sometimes, but the society is an ideal society where you share everything. You are part of a group where there is no competition, no exploitation. A human being is accepted and judged and participates in the life of the society not according to what kind of work he has, but because he is a human being."

This was an insider's view; an outsider's view came from British High Commissioner for Palestine Herbert Samuel, who regarded kibbutzniks as a peasantry with dignity. He felt they seemed "remarkably happy," because they knew quite well that they were working for the redemption of Palestine. "They read. They think. They discuss. There is among them a real activity of mind."

"You were young and you were creating something, creating a new ideal," wrote one kibbutznik. The kibbutz defined every aspect of their lives.

It surely defined Golda's life. She was fresh, feisty, and twenty-three, a magnet for more than two dozen vigorous bachelors. Though a full day's work often made Morris too tired to eat, it no longer seemed to faze Golda. "All they seemed to do was work, work, work," said Shana's daughter, Judy, who visited them there, "and then they had a meeting and all they talked about was more work." At this weekly *kumsitz*, the meeting after Friday night dinner, the group would discuss the upcoming week's work assignments. "The workers plan and the plan is worked."

"The evenings were truly unique.... There were moments when people burst into confessions of their past, telling how they viewed life, mankind, eternity. There were moments of tears, of laughter, moments of emotion which transcended gray daily life. It was very special."

Golda felt part of this intensity of talk, the constant excitement. At parties, when the frailer Morris was fast asleep, Golda was dancing as if she had unending adrenaline, singing as if she never wanted to stop. "She never seemed depressed, always managed to cheer the rest of us up when we felt low." "These were my kind of people," Golda said. "I felt absolutely fulfilled."

From a woman's vantage point, kibbutzim had a kind of utopian air: absolute equality, required involvement in the community, freedom from intense family life, from financial worries, from child-rearing, and freedom from sexual constraint.

"They were convinced that it was possible to create a relationship between the sexes on the sounder and more natural foundation than that which characterized 'bourgeois marriage.' " They viewed the bourgeois married woman "as little better than a chatteled servant." Esther Sternman, one of the early women residents of Merhavia, described this attitude as "a rejection of certain aspects of traditional sexuality ... a rebellion against the bourgeois norms of Eastern Europe." They rejected the norm of marriage and opposed "such a restricted conventional form as lifelong fidelity." They felt that sexuality should be anchored in spontaneous love, that "it was the freedom of each person to be in love with the person of his or her choice most appropriate at the time." So loose were some of the family ties at that time that kibbutzniks joked about whose children belonged to whom.

"We were all very young, in the real spring of our days," said Sternman of Merhavia, "and the spark of love burned strong in us, and more than once it would catch and burst into flame, but we always knew how to keep within limits, so that we should not be consumed by the flames. . . . A man knew how to overcome his desire when he saw that a woman did not return his love. . . . He did not use the woman's weakness and instability."

"Group sex, orgies, and multilateral relationships were not part of this freedom." Unlike the wild sex of the American Jazz Age, here they were forming a new society and simply wanted to reinvent the rules. Golda described the romantic relationships at Merhavia as "discreet." Sternman amplified this by insisting that "sexual relations were considered solely the business of those concerned." She similarly insisted that people entered into such relationships with "a purity of heart." While the place was too small for such secrets, there was the strong urge to keep any such personal affair private, as if to say, "This is mine!" The difference between a short affair and being regarded as a couple was when two persons asked to share a separate room. It was then assumed that they were not just lovers but that they were in love. Exclusive ties, however, were generally discouraged. This was part of the reason Golda insisted that there was a certain puritan attitude about all this. "You didn't live your life in the open. It was not on display." This followed the kibbutz code: "In essentials—unity; in nonessentials—liberty."

In terms of purpose, sex was an essential nonessential.

Nobody has revealed that Golda had any relationship there with anyone except her husband, but there are many former kibbutzniks who discuss this with a glint in their eyes. It would have been natural, they said; it would have been expected and it would not have been frowned upon. If her husband was too exhausted to share this with her, other young men were more available. Golda later admitted that she was not then worrying about her marriage, but frankly agreed that she should have.

Fighting for equality in everything, Golda similarly insisted on serving as a watchman. Even when she wasn't on duty, the restless Golda was often there at the early hours to greet the guards when they came off duty, to joke and talk with them, and share their prized omelette. They warned her "against wearing a white dress at night because that made too good a target for Arab snipers."

"At Merhavia, the nights were beautiful and the moon seemed different. On guard at night we looked at death and meditated on life. One night when I was on guard, Mirka Hazanowitz was killed, and we buried him in the morning. For the next few nights it seemed as if Mirka was riding up and down before my eyes, a kaffiyeh on his head, his rifle on his shoulder, smiling his enchanting smile."

Women and men also took their turn in the kitchen as part of job rotation. "Whenever one of the girls was due to start her month in the kitchen, she moped for a week in advance," Golda recalled. Kitchen work went against the women's idea of equality. They preferred using the pick digging rocks to prove that men were not monarchs but comrades. "For myself," Golda said, "American fool that I was, I couldn't for the life of me understand why this kitchen work should send them into a fit of depression."

Golda considered the kitchen as a challenge.

Golda also couldn't understand "why everyone was so careful with the feeding, care, and cleanliness of the livestock and not of the kibbutz members."

First she got rid of the bitter olive oil.

Then she decided to skin the herring. The so-called fresh herring—preserved in tomato paste—was a daily staple and never skinned. This obliged each one to skin his own serving and wipe his hands on his clothes, and the stink stayed.

"When the other women complained that the men would now always expect it, I told them, 'How would you have served herring at your own family table?' This is your home; they are your family."

Golda similarly decided that hard workers needed something hot for breakfast. "I bought Quaker Oats and cooked porridge in the morning," she said. At first, kibbutzniks were calling it "children's pap." They complained, saying, "We are not babies." But they soon grew to like it.

One of the main meals was chick peas soaked in water for twenty-four hours, then cooked with onions for soup. "The same concoction served for cereal," said Golda, "and later still in the evening, we ground it with onions as salad." A greater favorite was fried onions with bits of hard-boiled eggs.

Kibbutzniks always seemed to be hungry, "but as hungry as they were, food would often be left on the table because it was so bad."

On Friday night, the beginning of Shabbat, the men wore clean shirts and women put on skirts and blouses instead of pants. Golda discovered that even her simplest dresses were considered too luxurious. The field uniform was a piece of rough Arab linen, a hole cut for the head and two more holes for the arms, with a piece of rope around the waist. They called it the "sack."

"During the week nothing was ironed," said Golda. "I couldn't do that. I would iron them at night, not at the expense of my work." She used a heavy iron for her nightly ritual that dated back to Denver, Milwaukee, Tel Aviv. "I went out in the morning in a pressed dress and a pressed kerchief on my head." Kibbutzniks mocked it as "bourgeois weakness."

She could and would give most of herself to the kibbutz, but not her individuality, and not her will. She could discuss, participate, argue, but she could not simply conform. Why would anybody want to put a sheet on a perfectly good bare table? But Golda insisted. It was Shabbat, a time for formal dignity. She even put some fresh flowers as a centerpiece. The mockers claimed it created a small scandal among kibbutzim in the Emek, "gave us a bad name!"

The mockers were quiet about the cookies. Kibbutz tradition on Saturday morning called for coffee and cookies. Adding more flour to the recipe, Golda made an extra cookie portion for Friday night. For extra supplies, she earned a credit at the nearest grocery by giving English lessons to the owner's daughter.

Their enamel cups rusted so quickly that "they became repulsive" and she refused to buy more until the Haifa cooperative stocked a better brand. Instead she bought glasses which quickly broke. "All of us had to take turns drinking tea in the few remaining glasses, but I refused to give in."

The flour they bought from Arabs in Nazareth was rarely well-sifted and so their bread looked purple and tasted bitter—until Goldie came. She was determined to make good bread by sifting the flour more carefully and kneading the dough. "So when I finally learned how to make good bread, I was really proud of myself. After all, my mother used to bake her own *challeh*."

The food supply was a problem. Arabs often brought their caravans directly to the kibbutz. Kibbutzniks would select the desired livestock and the Arabs would slaughter them then and there.

Kitchen crises seemed constant. "One day we were looking through the window when we saw our comrades arriving with twenty more men who would have to be fed." They were en route to start another kibbutz nearby. At the time an oversized kettle was boiling water for tea. The water was simply poured into the already-thin soup and there was now enough to go around. It reminded Golda of when her father poured water into the wine barrel to make more wine for more guests at her Poale Zion meetings.

To show their appreciation, the kibbutz managers put Golda in charge of their flock of chickens. She hated chickens. "I was afraid to be in the room with even one chicken (or a living mouse)," she later admitted. Perhaps this dated from a time in Pinsk when a flood drowned the chickens, floating them down the streets. She had had nightmares about that for a long time.

The question of eggs became a major discussion at Merhavia. Why buy eggs from Arabs? Why not breed their own chickens, sell their own eggs? Golda soon found herself in nearby Ben Shemen taking a course in raising poultry. Her success came quickly. Merhavia soon bought one of the first 500-egg incubators in the country, and the egg business became a key to the kibbutz economy. Golda even started breeding geese, and that, too, became highly profitable.

This was a commentary on the woman. Give her a job to do and she would do it. She might hate it as much as she hated chickens. But if Golda saw it as a duty, conceived it as part of a cause, she would put all of herself into it, and do it well. No hedging, no self-pity, no re- proaches. That was Golda.

Golda saw it as a major disaster when a jackal sneaked into the coop one night and killed all the chicks. More major was the time she got sand-fly fever, known as *papatesche*, and her young woman replacement forgot to water the ducks. "And when I could go out again, I saw some ducks had died of thirst. My fever rose again and I had an attack of hallucinations in which I felt the entire room was filled with dead ducks."

Only those sick with a fever were entitled to such delicacies as lemons. When Golda had a high fever, the young man in charge of the mail brought back some lemon and ice for lemonade. "I have eaten many wonderful things in my life. But none which could compare with the exquisite taste of that lemonade." The ice was as rare as the lemon. Ice was available mainly in hospitals. Lemon was so rare that the kibbutz was scandalized when a young woman was discovered washing her hair with lemon. All citrus fruit was scarce, and kibbutzniks considered it a great gift when Golda visited Shana in Tel Aviv and lugged back a bag of oranges for everybody.

The months passed quickly for Golda. By the next year, 1922, she was a firm anchor in the kibbutz. She had proven her ability to work hard, as hard as anyone, without complaint. She had proven her initiative, her management ability, her dedication. Other kibbutzniks knew they could count on what she said. They regarded her as an attractive, spirited woman who enlivened their evenings with song and laughter, who brought some color into their drab, hard lives. Before the year was over, she was no longer "the American," she was "our Goldie."

"In the summer we went to work at four in the morning because it was impossible to stay in the fields when the sun came up because of the *barhash*." The *barhash* was an incredible mass of mosquitoes, gnats, and sand flies. "We used to smear ourselves with Vaseline, when we had it, wear high collars and long sleeves, wrap ourselves in kerchiefs, and come home with the *barhash* stuck in our eyes, ears, and nostrils. Even the cows used to stampede in the fields when the *barhash* came out. I had a solution for all my other problems, but not for the *barhash*."

Shana occasionally came to visit Golda at Merhavia, and especially remembered the *kumsitz*, the discussion groups, at an evening campfire, eating baked onions and potatoes, singing songs while somebody played a guitar or an accordion. Shana remembered thinking of the young kibbutzniks, "They had the goodwill but no experience. They were intellectuals and students." Shana was more caustic about the poor food quality, blamed it in part on the fact that "so many men worked in the kitchen."

Shana's daughter, Judy, made separate visits to Merhavia. "I loved it. I visited there every chance I had. And I guess my mother was really happy to get rid of me, too. I was then about eleven. I helped in the kitchen. I went out in the fields. I even got stung by a scorpion. I remember stuffing tiny eggplants. I learned to ride a horse—it was the only way to get around. And they started putting in eucalyptus trees to drain the swamps. We never hired Arab workers, and they discouraged closeness with the Arabs because you never knew. What are they going to do tonight? Are they going to come and fight?"

She told of the Arab men riding their donkeys while the women walked behind them, often carrying bundles of firewood on their heads.

She knew there were settlers who wanted to find a way of partnership with the Arabs "as a blessing for both peoples," but the idea then was not to depend on the Arabs. Each kibbutz was allocated so much flour and sugar and basics, and everything was made on the premises.

Judy's favorite memories of the kibbutz were the parties on Friday night. "I loved that! So did Goldie!"

Golda still didn't seem to have a solution for Morris. He was still the man she loved more than anyone, but it was a love now overwhelmed by this new life, a life into which he did not seem to fit. Compared to the vigorous young men of Merhavia, Morris now seemed increasingly fragile.

Morris had become lost in himself, resentful. All he seemed to have was his phonograph and his records that he had played a thousand times. For a while he had lost even this. Shana had borrowed the phonograph and they had had some difficulty in getting it back. Golda admittedly refused to recognize that she had edged Morris out of her life, "that Morris was struggling all alone." Writing exuberantly to her parents about the cow on the kibbutz giving birth to a calf, Golda received a letter from her father, asking mockingly, "And when are you going to be as productive as the cow?"

The mild Morris was adamant on the subject of children. Yes, he wanted children very much. No, he would never have any children on this kibbutz where the rules called for them to be raised by a rotating communal housemother, living in a separate house away from their parents who could visit only at certain hours. If Golda wanted children, the two of them would have to leave the kibbutz.

Golda was angry. Morris had known they were going to live on a kibbutz when they married, and he had also known the kibbutz rules on children. She felt he was now backing out of his agreement.

There is no question that Golda wanted children. She loved playing with Shana's children and the Shapiro children. She had enjoyed teaching children at the Folkshule, and they had enjoyed her. Still, given a hard choice of children or the kibbutz, what should she have done?

The quality of the marriage complicated the choice. Friends felt that the marriage was then stretching thin, beginning to break. The two cots in their room now seemed even farther apart. Morris must have written much to his mother about his complaints. To whom else could he have complained? He was too proud a man to have confided to mutual friends. An interesting note from a traveler among kibbutzim that year, commenting on those having the most difficult time, observed, "The most terrible . . . is the sight of a strong man, delirious with fever, calling and weeping for his mother, thousands of miles away." Morris had too much dignity to weep openly like that, even in fever, but he must have cried inside. A note from his mother offered to send him money for a ticket to the United States—if he would return without Golda.

"In Goldie's career," said one of her friends, "three things played an important part: First, she was very good-looking. Second, she spoke English, and very few in Palestine spoke fluent English in those days. And third, she had drive and talent and *mazel*."

Defining *mazel*, which means "good luck," Mike Green noted that the Hebrew equivalent for "M" meant "place." The "Z" meant time. And the "L" stood for knowledge. "In other words," said Green, "if you're in the right place at the right time and know what the hell you're doing—that's *mazel*."

Golda had *mazel* then. Merhavia selected her to represent them at the first kibbutz convention on the edge of Lake Kinneret at Degania.

"I made two fatal errors at Degania," Golda admitted.

"One, I spoke in Yiddish. Yosef Baratz said to me, 'It's bad enough you speak it in Tel Aviv; in Degania, no.' The crowd yelled at her in Hebrew, "Speak Hebrew! Speak Hebrew!"

"Oh, that was a real tragedy," Golda recalled. "I think I suffered more from that than from anything else. . . . I thought I would never understand Hebrew."

The other fatal error was to tell the other kibbutzniks, many of them women, "that I didn't understand why women working in the kitchen of the kibbutz considered it inferior to working in the fields . . . why giving food to people was no less an honor than giving food to cows . . . why you regard feeding your comrades as more demeaning . . ." The women delegates howled in anger. They had come here to build a new life, a new country. Whatever the men had to do, they had to do the same job, including harnessing themselves to a plough if the kibbutz couldn't afford a horse. They demanded not just equal rights but equal burdens. They felt almost a piety about working with their hands in the fields. They were pioneer women insisting on a principle.

A higher drama happened behind the scenes: the maneuvering of the men, the intellectual giants, who were shaping the future course of the country. "They were looking for someone who spoke English, who was good-looking, who was involved, who shed light on America." They heard this twenty-four-year-old Golda, saw her in action, and were amazed. The decisive men watching her included David Ben-Gurion and Yitzhak Ben-Zvi, who had both met Golda in Milwaukee. Two others would loom more important in her life—David Remez and Zalman Rubashov. Remez and Rubashov would shape her life with love in a way she would never then have suspected.

"You attend conferences, you speak." They had heard her speak, and approved the emotion, if not the language. In the course of the meeting, she had demonstrated her organizational abilities. They learned quickly about her loyalty to the Zionist cause. "They didn't want any feminists around in the leadership." Now they interrogated her at length.

"I can see us now," Golda remembered, "sitting around a smoky kerosene lamp, trying to solve knotty problems, many of which had not even arisen yet."

Golda was excited by the intellectual ferment at the kibbutz convention. These men were outlining the future she wanted. Mingling with leadership intrigued her, but she was still happier in the field with her comrades. When the Pioneer Women* later approached Golda to escort Mrs. Philip Snowden, wife of the prominent British Labour Party leader, on a Palestine tour, Golda replied with an emphatic "No!" "I was not going to waste my time traveling with somebody through the country." But then Berl Katznelson came to Merhavia to persuade her. Katznelson was the selfless philosopher of Zionist Palestine, the power behind the power. Even the proud, almost haughty Ben-Gurion deferred to him. Golda adored him. She would pay more attention to his words than to anyone.

Awed and flattered that Berl would come for her, that he thought this mission important enough, Golda quickly agreed. The tour turned out to be illuminating, exposing her to a country and people she had never seen—almost a revelation to Golda.

---

*Pioneer Women was a worldwide Labor Zionist women's organization that provided social welfare services for women, children, and the youth of Palestine. The group also helped new immigrants. It was begun in New York in 1925.

"We went to a Bedouin camp, my first introduction to the life of Arabs. They were very charming and very hospitable. I don't know how many cups of coffee we drank, bitter and sweet, sweet and bitter, and then they brought in these enormous bowls of *leben* [yogurt] with the *pitot* [bread] their women made. She and I had spoons—nobody else did, and, oh, there were sheep around. . . . Ben-Zvi joined us and he found an Arab he had gone to school with in Constantinople."

"We were not friends, but we were not enemies," a kibbutznik said of the Arabs. Another noted that there had to be an intermingling when he had to cross over an Arab melon patch to get into the kibbutz fields of tomatoes.

Returning to Merhavia meant returning home, "as though I had never lived anywhere else." Golda reported to her kibbutzniks as if she was their conduit to the outside world. They were all shelling almonds in the kitchen on a rainy day and "Goldie sat, looking a bit regal like always, telling us things." Golda once again had proven herself, and Merhavia soon elected her to its steering committee to help determine policy.

Once again Morris was the sad note in her success. Morris was proud of her, but regretful. The more important she became to the kibbutz, and the kibbutz to her, the further she pulled from him. He felt himself less and less vital in her life, more and more on the fringe. His depression was now both mental and physical. The distance between them never seemed to narrow. The crisis came with malaria. Morris got such a severe attack that he had to be hospitalized in Tiberias. Golda was suddenly his wife again, at his bedside, visibly distraught. The warning from the doctors was absolute: no more manual labor. If he stayed on the kibbutz, he could become chronically ill.

"He took up a way of life that didn't suit him but it was the kind of life that I couldn't do without. . . . It gave me such joy that I could have spent my whole life there. . . . He couldn't stand it either psychologically or physically. He couldn't stand eating at the communal table with the rest of us. He couldn't stand the hard work. He couldn't stand the climate and the feeling of being part of a community. He was too individualistic, too introverted, too delicate."

Golda added, "He was a wonderful person and with a different woman he could have been very happy. . . .

"It was a tragedy, a great tragedy."

The tragedy belonged to both. Despite the loosening of the marriage bond at the kibbutz, Morris belonged to the heart of her life. These young kibbutzniks these past two years were part of her spirit, but Morris was part of her soul. Deep within herself, she felt he was her anchor. This was an anchor she then could not and would not cut. An added factor was her difficulty admitting mistakes, or acknowledging to herself or anyone else that her marriage was a failure. Failure was something she could not accept. Failure reflected on her.

She could not cut loose so quickly from a man who had sacrificed so much for her, who had done so many things he hated simply for the love of her. Now his life was literally at stake. In every early choice between family and ideology, Golda always had chosen ideology. Ideology was her driving force. In a choice between children and kibbutz, she might have chosen the kibbutz. In the question of her husband's life, she had no choice. They would leave the kibbutz. Many of her political friends saw this decision as her tragic flaw, but it was also a humanizing flaw. This was probably one of the few successful demands Morris had ever made of her, and it was the last. Never again would she put her family before the party.

"I don't think I ever would have left if it were not for the fact that Meyerson took ill." She called him by his last name, in party tradition. "I hated leaving. It was a feeling of pain that still goes through me like a needle."

Even toward the end of her life, she would say, "The fact that I could not continue to live in the kibbutz still rankles, even after close to fifty years." Then she added, "I never felt I was making any sacrifice by being here and it never occurred to me that I deserved praise for being here. Since we did not stick it out, I have often thought that perhaps they were right when they [Merhavia] objected to taking us as members."

9

Tel Aviv after Merhavia was flat and dull. More than ever, Tel Aviv was growing furiously in an unplanned, ramshackle way, trying desperately to keep pace with the new surge of immigrants.

These immigrants of the Fourth Aliyah in 1924 didn't come because they wanted to, but because they had nowhere else to go. They weren't wanted in Poland, then suffering from an economic crisis and violent outbreaks of anti-Semitism. They weren't wanted in America, which shut its doors to any more mass immigration. So they came to Palestine, bitter about what they had left behind. An estimated 13,000 arrived in 1924, almost twice as many as the year before. Most of them were city people, with no interest in working the land. Golda sympathized with their problems, but could not relate to them. They were not Zionists, not pioneers. Many soon went back.

"They had no ideology . . . they were not partners in our ideal. There was a wide gap between us. I did not even consider workers in Tel Aviv as my partners—people who could walk around in white trousers with white shoes. I saw myself as a member of the modern aristocracy—like the aristocracy of the Middle Ages. A man who walks around with torn pants, with half his rear end showing, that's a man!"

These uninspiring arrivals further drained Golda's spirit. She missed the men with the torn pants and the big laughs. She needed their verve to uplift her own humdrum struggle for survival. She now felt utterly trapped as a drab housewife with a part-time job as a cashier. Her resentment was matched by her regret, a regret tinged with deep sadness. It made their marriage a misery, but if they blamed each other, they did so silently. This cold silence, boiling inwardly, became the pattern of their marriage. Golda later admitted that it might have helped if they had discussed openly their differences then, but they never did. The cracked marriage seemed to split even more.

Never had Golda been more vulnerable. At this critical point she again met David Remez. They had met briefly at the kibbutz convention in Degania, where he had been one of the dynamic leaders. Remez remembered her vividly. He had an eye for women and she had impressed him as a bright, lovely activist. As for Remez, he was hard to forget. He was a handsome man of thirty-eight, absolutely charming, and very important. He was head of the Solel Boneh, which meant "road-builder" in Hebrew, and fittingly concentrated on road-building, quarrying, home construction, and railroad lines.

Remez had a special talent for listening intently, and Golda was anxious to talk to some understanding ear. She could not have found a more sympathetic audience. Of course, he might help find Morris a job. As for her, he felt she was wasted as a cashier in Tel Aviv. There must be better uses for her talent. Shortly afterward, Solel Boneh offered Morris a job as bookkeeper in Jerusalem. Golda could not go with him because they needed the income from both jobs. Transportation was so poor that Morris stayed in Jerusalem and came to Golda only on weekends.

How often did Golda see Remez in those months? She saw him often enough to start some kind of relationship, a relationship that budded and flowered within the next few years.

Tel Aviv similarly had flowered from a little village to a hustling small city of 40,000 singing the song of construction. The motto of the permanent people was "Jew! Speak Hebrew!" Operas were sung in Hebrew, there were three daily Hebrew newspapers, and in 1925, 151 Hebrew books were published in Tel Aviv. Many felt that Tel Aviv reflected whatever the national mood was at the time, but that Jerusalem was stronger than the people who lived there because of its history and traditions. "Jerusalem was built on rock and Tel Aviv was built on sand."

Golda's life was more sand than rock, the sand shifting and uncertain.

She saw a lot of Shana and Sam during that time, and she envied them. Sam had arrived from the States and quickly gotten a job as treasurer in a shoe cooperative. The couple had had a third child, and seemed settled and happy. "My mother ruled the roost," said their daughter, Judy. "My father adored her, and followed her around." Shana was still compulsive about her housecleaning, "sterilized everything and washed down the whole house with disinfectant . . . *never* allowed any germs in the house." This traced back to her tuberculosis. Only Sam could turn off Shana when she became too arbitrary. He would do this "sometimes just with a word and she always listened and respected what he said. I think it was a tribute to their relationship."

Shana was still the strongest influence in Goldie's life, but Shana had changed. The political agitator had become the contented housewife, now urging Goldie to sublimate herself for her husband.

Morris's unhappiness matched Golda's. He kept pressuring Golda to find a job in Jerusalem.

"Morris? A many-sided man, completely self-effacing. Very taciturn. I don't know how many friends he had." His letters to his mother and sisters must have reflected what he felt because in their frequent responses they begged him to come home. He had become increasingly cynical about everything he saw. "Look what beautiful things God created and look what man is doing to it!" To a friend, he wrote, "Ah, Palestine, Palestine, you beggarly little land, what will become of you? How ironic sound the words at Poale Zion meetings about a free, workers' Palestine."

His weekend relationship with Golda soon changed. She was pregnant. "Morris had to follow me to Palestine to have a wife," she told friends. "I had to follow him [from the kibbutz] to Tel Aviv to have the child." Now, suddenly, David Remez found a job for Goldie with Solel Boneh in Jerusalem.

Jerusalem was a city of beauty and decay, inspiration and despair. The name came from Hebrew words meaning "city of peace," but it had never known peace. The deeper the archaeologists dug, the more layers they found of conquering civilizations: Philistines, Assyrians, Babylonians, Persians, Romans, Arabs, Crusaders, Turks. During all this, the Jewish Temple was destroyed and rebuilt, destroyed again and rebuilt again until only a retaining wall remained. The Hebrews declared their own kingdom in 1000 B.C., ruled by Saul, David, and King Solomon, claiming the land had been promised to them by God. Jerusalem later became holy to Christians because Jesus lived there, holy to Moslems because they claimed Mohammed made his ascent to Heaven from here on a horse.

A sixteenth-century map showed Jerusalem as the center of the world, the heart of a huge three-petal flower, with the petals marked Africa, Asia, and Europe. This prompted many to echo the view, "Jerusalem is closer to my soul than the place where I am now."

The Ottoman Turks ruled for four centuries, from 1516 until their defeat by the British in the First World War. There were always Jews here, and they began coming again in greater numbers from Russia in 1882.

Jerusalem was a city of stone, and the beauty of it came from the special glow of the stone in the sun. The rocky hills of the city enclosed settlements of different groups isolated from one another by stone outcroppings. Police gave orders in three languages to camels, donkeys, autos, and buses, "all trying to go in different directions at the same time." Representatives of the three religions named the streets. Housewives still drew their water from wells. Lamplighters lit the lamps at sunset, and old Arab cobblers and tinkers hawked their trade to Jews in Yiddish. Arabs attending the brand-new movie theater, seeing film for the first time, dashed for the exits when the villains started shooting.

Golda and Morris found a city without a café, without radios. But it had an opera company and a music school, and if you walked the streets you might hear someone playing hot jazz on a piano.

The Balfour Declaration of 1917 spread the fear among the 184,000 Arabs in Palestine that they would be "smothered . . . under a flood of alien immigration." Indeed, the persecution of Jews in Europe dramatically increased immigration into Palestine. But in 1927, unemployment was so bad that although 2,700 Jewish immigrants arrived in Palestine, more than 7,000 left the country. People abandoned their homes, closed their shops, and emigrated. A crowd of unemployed people almost broke up a meeting by the secretary of the Labor Federation, yelling, "Leader, give us bread!"

"I have no bread," answered the speaker, David Ben-Gurion. "I have a dream!"

Golda also had a dream, but needed bread.

"The next four years were the most miserable I ever experienced . . . the worst in my life," said Golda.

"It was a desolate place, the last Arab house available on the street," recalled Shana's daughter, Judy. "The kitchen was very primitive and the toilet was in the backyard. It was sad there, really sad." The house was unnumbered, on the edge of Mea Shearim, the enclave of a dozen Orthodox Jewish sects. Their dingy apartment had two tiny rooms. The bathtub was in the living room; the kitchen was a tin shack outside. An oil stove served for cooking and heat, and an antiquated, foul-smelling kerosene lamp provided light. Water from the cistern had to be boiled before drinking.

"We lived in more poverty than even back in Pinsk." But Golda had never gone hungry in Pinsk.

Solel Boneh was in serious financial trouble, paying salaries in *mashbir* credit slips instead of cash. "If you had a *mashbir* slip, you received one lirah's* worth of food from a *mashbir* store, but since we didn't have that store in our area, my grocery gave me only .80 lirah's worth of food and my poultry store gave even less," said Golda. Some local merchants insisted on an even deeper discount, and the English butcher, Spinneys, where Golda bought her bones for soup, would only take cash.

"They were practically starving. The question wasn't ever *what* to cook but that there should be enough to cook!" said Regina, who had to search to find them. Regina had moved to Jerusalem two years before to work for the Zionist Commission. "It was a hard, poor life. Morris worked very little. Golda had to quit her job before her baby was born. There was no money. Very few friends came to see them. She was desperate."

"I saw her cry once because she didn't have enough money to buy

---

*When the British forced the Turks out of Palestine, they instituted the same monetary system they had started in Egypt, then a British protectorate. The Egyptian pound was used as the basis, its value linked to British currency (about five dollars a pound). There were approximately one hundred piastres to the pound. After Israel became a state in 1948, it created the Israeli pound, called the lirah in Hebrew. In this quote, Golda is converting her past purchase into the then-current lirah.

oil," recalled a neighbor who lived above them. "It always captivated me that she cried over small things but stood strong as a rock over big matters."

"A Zionist doesn't make it conditional," Golda observed. "He comes to live here and, yes, suffer." But Golda did not always suffer in silence. "I was there when Morris got his first salary in money, real money," the neighbor related, "and he spent it all on a beautiful lampshade with goat's fur inside it. Goldie almost put that thing around his neck."

"It's the woman who gives birth ... the greatest privilege women have compared with men!" Golda repeated that often because she felt it so strongly. Nor did she even scream or moan during childbirth. "Your wife is a brave young lady," the doctor told Morris. The birth date was November 23, 1924, for the healthy boy, and they named him Menachem, the Hebrew word for "comfort." Golda hoped her baby would change her life. Morris only hoped it would help their marriage.

It did help, for a while. They took in a boarder in the spare room and that helped pay some overdue bills. Morris flowered as a father to his curly-haired son. Golda loved being a mother.

Golda was part of a group of new mothers who breast-fed their babies. They took turns waking up one another at feeding time. "One evening it was Goldie's turn and she stood by the bed of a mother who worked in the kitchen. Goldie tried several times to wake her up but she was sunk in such a deep sleep. When she finally opened her eyes, the woman imagined that she was still cooking in the kitchen. Goldie urged her, 'It's time to feed your child.'

" 'No,' the mother responded, 'the food isn't ready yet.'

"Goldie later retold that story a hundred times."

"Man's biological function is to do, woman's is to be," notes an Orthodox Jewish maxim. But the Talmud adds, "Women are temperamentally light-headed."

Golda was a serious-minded activist who confounded both these maxims. She also confused the Orthodox Jews who mentally consigned all women to a role as breeders of babies, and who prayed daily, "Blessed art Thou, our God, King of the Universe, that Thou hast not made me a woman." Inside Golda was a force "burning, broiling, whirling, getting ready inevitably to explode and create a universe." The explosion was inevitable. It came six months after the birth of her baby.

It had nothing to do with the poverty, the bleak lack of creature comforts. Nor did it involve her love for Morris, which was still strong despite the cracks and fissures. The explosion did concern the fact that she had expected motherhood to diminish her doubts about her life's direction, and it hadn't.

"Goldie should never have married," said Regina. "She certainly never should have had children."

Golda certainly didn't come to Palestine to be a wife and mother. She had come to Palestine to fight for an ideal, work the land, build a nation. The explosion came because the center of her life was Zionism. She wanted to go back to Merhavia.

The kibbutz for Morris was an old road to a dead end, and he would play no part in it. If Golda felt so strongly, he could not stop her. Nor could he prevent her from taking with her their precious son. If she wanted to come back, he would be waiting in Jerusalem.

Merhavia had grown considerably and changed much in the two years Golda was gone. More eucalyptus trees now drained the swamp. The vegetable fields were larger and more cultivated. There were more chickens and cattle. But the Arab village still loomed in the distance and there were still holes in the fence for guns.

Her return was not blissful. Many of her friends were still there, and their greetings were warm, but there were still the snide ones who sneered at the Americans who couldn't quite take it. None of them could fault Golda, though. She had paid her dues, and they knew it.

She had hoped to work the land, as before, but Golda was now put in charge of mothering five children, including her six-month-old son. Since they had no refrigeration, milk still had to be boiled. "Goldie's babies drink alcohol," kidded the kibbutzniks.

"We had only one bathtub for all the children," Golda explained, noting that infections were frequent, and so she was determined "about sloshing alcohol around the bathtub after each baby's turn and 'burning' it out to make sure it was sterile. ... I had many fights with comrades who thought it was not necessary."

Kibbutzniks sarcastically referred to them as Golda's "brandy babies."

"We took a large room for the infants that were there. I lived in a small room next to it. Now it never entered my mind to ask for somebody else to watch over the children at night because what did I do with my boy when I was in town? I would get up. So when the children would get up at night, I would get up. They were in my care day and night. . . . We did without a night-watch girl."

Golda should have felt fulfillment, but she didn't. If she hadn't come to Palestine to teach English, neither had she come to take care of babies in a kibbutz. She wanted to work the land, but the kibbutz leaders felt she was more needed where she was. There were still the young bachelors and the parties and the meetings, but all of it seemed so different now. The spirit had changed, and with it much of the fun. The singing no longer seemed as loud and the dancing was not as frenetic. No more did they dance until some of the shirts were ripped off their backs. If the kibbutz had changed, so had she. She was twenty-seven years old now, a mother, and she missed Morris more than she had expected. In the years to come, when she would reminisce about the kibbutz with longing—"There is nothing I've loved so much as the kibbutz life"—she remembered the first time she went, not this time. After six months, weighing everything, she decided to return to Morris in Jerusalem.

Kibbutzim were having a hard time. People left because they wanted to raise their own children, work on their own farms. Some felt the small kibbutz was a closed, limited club for exceptional individuals, and that it was too intimate, too exclusive. New and dramatic was a big kibbutz, Ein Harod, with 215 members, and the idea of transforming the whole country into one big kibbutz. In all the Jezreel Valley, there were only twenty kibbutzim, but they would one day help make it the breadbasket of the country.

"I hated leaving the kibbutz. I felt it was turning away from a degree of public life . . . to private life. It's something ironic, the way it finally turned out."

Her return made Morris more hopeful than ever that now she might really change. Sarah was born a year later, in May 1926.

Another baby meant dramatic changes. Reluctantly the boarder had to go because the other room was needed for the children. Sarah was sickly, and required a special diet and medicine. Medicine cost money. Where could they get it? Morris's paycheck was unpredictable. Store-keepers tightened on their credit and hunger was no longer a threatening word but a fact. A nosy neighbor even warned the milkman against extending any further credit to the Meyersons. Golda tore at him in a fury: "No one will take milk from my children!"

An American woman visited Golda and Golda served her some soup. The woman said, "At home we wouldn't eat this soup!"

And Golda cried.

She became an expert on poverty. Faigel Berkenblitt went to Golda, worried that Shabbat was coming "and I have nothing to prepare." The stores had no bread and no meat; she had nothing in the house. Besides, she said, "My kitchen was so small, I was in my own way."

Golda laughed and said it wasn't any art to do something when you have everything but "It's an art to make something of nothing! You go home and you'll think of something."

"And she was right," said Berkenblitt. "I had a few dollars and I bought some fish and vegetables, and I made a soup of the vegetables. Instead of meat, I used matzo meal and eggs to make *knaydlach* [dumplings]. I decorated the place with green leaves and branches. I didn't have a tablecloth so I used a white sheet. It was too long so I cut it off and made little curtains."

Golda and Morris were too proud to ask for help, but Shana and Sam knew what was happening. They made periodic visits to Jerusalem with a supply of dairy products, fruits, and vegetables. Shana's daughter, Judy, came even more frequently. She was a teenager now, having problems with her strict mother. "My domineering mother never approved of what I did. Whenever I wanted to run away, I'd run to Goldie. Or if my brother had a fight with me, he'd run to Goldie. She was our haven. I slept in the small room with Menachem."

Menachem was growing up. His earliest memory, when he was barely four, was of sitting on the stoop of their run-down, one-story house in Jerusalem, his mother handing him some toast. Imprinted in his mind was the searing heat, rocks, dried bushes, dust, and an Arab boy herding goats a few feet away. Golda and Morris both felt Menachem should go to a nursery school, but they couldn't afford the tuition. Golda made an offer the nursery couldn't refuse. In exchange for tuition, she would wash all the children's clothes. Fortunately, the British had installed plumbing in the area, so Golda no longer had to draw water from a well. She still had to heat the water, a pail at a time, and scrub all the clothes on a rough washboard.

"I laundered at night when the children were sleeping. The kitchen was outside and I laundered in the courtyard so I had to put a kerosene oil lamp in the window. I think there must have been fifteen or twenty children . . . little towels, aprons, diapers . . . whatever needed washing."

"I still remember her in that tiled courtyard," recalled a neighbor, "her long braids falling over her shoulder and her blue eyes still brimming with happiness."

Those blue eyes soon stopped smiling.

Still desperate for money, and with Menachem at school, Golda got the inevitable job teaching English at Miss Kallen's private school. "It was an experimental school of American origin with quite advanced educational views." She took Sarah along with her, since she couldn't afford to pay anyone to watch her.

Here she was, teaching English again, back to the start of the circle. What was the point? What had she really accomplished in six years in Palestine? An exhilarating interval at a kibbutz, and then zero. She and Morris could have had their children in Milwaukee and they would have been much more comfortable. They wouldn't have been so poor, they wouldn't have been so hungry, and Morris would have been so much happier. Would she have been happier?

Golda's high school yearbook had called college "a castle in the air," and now her Zionism was "a castle in the air." Her real world was washing clothes, teaching English, scratching for food. Morris took the brunt of her misery and frustration. "There is no doubt I made him very unhappy."

Regina dropped in occasionally for tea and Golda confided, "It isn't working out." Golda revealed something similar to another friend, "that she wasn't happy anymore as she should be, that she couldn't find herself." That friend afterward reminisced, "I doubt she ever loved anyone the way she loved Morris. But I'll be very frank with you . . . I've often wondered how these two people found love."

The wonder was not how they found love, but that it lasted as long as it did. Both Golda and Morris had come to Palestine with different delusions. Golda hoped that Morris would gradually catch her commitment to Zionism, that they both would do wonderful things together for their cause and their people. Morris had hoped that Golda's love for him, and any children, would make her "grow out of it," forget this obsession, return with him to the United States. Instead, they both now found these delusions shattered. Both felt themselves failures: Morris as an improvident husband, Golda as an insufficient wife and mother —insufficient only in that she was so unhappy in what she was doing. Their present seemed empty, the future ominous.

Golda needed *mazel*, some luck, and she needed it now. And she got it. "I did not choose a career. I did not choose a profession. It all just happened."

It happened one day at the open market in Mea Shearim. It was one of those accidental meetings that can change the world. An important man meets a depressed housewife and offers her a job. Golda was no longer the feisty young woman the man met at Degania or the spirited kibbutznik he had found in Tel Aviv. She was now the tired mother of two children, not yet twenty-nine years old, almost afraid to look into her future.

David Remez fired her with his own enthusiasm. She had a talent that the Zionist cause desperately needed. He had a vital job that fitted her perfectly, secretary of the Moetzet Hapoalot, the Women's Worker's Council. The organization trained young women for agricultural work and various trades, and they now needed to set up farms where women could learn the basics. "At that time the struggle for women's rights was to participate in everything that was done, any kind of work, no matter how difficult," said Golda. "Young women were even paving roads."

Would Golda do it? She knew what the job meant. It meant again leaving Morris in Jerusalem and moving back to Tel Aviv with her children. It meant constant travel. She would have to find someone to care for the children. It meant a vibrant life in a different world, but it was the life she wanted in the world she wanted. She felt a new kind of exhilaration.

Morris also knew what it meant. It meant the real beginning of the real end of their marriage.

10

Because you became a great woman
With strong features
Big nose
And heavy legs
None will believe how beautiful you were
Gray-eyed and slim-ankled

The men who loved you are dead
So I speak for the record
Indeed you were lovely among maidens
Once
In Milwaukee, in Merhavia
And sometimes in Jerusalem.
                                    —Marie Syrkin

And sometimes in Tel Aviv. Golda was almost thirty, more than ready for anything that might happen. Her frustration of the past four years had dampened her excitement, but her vitality and zest stirred quickly under the surface. Physically, she was most attractive, her figure still firm even after two children.

She had found an apartment on Gruzenberg Street, on the second floor, "very plain." Most Tel Aviv apartments then were much the same, simple and without style. Menachem recalled their flat as being light and bright, with a balcony overlooking the sea. No gas, no electricity, no phone, and their street was hot summer sand, but the beach was close and lent a feeling of freedom.

Morris stayed with his work in Jerusalem, joining them on weekends. The coldness between Golda and Morris had become an ominous quiet, but they succeeded in hiding their differences to maintain the frame of a family for the children. The children had one room, the other rented to two single girls, and Golda slept on the daybed, in the living room. For much of her life, she would sleep on a daybed in the living room. Whatever the children sensed about the relationship of their parents, they never really knew, until they were teenagers.

Sarah was only two years old in 1928, but she had the dim memory of Father painting their furniture. He also read to them, told them stories, filled them with music from his precious phonograph. He was usually there to make breakfast for them on Saturday morning, later would take them on long walks. As Menachem grew older, he would help him with his stamp collection, his Erector set. Shana's daughter, Judy, who visited often, recalled, "I remember going there for Morris to make me some fudge. He loved to make fudge." Golda was the first to admit that Morris enriched their children's lives with his knowledge, wisdom, and "with tenderness and warmth."

Motherhood unleashed a struggle inside Golda. Squeezing her time, she tried to be home when they needed her most, and she seldom was. She managed the chores of shopping for food, preparing meals, mending their clothes. But she was not always there when they returned from school. The children could not count on her to give them baths, tuck them into bed, read to them. Sarah recalled her mother reading stories to them from a book called *The Heart*, by D'Amicis, but it is significant that she could remember no others. Sarah was a particular worry with a recurring illness. She was in need of frequent medical attention and special diets, and was often ill for weeks at a time. With all this, Sarah somehow maintained a bright gaiety. Remez, meanwhile, was expanding Golda's duties to fit her talents. This meant even less time with her children.

Describing herself then, Golda said, "Your heart is rent. . . . A mother in public life—in her feelings—will never be the same as a man or a father in public life. . . . When the mother has to leave home in the morning for work and the child is down with a temperature, even if the best person is taking care, it is not the same. She leaves it in the morning with a temperature. She comes back in the evening; it's still sick, but she worries about her work. Or she's tired. Fathers also worry—I don't believe that mothers love their children more than fathers, that is nonsense—but there is something different there."

Always insisting loyally that Golda was a wonderful mother, Clara added, "I'll say this: she gave them a tremendous amount of love and affection when she was around. But she wasn't always around."

One of Sarah's early memories was of her mother returning late from a meeting, shouting, "Menachem! Menachem!" because she had misplaced her key. "I thought then what would have happened if he hadn't heard her and Mother would have remained outside."

"I worked for Goldie for a whole year," recalled Dora Volcani. "I'd pick up the children at four o'clock in the afternoon after kindergarten. Menachem was five, Sarah three. I'd bring them home, feed them, and if Goldie didn't show up in the evening, and she usually didn't, I would put them to bed. I would wait until midnight. If Goldie would come home then, I'd go home. If she didn't, I would spend the night with the children and leave the next morning.

"When Goldie did come home, she was always very tired. The children would often wake up after she went to sleep and march down the hall toward her bedroom. I would try to stop them and ask if there was something I could get them because I knew that Goldie needed her sleep. But they would say, 'No . . . no . . . *Ima . . . Ima . . . Ima . . . Ima . . .*' [*Ima* in Hebrew means "mother."] Because that was the only time they got to see her all day long.

"Their father wasn't around much when I was there. When he did come, he would come very late, but he would get up early to give them breakfast. When I did see him, he was always very affectionate with the children. I never saw Goldie with the children so I don't know how affectionate she was with them. I know the children were very lonely, starving for affection. I felt very sad for them.

"Weekends? Sunday, of course, was a working day. But even on Saturday, on Shabbat, Goldie always had meetings, meetings at the Labor Party, meetings with the public, meetings of all kinds."

One night Golda was at a late meeting while her children were waiting impatiently for her to return. Menachem remembered that he and Sarah busied themselves by singing all the songs they knew, then giggling and deciding to dress and go to the meeting. They knew the nearby Histadrut headquarters, had been there before. The six-year-old boy and his four-year-old sister climbed the stairs into a smoke-filled room crowded with people.

"It was one of my first memories," recalled Sarah. "My brother and I are sitting on a bench and my mother is chairman and puts some question to a vote, asking, 'Who is for?' And my brother and I lift our hands to vote."

Recalling the same incident, Golda recorded her "utter astonishment" at their presence, adding, "It was the most reassuring vote of confidence I ever got." But then she remarked ruefully that voting for your mother doesn't compare to having her at home when you need her.

Golda introduced her children to her associates. Then, on the way home, she tried to explain what the meeting was all about. "It was our first lesson in the political life of a democracy," said Menachem.

The memory of Judy Shapiro, then a teenager, who regarded the Meyersons as part of her extended family, was that "Morris was father and mother to their children." How did Goldie feel about that? "It ate her up."

"Golda once told me that the worst thing for a working mother was when she enjoyed her work. If she didn't enjoy her work, if she worked in a factory just to bring home food for her children, then she could be happy for all of her life. But if she enjoyed every minute of her work, then she felt guilty in leaving her children to enjoy herself."

Amplifying the inner struggles and despairs of a mother who goes to work, "the double pull" and the "inner division," Golda added, ". . . there is a type of woman who cannot remain home. In spite of the place which her children and her family take up in her life . . . her nature and being demand something more; she cannot divorce herself from a larger social life. She cannot let her children narrow her horizon. And for such a woman there is no rest."

Golda also noted, "A working mother could actually bring more to her children than if she were to remain at home." She claimed that it might be better for the children rather than having a mother "constantly hovering over them." She was referring to the mythical maternal figure of the Jewish mother, "the all-engulfing nurturer who devours the very soul [of her child] with every spoonful of hot chicken soup she gives. . . .

"But one look of reproach from the little one when the mother goes away and leaves it with a stranger is enough to throw down the whole structure of vindication. That look, that plea to the mother to stay, can be withstood only by an almost superhuman effort of will.

"At the best of times, in the best circumstances, there is a perpetual consciousness at the back of her mind that her child lacks a mother's tenderness. We believe, above all, in education by example, therefore we must ask ourselves: Whose example molds the child of the working mother? A 'borrowed mother' becomes the model. The cute things a child says reach the mother at second hand. Such a child does not know the magic healing power of a mother's kiss, which takes away the pain of a bruise. And there are times, after a wearying, care-filled day, when the mother looks at her child almost as if she did not recognize it; a feeling of alienation from her nearest and dearest steals into her heart.

"And having admitted all this, we ask: Can the mother of today remain at home all day with her children? Can she compel herself to be other than she is because she had become a mother? Is there something wrong with me if my children don't fill up my life? . . .

"My children have a very close relationship with me, but if I am to be honest with myself there is a little—maybe more than a little—pang of conscience over the injustice I have done to the children, days or evenings I should have remained with them but couldn't. . . . I know that my children, when they were small, suffered a lot on my account."

When her small son brought home a stray kitten to take to bed with him, Golda at first refused, saying, "It probably has fleas." She hated cats, but she suddenly remembered that her mother had said the same words to Clara when her little sister brought home a stray dog. Her mother had relented and let Clara keep the dog in the basement. And now, suddenly, looking at her pleading son, Golda relented, saying that he could keep the kitten so that "you'll never be lonesome."

"Look, she was too powerful a figure," said Marie Syrkin. "She couldn't be bound. She had to break loose. And, of course, she just soared. As for the business of being a wife and a mother, she took it so much more seriously than the average respectable woman does today because those problems bothered her far more than they would have if she had been born a generation later."

When Golda became secretary of the Women's Worker's Council, the Moetzet Hapoalot, the Histadrut was the "state within a state." The Histadrut managed a vast variety of economic enterprises, kibbutzim, trade organizations, the Solel Boneh, and even the Women's Worker's Council. The British Mandate took care of law and order, but the Jews were supposed to take care of themselves. The Histadrut was everything, there was nowhere else to go. It was responsible for employment, for the conditions of work, even for cultural activity. The Histadrut was the country's largest employer, an economic empire that produced more than one-third of the gross national product. It had the dual role of protecting the workers' interests and creating jobs. There was nothing more vital in a country where almost one out of four was unemployed. Its principle: the acceptable cure for unemployment is employment. This meant no doles. If there was not enough work to go around, you shared the work. This was not only their philosophy; this was their practice.

The common slogan was "Work is our life" and the highest praise was to be called "a good worker." "It's worth a lifetime to glimpse the work of Jewish hands . . . to see Jewish farmers."

"I am skeptical about people who say they are doing things for the public or for history," Golda once said. "Only one who feels he is doing something for himself and that he personally needs this done is doing something worthwhile and deserves praise." But then she added that a real state would be brought into being only if there were enough Jews willing to get their hands dirty in fields and factories.

At the Histadrut, they were all tied together by the tightest thing there is—a dedication so deep that they were willing to deprive themselves of family, friends, love, sleep, time, memory. The whole world suddenly had fit into a hard frame that nobody else could enter unless his blood was true, his eyes wide, and his heart full. In this, there was more heart than head, more hope than knowledge, more fervor, more faith, more love than anybody deserved.

Histadrut headquarters was compressed into a few rooms in a low, red building, where the paint peeled. Everybody including the janitor called one another by first names. There were only a few typists and one shared telephone. In such an intimate setting, where Golda rubbed shoulders with the emerging giants of her people, there was small wonder that she again fell in love.

"It was May first and we were going to a May Day meeting on the grounds of the Herzlia Gymnasia and there gets up a young man in a pongee shirt with a high collar buttoned on the side like a *rubashka*, with the sash; oh, and what a speech, and with what enthusiasm, something I had never heard before."

The young man modeled his oratory after a Frenchman named Jean Jaurès:

"He did not speak with his mouth but with both arms and legs, with his elbows and knees, with every rise and fall of his back, rising and quivering and leaping and filling the entire ambience of the stage. His every bone spoke. Spoke? Shouted, raged, threatened, exhorted, adjured. Fought the battle of the Lord...."

The young man was Shneur Zalman Rubashov—soon known as Shazar—"a wild man with an encyclopedic mind." He had studied at St. Petersburg and the University of Berlin, taught in Vienna. He wrote essays, books, poems:

So I went, caught
In a web of sad thought.
A captive of fear
In a tumult of desire.

Shazar was nine years older than Golda, a short man with piercing eyes, a handsome head, and an enormous drive. As one contemporary described him, "When Shazar walked into a room, the room would stop. People would gather around him to hear what he had to say." Another said, "He was a man who couldn't sit still. He wanted to do everything."

Discussing Hebrew poetry at a dinner party, Shazar began quoting from a new poem about a pogrom that had excited him. He was soon striding up and down the room, "waving his arms to the rhythm of the verse." He brushed a vase from the shelf, flipped a picture from the wall as he passed, and the hostess warned, "Shazar, calm yourself! Don't make here a pogrom!"

"Shazar" was an acronym of his three initials in Hebrew and meant "intertwining." As for his intertwining with Goldie, "the romance started right away in Tel Aviv in 1928," insisted one of Shazar's closest associates.

Golda's earliest attraction for Morris had been the remarkable range of his self-taught mind. In Shazar, she found a mind and a range much more vast.

"Shazar was a great scholar, fantastic, with a memory that couldn't be matched. Speak to him about any subject and he had so many associations of ideas. And he wrote poetry. Among friends we would always argue 'why does Shazar waste time in what he's doing because he could really be one of the great teachers of the new generation.'"

Shazar's teaching quality also showed up often on the Executive Committee of the Histadrut, and particularly as editor of the daily newspaper *Davar*. He also had great wit. One day when the news was particularly grim—war, revolution, economic collapse, famine—Shazar wrote an overall headline: WORLD COLLAPSING.

They had much in common. He was from the Minsk area, she from nearby Pinsk. When Goldie was listening to her revolutionary sister from the warming shelf above the stove in Pinsk, Shazar was in "the dawn of my youth," organizing self-defense forces of young men with lead-tipped iron bars and loaded revolvers to fight any pogrom. When the peasants arrived with their empty wagons to gather the plundered booty of prospective Jewish victims, and the mob readied for its attack, the young men shot their revolvers in the air and the mob panicked and disappeared. Goldie loved a story of Jews fighting back.

"When he was young, he was so skinny. No, he wasn't *that* good-looking, but he had enormous charm. Goldie? She had great eyes, wonderful eyes, out of this world!"

Palestine at this time was full of spontaneous combustion, people caught by the same cause, filled with the same romantic strain. This emotional interaction of people was typical of other dramatic places and times in history. Atomic particles collided in a charged atmosphere. Goldie and Shazar were two such particles, and the time was right. A symbol of its rightness for Goldie was that, in the summer of 1911, Shazar even had worked as an agricultural laborer at Merhavia, "and it was sealed in my spirit by the fire of love and the inspiration of those days has been with me ever since."

Everything about Shazar impressed Golda, especially the fact that he was translating her favorite poet, Rachel of Kinneret, from Hebrew into Yiddish. Shazar did not tell Goldie that he had had a love affair with Rachel. He did tell her of a trip to the Sea of Galilee where he first met Rachel, "a slim shepherdess, blue-eyed, lithe as a gazelle . . . stretched on a trunk of a carob tree." He was with a group in the valley and she was on the top of a hill: "golden in the sunlight, her white dress glistening, she raised her voice high in song toward us . . . we heard every note as if she were nearby and we heard not only her voice but a powerful echo . . . and the sounds came flying out of their stony hiding places, pure as on the day they were concealed, joyful as in the childhood of our people."

Shazar had the gift of expressing vividly everything Goldie felt. Shazar had Morris's same love of poetry and philosophy, but he coupled it with a vigor and a political commitment that Morris had lacked. Shazar was one who insisted that Goldie again visit the Wailing Wall.

"Perhaps we cannot really be called a people—not even a tribe?" wrote Shazar. "If your sense of history and analytic powers are not strong enough you expose the fallacies in this approach. Go to the Wailing Wall . . . stand there—and you will not only see but feel and sense with all your being the secret of our people's lasting life. . . . We are no stray flock. We are a people." The Wall was the only surviving remnant of the Second Temple "where the Divine Presence never departed." It became hallowed in Jewish history as a place for prayer, a center of mourning over the Temple's destruction and the forced Jewish exile. The Wall seemed soaked with tears, a place where you could leave all your sorrows. The intense praying of a dozen different Orthodox sects, the young and old; men fervently bobbing and weaving in loud enthusiastic prayer, some with their lips pressed against the stone, their eyes closed, their faces blissful; women covered with shawls quietly seeking the solace of God.

"We very soon became very good friends," said Golda discreetly of Shazar; ". . . he is a very loving person, very warm, and no airs about him of any kind."

Shazar was also a womanizer. In an assessment of Shazar, years later, the *Jerusalem Post* noted that he had "left more than one broken heart in the settlements of the Jordan Valley." His wife was older than he was and "very plain." Her critics, and even Shazar, called her "ugly." She was, however, very bright, very active in Zionism, a member of the Central Cultural Committee of the Histadrut, and edited its journal. She was also on the Secretariat of the Council of Women Workers, and her work surely overlapped Golda's. It was she who organized the book *The Ploughwoman*, in which Golda wrote her statement on motherhood. She had met Shazar in St. Petersburg and married him in 1920.

"He was quite a ladies' man—too much, terrific, impossible, really!" said an intimate who had worked alongside Shazar for many years. "His reaching out for women was just in him—he couldn't stop it, he just couldn't! I remember he once told me, 'I guess it's too late. I give up. No, I can't try to conquer another language, nor have another love affair.' But then he was introduced to a young lovely poetess and it didn't take him two minutes to get started with her.

"Yes, it was different with Goldie. Goldie was very important to him.

He went deeper with Goldie than with anyone else because she *was* extraordinary, and he sensed this. I know there was a strong feeling on her part, or she wouldn't have bothered. I do know that he said he'd marry her, and this is what she wanted.

"His own wife was not an easy woman, very distant. I liked her, in a strange kind of way. She was very clever, had a good mind. His marriage to her was a kind of debt of honor. It was a peculiar marriage. His mother couldn't understand why he had married someone so unattractive. But she subordinated herself to him completely, her world revolved around him. Still, she was a strong person, undeviating, and deviation was his middle name. That made it possible for him to play around. Yet I remember once, talking about his gifted sister, he said, 'I guess she was the only woman I ever really loved.'"

Golda's specific job at Histadrut was to train women workers, and she strongly believed in equal pay for equal work. But she was no feminist. "I never had sympathy for the women's organizations as such. That was not my basic interest in life." She considered "teaching girls various trades more important than women's rights."

"Mother complained that Golda was not a feminist," said Rivka Idelson. "Mother went more to the line of being a woman in the labor movement. Golda went more to the line of being among men. They had arguments but anyway, they didn't step on one another."

Beba Idelson, Rivka's mother, had settled in Palestine in 1926 and was general secretary of the Moeztet Hapoalot in 1930, then elected to all the central bodies of the Histadrut. Like Golda, she was tough, persistent, energetic. "Beba and Goldie were made out of the same material, both very strong and both understood each other. Beba stayed on as secretary of the Women's Worker's Council for forty-four years and was very loyal to Golda. Golda in return gave her much strength."

Both women admitted that being a woman was a hindrance to taking up public office because "the stereotypes of what's expected of women are implanted very early and take years of endless patient work to uproot them." Women had to cope with a deep-seated cultural resistance from men "and even some women" to gain acceptance of the notion that women are as capable as men in managing important jobs in government. "Although many men climbed the political ladder with the assistance of mentors, it was difficult for women to find mentors and when they did it was often perceived as 'sexually tinged.'"

"Of course I'm a feminist," Golda said years later. "But I don't call myself a feminist now with all the insanity of burning brassieres and that kind of nonsense." But she did accept the criticism of militant women. "Diehards would say that Goldie has been spoiled all her life, that she never had to fight for anything for herself, which is more or less true, I guess."

It was, indeed, more or less true. This was the time when a tight elite of Second Aliyah pioneers, the Eastern European intellectuals—Ben-Gurion, Ben-Zvi, Katznelson, Remez, Shazar—ruled the Histadrut. Generally, they were "very unkind to women near the top." Golda was a clear exception. Golda was their plum, their protégée, not simply because she was vivacious, talented, and pretty, but because they needed her. She was the only one among them who spoke fluent American English and had a similar fluency in Yiddish. They needed her as an emissary, a spokesman with the British rulers, the Europeans, the Americans. All of them groomed her for that.

"Men have always been good to me," Golda reminisced. "I've always moved within a circle of intellectual greats. I've always been appreciated and loved. And what else can you ask of fortune?"

Golda agreed, however, that for most women the trail was "harder, tiring, more painful. When a woman wants to become somebody . . . well, it's hard. Very, very hard. To be successful, a woman has to be much better at her job than a man." She also remarked, "I think that women get not so much an unfair deal as an illogical one."

She felt too many men had their cliché conception of women, the feeling expressed by a writer on why God created woman from man's rib:

"I shall not create her from the head of Adam, lest she hold up her head too proudly; nor from the eye, lest she be a coquette; nor from the ear, lest she be an eavesdropper; nor from the mouth, lest she be too talkative; nor from the heart, lest she be too jealous; nor from the hand, lest she want to touch everything; nor from the foot, lest she be a gadabout; but from that part of the body that is hidden, so that she be modest."

Golda was not modest. She agreed with the older Hebrew maxim: "Man is made of the soft earth and woman out of the hard rib."

"Goldie was a prime mover, doing a variety of jobs, outstanding in whatever she did," reported a man who worked with her. "She knew how to combine idealism and practicality. She knew how to get an idea across. And you just couldn't say no to Goldie." She later insisted, however, that "no one gave in to an argument of mine because I was a woman—except my husband."

Histadrut always had long meetings. If meetings lasted too late, there was no bus service. This meant sharing a taxi. Golda recalled that "everyone was ashamed to sign for the taxi" because Histadrut had no money for such luxuries, and a taxi item on an expense account involved much explanation.

Palestine then had no real economy, hardly a handful of industries of any size. The building trades soaked up half of the workers; the rest were scattered in orange groves, a salt factory, the Dead Sea works, some utility plants, and miscellaneous companies that made soap, concrete, edible oils. A weak link was the sharp fact that Arabs willingly worked more cheaply than Jews. The future looked grim. Unemployment was severe. In 1928, when Goldie went to work at Histadrut, emigration was higher than immigration.

Salaries were not based on work, but on need. "The woman who cleaned my office, and had more children, got more money than I did," said Golda. "We were all proud of that. Why should children be blamed because their mother was not secretary of the Histadrut?"

There were times when Golda felt the pain of poverty was too much. Her parents had made their *aliyah* to Eretz Yisroel in 1926. They sold their Milwaukee store and bought a plot of land, mostly sand, in Herzlia, just outside Tel Aviv. The good carpenter Moshe had built his own high-ceilinged house on a hill overlooking the sea. But that Passover there was neither money nor food for the family holiday dinner. Golda vividly recalled her desperate father looking "as though someone had beaten him over the head."

Golda got the money because she was bitten by a dog, and had to go to Tel Aviv for anti-rabies injections. While there she found a bank willing to loan her ten pounds if somebody would guarantee it. She finally returned home with the money, and they had their Passover dinner.

As soon as Golda's parents settled, they flourished. The tall, thin Moshe, who had lived so long in Bluma's short, well-filled shadow, now filled out like a late flower. The blooming had started just before Golda left for Palestine. Now gray-haired, dignified, with a short clipped mustache,

Moshe became a cantor in the local synagogue, a power mover in the carpenters' cooperative, and even a landowner with three acres of orange groves. Although he always remained a skeptic about religion, he felt strongly about traditions.

"My grandfather? He had a good heart," recalled Shana's son Yona. "He co-signed loans for so many people, and when the people couldn't pay, he had to pay it, or Goldie did. I remember him singing songs. . . .

"My grandmother was a very homey person, cooked a lot. She was the boss of the family. My brother remembers my grandmother as a tough woman, but she wasn't strict with me. I'm eight years younger than my brother."

Golda's energetic mother was soon back in business. Since there was no restaurant in that area, she made lunches to sell to workmen. She still kept kosher, with separate dishes for meat and dairy, even brought her own dishes with her when she visited Golda. When Golda's children developed scarlatina, and Golda quarantined herself in a room with them, it was her mother who brought food and passed it to them through the window. Bluma was still Golda's thorn: "Why are you smoking so much?" The answer was that Golda was so much in the company of men who smoked so heavily that she easily fell into the habit. She was soon smoking some sixty cigarettes a day.

Golda enjoyed describing herself at the time as "just a youngster, tagging along." There was no truth to it. She was not just a youngster and she never tagged along.

Besides Remez, the man most responsible for "lighting a spark" in Goldie was the spiritual father of the Second Aliyah, the untidy and unforgettable Israeli Socrates, Berl Katznelson, whom everybody called "Berl." He was trusted as the elder statesman because everyone knew he had no personal ambition. At any meeting, he sat in the body of the hall, not far from the entrance. Except for the newspaper he founded, *Davar* (*The Word*), he never accepted any executive office, stayed aloof from the hurly-burly of power politics. Self-taught in many languages, Berl sat in a shabby armchair in his book-lined apartment "and we drank in what he said." "His firmness was so compelling because one was always aware of the gentleness from which it issued." He was a gentle man with sad eyes.

"When his eyes were fixed on you in a hard and penetrating stare, it was as if the change in facial expression changed the entire atmosphere of the room. . . . He was never content with one answer to a question. Each question prompted him to ask another question and in the course of two hours I felt that I had been drained of all the information at my disposal . . . at the end of the conversation I felt as if I had been in a confessional."

"His mind is like a powerful searchlight. He knows how to pick out the most important means of the moment and to focus all his light on that one spot."

What Ben-Gurion and Golda took from Berl were the words "strength," "dignity," and "destiny." Ben-Gurion put them in a single sentence and repeated it often: "A nation must discover in itself its strength and its dignity if it is to achieve its true destiny."

Summarizing a three-day youth congress, Katznelson spoke for six hours with barely a pause, "and no one left the room."

Golda visited him often. "He gave me all the time I needed without once looking at his watch, and I loved him for that."

Berl was ten years older than Golda, curly-haired and handsome, with a womanizing reputation of his own. Men idolized him, too. Shazar and Remez regarded him as an affectionate older brother. Ben-Gurion, who was truly intimate with almost nobody, considered Berl his best friend and most important adviser. Ben-Gurion kept Berl's photograph on his desk—the only photograph—until he died. Golda, too, until the day she died, had Berl's photograph on the wall of her living room.

Katznelson was among the first to push for labor unity in the Yishuv, the Jewish community. He was the strongest supporter of an eventual Jewish state, the firmest believer in a Hebrew language and the strict maintenance of Jewish traditions as a binding force. To him, Zionism was a Jewish revolution. He was no orator, but his seminar speeches filled twelve volumes. His was the advice that fathered the heart of the Histadrut. As long as he lived, one would hear, "And what does Berl think?" And long after he died, people said, "If only Berl were here and we could talk it over with him." Ben-Gurion referred to him as "the teacher." At the time of Berl's death, Ben-Gurion delivered several six-hour eulogies.

It was Berl, as much as Shazar and Remez and Ben-Gurion, who promoted Golda for her various positions. She took over the Department of Mutual Aid. "The government wasn't doing anything for us so we had to establish our own fund for unemployment," she said, "and we had terrible unemployment." She took over the Sick Fund, and she made certain that if the head of a family died, the survivors would get some money.

"She had a very fertile mind," said Bertha Goldstein, known everywhere as "Bert." Her husband, Rabbi Israel Goldstein, was an internationally prominent Zionist leader, but Bert later became similarly important as president of the Pioneer Women. People considered her a friend and rival of Golda.

"Goldie could analyze a situation and she had the most proper response at the right time. She didn't get ruffled. And she had just enough of the feminine in her to be able to use it to advantage—not deliberately. But it became a combination of logic and emotion."

"Goldie was strong enough to show her weakness," said Rivka Idelson. "She didn't cover. I remember a meeting of some twenty people when Golda burst into tears. Very few people saw her weep, but she was emotional, very much. Sometimes she couldn't hold against her tears."

"It used to be a scandal in the movies, the sad movies, how she wept," recalled her friend Shulamit Nardi. "And when she needed something and didn't get it, she'd cry like a high school girl."

"I didn't use that as a weapon," Golda later insisted, "but in my youth I was much more sensitive. Like anyone else, I prefer that people agree with me. But when they don't, they don't. And I think I can take these personal attacks better than I did when I was young. I don't cry anymore these days."

The Yishuv was so small that Golda became prominent quickly. She had set a precedent—the first woman to reach the top executive level. An observer placed her even then as one of the country's one hundred most important leaders.

"You couldn't say Goldie was just a woman," declared a man who worked with her at that time. "Goldie was a first-class politician, a real serious heavyweight, respected by everyone."

"Goldie to me was someone who was always held up as the golden light you have to strive for," said a younger friend. "Even in those days, she was pointed out as the physical embodiment of what a Zionist should be. She was a model for all the kids, so much so that it was coming out of our ears, so that most of us kids were turned off. Because who could compare to that image, or even try?"

Golda had her enemies; they came mostly from a group whose ambitions were spoiled by her stubbornness and by her ability.

Again, because the Yishuv was so small and close, gossip was a way of life. The many who envied Golda openly smirked at the fact that this young woman was settled snugly in the small offices of the Histadrut with a well-known group of womanizers. For a time, someone had circulated a nickname for her: "the Mattress."

"A man told me—somebody who really knew Goldie, and I won't say who—that she was 'easy to get,' " said the daughter of an old friend.

"People loved to gossip. It gave a little spice to life. Whenever I went to Tel Aviv and stopped in at Goldie's for a coffee, everybody pumped me for the latest gossip when I came back to the kibbutz. Everybody knew Goldie because she was an American, and there were very few Americans in those days, especially among the leaders. And especially among the women. So they would ask me, 'Who was there when you saw Goldie? Was her husband there? Was her son there? Who else was there? Were there any strange men there?'

"They really tied Goldie up with any available man, or nonavailable man. And there was a lot going on. The point is these leaders were extraordinary men, men of power, the men who created the country. They attracted all kinds of women, and they needed the relaxation of women. And the women were available. For Goldie, it was the other way around: the men were available, and for the same reason."

Much more serious than gossip was her relationship with David Remez. He had started by being her sponsor and patron saint, then her confidant and strongest supporter. The depth of their flowering intimacy revealed itself later in a remarkable letter.

"I was no nun," admitted Golda. She was a normal human being with normal desires who no longer had a physical relationship with her husband. The concept of freer sex was an accepted socialist principle. The country was small and everybody knew everything, "but people let people live." Golda never resented being a magnet of men, and she was one of the few women constantly intermingling with Histadrut leaders in their pressure of never-ending work. Rumors even included Ben-Gurion and Katznelson among her lovers.

Rumors often became more real than reality. "While Freudians maintain that there are four people in bed every time a couple make love —the couple, his mother, and her father—in Israel there are dozens, if not hundreds of people . . . linked to the original ones who gossip. . . . One often has the impression that what happens between two people within four walls is irrelevant compared to what people outside those walls imagine is happening."

Golda explained her own view of the sex of the time. "There was a certain puritan attitude. You didn't live your intimate life in the open. It was not on display. In those days it was not done. Private affairs were not talked about then. There are people who generally don't talk about their intimate affairs, and I am one of them."

What about her closest women friends? Did she talk about her intimate affairs with them?

"Never! Never!"

Well, hardly ever. Her oldest friend, Regina, asked her why she didn't get a divorce.

"He won't give it to me," she replied simply.

Friends who knew her best feel that if Golda really had wanted a divorce, really insisted on it, pressured for it, Morris would have given it to her. Perhaps her reluctance for a final cut of the cord in part stemmed from her residual love for the man and partly because her marriage served as a protective armor in her relationships with other men, relationships she didn't want to consummate, relationships she might want to avoid. A divorced woman working among so many men might have been a red warning light for their wives, might even have been a social stigma. Even the veneer of a marriage served as some cloak of convention.

"I think Morris and Goldie didn't divorce because of the children," noted Rivka Idelson. "My mother left my father because she was interested in somebody else, but she was puritan otherwise. Most of their education and background was puritan. Absolutely. It complicated their lives in a way. Look, Israel is a male community, all male-dominated."

Except for the inner circle, Golda's romance with Shazar was indeed a private affair. Regina agreed that Golda almost never talked about her love life, but added, "Look, we all knew! I used to meet him in her house, but then I'd clear out quickly."

Shazar was often at Golda's house. For one thing, everybody lived near everybody else. Tel Aviv was still so small and sparse. Houses of Histadrut executives, like their lives, were in a close huddle.

Nor did people telephone before they dropped in to visit. Few people had telephones, but that was not the real reason. They simply felt themselves part of an extended family—and besides, they had much to talk about. So Golda learned to expect a stream of visitors on Shabbat and had her cakes and cookies baked and ready. "There was an endless series of these characters who come in, eat—it was taken for granted, that was the style of their life."

There was something else that simplified a secret courtship: there always seemed to be international conferences, conventions; and English-Yiddish–speaking Golda was most often included in the delegation. She got an added traveling job when the head of the Department for International Relations was killed in an auto accident.

In the spring of 1928, Golda was on a delegation to a meeting in Berlin, one of her first trips outside Palestine. The contrast between the highly sophisticated Berlin and the dusty, primitive Tel Aviv hit her with a dramatic shock. She saw sleek-looking women, chic shops, store windows bulging with every kind of food fantasy. "What a world!" Golda wrote home. Making it more wonderful for her was that Shazar had maneuvered himself to be there, too.

Going to the central square in Berlin, she described it as "a world that I had actually forgotten . . . the fruit, cherries, apples, flowers and trams and trees." Then she thought, "So all right, there is this world for the *goyim* but we have to do it just for ourselves." Shazar had studied in Berlin and knew it well, and he took Golda to all his favorite places. With her high school German, Golda also could order her own food, but still needed some interpreting at the opera and the theater.

The two went together soon afterward to another international meeting at Brussels. Those trips now seemed, for both of them, like a succession of honeymoons.

"It was certainly no secret about Goldie and Shazar," said Shazar's longtime personal friend. As another intimate observer put it, "This was no kibbutz quickie."

It lasted long after their passion was overpowered by greater passions, long after their physical connection was supplanted by something more. For those interested in historical trivia, it was perhaps the only time in the history of the world when a future president of a country had a love affair with his future prime minister.

While abroad, Golda received a cutting letter from her sister Shana. Shana was still the austere center of the family, the self-proclaimed critic and conscience, and, even now, the one person whose praise Golda most desired.

Shana now had no praise. Once the paragon of Zionism who put its principles above everything else in her life, Shana now felt that Golda was sacrificing motherhood.

"She is a public person, not a homebody," Shana said of Golda. "Should we rejoice in this?"

Shana's answer was a loud no.

Inevitably Shana found herself picking up some of the supervision of Golda's children. While Golda always provided for women to fill the gap with Menachem and Sarah, especially when she went on trips, and while Bluma also came occasionally to be with them, the bulk of responsibility seemed to sit with Shana.

Shana's children and Golda's played together like brothers and sisters. "We lived a block or two from Goldie," said her nephew Yona, "and so we played together with her kids all the time, in one house or the other."

Unlike Golda, Shana was a strict disciplinarian, rigid in her schedule and expecting instant compliance. Children had to have a hearty breakfast, were permitted only a half hour of radio, "The Children's Hour," and the only films they ever saw had to be educational. Any children in her house were constantly questioned on whether they had done all their homework, practiced their music. Menachem enjoyed joining Sam for an early swim at six in the morning.

Golda was in Brussels in 1929 when she received Shana's caustic criticism. Shana's letter had scraped at her conscience, and she replied:

> I ask only one thing, that I be understood and believed. My social activities are not accidental; they are an absolute necessity for me.... Before I left, the doctor assured me Sarah's health permits my going, and I have made adequate arrangements for Menachem.... But in our present situation, I could not refuse to do what was asked of me. Believe me, I know it will not bring the Messiah, but I think we must miss no opportunity to explain to influential people what we want and what we are....

What if she were to cut off all public activities? Golda asked. At Morris's insistence she had done it once after leaving Merhavia. Would it now be "more wholesome for the children?" Golda doubted it.

She *wanted* to doubt it. She had never had so much fulfillment. At

Histadrut headquarters, she could feel everyone's respect and warm encouragement. Every day brought unexpected excitement, challenges, satisfaction. On the foreign trips, there was the stimulating contrast of the soft world, the unexpected small luxuries, the constant interplay of challenging minds and opinions. Above all, there was this great exhilaration of a highly special love affair.

When she came home, Golda had increasing concern about her daughter. Sarah could only eat carbohydrates. Doctors could not seem to diagnose her frequent illnesses, and she was often in bed for weeks at a time. "There was always a lot of anxiety about her." Golda herself now had more migraine headaches, the pain so intense that she had to quit work and go home. It pained her even more when the children danced around her, delighted that she had a headache and would be home with them that afternoon. Otherwise her work schedule was so packed that she had to make appointments with her children to take them to the movies. She usually arrived just before the film started, Menachem and Sarah both guessing how late their mother would be.

Reminiscing about those years, Golda later said, "I often wonder what do they [the children] really have in their hearts? What do they feel toward me? Because there's no doubt that I neglected them."

Defending his mother, Menachem insisted, "The last thing one would call my mother is a career woman. She did these things because she felt it was her duty. She would always say, 'If you want things, you have to go and do them.' But if we really needed her, she was always there."

Taking a different tack, Sarah said that she "was orphaned of her mother," and amplified it by adding, "Well, we did suffer because Mother wasn't home, but—in the long run, looking back, I feel it was worthwhile. There was always interest in the home ... something always going on. ... For such a mother, it was worth it."

To maintain their façade of marriage for their children, Golda and Morris still had some contact, usually on Saturday. "My parents spoke Yiddish to us," Sarah recalled, "because they felt Jewish children should know Yiddish, and besides their Hebrew was still not very good. They also still spoke some English between themselves when they didn't want us to know what it was."

Golda's poor Hebrew was a problem at work. She shared an office in the expanded Histadrut headquarters on Allenby Street near the central bus station with Heshel Frumkin, who later helped organize the

Jewish defense forces. Frumkin "wasn't the neatest man in the world," Golda remembered. "I always said to him, 'Frumkin, if you throw all the paper on the floor, what do you need a wastebasket for?' And he said, 'That I know in what direction I should throw the paper.'"

In those days, there were no such things as formal appointments at the Histadrut. "Appointments were usually made by somebody just opening the door and saying he is here," said Golda.

In 1929, Golda returned to the United States for the first time since moving to Palestine. Herbert Hoover was the new President. Wall Street was peaking in its money-making frenzy just before the great crash on Black Thursday. People were singing "Tiptoe Through the Tulips," and the favorite novel was *All Quiet on the Western Front*. Golda was probably aware of none of these things because she was too filled with fear.

"I was speaking at a convention for the Histadrut campaign and I was scared. It was the first time I had spoken in New York since my arrival, my first really big audience, and here I have to tell about my world to the American world. My knees were shaking. I didn't know what happened to me."

Her knees were also shaking in Chicago when she addressed a very large audience and noticed a famous Zionist speaker in the front row, an elegant intellectual whom she had much admired. "My God, how can I open my mouth when Shmarya* is sitting there?"

She was not concerned about opening her mouth when she had dinner with Arthur Goldberg, an ardent Zionist, a brand-new lawyer. Goldberg, who would one day become a member of the U.S. Supreme Court, still remembered her vividly as "a firebrand." She was a firebrand because she felt she had an urgent message about the needs and hopes of Palestine pioneers.

Now she could tell her audience to separate the romance from the

---

*Shmarya Levin (1867–1935) was the best known of a select group of speakers known as *Magidim*, who resembled the Baptist circuit riders of the nineteenth century, roaming preachers. The Magidim preached Zionism instead of religion, speaking mainly in synagogues on Saturday mornings. Levin's speeches were a blend of Jewish heritage and European culture, spiced with Jewish wit. Golda said of him (Samuel interview, August 9, 1974, Lavon Institute): "He was so wise, but you know there is a wisdom that is cold. The man had a good head but his wisdom was so warm and sparkling, and a sense of humor which was fantastic."

reality, tell them that a kibbutz coupled sweat and hope, that the work was hard, the rewards slow in coming.

Golda crossed a long bridge in her life when she went to Cleveland to see her sister Clara. They never really had known each other and now truly belonged to two different worlds. "Neither of us is an expert at writing letters," Clara observed. "We don't write, so we really knew very little about each other." Other Palestinians excused their lack of writing home with the excuse "Life is too big for letters."

The little Tzipka/Clara was now a married woman with a mind of her own. When she was a student at Marquette University, she still had vague plans of going to Palestine with her parents. Another student changed her mind. His name was Fred Stern, a brilliant young man and a bitter anti-Zionist. The two went on together to the University of Wisconsin and married. Clara had been following her sister's career long-distance, and was proud of her, but her husband gave her the firm belief that American Jews should stay in America. The two sisters were much alike in temperament, both strong and stubborn, but Clara more outgoing and verbal. Fred greeted Goldie's arrival with hot, unpleasant arguments. The bridge between the two sisters now seemed longer than ever.

In August 1929, thousands of Arabs swarmed into Jerusalem at the bidding of their mufti, Haj Amin-el-Husseini, in a *jihad* (holy war), starting a murder spree that soon spread into nearly two dozen settlements, killing more than 130 Jews. In Hebron alone, Arabs went from house to house killing sixty-six Jews, including women and children, with knives and hatchets. Some felt that the British soldiers put down the violence with more reluctance than zeal: "We had no confidence that the British were prepared to save us." The charge was made that British officers felt more socially comfortable with Arab leaders than with the Jewish ones. The truth was more mixed. Many British soldiers felt a great sympathy and understanding of the Jews and made their own friendships with them. But the primary British attitude of pacifying Arabs, not Jews, came from the anti-Zionist colonial secretary.

In the course of the riots, Jewish children in the areas of attack were collected in a refugee camp. Shana was one of those who volunteered to help. In feeding the children, she decided that herring was unsuitable for them for lunch on a hot day. A sneering nurse questioned: what did Shana know about dietetics? Shana considered this a challenge. She researched the subject, decided the best place to study dietetics was the Kellogg Institute in Battle Creek, Michigan, and decided to learn. Sam was on one of his periodic trips to the United States, earning more money for his family, when Shana wired him her fresh intention. His answer came quickly: "Come." Shana hurriedly made arrangements for the care of her two older children and took her youngest, Yona, with her.

"Perhaps you understand me now?" Golda wrote her from America when she heard the news.

The Arab riots gave an urgency to Golda's first visit to Great Britain in 1930. She was a fraternal delegate to the Women's Labor Convention, trying to alert British women to the fact that their country was veering away from its Zionist commitment and becoming increasingly pro-Arab.

Audiences liked what she said, and invited her to tour England, making speeches to smaller groups of mixed audiences. While she found many women fascinated by pioneering in Palestine, she also noted that many of them obviously preferred the "more charming picturesque Arabs."

Reporting on her reception, she wrote, "I found the same hazy or wrong information about a war between the Jews and the Arabs, and of course the poor Arabs were right." She told of a seventy-five-year-old woman at a meeting who said, "We didn't know that was what you were doing. We thought that you're chasing out the Arabs."

Golda observed that her audiences seemed attentive, "they wrote everything down," and added, "I felt that I'm among friendly people." She noted that she was also hoping to meet some women members of Parliament. The miners of South Wales invited her to visit and she found it "an exceptional experience . . . I saw their life." It also reminded her that Wales and Palestine were the same size and that the Welsh were also an oppressed people. Summing up the situation, she noted, "It isn't very cheerful. Sometimes I think something happened and there's a chance for the better and the next day information comes that shows the opposite. It's very hard not to be pessimistic."

A crucial convention for Golda was the annual Imperial Labour Conference of trade unions from all over the British Empire. David Ben-Gurion joined her there as another delegate. Golda had asked to speak to the conference and was scheduled for five minutes. Ben-Gurion, also scheduled, was equally nervous because his heavily accented English was not exactly Oxonian. "So we didn't see anything of him until the conference. In those days, he ran to the movies or read thrillers to relax."

The international conference had a heavy representation of Arab delegates who were prepared to yell down any Jewish delegates. Ben-Gurion made a speech against an Arab uproar, then told Golda quietly, "Don't speak." Other friendly delegates were similarly worried about Golda. "They will stop her. This is going to be shameful. What is going to happen?"

Golda felt inflamed about the impact of the Arab riots and the need to explain them to the world. She felt nobody understood that the British were preparing White Papers backing away from their promise to give the Jews a national home in Palestine—and the world didn't seem to care. She wanted them to understand and she wanted them to care. Here was one of her heroes, Ben-Gurion, advising her that the spirit of the convention was against them, too tough to buck. But she was defiant. "I think I can honestly say that I was never deflected from doing something because I thought I might fail."

"But I asked for the floor!" she declared to Ben-Gurion.

"I decided they can *platz* [explode], but I am going to speak, exactly five minutes, not a word more. This was after the Arab riots and I wanted to tell them what it was all about, and I did."

A woman delegate afterward commented, "I have never heard a woman speak so quickly. And I never saw such sad eyes."

Golda and Ben-Gurion were driving back to the National Hotel on Great Russell Street when Ben-Gurion said, "I don't understand. Until now I thought we had only two people who could explain things to the outside world and that was Weizmann and Shertok (later known as "Sharett") but *you*!"

Golda laughed. "You underestimated me."

Ben-Gurion was lavish in his praise of her in his article in the *Hapoel Hatzair*:

". . . I trembled at her daring words. Her speech shook the convention. She spoke with genius, assertively, bitterly, with hurt, and sensibly."

Golda caught the convention delegates, but she could not change history. British Prime Minister Ramsay MacDonald, from whom the Zionists expected support and sympathy because he was a Labour Party man, issued another White Paper in October 1930, seriously restricting

Jewish immigration into Palestine and limiting the amount of land that Jews could buy. This seemed to guarantee that the 150,000 Jews there would remain a permanent minority to the 800,000 Arabs. "No white papers or papers of any other color will decide our fate!" declared an infuriated Ben-Gurion. "We will determine our own destiny. We *must* resist!"

Golda reserved her bitter comment for the prime minister, saying it was hard to learn that just because a man was a socialist didn't mean that he was necessarily an honest man. What particularly angered the Zionists was that Britain gave away a great slice of their Promised Land, almost two-thirds of it, to the newly created state of Transjordan. It hurt to remember a few years before, when the British high commissioner dedicated Hebrew University in Jerusalem. Then the people had thrown flowers in his path and danced in the streets when he told them, "Today you have become a nation!" For the British now, the whole area had become "a little colonial backwater."

"I remember having tea with Victor Adler and some of the British Labour people," said Golda. Adler was head of the Socialist International, an Austrian Jew but not a Zionist. "I remember him standing at the window and he said, 'You know, the trouble with you is you want a national home but all you're getting is a rented flat.' "

Golda's thoughts were in another world when a letter cut her down. David Remez, who had picked her out of obscurity and guided her life into power, a man she adored and confided in completely, wrote her a bitter letter, indicating that their long-term intimacy had come to an end. Remez was Zalman Shazar's best friend, and they remained so until Remez's death, but it was a letter of obvious jealousy. She and Remez used some code names for people. "Gershon" referred to Golda's husband, Morris. Remez's pet name for Golda was Chaya.

June 14, 1930

. . . If I wanted to hurt you, I probably wouldn't say what I am going to say to you. To hurt someone isn't very comfortable, not to take into consideration that the one who causes the pain suffers, too. I once wrote you perhaps that sweet words are easy, they don't cost anything and are pleasant to hear. We always avoid talking about serious things. I don't know why, but first there was no opportunity and then I don't want to cause a scene, and Zalman had the same feeling. Talking to you would make a scene. If it would help, it would be worth it. My opinion, Golda, the trouble with you is you were raised on praises. No question you are successful. I don't question you in your social earnestness. You are not a *mensch*. For you, there is no individual. It's only the masses ... also you are standing for something high and that makes you small. You are always pushing everyone aside and this makes you unsympathetic. Particularly the way you act to your friends is unforgivable.

... You're impressed by Zalman. I dare say Zalman has a wife that loves him. Zalman is everything to me. Gershon has a wife that ignores him.... True, Gershon is a very difficult person, but you made him what he is today.... Put yourself in Gershon's place ... think about the way you acted. Yes, I accuse Gershon. If he would have been a stronger person, he wouldn't let you spit in his face. It should have happened to the good Zalman. You would come and leave him the next day at two or three in the morning. Zalman wouldn't have remained silent like Gershon. He would have done something, or made me talk. If Gershon would have done the same thing, you'd respect him more.

... Before you were famous, it wasn't any better. There is a deeper cause and that you should search your own soul for and give a true answer. You are ready so you say to give your entire life to Gershon for the sake of the children. Why do you make yourself ridiculous, Chaya ... what kind of atmosphere can there be in the home when the mother surrenders, when the father comes home and she rests on one sofa and he on the other? I must tell you, Chaya, the truth, that I care very little for you because you became friendly to other subjects, which is painful for Gershon, and still more painful for the children ... you had no right to leave ... someone else should have gone to Berlin.... Tomorrow I'll find out from Gershon how she [Sarah] is feeling this week, and it's about time to take her to the doctor, who will arrange this if not you? There's no one else who can do it.

... Chaya, even the closest person, a sister, can't advise you. This no one else can decide. It can all be decided calmly and not with anger. Zalman will help you because you had good times together. Don't forget in the nice words Gershon said to you, there's more love and devotion than in the beautiful phrases your friends give you.

... In the small world for me, the individual is important. For you, the majority is important. Maybe you are right.

... We'll end our friendship, which is so tragic, with misunderstanding and friction.... I believe of your modern feminism you recognized only the surface and unimportant matters.... If I'm the last person that you find to tell of the sudden decision to leave the house ... has life become too modern for my concepts? Is the best thing to take a modern step and get divorced? If you don't need more to fulfill your life, and I am for you much less than nothing? This I've known for a long time . . . I'll suffer. I'm used to suffering . . . you ran away with him. If you continue this way, you will never come home again because I have no home. . . .

Why would Remez write Golda such a letter? The tone and use of pet names and code names indicated an intimacy few had suspected. His conspicuous jealousy of Shazar would have shocked many. Shazar had been his best friend, and would remain so long afterward. Perhaps they never before had courted the same woman at the same time? Another possibility is that Golda's relationship with Remez grew more slowly, first as a friend, while her romance with Shazar had started with a rush, Shazar-fashion. It is difficult to believe that Remez had such great concern for Morris when Remez himself had played so loose with his own marriage. Some of the Remez darts dug deeply in terms of character, and Golda surely read them with hurt, but Remez would soon eat those words.

Shortly after that, however, Golda received a greater shock, a cable from Morris: SARELE DESPERATELY ILL. COME HOME AT ONCE.

11

All the doctors said that Sarah was dying. The most optimistic suggested she might live until she was twelve, but the others predicted quick doom. They had diagnosed the cause of her ill health as a rare kidney disease, incurable. Earlier they had put her on a strict carbohydrate diet, saying, "She mustn't walk up the stairs, she mustn't run and she mustn't go to kindergarten." For a while, she seemed to survive on six glasses of sweetened tea. The imaginative five-year-old girl pretended each cup of tea was a different food, ". . . and this is meat and this is soup. . . ." As Golda described Sarah, "Her face was swollen, sometimes you could hardly see her eyes, oh, she suffered."

Golda suffered with her.

Sarah later recalled being stretched out on the kitchen table, a doctor drawing blood from one of her veins. This was one time when Golda could no longer put on a brave, smiling face. She burst into tears.

Sarah looked at her and said, "Mama, don't cry."

One of the first friends Golda contacted about Sarah was David Remez. They had repaired their relationship, despite his bitter letter. She told him about her tragedy with Sarah, that she needed heaven's mercy and needed friends. She asked him to please find Shazar and tell him.

Remez was having his own problems. He was a strong family man with a lovely wife and son, but his heart wandered. His longtime mis-

175

tress, named Gusta, was pregnant and about to give birth. She lived in
a house behind his, and worked with him at Histadrut. The name
"Remez" in Hebrew means "hint" or "clue," and when Gusta's pregnancy became obvious, the whispered word at Histadrut was, "Ah, Gusta
has a *remez*!" The rumor then was that Gusta expected Remez to divorce
his wife and marry her. Those who knew Remez best knew he would
not do this. "There was something special in his family—they were all
so close. Everybody spoke of it. Everybody accepted it, yes, Golda, too."
All this had an obvious impact on Remez's relationship with Golda.

The Remez situation accentuated Golda's wish to be elsewhere.

The myth is that a desperate mother flouted the doctors, begged the
Histadrut for an assignment in the United States so she could see what
Americans could do for her Sarah. The truth is, as Golda later admitted,
she didn't have to ask for the assignment. "They wanted me to go and
I accepted it." What moved her to accept, of course, was the hope of
fresh medical treatment, "because I think that otherwise I wouldn't have
gone."

There was, however, an additional factor, something that did not then
surface: Shazar, by some strange coincidence, had arranged to be in
New York at the same time.

Golda's assignment was to become secretary of the Pioneer Women.
Her specific mission was to broaden its base, converting it into a national
organization in the United States, organizing chapters all over the country, giving members projects and functions, stirring their blood with
stories of Palestine pioneers, and raising funds for their vital needs. It
was a two-year term.

Pioneer Women was a U.S.-based worldwide Labor Zionist women's
organization founded in 1925, whose purpose was to provide social
welfare services for women, young people, and children in Palestine,
and also to help new immigrants become productive citizens there. It
sought to involve American Jewish women more actively in Jewish
community life. By 1936, it would have 10,000 members with chapters
in sixty American cities.

The Pioneer Women were a mix of Zionism, Yiddishism, and feminism. The organization was born in the wake of the so-called living
well. A cry for help had come in 1924 from a Jerusalem girls' agricultural
school which needed $500 to dig a well. A group of seven New York

women, wives of Poale Zion leaders, raised the money, then decided to stay together and fill other needs.

Shazar was going to Columbia University at the suggestion of Berl Katznelson. He had discussed with Berl a dissertation he had once started and Berl had told him, "You better go finish it." Columbia had created a new post of Professor of Jewish History taught by a man named Salo Baron, who was busy writing a social history of the Jewish people. Shazar had known Baron in Vienna and planned to work with him. As Berl had suggested, Shazar also planned a speaking tour of the country. He and Golda occasionally, but not surprisingly, would find themselves in some of the same cities at the same time.

The doctors were unanimous in condemning the trip as "extremely dangerous" for Sarah. They told Golda, "You're crazy to cross the ocean with her . . . the salt air is dangerous for her condition." One bluntly said, "The trip will kill her." Golda's parents also considered it "madness."

But Golda and Morris discussed the trip at great length. The situation might be different if the Palestinian doctors had offered some hope, but they offered none. Golda planned to fight for their daughter's life. She had to try everything. Morris agreed.

It was a long trip, two weeks. They took the train to Port Said, then a ship to Marseilles, then sailed from Cherbourg to New York. The first-class section of the S.S. *Bremen* had no children, and Golda got permission for Menachem and Sarah to use its beautiful children's playroom.

For eight-year-old Menachem, it was "a glorious voyage." The playroom was a wonderland "with trains, bicycles and games such as I had never seen before." As for little Sarah, Golda felt "it was as though she knew how frightened I was and felt she had to reassure me." Mostly, though, whatever fear and tension Golda had she managed to keep within herself. In her own way, she later admitted, she was quietly praying.

The children regarded this interval as a thing of wonder because they had their mother completely to themselves—no other people, no other meetings. They could talk and read and sing together. "And Mother played shuffleboard with me for hours," Menachem remembered.

Their own cabin had only two beds, "so Mother slept on a cot."

Golda needed help. Her old friends, the Goodmans, willingly offered their home and their care. Moshe, then in his sixties, and sickly, was no longer an editor but still had his restaurant where he fed his free-loading political friends. He was the Grand Old Man of the Movement, the one to whom the young Zionists came with their questions of conscience. And Fannie was exactly the kind of motherly woman the children needed. Golda described them as "a wonderful family . . . they really loved the children as though they were their own." Golda arranged to stay for a year, paying minimal rent.

"We lived in Brooklyn, near Prospect Park on Clarkson Avenue in a big apartment house, on the sixth floor, the top floor. You opened the door and there was a long hallway. On the right was the kitchen, on the left the living room. That's where I slept," said Judith, the Goodmans' daughter.

"Behind that was a room meant for the dining room, and Sarah and Menachem had that. There were doors from each room onto the hall. As you walked down the hall, there was a bedroom on the left, that was Golda's, and a bedroom on the right, which was my parents'. Behind that was the bathroom. I was thirteen then; I was going to high school.

"I remember that Golda told us that in Palestine the doctors just didn't know what to do with Sarah, and they put her on a diet of just spaghetti. That's all she ate. Well, my mother was one of those dear old-fashioned Jewish mothers and she would say, 'You've got to eat good nourishing food . . .' "

The first priority now was to put Sarah in a hospital, Beth Israel, on the Lower East Side. From her room on the third floor, she could see some trees in a small park. Doctors at Beth Israel quickly diagnosed her problem as chronic glomerular nephritis. It was indeed a disease of the kidney, but different from the one reported in Palestine. "There are two types of kidney disorders which are very similar," Golda later reported, "but the treatments are just the opposite. The other treatment could have killed her."

On her first day in the hospital, Sarah clutched at her mother, begging her not to leave at the end of visiting hours. She was a small child speaking a foreign language in a huge, strange place, fantasizing her fear of the unknown. Menachem was equally miserable. His mother was not permitted to take him to the hospital. Nor could she take him to work. He would not play with other children in the street because he couldn't speak English. At the same time, he refused to go to school and face ridicule from other pupils. Mostly, then, he stayed in his room, on his cot, reading and rereading the few books he had brought. Golda spent little time with him then, since she stayed mostly with Sarah at the hospital.

Sarah's recovery was almost miraculous. Within six weeks, she left the hospital completely cured, able to run, swim, roller-skate, even knowing some English words and phrases the nurses had taught her. Writing of the transformation to Morris, Golda later recalled how she found herself crying at the joy of it. "I was scared stiff," she remembered, afraid the recovery wouldn't last. "We had to go back from time to time for tests, but she was perfect."

Pioneer Women were all fully aware of what Golda was going through. "I remember this Pioneer luncheon when Golda brought Sarah with her. One woman gave her a doll."

Many of these women became Golda's lifelong friends. Most of them came from the same seed: refugees from Europe, self-made young women who wanted more of life than marriage. Sometimes Golda would scold them, "in an elegant way," telling them they "should be more modest," and instead of saying, "I want" or "I deserve," they should concentrate on their contribution.

Jealous of Sarah's growing English vocabulary—"She picked up English, snap, just like that"—Menachem was now willing to join her at school. At the start they were both put into the same first-grade class, and Goldie sat with them the first full week, translating into Hebrew everything the teacher said.

"We had a marvelous teacher, very marvelous, Mrs. Allen. She was not young. I feared her at first. But we learned English very quickly, really. They used the global method where they teach you whole words, using cards."

At home, though, Golda spoke only Hebrew to her children, so they couldn't forget it. "Neither my mother nor I knew Hebrew," said Judith, "but my father spoke Hebrew to them so that was okay. Menachem was quiet and I was quiet. We were sort of very shy of each other."

Judith remembered Golda asking her mother, "Fanny, please ask Judy to come out of the bathroom, I've got to go to work." "I was sitting in a chair in the living room, hunched over, reading a book, and I said, 'But I'm not *in* the bathroom.' It turned out that Menachem and Sarah had locked themselves in the bathroom. They were like two peas in a pod, always stuck together. Menachem could be a terror, he had a bit of a temper and I guess I used to fight with him a little bit. But Sarah was a sweet little girl, a blond beautiful child with big green eyes, always smiling, always cheerful. I think she was a little smarter than Menachem in many ways. She was very sharp. Yes, it was a terrible position for both of them. They knew no one here, no one. And their mother was away so much of the time. We always knew where Golda was when she traveled, and she would call all the time to speak to the kids, and to my mother, almost every other night.

"There was a man named Gold—I don't remember his first name— a personal friend of Golda's and my parents, a constant visitor. He came for dinner one night and it was getting late and he said he had to go home. I remember Menachem saying, why couldn't he stay in the bed with Golda? There was plenty of room . . . it was a big bed! Nobody knew what to say. But he did go home."

Golda took them to the zoo, the museums, the planetarium, concerts, movies, and the sights of New York. They visited Clara and her husband, who had now moved to nearby Bridgeport, Connecticut, and they made a trip to Philadelphia to see their father's family, their grandmother and aunts. Sarah remembered her grandmother as a small, frail old woman with white hair and glasses, a pleasant face. "I don't remember if she spoke English."

"Menachem and Sarah thought everything in the United States was terrible," recalled Golda. "Everything was bad, nothing was good, everything back home was good. They did like American chewing gum. Maybe they didn't have any in Israel, maybe it was new to them. It was so precious to them that every night, before going to bed, each of them would put the used gum in their glass of water on the night table between their twin beds to save it for the next day!

With Sarah cured, and the children settled and in school, there was now Shazar. The two were most discreet, but saw each other often. Shazar's friend recalled his constant references to Golda, quoting comments she made "when she was here the other day" or "when I saw her." What happened between them was their secret, but what is known by one of Golda's closest friends is that Shazar had proposed marriage—he would divorce his wife, she would divorce her husband—and they would marry when they returned home.

Gershon Levi sat next to Shazar, still known as Zalman Rubashov, in Baron's seminars on Jewish history at Columbia. Levi recalls that Zalman was interested in movements among people and in Messianists, about whom he was writing a thesis. He had promised the Jewish poet Bialik that he would study and publish a book on one of these Messianists, and he was then immersed in a diary of one of them. "He asked me if I could help him translate his Yiddish into English," said Levi. "He was staying at a hotel on Seventy-second Street and he would write out the stuff on hotel notepaper and pass it on to me. I'd sit at a typewriter and bring him pages at a time. I don't know how long that lasted.

"At night he used to make speeches right and left. He talked in a very fiery Yiddish, of which he was a master. They called him a speaker who never knew when to stop. I once saw him address a synagogue during services. Because of his background and principles, he wouldn't go into the pulpit but stood at the side.

"I had some material for Rubashov. I didn't know where he was but I knew he knew Golda. So I found her at the Mount Royal Hotel and knocked on the door and asked if she would bring it to him. And she took it."

Shazar was then at his enthusiastic best. He was still lean and handsome, still without a mustache (that would come later). When he spoke, he was emotional, almost lost in his imagination and his words, almost unable to stop. Some people who heard him were worried that he might fall off the platform.

Shazar's influence on Golda was pervasive. His language was rich and he tried to enrich hers. He made her read things she might never have read. New York was a hub of culture, lectures, museums, and music, and Golda was a willing learner and listener. If there was a word for Shazar then, it was "scintillating." With any audience of women, Golda talked; with her adored Shazar, she listened.

Shazar being Shazar, he was scheduled to speak, mostly about Zionism, almost every night to some group, and was invariably late. Jacob Katzman remembered being hired simply to make sure that Shazar didn't detour from his speech assignments. Once Shazar managed to elude Katzman, who finally caught up to him. "I was literally in tears," said Katzman. " 'What are you doing to me?' I said to him. 'They'll hold me responsible if you're late.'

"Shazar looked at me with a sweet smile. 'Do you regard me as a rational man?'

"I said, 'Of course I do.'

" 'So you think a rational man can let his life be governed by a little tin box with cog wheels and springs?' he said, pointing to his watch."

But whenever he got to wherever he was going, Shazar was an extraordinary orator who almost hypnotized his audience. "He pranced all over the platform. He'd lean on the back of the wall, with his back to the audience. He'd sometimes talk to his fist, to his fingers, gesticulate like nobody's business. But what came out of his mouth were pearls, gems of wisdom. This was a brilliant man with a trigger mind, extremely erudite. All his life he had absorbed information like a sponge, especially in history. Basically he was a historian, taught it, wrote about it. He knew more details about every living scholar and Jewish dynasty in the Hasidic world than any man I ever knew. He was a superior intellect of the movement, an intellectual force. And a sweet man, yes, who liked the ladies.

"Shazar was a talker. He said everything ten times as much as he had to. Golda didn't talk much. Even her speeches were short. There was always the sense of holding back something, and giving you only what was necessary. And she didn't gossip, either. She always did the right thing at the right time. Shazar, bless him, was the world's least practical man. He was an extraordinary man, no question, but he was always thinking of so many things and he'd sometimes go off on a tangent. I don't think Golda had tangents."

Shazar was also a man who lived with an inner struggle. For all his intellect, he was constantly trying to come to terms with his Hasidic heritage. The Hasidim were a close-knit Orthodox group who merged ecstasy, mass enthusiasm, and mysticism, "serving the Lord with joy." Once a persecuted sect believing in leaders with supernatural powers, the Hasidim became a more organized, recognized movement, still maintaining their joy in God. Shazar was named after one of the most important Hasidic leaders, Schneur Zalman. Shazar's conflict was that the Hasidim strongly opposed the Zionist movement, and Shazar felt pulled by both forces, and this conflict lasted his lifetime. Whenever he was in New York, he always spent some time with the growing Hasidic group in Brooklyn.

Golda was a beautiful young woman and the men were waiting in line

...but she had fallen in love with Morris Meyerson, who had "a beautiful soul"— and married him.

Shana decided to take her two children and join Golda and Morris on their *aliyah* to Palestine. Shana's husband, Sam, would come later.

Here they are in Boston in 1921, just before embarkation. Golda is first on the left in the second row, alongside her friend Regina Hamburger; Morris is directly behind them.

From the teeming New York Lower East Side, where Golda worked for almost a year

...to Tel Aviv, the city built on sand.

She and Morris lived in an agricultural
cooperative, the kibbutz Merhavia.

She fed and bred chickens

...worked the land. She loved it; Morris
hated it.

...washed clothes

They sent her to the United States to organize pioneer groups and raise money.

She took her children, returned home after more than a year

...along with a new American friend, Leah Biskin, who moved in with them.

They seemed a happy family, but the marriage was breaking up. Golda had made her choice: her cause came first.

Many of the Zionist organizations had their offices in the same place, the ninth floor at 1133 Broadway, a big building in the heart of the garment district, or, as they called it, "the needle trade."

"We were terribly cramped," noted Katzman, then the national secretary of the youth group of the Labor Zionists. "We just had little cubbyholes. When a secretary came in to take dictation, one of us had to stand. Golda's office was right next to mine, and we'd see each other every day. She made lots of friends right away. She was a very simple, outgoing person, never put on any airs. She was the kind of woman who made other women feel they were her sisters.

"You'd go to a meeting night after night. You'd take along copies of a Yiddish weekly and try to sell a few. If you were that lucky, you could go out and eat afterward. If not, too bad. Yes, there were always meetings. We never lacked meetings. If you didn't have one, you had two.

"None of us had any money. I remember walking up to the Bronx once because I didn't have a damn nickel for the subway. But that was the depth of the Depression, with breadlines, and nobody complained. There was a little hole-in-the-wall shop around the corner which sold sandwiches for seven cents. Or we'd grab a hot dog for a nickel at Nedick's. The Pioneer Women were the fund-raisers and they had the only money, so sometimes I'd join Golda at the Jewish deli across the street. They'd have cole slaw, sour pickles and sour tomatoes, pumpernickel and rye bread on every table. That was on the house, and so I'd start making my cole slaw sandwiches. To this day, I love them.

"I even used to baby-sit for her kids in Brooklyn when the Goodmans had to go somewhere. I found Golda's kids both very lovely, well-mannered. Sarah was a beautiful little girl; Menachem a very delicate boy, very quiet, withdrawn."

It was easy for Golda to relate to the American Depression. She remembered vividly her own hunger in Jerusalem after leaving the kibbutz. She could empathize with desperation. What she found difficult to understand was that young Jews, faced with a bleak future in the States, even then wouldn't accept the challenge of Palestine. After arranging her own priorities of life so securely, putting country and cause above all else, she could no longer fully understand the reluctance of mothers to let go of their children.

This job with the Pioneer Women was never anything Golda wanted.

She would have preferred being back in Palestine, part of the real pioneers, busying herself in the business of creation, the intense party politics, the constant challenge of problem-solving.

These Pioneer Women were "ideologically uncomfortable in their physically comfortable city lives." They saw the life of the Palestine pioneer, the so-called *chalutz*, "pure and untainted by bourgeois softness and selfishness." Golda to them was living their dream. She was their *shlichah*, an emissary, from that dream. Around such *shlichahs* "there was a holy feeling! They were the ones who gave it content, who gave it wings, who gave it imagination!" Pioneer Women members described themselves as wood laid for a fire, needing a spark. Golda was one of their sparks.

Golda was in her prime, thirty-four years old, and growing increasingly confident of her leadership. Her mission was not easy. These women were Yiddishists, intent on maintaining their language and origin. If a speaker spoke to them in English, they would cry out, "Yiddish! Yiddish!" In a way, they were defying the uptown Jewish women assimilating into America. Pioneer Women were insistent on maintaining their Jewish identity.

But they were not simply middle-class, middle-aged women. Many of them had children who were grown and gone and they had a choice of being bored to tears, going to social engagements, or joining organizations and finding causes. Most of them were self-educated women, and militants. In the United States, in these early years of the women's vote, there was the growing feeling of women coming into their own. Homemaking was important, but not enough. They wanted more purpose in their lives. If they couldn't uproot themselves for an *aliyah* to Palestine, they could and would help those who were there.

It would not have occurred to them then, as it would today, that men should have an equal role in the care of children and housework. Most of them did not want to overturn the world that men had made—they simply wanted to participate equally in it. "The time for a fundamental questioning of sex roles had not yet arrived."

But they had their own passion. In their journal, one wrote:

"To this very day, the human spirit that seeks creative expression is a masculine one. . . . Women seek the opportunity now to come into their own field of expression. This can be accomplished only by a struggle. She must wage war against man in order to uproot herself from the dingy corner into which history and nature have set her during thousands of years and the development of civilization."

Golda had no interest in waging war against men. Nor did she believe in their ideological purity in Yiddishism—as she had ten years before. Her aim now was to create a power of American Jewish women to help the Yishuv, the Jewish community in Palestine. She wanted them to broaden their membership to welcome young American women who knew only English. "For some who were spineless, Golda gave them starch." She criticized their lack of information and political understanding, the lack of an organized cultural effort, the poorly planned financial activities.

She knew what she wanted and could be tough.

"She was a person of monolithic mind who took her cue from what the Labor Party said. She later helped formulate what the party said, but once it was said, she followed it blindly, stuck to it."

She praised the Pioneer Women's sense of concern, their warmth, their feeling for the world family of Jewish people, and she filled them with her own vision of Palestine. She conjured up "the smell of toil and sweat," as well as hope.

"Goldie brought us a waft of fragrant orange blossoms, sprouting vegetables, budding trees, well-cared-for cows and chickens, stubborn territory conquered, dangerous natural elements vanquished, all the result of work, work, work ... work, just for work's sake ... just for the ecstasy of creation."

She stirred them with stories, gossip, speeches, anecdotes. She even suggested the fund-raising sale of products "made in Palestine." Pioneer Women delivered orders of Jaffa oranges in their baby carriages. Golda herself helped pack Palestine matzos in a Bronx warehouse. She was a great believer in not wasting time, "so while we packed I taught the women the latest songs from the Yishuv." She also taught them the latest dances "and she danced with us until the wee hours of the morning."

Golda moved them most when she told them about the struggles of the Jewish women pioneers in Palestine, their struggles in the fields, their struggles to bring up their children, their struggles to survive. This had the most potent impact, and "really built us spiritually."

This was the time Golda started her unique approach to speech-making. Her language was the simplest, almost basic English. Her imagery was emotional, somewhat romantic. She aimed at the heart rather than the head. Despite the fact that she was realistic about the problems Palestine pioneers faced, she gave these problems an inspirational glow. Often she was most personal. Her own control was superb, but she had a way of touching tender places in people, making them want to help, making them want to give. Women listened and often cried. Men squirmed and felt guilty and reached for their wallets. Young people often felt impelled to go and see for themselves, to be part of what was happening. She stirred pride. Not hate, not pity, not bitterness, but always ending on an upbeat. She did it so well, without any notes, talking directly to the people, searching their faces, their eyes, that it became a kind of magic.

"She was really a very natural orator, even though she had a monotonous voice. She had a sincerity about her, an ability to put things in such a direct manner that you actually visualized what she was talking about. You could actually feel things that she spoke about. Her audience believed her. She had a way of reaching you directly."

Wherever she went, the young women followed her. She was what they wanted to be, if they had the courage. One of those who adored her most was Leah Biskin.

Leah Biskin had served as Pioneer Women's secretary until Golda came. Leah had come to the States via Lithuania and London. She was a plain, unpretentious woman who wore glasses and was thought of as "the spinster type . . . somehow you couldn't imagine a man in her life." She never pushed herself, or anybody else. "She was a very pleasant person," "very skinny, very tense, 'schoolmarmish,' younger than Golda."

"She was tall, and not terribly articulate," said her niece. "She could be curt and rather cold."

Leah seemed to attach herself to Golda, being always available, even trying to anticipate her wants and needs. Whatever Golda wanted, she wanted. Whoever Golda liked, she liked. Golda's family was her family. Golda was not only her intimate friend, but her model. If Leah needed a purpose in life, she now had found it: to serve Golda. She returned to Palestine with Golda, moved into her apartment, shared her bedroom, and served her for the rest of her life.

Golda then seemed to need this understanding relationship. Whatever she told Leah was a confidence she knew would be kept. Leah was absolutely loyal and always supportive. Leah would always tell Golda what she wanted to hear.

Golda treated Leah like a small treasure. In turn, Leah invited Golda and her children to share her family's Passover services in Detroit in 1933. Leah's father was an old religious man with a beard, and she had brothers and sisters who were there, too. "My mother went there from where she was in the United States," said Sarah, "and we went there with Leah from New York." As part of the evening, Leah's family would cluster around Golda with questions about the Promised Land. "Goldie," one of them asked, "do you really think women can work as hard as men on farms?"

"Leah was a lovely, sweet person, just a darling," recalled the Goodmans' daughter. "She moved in with us, too, and she and Golda shared a room."

"Sometimes weeks would pass and we didn't see each other," said Sarah. "My brother suffered a great deal from this. He quarreled with Mother and tried to stop her from leaving the house. I also felt lonely without her. We were always lonesome for Mother because we saw so little of her."

Golda never denied this. "In those years, one didn't fly and I would start out on a tour of the country and be away for several months . . . you didn't shuttle back and forth because it was too expensive."

Sarah once asked her mother what she did. Golda said she went to meetings and talked to people, traveled and talked to people. Sarah burst into tears and said, "So why can't you stay home and talk to me?"

Golda herself told that story. Some friends felt that she told the story as another way to punish herself, another act of contrition. The pain was there.

During their two-year stay in the U.S., Sarah and Menachem went to one of the summer camps for children that Pioneer Women maintained near Highland Park, New York. They were soon known as "Goldie's children," and reacted with "pride and annoyance." Golda visited them, especially during the week-long seminars she conducted at a neighboring camp for young women. The young women, mostly college-educated, knew little about Jewish history and traditions, and almost nothing about Palestine. Golda inspired them with challenges far different from any offered at college, and the "soft city girls" regarded Golda as a pioneer activist "and idolized her."

Another more primitive camp for young people, from ages twelve to twenty, up in the Catskill Mountains, near Kingston, New York, tried to duplicate some of the life on a kibbutz. Water came from a running creek, and everybody showered under a waterfall and lived in tents. Golda stayed for a week, slept in a tent just like the campers did.

"We'd sit around a big flat rock where we had a campfire. You could see the glow of the fire on the kids' faces when Golda started telling stories of the pioneering days. And then she'd teach them songs. She had a warm contralto voice and knew a lot of songs. She was beautiful."

This primitive camping was something Golda liked best of all about this New York tour. It was a shot of nostalgia, reminiscent of a less complex time of her life. She may have wanted to shake these young people and say, "Come with me . . . come with me . . . join me in my adventure." And maybe she did. But not many came then.

David Breslau also thought she was "beautiful."

"I remember at a convention in Philadelphia, I always found her challenging and impressive. But then I was only fifteen and I was ter-rified at having to go and talk to her, because to me she was a great important person." Breslau was with a splinter Zionist group seeking autonomy and Golda was persuading them not to break away. "A lot of what she was saying made sense. She never talked down to us, always spoke to us as equals.

"Our second meeting was in 1933, a convention of the Young Poale Zion. She made an impressive talk, saying that the greatest achievement was to make an *aliyah* to Palestine. Sometimes in the middle of the speech she wandered off a little, but her beginnings and endings were tremendous. I remember how she swept the audience of young people to tears."

The travel for Golda was reminiscent of a dozen years earlier when she most remembered the smell of railroad stations and the sound of her own voice, the long bus rides, sitting up all night in railroad coaches, sleeping with families instead of in hotels. ("I slept in a hotel only when I was sick.")

Evoking memories in her audience of the crime-ridden 1920s, Golda made a sharp point: "Palestine today is a place where there are no gangsters, policemen, or flappers, and men and women work side by side in the fields. . . . There are over 40,000 people in rural districts of Palestine who never have seen a jail or policeman."

She talked to all kinds of groups, immigrant groups and college graduates. She talked about "what it means to work side by side with your man . . . your comrade, sharing everything with him, a full partner." She presented a picture of these women with "deep furrowed, grim and determined faces." And she talked about the independence "for the woman's own consciousness that grows from within."

Long afterward dozens of chapters around the country called themselves "Goldie Meyerson Clubs," members joining the growing line of women who always approached Golda to remind her, "Remember me? You slept in my bed."

Such adulation was heady stuff for a young woman in her early thirties. She liked these women, but the trip frustrated her. Most of these people were not true Zionists—they would never make *aliyah*. They would send their money, but not themselves, and only a few would send their children. Asked her reaction if her son made *aliyah*, one Jewish woman leader said angrily, "Over my dead body."

The incoming money then was not much. America was no longer the *goldena medina*. The United States was deep in the Depression. Fully 25 percent of the American labor force was unemployed. Millions were shabbily dressed and poorly fed. Thousands of people wandered aimlessly across the country in boxcars. Banks wobbled on the edge of collapse. Democracy itself seemed in peril, and there were many urging President Franklin D. Roosevelt to assume dictatorial powers. It would take time before "a crippled President would teach a crippled country to walk again."

So it was understandable that the Newark chapter of Pioneer Women, pledging to raise $165, accumulated only $17.40 in ten months. Or the Wilmington, Delaware, group sent in only five dollars. It meant a great deal for a group in Columbia, Missouri, to donate forty-five dollars.

In spite of her youth and perhaps because of her high principles, Golda could be puritanical. She found it unseemly when a small midwestern town raised funds by playing cards. "For Palestine, you play cards? This is the kind of money we need? If you want to play cards, you can play as long as you like, but not in our name!"

They wanted to know: Didn't women play cards in Palestine?

"Never!" said Golda indignantly.

She later changed her mind. Ultimately Golda decided it was just as proper to raise money by cards as it was by charging twenty-five cents to a masquerade dance, or to hold raffles, bazaars, picnics, and treasure hunts. She still stubbornly added, "I think it's silly . . . and if my *chaverim* in Palestine find out that I was sandwiched between lunch and cards, I'll never live it down."

Golda was not a letter writer, but she did manage an occasional note to Morris about their children. She also wrote more frequently to David Remez, careful not to mention Shazar. Her notes to Remez were a mix of factual reports and wistful reflections. There were two families she knew well making their *aliyah* to Palestine. Whether or not they stayed permanently depended on how their children adjusted. Did he know anyone to help them? She promised that they would talk about everything that happened to her that year, and everything she hoped would happen next year. She was still uncertain about many things and was anxious to return home and get his wise counsel.

Never heavy on nostalgia, Golda made stopovers in Milwaukee, Chicago, and Denver. A seven-year-old Dorothy Ziperstein vividly remembered her arriving in Milwaukee "in a heavily beaded silk dress with a V-neck, styled like old Russia, her hair in braids wound round her head, smoking incessantly." Dorothy then assumed Golda was an Indian squaw. Many of Golda's friends had scattered, but she always found enough left to make her welcome warm. Yet when someone asked her later whether she ever missed America, she answered firmly, "No, never!"

She and Shana had a short reunion. Golda knew better than to mock her for doing the same thing for which she had so much criticized Golda—separating herself from her children. Shana continued her studies in dietetics at the Kellogg Institute, keeping her youngest child with her while the other two children remained in Palestine.

Kudos to Golda came from everywhere. San Antonio, Texas: "We, the younger element, have been charmed and inspired by *chavera* Meyerson. We are seriously interested in organizing into a group." Kansas City: "Huge success . . . sending $100 toward our quota." Memphis, Tennessee: "New group now started." One member recalled Golda scolding them at the Pioneer Women convention for not sending their children to Palestine. "Members left with a feeling of guilt. It wasn't a pleasant experience."

Golda also tried to get them to reach out beyond their own lives into their own society and the problems of their world. "Younger people saw in Goldie somebody who was approachable, who had accomplished something, who had an ideal—and they wanted to be part of it. What we decided was that whatever goes on in American life cannot be foreign to us. American life, American Jewish life—that's us. We're here! We had to reach out! We couldn't isolate ourselves and just be Pioneer Women."

Golda agreed. What she tried to do, though, was not simply describe the Palestine Jewish woman, but the whole ferment, economic, cultural, political. "We welcome private capital in Palestine, but private capital that does not employ Jewish labor is not welcome." A man in her audience, a prominent Jewish writer, came up to her afterward, slightly incredulous. "I don't understand. This was a *political lecture*. After all, you are only a *woman*!"

The president of a Pioneer Women group in Winnipeg, Canada, also came to her hotel room afterward to protest: "Look, you speak very well, but you don't speak like a woman!" She explained that the previous speaker "wept and we all wept."

"I remember that hour because I was dead-tired," said Golda, "and she sat there on my bed repeating over and over again that I should talk like a woman and not like a man." Golda's reply was that tears don't have to be pulled out of anyone in the Zionist movement. "God knows there is always enough to cry about."

Indeed, Golda had no fear of being emotional. Shazar was the perfect model. Ben-Gurion had told her, "Sentimentality is no sin." And one listener vividly recalled Golda's speeches: "We always had to have our handkerchiefs ready."

There she was, so often bone-tired. Tired of saying the same things over and over again, tired of trying to say them with emotion that sounded fresh and warm when she felt dry and cold, tired of meeting the same kind of people, tired of always being en route to another city, another bed, another late night with people who wanted to talk, talk, talk while she wanted to sleep, sleep, sleep. She wanted to be back in her Tel Aviv flat that overlooked the ocean, with *chaverim* who had proved their faith with deeds, not money, who shared her feeling for action.

When she and Shazar found themselves in the same city, they would make the most of it. The lecture tour was almost as repetitive to him as to her. Less so, perhaps, because he loved to speak more than she, and he was more of an actor than she was an actress. She could only say what she felt. He could say anything and *make* them feel it.

Golda and Shazar both knew that they belonged to another place. Golda no longer had roots in America; she only had memories.

Wherever she went, there was always a warm, welcoming party. Informed that she could not park right in front of the railroad station, the Cleveland Pioneer representative told the porter she was expecting a Very Important Person. The porter, conjuring up a Hollywood celebrity, willingly watched the car for her. When the woman finally arrived with Golda, the porter exploded in frustrated anger. Perhaps, two decades later, he might not have been so disappointed.

In Winnipeg, her train arrived early and there was nobody to greet her. The morning was wintry, blustery, and Golda went directly to her hotel. She was taking off her shoes when the phone rang, and she heard a voice in despair saying that there was now a large delegation waiting at the station and what should they do? Golda quickly repacked her suitcase, took a cab to the station, allowed herself to be enthusiastically greeted and proudly paraded back to the hotel.

Golda impressed men, too. "When I first met Golda in Toronto in 1932, she looked like a *femme fatale* with a big fluffy hat and a long cigarette-holder," recalled Meyer Steinglass, who then worked with the Zionist Organization of America. "She was very striking, very good looking and she had this certain air of mystery about her, always. Did she carry herself like someone who thought she was attractive? Yes and no. She *appeared* to be unaware of it—I could never guarantee that she was or wasn't. But I was rather smitten with her."

After a year with the Goodmans, Golda and her children moved to Hamilton Street in Manhattan, to stay with Malka Shenkman. "It was just too hard for my mother," said Judith, "because she was helping my father in the restaurant and taking care of the house."

Malka Shenkman was divorced and had a son at home about the same age as Sarah. "Malka was quite young," Sarah remembered. "I think she worked part-time. She was a good woman, but she was not our mother and sometimes we used to behave quite badly. I remember, when she had enough of our hard times, she'd sit down and say, 'Now I'm writing to your mother.' Yes, that frightened us, that stopped us. Anyhow this gives you an idea for how long a stretch of time we were without a mother.

"But Mrs. Shenkman was friendly. She'd take us to Chinese restaurants

and the cinema. My brother was all excited about the underground
trains. And we saw Japanese children and Negro children. Mrs. Shenkman's son and I became friends. He's now a pianist, really very good."

Among her other duties, Golda became editor of the Pioneer Wom-
en's magazine. Writing was difficult for her. Speaking came as easily as
breathing, but writing—even letter-writing—was almost painful. When
she did write, it was always plain and to the point.

Marie Syrkin became one of her most intimate friends. Marie was
one of the few women to whom she could talk about her personal life,
even her love life. Forever after, when Golda came to the United States
she always met with Marie. And Marie would always stay with Golda
whenever she came to Palestine.

It was easy to see why these two women became the firmest friends
so quickly. They met at a time of their lives when both needed each
other. Marie saw in Golda the activist she herself would like to be, the
woman who pulled out of herself the utmost of her potential. For Marie,
Golda was a waving banner. Golda saw in Marie an educated, sophisticated mind that she herself would have liked to have. Marie then was
a teacher, a poet, one of the editors of the *Jewish Frontier*, the first
Labor Zionist journal. Her father, Nachman Syrkin, had been one of
Golda's gods. Poale Zion was his concept, the merging of socialism and
Zionism geared toward the founding of a Jewish state in Palestine.

"I would have met her naturally," said Marie of Golda. "It was a small
movement and I was already in it. She was a year older than I was. We
were just talking, as two young women talk. She had to go make a
speech and she didn't want to go—she was sick of making speeches.
Then in the afternoon she went to Lerner's, a very cheap store, and
bought a new white dress for ten dollars. And she liked it so well that
she decided to make the speech after all, so that she could wear her
new dress!"

Few people were close enough to Golda to note the normal vanity
in her. She was not only vain about her long, lovely hair, but about the
polish on her nails, the freshness of her clothes, her clear skin, as well
as the occasional new dress.

"I went to that meeting," Marie continued. "That extraordinary earnestness! I remember writing, 'When you listen to somebody else, you

may say, "What a brilliant speech!" and you see the audience grinning at the felicity of the phrase. When you listen to Golda, you are never involved in the manner of speaking. You simply know what to do.'"

Syrkin recalled Adlai Stevenson introducing John F. Kennedy, saying a similar thing, comparing himself and Kennedy to Cicero and Caesar. Cicero might make a brilliant speech, but after Caesar spoke, the crowd yelled, "Let us march!"

Syrkin noted that Golda's least effective speeches were those few she had written and had to read. "But her *great* speeches were when she spoke impromptu, when she even said, 'I don't want to speak ...'"

Leah Biskin was one kind of friend, generous, simple; Marie was somebody more special. Marie would challenge, question, probe. Leah was like a warm bath; Marie more often like a brisk shower. Marie stretched Golda. Marie had a provocative mind with as many questions as answers. Leah adored Goldie blindly; Marie loved Golda, but understood her frailties as well as her strengths. With Marie, Golda could discuss anything from poetry to the issues of the world. Marie had a keen, sophisticated mind and Golda liked to sharpen herself on it. But it was an easy, flowing friendship, a friendship with much laughter. What Marie offered Golda most of all was her intellectual honesty. This was something from which she would not deviate, not even for Golda, and Golda knew it, respected it, and loved her for it.

Like Golda, Marie came from Russia at an early age, but was already fluent in three languages. By the time she was a teenager, her father was teaching her the Bible in Hebrew and Spinoza's *Ethics* in Latin. Marie's mother, like Shana, had been a revolutionary and tubercular.

In the United States, Marie had graduated from Cornell, married a college instructor, and mothered two boys, one of whom died. By the time Marie met Golda in New York, Marie was teaching high school English there, caring for her surviving son because her marriage had dissolved.

"I didn't know what was going on then between her and Shazar, but I did see him often with her," said Marie Syrkin. "He translated my poetry into Hebrew." Nobody knew the working of Golda's mind more intimately than Marie. This is why she could, and did, write for Golda on any issue for any publication—sometimes without even discussing it with her first. There was no one else Golda trusted to do this, and Marie never failed her. Marie became Golda's written voice.

A great asset of Golda's was her ability to cope with almost anyone anywhere. The Pioneer Women received a surprising invitation to participate in a women's fair at the Seventy-first Armory on Park Avenue in New York. They were invited to set up a booth and display their artifacts and literature. The fee was a hundred dollars. In the depths of the Depression, this was a considerable sum. Golda, however, insisted they do it.

Observers noted this was the first time Israeli handicrafts were shown at such a fair—dresses, needlework, aprons, towels, dolls, tablecloths. The invitation was surprising, because the sponsors were the DAR, the Daughters of the American Revolution, surely one of the most austere and aristocratic women's institutions in the country. "They had searched the phone book for women's organizations of American patriots and lo and behold came across the name 'Pioneer Women.' Everyone there was quite embarrassed when the Pioneer Women appeared. But here again, the personality of Golda shot above everything else there. The fair lasted a whole week and she became the darling of the fair. She was touted around and introduced to everyone. From that time on, Golda had a number of friendships among those society dames."

Golda didn't tell her other audiences about the DAR, but she told them about the beginning of Degania, the first kibbutz in Palestine. One of the original ten kibbutz members told Golda he had proposed that members work for five years before any thought of marriage. "So what happened? Came two girls from Russia. And five months later, he was married—the fellow who proposed the plan. But he was not the first. I was the first."

Going home in 1934 after two years meant great excitement for thirty-six-year-old Golda. The work had been difficult and she had confided to friends that she was often depressed "and not very good company." Never had she been away so long, and never more lonesome, particularly since Shazar had returned home long before she did. Her children were even more lonesome. With all its comforts and conveniences, nothing in America had seemed to measure up to what they had left behind. Mostly what they all had missed were family, friends, and heritage, and home.

Golda did create a cadre of friends in the Pioneer Women and elsewhere who would anxiously await her every time she returned, friends who sensed "she would one day be outstanding because she was so remarkable even then," who expected her career "to surprise us," who editorialized, "We shall never forget her."

A few, including Leah Biskin, returned with her to make their own *aliyah*, and Golda spent much time aboard ship uplifting them with her own spirit, "constantly leading them in Hebrew and Jewish songs."

When they docked at Haifa, Morris was waiting.

12

Be patient toward all that is unsolved in your heart . . .
                                                    —*Rilke*

Homecoming for Golda was not what she had expected. She had hoped that Shazar would get his divorce and she would get hers, and they would marry and live happily ever after.

Shazar had changed his mind about a divorce. He was forty-five years old and his life had grown too respectable, his pattern settled, and his wife had accepted whatever he did outside of her life, as long as he came back to her.

Golda was bitter about it. When Regina asked again, "Why didn't you get a divorce?" Golda replied, "First of all, Morris wouldn't give it to me. Secondly, I didn't want it. What did I need it for? I wasn't going to marry anyone."

Why wouldn't Morris give her a divorce? "Why? Spite!" declared Regina. "Look, he was very angry. You can't blame him. He knew about Goldie's other men. But he still loved her."

Asked what went wrong with their marriage, Morris told a friend, "I came to Palestine for one reason only—to be with Goldie. But she was never there."

Golda had her own explanation: "If your husband is not a social animal like yourself, and feels uncomfortable with an active wife, a wife for whom it's not enough to be a wife . . . there has to be a clash." She gave similar explanations often, but never without sadness.

The truth is perhaps simpler: she grew in giant steps and he didn't.

There was no sharp break between Golda and Shazar—their relationship would last into their old age. But there was then a gradual easing away from each other, an emotional distance. Shazar had been a large part of Golda's life. Golda could not tolerate any gap of loneliness in her life. She was a private person but never a loner. She needed the feedback and warmth of friends, and lovers. This new gap in her life did not long remain empty.

Sarah remembered her mother talking nostalgically about "her hidden yearning to return to the kibbutz." Golda actually applied to Ein Herod, a large kibbutz where she had many friends. "But nothing came of it," said Sarah. "They didn't have any vacant housing for me," Golda explained.

Golda and her children moved into a friend's empty apartment for a time. She later lived for a while with her friend Beba Idelson, one of the few other women prominent in the Histadrut. "Both were closed people," noted Beba's daughter, Rivka, "but they would confide in each other." Golda then found her own apartment on a new street in northern Tel Aviv, a street with young trees and three-story concrete block buildings.

Tel Aviv then was called the "Wonder City," a modern metropolis of 150,000 people, complete with Viennese coffee shops. Zionist founder Herzl, who believed, at the turn of the century, that Zionists should comport themselves like upper-class gentlemen with frock coats and top hats, would have been amazed at the open-necked-shirt informality set by Ben-Gurion.

Morris still had not given up hope about Golda. Friends noted that Morris seemed more attentive to Golda than ever, "almost too cloying." If she was planning a trip while he was home, he still packed her bag. When she wondered where to put all their books, he built a bookcase, "and it looked like a Morris bookcase . . . he was very handy."

He now worked and lived in Haifa—where he had a new job—but returned to Tel Aviv early every Friday evening. His children would wait for him at the bus stop. Their ritual was to stop off at a store where Morris bought the *Manchester Guardian* and the London *Times*, perhaps stop to check inside a bookstore, then go home, where Golda would have dinner waiting. The children both remembered that no matter how busy Golda was, she invariably came home to prepare Shabbat dinner. She made all the traditional dishes including *challeh*, the braided bread. She never seemed to make any new recipes—nor did she want to—but she always made enough cookies and cakes for the open-house weekend.

This façade of a marriage was maintained primarily for the sake of the children. "What was so strange was that there was almost no conversation between Goldie and Morris. . . . Goldie froze Morris. No arguments, no shouting. Simply silence. . . . She had a way of tightening her emotions. There was that phrase 'I close my eyes on you.' That was Goldie. If she wanted to freeze you out, brother, you got frozen out. And she did that to Morris. It was so sad."

Replacing conversation was the music of Brahms, Tchaikovsky, and Beethoven on their many classical records, while guests sat on pillows on the floor. With Saturday sunset, the end of Sabbath, Morris would take his bus back to Haifa.

Golda had enrolled her children in the Beit Hachinuch, "School for the Children of Working Parents." The range of courses included workshop classes in gardening and the kitchen. Other children teased Menachem and Sarah because they now spoke Hebrew with an American accent, and many called them "the Americans." "It was not a very big school," Sarah remembered, "and I think it was quite expensive. Not everyone could send their children there. It began at eight o'clock in the morning, even earlier in the summer, till three o'clock every day. We ate lunch there. That made it easier for Mother."

It never seemed easier. At the Histadrut, she could see an issue quickly, and decide. At home, there were too many emotional challenges to her peace to permit her to relax. Leisure was a word outside of her experience. She demanded so much of herself that child-rearing loomed too large for her. She somehow managed to cook their meal for the next day, and mend their clothes, no matter how late she came home from meetings. But she felt frenzied at the idea of bicycles, wouldn't buy them any, or let them ride, "but we did it on the sly." Coming home by bus one day, she looked out of the window and saw Sarah riding a bicycle loaded with bouquets of flowers. Sarah belonged to a youth group, and they were delivering flowers to raise money for a trip. "And she had borrowed somebody else's bicycle to do it."

Sarah was the undemanding one, pushing all her loneliness inside. "She had all her emotions battened down, hard." Menachem was more verbal in his complaints, in his demands for her time. For these two young people, it had been a painful, lonely time. If there was much they did not understand about the home scene, there was also much that they didn't want to understand. For Golda, the pain was often sharper. Menachem remembered that his mother sometimes yelled at him "like any other human being." But, much more often, Golda silently yelled at herself.

Menachem had caught his father's love for music. At a previous Passover service at the Biskin home in Detroit, a young man had played the cello "and all of a sudden, Papa, I *knew*!" Golda and Morris combined a month's salary to buy Menachem a cello, and it was Golda who carried the heavy cello to his biweekly lessons until he was big enough to carry it himself. They also bought Sarah a violin but she never liked it. "It never occurred to me that I could tell my mother I wanted to stop lessons." She finally did, in the fifth grade, "because it was difficult to pay the fees."

"We often walked with Mother and visited friends," said Sarah, "and they visited us. People like David Remez."

Golda's relationship with Remez had warmed again. "Yes, large piles of anger are piled between us," he had written her. "These are only nightmares, a bad dream at the hours when our hearts tended to light—I still believe that there will be light between us because in this shadow that defines the past and the future, we won't be able to live. G., these were only nightmares. . . ."

The nightmares were over and the light brightened. Realizing how much she had hurt him, Golda asked his forgiveness. Her excuse was that she was going through a difficult period on a complicated road searching for her own emotional truth. She stressed that she needed to see him, talk to him, that everything between them was very dear to her.

Remez was now secretary-general of the Histadrut, one of the most powerful men in the Yishuv.

A dozen years older than Golda, he had also been born in Kiev. He was a young chef when she was a child. He then became a printer, a teacher of Hebrew, a law student at the University of Constantinople— where he met Ben-Gurion and Ben-Zvi. The three enlisted in the Turkish army in the First World War, but quit when they were kept out of combat. Remez married a pretty wife, nine years older, and they made their *aliyah* to Palestine in 1914. He worked on farms, dug ditches, drilled wells. Berl Katznelson plucked him out and transformed him into a labor leader.

"My father never belonged to any group within the party," said his son Aharon Remez, "but he could establish trust from all sides. If there was a clash of opinion at a meeting, he was the best possible chairman to prevent a breakdown. He could take opposing opinions, find a common denominator, and bring them together. They called him the Great Mediator and the Great Unifier, and he was."

Few leaders had greater patience. Unlike Ben-Gurion, who fixed on an idea and charged with all his might, Remez was a careful planner with an almost seismographic ability to feel all the tremors of a problem before making his move, and always probing other leaders for their apprehensions. Once decided, he was an action man.

Remez had his ideals, but he was pragmatic. Anything that helped the future Jewish state was beneficial; anything that put it in danger was harmful. While he was not an academic or a scholar like Shazar, Remez had a love of language. He created new words in Hebrew from old root forms. He was a quiet speaker, seldom raised his voice, but his speeches were always carefully wrought, filled with poetry and rhythm. In one of them, he said: "There is a place in the world that bestows its glory on every foundation established in it. That place is Jerusalem. There is a time that adds charm to all existence. That is the time of youth."

For him, Golda was youth. He once described a woman who might have been her:

". . . who dared to oppose the conventional. She would not accept the love of humanity if it served as a cover for escaping the love of Israel. The living truth in her heart led her to love humanity, Israel and Zion. Thus the heart of this daughter, too, was reunited with the heart of her forefathers."

Remez's short stature seemed to enhance his handsome head. "Many, many women were in love with Remez. I know two women who wouldn't marry anyone else because they were so in love with him. He had great charm, an impressive mustache, warm laughter. Most of all he had a romantic way with words."

"My heart still moves to meet you," Remez wrote Golda. He spoke of their relationship as being surrounded and separated in secrecy by a wall of Chinese fabric. "Isn't it too torn? You can cut into it windows and openings as you wish. I will accept the verdict."

"Remez lived ten minutes' walk from Goldie, no more. Remez had many affairs but he was no Casanova. When he was connected with a woman, it was very serious."

Remez still had his connection with Gusta, who had given birth to his son. The *bris*, the circumcision, had been a big affair at Histadrut, and everybody brought presents. But long before the *bris*, there had been an easing off also between Remez and Gusta. She had realized that he would never divorce his wife and marry her because his basic family was too important to him.

"When Golda came into the picture," noted a mutual friend, "there was nobody else for Remez but Golda. And no other man for Golda but Remez."

"There was a kind of chemistry between him and Golda," said Nomi Zuckerman. "They didn't have to explain things to each other. They were on the same wavelength. They were good for each other, helped each other, supported each other. And Remez realized the flame that was in Golda."

There was something about Golda that caught people—an intensity. She also always had a presence. When she walked into a room, people knew it, felt it. Some people claimed it was a kind of magic. Whatever it was, it quickly caught Remez. Their romance flowered. Again, it was not flagrant; it was not discussed. Indeed, as one observer put it, "It had great dignity."

In many ways, they were vastly different. Golda had more of a gut reaction to things. She had little patience with those with whom she did not agree. She would dismiss some of them as "too solemn, too academic, too impractical . . . let's forget them." She had an instantaneous understanding and grasp of situations, a great intuition, an ability to catch essentials, but she did not have the Remez willingness for the very careful weighing of alternatives.

"We saw a great deal of each other," said Golda of Remez. "Remez was one of the few comrades with whom I discussed any personal, nonpolitical matters, and I relied a great deal on his advice and guidance."

Shazar had had a great impact on Golda. He was an intellect, a teacher, a moral force. "But he was not a guiding light. You could go to him when you were in a very bad mood and needed uplifting, but you didn't go to him for his political opinion. Golda went to Remez for everything. Without Remez, she didn't move." Another observer noted, "Remez gave her not only intellectual support, but the guiding assurance that she was doing what was proper. He was truly the strong man in her life, the mentor, and she needed him."

"He was my real compass," Golda told Remez's son.

"They had something going that was good," noted another mutual friend, "and for a long time."

The long time was the rest of his life.

The David Remez hand guiding Golda's future was firm. In 1934, shortly after Golda returned from the United States, she became a member of the Vaad Hapoel, the Executive Committee of the Histadrut. If the Histadrut was the secret government of an unborn nation, the Vaad Hapoel was its cabinet. Unless the Vaad Hapoel supported a policy, it could not be implemented. Golda was now one of the dozen shakers and shapers of policy that detailed most of the life of the Yishuv. She was not only working alongside the Jewish giants, she was one of them.

"The inner circle was like the nucleus of an atom. Each person had something in common with the rest to make it a cohesive group, but the members were also very different from one another, similar on one side, different on the other, a very compact, concentrated group."

One of Golda's initial jobs was to set up a tourist bureau for Very Important Persons, to show them physical proof that Jews could govern themselves. Shortly afterward, she was elected to the Histadrut Secretariat, even closer to the center of power. She became chairman of the Kuppat Holim, providing medical service for almost half the Jewish population, intimately involved in the "womb to tomb" welfare of the Histadrut, as well as labor conditions and unemployment problems. While still in her thirties, she was made head of the Histadrut Political Department, which she later referred to as the most creative time of her life.

"They thought I was a good speaker, a good organizer, and a hard worker. They got to know me and they gave me plenty to do." She jokingly referred to herself as "made of steel." Nobody any longer viewed her as an immigrant. They smiled at her simple Hebrew, but

R A L P H   G.   M A R T I N

she had come a long way from the time when she returned from a Hebrew lecture "and cried a little because she didn't understand a word he said." She was now rooted.

Unkind critics still claimed that Golda's lovers had pushed her into prominence. It was true that Remez, Shazar, and others helped open doors for her to prize assignments, that they did help shape her, but not as much as she shaped herself, and proved herself.

Her children knew only that they saw less and less of her. "It wouldn't be the right thing to say that I was proud of my mother," said Sarah. "Whenever I had to fill out a questionnaire, I always understated my case. I would write that 'my mother works in the Histadrut' and that is all." Sarah had her own pride and wanted no special treatment because of her mother.

"When they lived with us in the same apartment," said Rivka Idelson, "and Golda was running around the world, Morris used to come and sit with the children, tell them what to eat and what to do. He was very tender, very gentle. He was a round-faced man with rimless glasses and he always had something nice to tell you, to show you. He knew every new book; he was very cultural. He used to tell stories to the children before they fell asleep. Sarah took things more easy, Menachem more hard. But neither had any tension with their father. I used to consider him very sad."

Histadrut pressure was intense. More often now, Golda came home with a painful, enervating migraine headache, which forced her into bed for twenty-four hours. Otherwise the work was seamless, no hours, no days or nights, no vacations. She loved it. She was constantly giving birth to programs, policies for a future nation. Unlike her peers, she was not an intellectual. She had little of their knowledge, less of their abstract philosophies.

"Look, all right, she was no great intellect, but she had an enormous intelligence, *enormous*! I know she didn't read too much, didn't have time, but she got her education by *ear*. Look, when you sit at meetings day after day, year after year, with these giants—where you participate actively yourself—believe me, that's an education you can't get at a university," said Dr. Jacob Katzman. "So she had *that*."

Golda also learned from crisis. One such crisis was the closing of the port in Jaffa in 1936 when Arab workers went on strike. David Remez had a sudden vision. Why depend on Arabs in Jaffa? Why shouldn't the

Jews have their own port in Tel Aviv, train their own dockworkers, buy their own ships? An enthusiastic Golda told Remez she had had a similar vision sitting on the veranda of her apartment overlooking the sea. Her vision was a fleet of ships flying the flag of the Star of David all over the world. After all, why not? Two thousand years before, the Jews were a seafaring nation. Why not now? "We must train our people for work on the sea just as we have trained them for work on the soil," she said. All they needed was money, and the only place for that was the United States and the only one to get it was Golda. Would she do it? She was so confident that she even agreed with Remez on an approximate date when they would rendezvous in London to buy ships. Remez supplied a name for their project: Nachshon. That was the name of the first Israelite to jump into the Red Sea at the command of Moses after the Exodus from Egypt.

On her American tour in 1936, "speaking over the chicken," Golda told her audiences, "Believe me, my friends, that's all we ask of you— to share in this responsibility with everything that it implies—difficulties, problems, hardships, but also joy, a lot of joy!"

In telling of other accomplishments, Golda declared that the Histadrut had brought more than a thousand Jewish children from Germany, placing them in settlements, that the Histadrut had sent men and women to some thirty countries to help train young people culturally and physically for life and work in Palestine.

During her trip, Golda found herself at the same hotel in New York with her friend Beba Idelson. Both had been invited to Passover services with good friends. One of them was Abraham Cahan, editor of the Jewish daily newspaper, the *Forward*. Cahan pulled aside Beba Idelson's daughter Rivka and whispered the news that Moshe Beilinson had died, told her not to tell Golda. Beilinson* was a chief spokesman of the Labor Party who had written voluminously on Zionism. "Beilinson and Golda had been very close, intimate," Rivka explained. Cahan didn't want Golda to know then because it would ruin the evening "and the show must go on. It was the first time I ever had heard that phrase, but

---

*Moshe Beilinson (1889–1936), born in Russia, a protégé of Shazar and Katznelson, on the editorial board of *Davar*, translated books of Jewish interest into Italian, wrote books on the Arab-Jewish question. One of the main hospitals in Tel Aviv is named after him.

I couldn't hold it in and I went upstairs to her room and told Golda, privately.

√ "Golda had such a head of hair, like a lioness. She started screaming, screaming, scraping all the hairpins out of her hair, tearing at her hair, tearing at herself, her long hair falling down to her waist. She looked so wild, wailing all the time, her hair falling all over her. I tried to persuade her to calm herself and come downstairs to the services because they were waiting for her, but she wouldn't do it. 'We must keep smiling when Beilinson is dead?' she asked incredulously. So I came down and told everybody else and a few people went up to try to calm her down. She finally did come down, perfectly controlled. I don't know how she did it. But after the Seder was over, she and a few friends went out into the street, all of them weeping. Beilinson? I think he was younger than she was. Good-looking? I don't know. But it's nothing to do with good-looking if you love somebody. But I don't think there was a love affair there, and I think I know most of her love affairs."

Golda raised the money, kept her rendezvous in London with Remez. "We stayed quite awhile in London," said Golda. "Several weeks. We didn't have very much to do, and we would sit up all night at the Lyons Corner House in Oxford Circus. It wasn't expensive and it was interesting to see the clientele change from hour to hour into the early morning when the people came in before they went to work. We used to walk for hours in the night. It was fascinating. I loved London. I just loved it!"

She also loved Remez. She confided to few friends about this, but did tell one, "I loved him very much."

"The thing to remember is that Remez was not known as Golda's lover—she was known as Remez's girlfriend because he was then much more important than she was." As director of the Histadrut, Remez could send Golda to conferences in Basel, London, Prague, Geneva, Amsterdam, and Copenhagen, and he could send himself, too.

Whenever it came time for another trip, Golda claimed she always felt the same about leaving her children: "Your heart goes to pieces!" Wherever she went, there were usually letters waiting from her children. Menachem had received books and shirts she had sent but now wanted an electric set "so I can build a radio." He had read *Treasure Island* in English and was now interested in painting. Golda suggested he find a good teacher. "Ask someone who knows." She asked Sarah what she did while her brother was away in camp and Sarah replied that she had spent some time with her grandparents. Golda sent a record player to Sarah via a friend and got the report that Sarah had said, "I don't want a record player! I want Mommy!" And then wept.

Golda wrote them about her first plane trip: "To tell the truth, I was excited and a little nervous ... this was the first time I'd ever been in such a contraption."

More news from Menachem was that he was learning how to bind books at school and Sarah was learning embroidery. He suggested she bring him a children's encyclopedia as a present and he was glad she had gone to the dentist.

Gossip about Golda and Remez circulated within a small group. An American visitor, dining with friends in Palestine, was surprised to hear it. They were surprised that he was surprised. "You must know *that* gossip ... what kind of Movement is this that you don't know these things!"

Nobody knew it more clearly than Gusta. She had been in charge of the Pioneer Women's Home in Haifa, her son in first grade at a nearby kibbutz. Remez thought highly enough of her ability to put her in charge of his pet Nachshon project. He tried to manage a fairly regular visit to see their son and Gusta returned to Histadrut headquarters in Tel Aviv once a week. There was jealousy and bitterness, but she and Golda respected each other as co-workers, and there was more hurt than hate. Many years later, Golda asked a mutual friend about Gusta: "Is she still so beautiful—inside, too?" The friend's answer was yes, and Golda sighed audibly and said, "Always I was jealous—she was so good-looking." Then she added, "And a good manager."

Remez's wife's understanding also seemed boundless. Her name was Luba. "She was a very nice woman, very kind, and beautiful." She not only accepted Golda's presence in her house, but their children played together. Rachel Shazar similarly highly admired Golda, despite her jealousy about Shazar's love affair with Golda. Golda had helped publish and contribute to an English edition of Rachel Shazar's book *The Ploughwoman*. "I didn't keep a diary of her loves," Rachel once told Yehudit Simchoni, "but Golda had enormous personal magic."

"The silent understanding was that you could have lovers, but they should not rock the boat, should not break up marriages." Shazar also had fallen in love again, with a woman who was a good friend of his wife's, and he still maintained his close friendship with Remez and Golda.

The common glue that kept them all together like this was the strength of their commitment to the party and the cause. This commitment was strong enough to absorb all personalities, all relationships, all individual trauma. In this sharing of everything, private affairs were respected as highly private. Golda's relationship with Remez "was a very natural thing, and it had dignity. They met together, openly went together, and everybody *knew*."

Everybody knew not only about the remarkable number of missions on which Golda and Remez managed to go abroad together, but also that they had an available apartment of their own, aside from their private homes.

Golda still didn't wear lipstick or makeup. Her daughter recalled Golda having only two dresses in those early years. "She washed one and wore the other." But she had her own vanity. She needed a warm blouse for the winter. "A friend of mine went with me and we saw a beautiful, deep red cashmere blouse, and she talked me into it. It was sixty-five piasters and I can't tell you how I later ate my heart out at this fickleness to pay sixty-five piasters for a blouse!"

Except for the occasional Russian embroidered shirt, the standard informal summer clothes for men and women were shorts and open-necked shirts. "It would have created a sensation if somebody walked down Allenby Street in a suit. I remember when the casino was built and a half dozen women were foolish enough to go there in long dresses—that was the most ridiculous thing in our eyes that anyone could imagine."

Elsewhere in Europe, the seeds of the Holocaust had been planted. Hitler's Nuremberg Laws in Nazi Germany in 1935 stripped all Jews of their civil rights. They could be beaten at whim, their shops vandalized and looted, their synagogues set afire. They could not sit on a bench in a public park unless it was plainly marked JEW BENCH. An increasing number of stores had signs that read WE DO NOT SELL TO JEWS. One woman was forced to wear a sign saying, "I am the biggest pig of all . . . I only sleep with Jews." German citizens whose families had fought and died for Germany for many generations, who conceived of themselves as more German than Jewish, who had been integrated and thoroughly assimilated into every creative level of the country, every part of the government, every section of the nation, now suddenly found themselves pointed out as Jews even if they had only a single Jewish grandparent. Within a year, half of them had been fired from their jobs. Europe had eight million Jews, more than seven million of them not yet under Hitler's rule.

Almost 69,000 German Jews made their way into Palestine that year, despite stringent British restrictions. Mandated by the authority of the League of Nations, the British seemed more intent on keeping Jews out than letting them in. The total Jewish population in Palestine in 1935 was about 400,000, 23 percent of the population.

Heightening the tension, Palestinian Arabs rioted in the spring of 1936. Inspired by the Haj Amin-el-Husseini, the grand mufti of Jerusalem, their spiritual and political leader, Arabs burned farms, ambushed buses, derailed trains all over the country. A special pang was caused by Arab destruction of hundreds of thousands of freshly planted trees. All travel was unsafe. The Arabs attacked everywhere, killing eighty, wounding hundreds.

"I kissed the children good-bye in the morning," Golda recalled, "knowing that I might well never come home again."

Golda remembered that time as "one funeral after another." "Two nurses were killed in a Jaffa hospital where patients were almost 100 percent Arabs. After all they did for the Arabs, and the Arabs killed them." Arabs attacked Tiberias, setting the synagogue afire while there were people inside. "There were five or six children and they shot at them . . . killing two daughters, and then stabbed the mother in the chest. A mother begged them, 'These are children! . . .' and one of the Arabs answered, "They'll grow up . . . kill the Jews!' "

Reacting against Arab attacks, some Jews attacked an Arab bus and were promptly arrested by the British. Brought before a judge and sentenced to death, the unrepentant Shlomo Ben-Yosef wrote: "Am not sorry at all. Why? Because I am going to die for the sake of our land."

The British called the riots "disturbances" and sent the Peel Commission in 1937 to reevaluate its position on Palestine. One of the commission members, Sir Horace Rumbold, was surprised to meet a very prominent musician he had known in Germany, now a recent Palestinian immigrant. "This is a very great change for you," he told the refugee. "Yes, it is," the man replied. "It *is* a change from hell to heaven."

The Peel report reaffirmed the primary purpose of the British Mandate: "to promote the establishment of a Jewish national home." It praised the energy and effort of this "going concern," noted its economic advantage to the Arabs, but saw the eventual conflict of Arabs and Jews over sovereignty. The only hope "lies in surgical operation . . . partitioning the country into Arab and Jewish states."

Testifying before the Peel Commission, elder statesman Chaim Weizmann was asked how many Jews in Europe saw Palestine as their sole hope of salvation. "Over a period of years, no more than two million —of the youngest and the strongest. . . . the old ones will pass; they will bear their fate or they will not." Frightened by the Arab riots, Weizmann even agreed to a British proposal for a temporary halt in immigration. A horrified Ben-Gurion unsuccessfully tried to dissuade Weizmann. "It is hard to see a man in his downfall," wrote Ben-Gurion. American Zionist leader Stephen Wise was more pointed in his criticism of Weizmann: "You have sat too long at English feasts."

Golda had her own question: did not the old Jews have a right to live? Available at that time were professional reports that Palestine could shortly sustain a population ranging from eight to twenty-two million. She also had a sharp critique of the inadequacies of British colonial control in Palestine: the lack of an unemployment insurance plan and the minimal amount spent on education. "Our people are such that they consider education is a primary need for the family."

The Peel Commission proposed partition: a Jewish state confined to 2,000 square miles, an Arab state of 48,000 square miles, and an international enclave at Jerusalem.

Golda was against it. Sarah wrote her "Good for you." Golda, among others, felt that a Jewish state without Jerusalem was a body without a head. Berl Katznelson agreed with Golda, felt it was a betrayal of the British Balfour Declaration. Ben-Gurion reluctantly accepted the Peel report, claiming that any state was better than none. He conducted his own private negotiations with an Arab friend, a former attorney general of Palestine, to implement the separate-state idea. Ben-Gurion was now chairman of the Jewish Agency. The internal quarrel became academic because the Arabs bluntly refused the Peel offer. Golda later admitted that Ben-Gurion had "the greater wisdom" on this issue. A Jewish state of any size could have absorbed hundreds of thousands of refugees that the world didn't want.

Golda wrote her "dear children" how interesting their opinions were to her about the partition and the vote and promised to explain all the details when she got home."

Menachem replied that he hoped she would come home on a Nachshon ship with a Jewish flag flying at its mast because he now had decided to become a sea captain. He had watched the incoming ships from their terrace and knew all their names and flags.

When Arab longshoremen stopped the ships at Jaffa, volunteer Jews unloaded cement from a Yugoslav freighter at a primitive wooden jetty they had built in Tel Aviv, while a huge, proud crowd of Jews watched, cheered, and sang. Arab riots coupled with British complacence confirmed once again for Histadrut leaders that they must depend only on themselves. When Arab bus drivers went on strike, Jewish volunteers armor-plated the buses and drove them on schedule. When Arab farmers kept their produce from the market, the kibbutzim delivered their own crops. In the face of Arab riots, Jews built fifty-two settlements within the next three years. Since Arabs never attacked in the daytime, settlers spent the first day constructing a stone-filled wooden watchtower and stockade to repel the inevitable nighttime attack. "Tower and stockade" became symbols of the time.

At home, Golda got a new boarder. She was Nomi Zuckerman, now a sensitive teenager and a gifted pianist, studying music at a nearby school. Nomi's father had been one of the men who had persuaded Golda to leave Milwaukee and go to Chicago. Nomi had witnessed the divorce of her own parents and now had to watch the final disintegration of Golda's marriage.

"Golda was often away and I tried to help as much as I could." Nomi noted how Morris acted as father and mother during that time. He had done the same thing some years before when the children moved in with him in Jerusalem while he managed a bookstore belonging to Sam and Shana. The children had then attended an American experimental school in the Russian compound and Morris cooked their dinner, taught them history and art, and walked with them through the Jerusalem hills. The children remembered their father sitting in the store "always reading a book," never pressuring anybody who came and browsed. He was in his ultimate element, the happiest work he ever had. "But he was not a good businessman at all," said Nomi Zuckerman. "He was too honest, too trusting, too unconcerned with selling." The one thing that energized him was the arrival of his children. They recalled what fun they had each time in picking books for themselves. When Shana and Sam returned from the United States, they had to sell the store at a heavy loss, and Shana never forgave Morris.

Morris's intellectual life, his books and his music, were empty without his children and his wife. Life with his wife was now nothing more than stretches of silence finally exploding into heated arguments. After one such final argument in 1938, Golda fled from home to stay with her friend Raziel Shapiro.

"I remember how she was crying when she came," said Raziel's daughter Judy. "She stayed for two weeks."

Morris was gone for good when Golda returned home. The façade was finished. No more weekend visits. The children now would visit him. It would be years before the two would again talk to each other. Menachem pleaded with his mother. "Why are you doing this? . . . Why are you leaving my father? Why? Why?"

Sarah, with the sad eyes, watched, listened, said nothing.

What answer could Golda have given Menachem? Her simplest might have been, Your father is an excellent man, but he and I now live in different worlds.

Golda's world was fraught with anger. Bitter critics now accused Golda of being "against the workers." Some even said, "She enjoys being in the opposition. There is a sadistic streak in her." This feeling stemmed from Golda's proposal for a *mifdeh*, a day's pay from all Histadrut workers to help repair the damage done by Arab riots. The Hebrew word *mifdeh* meant "ransom" or "redemption," a debt of honor for a man at work to help others. She earlier had pushed through a similar *mifdeh* to create an unemployment fund. "I remember a very, very dear friend of mine telling me, 'Golda, you are destroying the Histadrut. You are demanding something that is impossible.'" At that time, people proposed that she go back to America for money rather than soak the Palestine Jewish workers. Golda's answer then was sharp: she would raise money in the United States to "aid the building of a country" but she would not ask American Jews "to pay doles for our poor." For her, it was a point of pride. The Yishuv must prove to the world that it could take care of its own. To do otherwise would be a blot and a shame. In this, she had the full support of Ben-Gurion, Katznelson, Shazar, and Remez.

Golda fought for her *mifdeh* ideas with a will "as strong as iron." To sell the unpopular *mifdeh*, she toured from one factory to another, trying to persuade workers to think outside of themselves, to realize that they were part of a people, part of a future state. In doing this, she answered the critics who claimed "she had no ideas of her own," that she was "merely the popularizer of the party viewpoint."

"When Golda was in a dilemma," said Aharon Remez, "she'd talk it over with my father, without any reservations. When he said something, she'd consider it more or less a moral license to do it."

Her final break with Morris—even though she never got a divorce —meant that she now needed Remez more, expected more from him. Remez quickly and completely filled her need. No more would he moralize, as in that earlier letter, about what she had done to poor Morris. Nor would Golda expect any discussion about his own wife, or Gusta. Remez was now her rock.

"I became aware of Golda very early," said Aharon Remez. "I have childhood memories of her. We lived near each other and Golda came to our house very often, and we went to hers."

Remez once returned from a ten-day trip to Paris, "obviously ill." Instead of going directly to bed, he asked his son, then a boy, to take him immediately to Golda's. It was in the early hours of the morning before he returned.

The word "love" in Hebrew encompasses much, the spiritual as well as the sexual. A close friend who had read Remez's correspondence with Golda remarked, "My eyes were filled with tears." Friends who regarded Golda as purely pragmatic would have been amazed at the tenderness, the deep sensitivity, the revealed aching loneliness and the poetry in her letters. Poetry came natural with Remez. "I found one poem he started that was three or four pages long," said his son. "I found over thirty versions of that same poem, the last one only five lines. He tried to think everything out to its purest form. . . . Every word like a pearl, every sentence like a diamond."

Golda's romance with Remez, however poetical, still had to fit in somehow with their consuming political responsibilities. Remez was the one who urged Golda to make her first short speeches in Hebrew, then acted as her cheering section, persuading her to do more. He also persuaded her to work on a text of a film of Zionist accomplishments in Palestine, a film to use in fund-raising in the States, and she wrote from Paris how difficult it was and how she was working on it day and night. Writing was the most difficult thing she ever had to do. Remez was also the one who taught Golda how to listen. "My father tried to talk with people who didn't think like him—while Golda liked to discuss issues with friends who did agree with her. My father would listen to other opinions, pick up the right points, and react, trying to bring them to his view. It took a long time before Golda could do this, too."

As Golda's responsibilities kept increasing in the demands of work and home, she told her son, "What I need is a wife."

Leah Biskin moved in as soon as Nomi Zuckerman left. "Leah was one of the whiniest persons I've ever known," said Nomi. "Her voice went 'Ya-ya-ya . . .' She was a loner. I don't know of any connections she had with any men."

Leah's ties with Golda were tight. They had the same background, knew the same people, had the same interests in everything from politics to music. "They always had a lot to talk about. I don't think it was good for Golda to be alone with her children at that time. She had too much guilt, and it showed." Leah became the proxy parent when Golda was away and the children resented it. Their father got a bookkeeping job in Jerusalem and boarded with the Zuckermans.

Morris's room in the Zuckerman house was very simple—a metal bed, and an old kneehole desk with his children's pictures on it. "I can see him standing before this picture of his children, for hours, with a cigarette in his mouth, humming, and it would break my heart," said Nomi.

On his wall, he still kept the print of Dante and Beatrice, an identical print of the one that Golda still kept on her bedroom wall, the two prints they had bought shortly after their marriage to symbolize their love and relationship.

Also in his room were British magazines on literature and music, some of them bound and lettered in his beautiful handwriting, an *Oxford English Dictionary* "that thick!" He loved crossword puzzles.

"He was like a father to me," said Nomi, whose own father, like Golda, had been away from home so much with his Zionist activity. "Every weekend we used to go for a walk all over Jerusalem. He knew it all, and he had such pride in it, such love for it.

"He was a love . . . he was simply an angel. We all loved him dearly."

Golda and her own parents had become closer after they had settled in Palestine. They both realized Golda's growing importance as a national figure, even came to her for financial advice. They also sat in with their grandchildren more often when Golda was away.

Shana, back from the United States, also moved into the breach, sharing her home and family with Menachem and Sarah. "My mother envied Golda, oh, yes," said Shana's daughter, Judy. "I even felt it then. That's why she tried to get her own reputation. She got a job in the Hadassah hospital as a dietitian."

Shana's relationship with her parents was still distant. When her mother was staying with Menachem and Sarah, Bluma suddenly started gasping for air. A young woman there rushed to the drugstore to call a doctor. The doctor thought it serious enough to call the family together. A stomach pump, however, revealed that Bluma had overeaten green grapes. Shana arrived, casually asked, "Mother, you don't feel good?" then quickly walked into the kitchen, showing no further concern, saying, "I'm hungry." The unfriendly observer described Shana as cold, hard, more difficult than her mother, a frigid personality—always a pall to everybody. More friendly critics recalled how willingly and how often Shana took care of Golda's children, how open her house was to many friends, and how fully she gave of herself for any community need.

Whatever quiet envy Shana had for Golda, her growing pride in Golda's accomplishments was even greater. She even started keeping a scrapbook of newspaper clippings about her. In a way, she saw Golda as a product of her creation, and Golda was the first to agree. Shana had a new house now and Golda and her children visited often. Shana was not one who changed much over the years—she was still as precise and orderly as always. Even in her cooking, she never deviated from a recipe. Golda also had an orderly mind but she was always ready to try anything new.

Golda seemed to move to different, but similar, apartments almost annually, a kind of Tel Aviv tradition. With her life so rootless, she needed to settle somewhere and bought an apartment in a housing project on Nardou and Hayarkon streets in north Tel Aviv, again with a veranda overlooking the sea. The heart of her home was still the built-in bookcase, a whole wall, for books, records, and the record player.

The language of the home was only Hebrew now. "Mother was adamant about that," said Sarah. Menachem and Sarah still played music together. "Sarah loved music but she didn't have the dexterity that Menachem did. He always had a great deal of bravura as a performer."

The emotional hurt of his parents' separation not only colored Menachem's character but visibly affected his work at school. His teachers overlooked much, and tried to be helpful, partly because his mother was Golda. "His life was terrible for years," recalled a family friend. "He suffered deeply."

"Sarah never spoke about it," Golda admitted, "but Menachem resented me for quite a few years." Years before, she said, Morris had left home "and the children suffered so terribly that I went and asked him to come back. It was my fault."

Asked if she had cried then, she answered, "Not really."

Nor did she cry this time, nor did she ask him back again. Many years later, discussing this, she said quietly, "I regret that we parted."

There was no regret then. With the façade finished, her open house was now even more open. "You never went to her house when somebody wasn't there. She had good taste in men and she liked the attention she received from them. It was all very natural and she didn't try to hide anything. Yes, she was beautiful then. She was no Marilyn Monroe but she was really terribly attractive physically. It was almost like looking at somebody else."

At that time, Golda seemed unconcerned about her public image. She surely never worked at it. Shazar made certain that Golda and her projects had proper publicity in *Davar*, the country's largest newspaper, of which he was an editor. Many of Golda's projects were not popular at first. They involved sacrifice, taxes, hardship. "She was, however, everybody's role model, everybody's ideal. People respected her. And her private life never became a matter of public interest. Nobody ever censured her for what she was doing, nobody ever pointed a finger at her as they later did with Moshe Dayan, because of his active love life."

What was most important to Golda was loyalty. It did not matter whether somebody agreed with her on everything, but it mattered completely whether or not she personally trusted that person. This to her was the most important element in the consideration of a person. She had been burned often by people who agreed with her privately on an issue and then disagreed with her publicly. Those people were on her black list. "And once you got on that list, you never got off. She never forgot. But, on the other hand, if you were on her white list, she welcomed you like a real Jewish mother and she'd go to the mat for you every time. If you were on her white list, you could do no wrong. There was no gray list. She was incapable of gray. It was always either black or white."

In the spring of 1938, the world of horror seemed to intensify for Jews. Hitler's Nazis had taken over Austria, and that country seemed to need no prodding to harass and arrest their 400,000 Jews. Gangs would force old people to scrub latrines with water laced with acid, mock them and beat them, vandalize Jewish shops and homes.

Whatever the world later believed of all this, there seemed general agreement that something should be done about the remaining Jews still alive in Germany. President Franklin D. Roosevelt organized an International Conference on Refugees, inviting delegates from thirty-two nations. The event was to celebrate the fiftieth anniversary of the Statue of Liberty. They met at the Hotel Royal, a posh French resort and spa in Évian-les-Bains, overlooking Lake Geneva, in July 1938.

The Grand Salon was magnificent, the horseshoe-shaped conference table most impressive. Behind the diplomats were two semicircular rows of assistants. Farther behind were the chairs for the audience and observers. Golda was an "observer." She was not used to sitting silently in the back of a room, unable to express herself on a burning issue.

The American delegate made an inspiring speech, then announced a slight rise in the United States immigration quota from Germany and Austria to 27,370 persons a year. He neglected to add that the quota had been filled for the next two years. One after another, delegates of other nations said it was a shame, and they were really sorry, but there was nothing they could do. Bolivia was more blunt: no Jewish immigrants would be permitted into their country. The Australian excuse for not accepting Jews into their enormous empty spaces was that Australia didn't have any anti-Semitism in the country "and if Jews come in, they will cause it." Only Santo Domingo agreed to accept some Jewish refugees into their tiny country.

Golda felt "sorrow, rage, frustration and horror. . . .

"I wanted to get up and scream at them all, 'Don't you know these numbers are human beings, people who may spend the rest of their lives in concentration camps, or wandering around the world like lepers, if you don't let them in?' ''

Golda also knew that the British had refused even to discuss the possibility of permitting these refugees to flow into Palestine, that the Jewish homeland dream would fail without immigrants. To make the dream real, they needed people more than they needed money, more than they needed land. The failure of the conference loomed as the failure of their Zionist future.

Reflecting years later, Golda said, "I realized that a world which is not necessarily anti-Semitic—because Hitler was denounced at that conference, and there was considerable pro-Jewish sentiment there—could stand by and see others who were weaker victimized." The lesson she learned: "We can't depend on others."

Nor did the world press see it as an important story. *The New York Times* only gave the conference a half column on page thirteen. The opening of an art exhibit by Hitler in Munich was reported in a story twice that size. The Jewish Agency held a press conference and the Agency representative gave "very, very acceptable answers" to reporters' questions "but Goldie was fabulous." "There is one thing I want to see before I die," the indignant Golda told reporters, "that no one will have pity on the Jews." She explained later that she had said that "because I felt that pity was the most Jews could ever obtain in their hour of need."

Golda's words echoed all over Palestine and she returned home a heroine. More and more now, she was "Our Golda." Only in her own home did she still feel the resentment of her children. Remarking later on the price of celebrity, she said, "Oh, yes, I paid a price to be what I am. I paid for it dearly."

But the newspapers were full of her, and her pictures were everywhere. "Morris had to pass a photographer's shop on the way to work," said Nomi Zuckerman, "and there was a portrait of Golda in the window. So every time he walked to work, or came home, this portrait of Golda met him coming and going."

This sudden celebrity did add to Golda's growing self-confidence. She still went to Remez as her personal supreme court on morality and wisdom, but she was now moving faster out of his shadow. Her voice at meetings was stronger and more certain. She never had compunction in saying what she felt, but now she had more faith that she was right.

The horror news out of Hitler's Germany never stopped. A Jewish boy had killed a Third Secretary at the German Embassy in Paris and the Nazis in Germany instituted its *Kristallnacht*, the "Night of the Broken Glass," setting 191 synagogues on fire, dragging Jews from their homes to beat them and hang them. Some had their feet tied to horse-carts on cobblestoned streets, so that their heads would bounce and crack on the stones.

Golda added her stronger voice to the need of a Fifth Aliyah, getting Jews out of Germany to Palestine, legally or illegally.

The head of the Intergovernmental Committee on Refugees proposed a number of plans afterward, one of them suggesting that the thirty-two nations each accept 25,000 refugees. All of them answered, "no, thank you." Dr. Chaim Weizmann had a bitter comment: "The world is divided between those countries that expel the Jews and those that won't let them in."

Golda stayed up all night writing an article for the Histadrut periodical saying that Jewish mothers in Germany "are asking for only one thing: take our children away, take them to any place you choose, only save them from this hell." In her plea to the Jewish community in Palestine, Golda emphasized, ". . . if we bring them here, to this country . . . here they'll be safe: safe for their mothers and safe for the Jewish people."

The British had other ideas. In their White Paper of 1939, they declared:

"His Majesty's Government therefore now declare unequivocally that it is not part of their policy that Palestine should become a Jewish state."

The Balfour Declaration seemed dead. The blunt Weizmann noted sadly, "We have been betrayed. . . . Ours is the sorrow, but not the shame."

The British could not have spelled out their new view more clearly:

Fifteen thousand Jews a year would be allowed into Palestine for five years. After that, "No further Jewish immigration will be permitted unless the Arabs of Palestine are prepared to acquiesce in it."

Why?

The answer was simple: the world didn't care.

Golda helped frame the Zionist reply:

"It is in the darkest hour of Jewish history that the British propose to deprive the Jews of their last hope and close the road back to their homeland."

The British plainly had decided that the problem of separate states was "impracticable." Critics noted the greater pro-Arab influence in the British Foreign Office, the increased British concern for Arab oil, and the general mood of appeasement of the Arabs in the same way that the British were then appeasing Hitler.

Jews all over Palestine paraded in protest. "I was thirteen years old," said Sarah, "and I went to all the demonstrations. Not my brother. He was an individualist, more interested in his music, in his cello. My father was like Menachem—he didn't like crowds."

Golda wrote her children in August of 1939 that there was a heavy feeling of the danger of war, but if war broke out, "Don't worry, I'll come home at once."

War came within weeks, in September, when Nazi Germany invaded Poland. Golda hurried home on a Jewish ship by way of Marseilles.

David Ben-Gurion once had told the Yishuv, "Jews should act as though we were the state in Palestine, and should so act until there will be a Jewish state." When the British exercised their mandate in their White Paper, and when war came, he said, "We do not regard the Mandate as our Bible, but the Bible as our mandate.... We shall fight the war as if there were no White Paper, and the White Paper as if there were no war."

"It was a very nice slogan," said Golda later, "but not so simple to implement."

13

Much of the world was still having its last innocent summer in 1939. The United States was so unprepared militarily that the army still used horses to pull artillery. That year Sikorsky built the first helicopter, the first nylon stockings went on sale, and the first baseball game was televised. *Gone With the Wind* was the big movie, *Grapes of Wrath* the big book, and the most popular songs were "God Bless America," "The Last Time I Saw Paris," and "I'll Never Smile Again."

But in Europe, a war was being fought. Nazi Germany had signed a pact with Soviet Russia, and Poland was attacked from both sides. Italy invaded Albania, Germany swallowed Czechoslovakia, Russia attacked Finland. The British sent an expeditionary force to France and evacuated the children from London.

The British concern for 20,000 Jewish refugee children from Hitler's Germany was not so keen. Chaim Weizmann pleaded with the British to permit these children entry into Palestine where they would be cared for. British officials weighed the matter, then decided against it because the Arabs would not like it.

A bitter Ben-Gurion told a secret meeting of his party, "If I knew that it was possible to save all the children of Germany by transporting them to England, and only half by transporting them to the Land of Israel, I would choose the latter, for before us lie not only the numbers of these children but the historical reckoning of the people of Israel."

Jewish children did not appear on the British military map. The Foreign Office was more enthusiastic about the slogan "Arabia for the Arabs." Their vision was to unite all Arab countries into a single force alongside the British. The British miliary saw this combined force standing up against the Germans if and when they swept through North Africa into Egypt, captured the Suez Canal, then fanned out into Palestine.

The grand mufti, who directed most Arab action in Palestine, had his own vision of the future. He flew to Berlin, pledging full Arab support to the Nazis. As Hitler's permanent guest, he made frequent radio appeals to all Arabs everywhere. The Arabs listened. When the British permitted voluntary noncombatant recruitment of Palestinian Arabs and Jews into the British army, not many Arabs volunteered. Since the British had an urgent need for doctors, drivers, ordnance help, they reluctantly accepted more Jewish volunteers but classified them as "Palestinians." It became a matter of irony that Jews had been known as "Palestinians" long before the Arabs. Since the early 1900s, Jews in Palestine had been referred to as "Palestinians," whereas Arabs sneered at the term, considering themselves part of Greater Syria.

Golda played a key role in urging Jews to volunteer to serve alongside the British. One of her many jobs was to represent the thousands of Jewish and Arab workers, all members of the Histadrut, who worked on British military bases. Some still called Histadrut a "dictatorship of the proletariat," but it remained a federation of Jewish and Arab workers of every political faction, freely electing their representatives in hotly contested elections. "I always considered myself part of a group," Golda later explained, then added, "It is significant that the first organization of Arab labor in this country was done by Jewish workers." During one negotiation for better wages and working conditions, Golda arrived at the office of a British major, heading a delegation of Arabs and Jews.

"The officer stayed seated while our delegation walked in. When Golda came in, he was the British gentleman offering a seat to the lady. Golda said no, she would not sit down until there were seats for the rest of her delegation. Seats had to be provided for all of them, including the Arab workers."

A Jew demanding chairs for Arab workers? Many were incredulous.

Golda saw it more simply. These Arabs in her delegation were Histadrut workers first, Arabs second.

Golda never had studied Arab history and her attitude toward Arabs was ambivalent, more instinctive than deep. As much as she accepted Arab Histadrut workers, she would not wipe out the memory of Arab snipers at Merhavia or Arab rioters killing and looting in Haifa and elsewhere. She had to compartmentalize these two views in her mind and it became increasingly difficult and tenuous.

More and more, Golda became the leading Jewish representative to the British occupation forces in Palestine. "I think they invented the post for her."

"Who else did we have?" asked Gershon Avner, who later became her assistant. "Golda was one of the few who could speak fluent English, who could cope with British officials, who had the confidence of our leadership, who had the full Histadrut background. We had many gifted people, but few who could do that job. And she had the added capacity to explain Jews and Jewish Palestine to non-Jews, most of whom knew nothing about us."

As a spokesman, also, for Jews everywhere, Golda became part of a secret committee organizing a network over all of Europe, warning Jews, "The ground is burning beneath your feet ... come to Palestine. ..." Golda and others busied themselves buying any available ships, usually antiquated cargo vessels and dilapidated river boats, and sneaking them into quiet French ports to pick up refugees. Golda's balcony, with its sweeping view of the sea, became a watching post for arriving ships. Those escaping the British gauntlet were hurried to different parts of Palestine with forged identification papers. Golda often went with Ben-Gurion or Remez to greet the incoming illegal immigrants in the dark of night on isolated beaches. She quickly learned how to use a pistol.

Sticking always in Golda's mind was the memory of those thirty-two nations in Geneva all piously saying how sad it was about these poor Jews, but most countries refusing to accept any refugees. Protesting this world apathy, Golda proposed a parade, similar to the one she had organized as a young girl in Milwaukee to protest pogroms in Poland.

"Look, you must do this," Golda told a reluctant British general, "or you will have constant disturbances among your Jewish workers." The threat worked. It was a spirit-lifting parade that deepened the determination of all those involved with the illegal immigration process.

The British attitude stiffened.

A Jewish worker in a British camp who had trained himself to read things upside down noted a cable from London on the desk of his British superior, advising that the political disadvantages of creating obligations to the Jews far outweighed the tactical advantages. This changed when the war worsened. Individuals such as Aharon Remez were permitted to enlist in the Royal Air Force.

"We had to struggle to get our men accepted to fight in the war against Hitler," recalled Golda. "They had this ridiculous, absurd idea that they could take only as many Jewish volunteers as Arab. But the Arabs weren't volunteering to fight against Hitler."

Of the 33,000 Palestine Jews who ultimately enlisted in the British army, many fought in North Africa, Italy, Austria, Crete, Syria, and Iraq. A total of 9,000 Arabs enlisted; half of them soon deserted or were discharged.

Part of Golda's job was to remind the British of all this, to prick their conscience when she could. Golda had minimal writing skill, but she had a way of packing considerable emotion into simple words in posters. One such poster concerned the sinking of the *Struma*, an "illegal" refugee ship filled with 769 Jews. The British had refused to admit them into Palestine, and the ship was later accidentally torpedoed by the Soviets in the Black Sea. It sank, leaving only a single survivor to tell the stark story.

Golda's daughter, Sarah, belonged to the Youth Movement and several afternoons a week, after school, went to secret meetings. Forbidden to discuss anything they did, even to parents, Sarah told her mother one night that she would be home very late. "We used to put up posters in the middle of the night, right under the noses of the British." Only this time Golda knew that it was her poster on the *Struma*.

"I stayed awake until dawn waiting for her to come home." The next morning neither of them mentioned what had happened, what each had done, "although I was dying to say something," said Golda.

"When Mother was with us, she always gave us the feeling that everything would be all right. She was so outgoing, so very optimistic, and she always laughed a lot," Sarah recalled. "She used to say I was pessimistic, and I think I was. I wasn't very open with my mother about private things, but my brother was. He was very loving, very close, and often demanding."

The strangeness of it was that here was Sarah, supposedly similar to Golda in many ways, fighting the same fight as her mother, completely dedicated to the same cause, demanding little from Golda, and getting less. Menachem, on the other hand, was more like his father, primarily preoccupied with his music, demanding much from his mother, and getting more. Partly it was perhaps because Menachem's original resentment toward his mother at the breakup of the marriage had turned into an adoring affection. He could show it, while Sarah—who may have felt the same—was still too private with her feelings.

Morris had gone back to the United States to visit his family in Philadelphia. His brother-in-law remembered how absolutely desolate he looked, "hunched over, brooding." His was then an empty life. There was no longer any poetry in it. The bridge to Golda had grown impossibly long. His children were emerging into their own persons, would soon have their own private lives. He had few close friends. His Philadelphia family seemed as devoted as ever, but they no longer depended on him, or even needed him. He felt like a loose pebble on a beach. He had not spoken to Golda for years. Nor would he talk about her to his sisters.

Six months later he returned to Palestine, mainly because of his children. Soon afterward Solel Boneh found him a job in Persia. The knowing elite smiled at the power of David Remez.

"Remez and Golda didn't live together, but Remez spent more time with Golda than he did at his own home. It was very discreetly covered with work. Even when they wrote letters to each other, it would start with the work they were doing together, then, inside the lines, you could read the private things, you could smell the love."

Increasingly often, they now expressed their love frankly and openly in their private letters.

When they were apart, or when one of them traveled, they wrote of their pain of separation, the sleeplessness, the longing, the terrible loneliness, the wish for touch. Golda repeatedly referred to the need for his strength.

"Remez created Golda, like Pygmalion and Galatea," insisted a mutual friend. "He tried to make her a carbon copy of himself, of what he was and what he thought and what he wanted done. He taught her how to manage politicians, how to read things, he gave her all the supply, all the basis to be what she became. He not only pushed her toward high things from the beginning, but he walked beside her. He was a good teacher, a constant adviser. He gave her his soul. Golda had Remez's soul in her body in everything she did, until she died."

The place in Jerusalem where they spent so much time together was a small hotel, a pension, on a little side road, where many visiting Histadrut executives stayed. "When people want to be together, they can be together. They found ways."

"She was a person in her prime, a human being. Who would expect her to be alone?" The more caustic critics commented, "Well, Golda didn't read books so she had to do *something* at night."

"She is worth a sin," said Tehilah Shapiro, quoting a Polish expression, referring to Golda's love life. "She had so much charm, the way she spoke, dressed, even the braid in back of her head. She was also a bit of a coquette, and she had taste. Every morning she would put on a corset, straighten out. Yes, yes, there were romances, the first with Shazar, then with Remez. Berl, too, would arrive, knock on the door and ask if Golda was home."

"There was always jealousy around her," added Yehudit Simchoni, a member of the first Knesset. Simchoni added that Golda once had told her, "with much embarrassment," that it took Berl's wife a long time to be convinced that there was no romance between her husband and Golda.

Golda was so private that she told nobody everything. Regina admittedly never asked Golda about the men in her life "even though I knew." She knew only some of them. Most of her intimate friends knew even less. Marie Syrkin, who knew more than anyone, admitted knowledge of only two of Golda's "long-lasting relationships," and insisted that Golda never had any overlapping love affairs.

Golda belonged to a generation for whom an emotional commitment was a serious thing, even at a time when the free-love concept presumably flourished. Seemingly casual affairs were seldom trivial. With all this, most marriages remained intact, even when an affair grew more public. Ben-Gurion told the weeping, jealous wife of a Jewish leader, "You have to get used to it." Elsewhere, B-G added, "Great men's private lives and public lives are often conducted on parallel planes that never meet. . . . A man may be a saint all his life and be unfitted to public tasks; and the opposite is also possible...." The fact was that Ben-Gurion's own love affairs had driven his wife to such despair that she had threatened to kill herself.

As much as Remez loved Golda to the end of his life, he was an overwhelming romantic whose roving eyes never grew dry or cold. Nor was Golda one to cry in a quiet corner. As an aphrodisiac, power worked for women as well as men. Gossip about Golda was a constant in a country where so few women were in positions of real power.

A French reporter once asked Golda, "Has love had a major role in your life?"

Golda seemed surprised. "Love?" The reporter then noted there was a long silence before she finally replied, "I think so."

At forty-one, Golda was at her peak when Zalman Aranne came into her life. If Shazar enriched her mind and soul, and Remez broadened her political mind and enraptured her heart, Zalman Aranne filled her with fantasy. His intensity was his most irresistible quality to so many women.

Aranne deeply felt that the fate of the country was on *his* shoulders, that action must be taken on everything *instantly*, and there was not a moment to be lost. So overwhelming was this feeling that he occasionally seemed almost wild. The comment he himself often repeated was, "I am crazy one day a week, but I never know which day."

Aranne was so unpredictable, so outrageous that he would make Golda laugh out loud. Aranne adored Golda. In his office, he was often a martinet, but in Golda's presence "he was the complete courtier, almost a romantic adolescent." "The only time I ever knew him to change his shirt deliberately was when he went to see either Ben-Gurion or Golda. Whenever she came to him or he went to her, the two would sit for hours in an intimate, laughing way, talking freely as if there was nobody else in the room."

"I remember asking Aranne about Golda," said one of his closest friends. "I said, 'There are all kinds of stories that you are having an affair with Golda. Is it true?' And he smiled enigmatically and spread out his hands and said with a twinkle, '*Vox populi.*' It was his way of saying that if the people are all saying it, then it must be true. And it was.

"There was a conference on something in a hotel in Jerusalem. I don't even know what it was about anymore. But we all had rooms on the same floor. One of our people told me that he got up very early in the morning because he couldn't sleep and decided to take a walk. As he walks down the hall, who does he see coming out of Golda's room but Remez. That was no news. We all knew about Remez and Golda. But then he comes back from his walk, going to his room, and who does he see going *into* Golda's room but Aranne. Well, I knew about Aranne, too, but *one after another!* If anybody else had told this to me, I might not have believed it. But the man who told it to me was David Hacohen,* the head of the Solel Boneh, a very conservative, respectable man who was much more shocked by it than I was."

With a small smile, the storyteller remarked that all this happened long before breakfast, "but of course they could have been just *talking*."

"Zalman and Golda would often meet at my house," said Golda's close friend Masha Rabinovich. "Zalman lived not far from me and I worked with him in organizing a labor college for workers. Zalman and Golda were very close. It was difficult for most people to work with Zalman, but not Golda. They worked well together. Zalman was crazy in the whole head, but crazy in a good meaning, a nice craziness. He was a very intelligent man. He had a full heart but not the capacity to talk about it with people. He was a very closed person, private like Golda. I remember him standing by my window, talking aloud to himself, saying, 'The soul of another person is a dark thing, but your soul is darker than dark.'"

Zalman Aranne (originally Ziama Ahronowitz) was a year younger than Golda, born in the Ukraine. He received a religious education, studied agriculture at Kharkov University, and came to Palestine in 1926. His wife was much older than he, and he did not have the loving family life that Remez had. When Golda met Aranne, he was secretary of the Labor Council. He had been secretary of the Mapai Party when it was founded in 1930, the party to which Golda and Remez and Ben-Gurion and Shazar all belonged.

"Aranne was very beautiful—not good-looking, beautiful," said Rivka

---

*David Hacohen (1898–1986) came to Palestine from Russia in 1907, served in the Turkish army during World War I, one of the founders and directors of Solel Boneh. During World War II, he was Haganah liaison officer to the British army. He was later a Mapai member of the Knesset and chairman of its Foreign Affairs and Security Committee, and later, Israel's first ambassador to Burma.

Idelson. "We came from Russia. I was a kid of five and he was twenty, or something. So beautiful he was, I can't forget it."

He loved his mother, but hated his father, a rigid, fanatic Jew. A rabbi slapped his face when he was ten years old and he never believed in religious leaders after that.

"And it was like he came from the jungle. He didn't know what electricity was. He was sent to us. I was the interpreter. I told him about the buttons to call the police, the landlady, the fire department. He was like a kid, a grown-up kid. He called in a false alarm and had to pay a fine. Excited about everything. Ashamed that he didn't know it.

"He was very concentrated with himself. Wanted to prove to everybody that he was better than Berl Katznelson. He was always frustrated with himself that he didn't do more. He was frustrated all the time.

"He was an educated man, a self-made man, an interesting man. He tried to write poetry but he was no poet. He once had a passport picture taken and he said, 'Such a beautiful picture.' And it was. And I wanted it. I must have it somewhere.

"He was sensitive, easily insulted. He never said, 'Why don't you agree with me?' He would say, 'Why do you insult me?' Always defiant."

Aranne was not at the hub of power like Remez, but he was close to it, and jealous of it, and jealous of Golda. Golda herself was torn. Aranne was so much fun, so persuasive, with all the brilliance and idealism of Remez. But Remez had reached a deeper chord, and was there first. She pleaded with Remez not to ignore her, not to harden his heart. She tried to explain her tension, how hurt she was when they were alone together at a meeting and he wouldn't talk to her. She couldn't stand being scorned by him, she said, because she loved him so much, his wishes were her wishes, their love shone for her in the dark.

Who would ever have suspected that Golda had all this romantic poetry within her, that this decisive, pragmatic woman was filled with so much loneliness and jealousy and love? While many in her inner circle knew about Golda and Remez, and some knew about Shazar, only a handful knew about Aranne.

But nothing consumed Golda so completely as her cause, her party, her country—more important to her than family, friends, lovers. She was not one of those who could successfully compartmentalize her life. If her cause called, everything else was squeezed into a corner. What she could do, better than most, was to maintain a tight mask over her private passions. "Some people are surrounded by many people, but are alone."

In a country so small and so open, privacy in any form was unusual, especially on her level. It made the tight mask understandable. She wanted to cherish any small privacy she might manage. Perhaps it was also the only way she could function professionally, since these were people she dealt with almost every day.

She told friends repeatedly how much she loved her independence, "not having to call anybody to say she would be late," the freedom of impulsive decision, the ability to get up in the middle of the night to listen to the radio, or work, or even wash the floor—a kind of thinking-time therapy for her.

Masha Rabinovich was one of Golda's few intimate women friends. She held a special place in Golda's soul. Masha was much younger than Golda "but we were *chaverot.*" "I'm only a housewife, a friend of the kitchen—of her kitchen and my kitchen. We spoke in Yiddish. Hebrew we talk, but Yiddish talks by itself. My family is from Minsk and my mother language was Hebrew but that great writer Sholem Aleichem once took my hand and spoke to me in Yiddish and he said he couldn't understand a girl who didn't speak Yiddish. From that moment on, I learned the language.

"The best place to speak is over a cup of tea or coffee. Golda had a whole collection of kettles of different sizes, a kettle for four glasses, for five glasses, and she had one *enormous* kettle. She had a sensitive side and it was very good to sit with her and talk about all the little things in our lives, the daily interlocking things. Like threading a needle—soon you have a carpet. A carpet on a stage. Life is like a carpet.

"She had a good touch of hands. It was a good feeling when we held hands. You could feel the running of the blood, a warm thing. She had wonderful hands. And she had a very good laugh. Yes, we laughed together. And we also cried together."

Invisibly eavesdropping on these two women drinking tea, who would imagine that Golda was now one of the fifteen people in Palestine deciding the daily fate of the Yishuv. Masha saw mostly her soft side, most others felt her *chutzpah,* her brassy kind of courage. (*Chutzpah* was best defined as "that quality enshrined in a man who, having killed his mother and father, throws himself on the mercy of the court because he is an orphan.")

Golda faced problems without flinching. "She had this uncanny sense of getting at the heart of a problem, making quick decisions, one, two, three. It was her great gift and her great strength." She hid little in her public face; she was "of a piece." "There is no recipe," Golda explained. "The only thing I tried to do was differentiate between what is basic and essential, the things one could fight for." She might have added: fight and win. Whatever qualms and doubts she ever had on issues were usually hidden under a constant face of self-confidence. She had learned early from Remez and Ben-Gurion to make a decision decisively, no matter how indecisive you might feel.

The pull of power is a vortex, almost a gravitational force. Everybody on the rim gets sucked in. Golda was no exception.

"I have no ambition to become somebody," she once said, and may even have believed it. She was uncomfortable with the very notion of being a seeker of power, a friend insisted. Perhaps it was true when she first went to the kibbutz, but it changed. Her closest friends felt her ambition. Golda never refused a position of power, even if she sometimes mildly, modestly protested.

Yishuv women proudly followed Golda's upward career—she was their shining example of the potential. Feminism was not Golda's fight, and she often stubbornly insisted she was not a feminist, but she gave mixed signals. She did say, "To my great sorrow, there are fewer women, very few, working in so-called men's jobs."

"The thing is," Golda said, "even among the best of men, the most liberal, it is assumed that if a woman is to be elected to anything, she must be so much better than anyone else. I remember so many women saying we will do this and we will do that, and we will do it better. I got up once and said, 'I don't promise to be better.' I don't know why I should promise. A woman does not have to prove that she will do wonders. If she is capable and accepted and will do her work well, and is devoted, then she will do it better. All for the good, but she should not get selected because she will be better than all the men. No."

In a world at war, Palestine was an isolated, remote footnote in 1939. But to the people there, problems were still real and immediate. Things were happening too fast for rule books or bureaucracy. There was no time to pass the buck. Decisions had to be made directly, immediately. Where to place a factory or a kibbutz or a stockade? Where to get more arms and where to hide them? How to speed up the flow of illegal immigration? How to share the work when there wasn't enough work for everybody? Her prime principle was that the only acceptable cure for unemployment was employment. In sharing available work you minimized doles and maximized self-respect. "Our deeds are better than our words," she liked to say. "Come to Palestine and see for yourself!"

With so many decisions affecting so many people, she sometimes felt overwhelmed and confided to Remez that friends thought her strength was limitless, but the truth was that she was experiencing a terrible tiredness.

Too many people still visualized Palestine in terms of picture post-cards, high drama, and biblical references remembered from their youth.

According to a brochure at the 1939 World's Fair in New York, "the heartbeat of Palestine is the rhythmic stroke of hammers of Jewish pioneers building a country, transforming wilderness into civilization ... strong, brawny bodies hewing a glorious, pulsating tomorrow out of a barren listless yesterday. The new Palestine is the triumph of life defeating death. The victory of idealism and heroism over unwilling, reluctant elements. The history of Jewish Palestine is an epic that sings of the courage and tenacity of the Chalutzim who conquered swamps, stamped out malaria, harnessed rivers, fertilized deserts, built schools, hospitals, factories ... a nation on the march. ..."

Mixed with the glowing adjectives was much truth, but what was missing was the bleakness of so much of this barren land, this dry, rocky place with tiny scattered settlements. A newly arrived Italian-Jewish refugee that year caught some of it as he arrived in Tel Aviv:

"Facing me, rising from an expanse of sand, were lines of flat roofs, colorless cement cubes, with a splash of green here and there. The entire harbor consisted of a small jetty ... a few cargo ships waiting beyond the shallow water.... The people I saw outside the tiny port all appeared perspiring and scruffy, the men in sandals and shorts, the women in sandals and khaki bloomers, hitched up to the tops of their thighs with elastic. Women covered their heads with faded scarves of coarse blue cotton, men wore peaked caps....

"I perceived ... the power of the people who, from ideological choice rather than necessity, wanted to appear poorer and rougher than my father's peasants. They exuded an affluent misery. They displayed a life-style that signaled to me unequivocally that I had fallen into a world of frenetic action . . . with no hiding places for the soul . . . a living collection of tattered styles, languages, customs, costumes, and habits. It was a history that jumbled together in disorderly, unharmonic, unblended terms. All the passions and hopes were here. . . ."

He described the "squat, dusty-brown buses with rows of hardwood seats and dirty windows with wire netting on the outside, to protect against the stones and sometimes the bombs that the Arabs had gotten into the habit of throwing." His memories included a shuffling man with baggy black Turkish trousers selling an orange drink, clapping metal castanets to attract attention, pouring the drink for customers in a common cup which he moistened with a little water afterward, "erasing with his thumb any trace left by the customer's lips."

Palestine coins, he said, bore the word "Palestine" in English, Arabic, and Hebrew, the Arabs objecting to the Jews using the words "Land of Israel" and settling for initials, and the Jews objecting to the Arabs using the words "Land of the Philistine."

He described the lounging Arabs in front of hovels, sucking on their water pipes, selling sugar cane, in contrast to Jews sitting on wooden benches in a kibbutz, talking politics while they washed their feet.

He quoted a woman who said, "Palestine is a land where caresses are made with sandpaper," and a writer who noted, "The people laughed in Hebrew during the day and cried in many languages at night."

Golda explained why the Arabs got along better with the British officials and the Jews got more of the "sandpaper caresses." "Arabs recognized the British as their superiors. We looked upon ourselves as their equals, and that they couldn't take. And the Arabs were so *nice*."

Golda often bent over backwards trying to understand the British position. She was, after all, the Yishuv liaison, and her contact was persistent. "What could they do?" she asked rhetorically, when the British were ordered to search houses and the people refused to let them search. "Look, I told the high commissioner that I don't think any other army would have behaved better."

If there was one thing the British resented most about Palestinian Jews at that time, it was the fact that they "were meant to be a subject of British rule; instead they behaved as if they were an independent nation."

The British use of force varied, minimal in some places, brutal in others. In their need to maintain order, their own forces stretched thin, the British finally established the Notrim, the Jewish Settlement Police. Understandably, most such police also belonged to the Haganah. The Haganah (earlier called Hashomer) was an underground Jewish military organization born in 1920 during a time of Turkish control, primarily for self-defense against Arab rioters. Jews decided they could not depend on the Turks, or later the British, to defend them from the Arabs. Unless stirred up by the mufti, most Arabs lived peacefully alongside the Jews. But the mufti seldom kept quiet for long.

Arab terrorists concentrated on isolated Jewish settlements until the Haganah fortified such areas with barbed-wire fences, concrete positions, trenches, floodlights, and specially trained night squads. Then terrorists turned to the roads, disrupting transportation, killing passengers in buses and cars.

Before World War II, the Haganah had grown into a force of 25,000 men and women, all volunteers. A British captain, Orde Wingate,* helped train them into professional soldiers. Guns were smuggled in with barrels of cement but soon there was a secret arms industry producing its own hand grenades, mortars, shells, submachine guns. Arms caches were hidden in selected parts of the country. Even Golda's father built a secret room in his house to hide Haganah arms.

Out of the Haganah came the Palmach in 1941, an elite mobile assault force available on twenty-four-hour notice to serve anywhere as a regional fighting reserve. Palmach units generally located at key kibbutzim, earning their keep by working on the farms.

No longer were the Jews in Palestine just a ragtag bag of idealists. They had formed their own shadow government with its secret army and its well-organized institutions functioning under terrible conditions. The Yishuv was now flexing its political muscles, readying itself to step across the invisible line to statehood. In May 1942, at the Biltmore Hotel

*Charles Orde Wingate (1903–44), British army officer who served in Palestine during the 1936–39 riots. Became strong supporter of Zionist cause, known as He-Yedid (The Friend). Trained special night squads of Haganah fighters to combat Arabs. His grandfather had conducted a Church of Scotland mission in Hungary for poor Jews, and his parents served as missionaries in India, where he was born. The British transferred Wingate out of Palestine, forbidding him to return. Wingate Square in Jerusalem is named after him, and so are a children's village, a forest, and a school.

in New York at an Extraordinary Zionist Conference, David Ben-Gurion, as chairman of the Jewish Agency Executive, insisted that Jews could no longer depend on the British to establish a Jewish National Home in Palestine, that Jews should plan for their own "Jewish Common- wealth" with unrestricted immigration. This was the first time since Balfour that the idea of a Jewish state for all Jews became the official policy of the Zionists. Not only was Palestine the place where Jews *should* be, but it now seemed the only hope for their survival. The new Nazi nightmares added frenetic immediacy to the question of *aliyah*. "The hosts of time cannot subdue it," the poet Rachel had once said of Zionism. "To be a Zionist, it is not necessary to be mad, but it helps," said Chaim Weizmann.

There was blood all over the world in 1941 when the Japanese bombed Pearl Harbor and Germany declared war on the United States. Italy sided with Germany and even bombed Tel Aviv. "Well, Mother, you never gave us a toy gun. You believed there would be no use for guns," Menachem said. "But here we are, we live all our lives with them." Even Sarah now learned how to use a pistol.

Golda's work consumed her more than ever, and her children saw less and less of her. "She always felt she had wronged them by not being with them day and night, which of course is ridiculous. Her children admired her tremendously. They adored her and obviously were a thousand times better off with the mother they had," said Marie Syrkin.

Golda doubted this. "Even after they grew up, I often wondered, what do they really have in their hearts? What do they *feel* toward me?"

Sarah had a sad way of describing her mother's too-frequent trips abroad: "She always brought us presents." The intimation was clear. She would have preferred so much more the greater gift of Golda's time. Even on Shabbat, when Golda invariably stayed at home, they still had to share her with a never-ending flow of visitors.

Menachem had quit high school to attend night school so that he would have more time during the day to practice his cello. On a rare Shabbat afternoon, Golda enjoyed sitting on her balcony in her house- coat, endlessly chain-smoking her Chesterfields, surveying the sea, and listening to her son play the cello. The children hated her smoking, "but only Menachem spoke up about it."

Sarah was more caught with the Zionist cause and her Youth Group, and was increasingly determined to make her future pioneering the land on some frontier kibbutz.

The British had forbidden the creation of new settlements, but where else could they put the large number of new immigrants, legal or illegal? Once such settlements were built, did the Jews not have a right to defend them? Their answer was yes. "We have no alternative," Golda emphasized. A slogan circulated throughout Palestine about this time: "One more rifle, one more plow, one more horse, one more *dunam* of land."

Zionists had a strong supporter in the new prime minister of Great Britain, Winston Churchill. He firmly believed in a Jewish national homeland, and felt that Britain already had treated the Arabs most generously in creating independence for Saudi Arabia, Iraq, Syria, and Transjordan. With the exception of a few leaders, he said, "The Arabs had been virtually of no use to us in the present war."

More horror news seeped out of the Nazi concentration camps. The Polish government in exile in London published recent reports from Auschwitz: 4,000 dead by shooting, 2,900 by gassing, 2,000 by phenol injections, 1,200 beaten to death, "and 800 had committed suicide by walking into the camp's electric fence." This did not stir the compassion of Viscount Cranborne, who refused to relax immigration quotas of refugees into Palestine "because there might then arise shortages of housing accommodation and food . . . there are not unlimited supplies."

Let them come, Golda insisted, we Jews will take the responsibility of feeding them, of finding them homes.

Cranborne was more concerned about the number of refugees coming into Britain. His suggestion was the creation of a Jewish state in Africa "but not for any love of the Jews." "Only thus will we be able to get some of the Jews out of this country, in which there are now far too many."

Zionist leaders quickly dismissed the African proposal: "Any such idea was like asking children to forget their mother when they know she is alive and longing for them."

Chaim Weizmann, who felt both befriended and betrayed by the British, now warned: "We are a stiff-necked people, and a people of long memory. We never forget."

When the first detailed news of concentration-camp murder was made known, Golda raised the question at Histadrut meetings about the refugees. "What can we do, first of all, to let them know that *we* know and we're doing something about it? And second we need to do *something*." "At a time of such tragedy, there's a feeling that one should be part of it. And if you weren't, well—it's as though you weren't where you should have been."

The British reluctantly agreed to train several hundred Jewish paratroopers to drop into Hungary for sabotage and refugee rescue. Increased pressure from the British Foreign Office canceled this operation. It was later reinstituted, with only several dozen paratroopers. The American Office of Strategic Services sent Major Arthur Goldberg, an old friend of Golda's, to help organize the drop.

One of the paratroopers was a handsome man who had endeared himself to Golda during her kibbutz days. He was Enzo Sereni, whose father had been physician to the king of Italy. Sereni was one of those highly sophisticated men who became kibbutz pioneers, and he always volunteered for missions of danger. He was one of the few who went among the Arabs during their 1937 riots, trying to cool their heat with reason. He repeatedly went into Iraq to rescue Jews during the anti-Jewish riots there. "Don't go," Golda pleaded with him now. "You are really much too old. [He was forty.] You are much too valuable here." Sereni smiled, kissed her good-bye, and never returned. He was later killed in a gas oven in the Dachau concentration camp. Two of the paratroopers were women. One of them, the poet Hannah Senesh, twenty-three years old, was caught, tortured, and executed in Budapest. The mission had failed.

The German lyric poet Rilke had said that the greatest power of self-respect was "learning to live with the questions that have no answers." One such unanswerable question now came from the beleaguered Jews in the Warsaw ghetto, who were being systematically murdered by the Nazis in 1942. Their question of Palestinian Labor Zionists: should they surrender or die fighting?

Party committees debated the issue. "How could we in Tel Aviv tell them to die?" Golda wondered. The question was still being debated in Tel Aviv when word came that Warsaw Jews had made their own decision: to die fighting.

"I remember when we got the news," said Golda. "We broke off our discussions and without any speeches, without anyone saying a word, it was absolutely clear that our lives had been given fresh meaning."

A slim, dark girl, Zivia Lubetkin, a Warsaw ghetto fighter and survivor, finally made her way to Palestine. At a meeting of Vaad Hapoel, Golda told her how desperately they had tried to make contact, to give some sign of solidarity, to provide some help, any help, and how helpless they had felt when they couldn't. They were part of one movement, she said, "we the parents and you the children, but on that day we felt that the parents were unworthy of the children."

"In Warsaw's attitude toward the ghetto, there was disgust and compassion, shame and anti-Semitism." There were many Poles who saved Jews from death, but there were many more "who exhibited a mindless lack of feeling. The carousels full of laughter, turning around as clouds of smoke rose from the adjacent burning ghetto ..."

More detailed stories were coming out of Nazi-occupied Poland. "Pious Jews had their beards removed by blunt instruments, which tore their skin, or had their beards burned off. Swastikas were branded on the scalps of some victims, others were subjected to "gymnastics" such as "riding on other victims' backs, crawling on all fours, singing and dancing, or staging fights with one another.... The Nazis took a special sadistic pleasure in violating religious feelings ... burning down synagogues ... or turned them into stables, warehouses, bathhouses or even public latrines.... Several hundred synagogues were destroyed in the first two months of the occupation.... People were dragged from their homes, tortured and beaten, cleaned latrines with their bare hands, or in the case of women, washed the floor with their own underwear."

The pattern was humiliation, torture, and death. In a single day, as many as fifteen thousand unarmed men, women, and children were slaughtered. The world had been horrified in 1906 when a czarist pogrom in Bialystok killed seventy Jews. On June 27, 1941, a thousand Jews were burned alive in the synagogue; a month later 3,000 more were killed in a field outside of town.

Golda heard the story of Rivka Yosselevska, a young woman from Pinsk who had escaped to Palestine. She told how Pinsk Jews "were chased like animals to the central square of the town, where they were kept until the next morning without food or water. Then, when they were exhausted by fear and fatigue, all were marched outside the town. They reached a huge ditch and were told to stop and undress.

"Even when I saw the naked people who had arrived before us, I still did not believe they would kill us. I hoped it would be just torture," she said. Taking off her clothes, she stood there clinging to her six-year-old daughter. Her mother, her grandmother, and her sister were all nearby. Her hopes were in vain. The SS started shooting the Jews one by one, firing point-blank into the back of each victim's head, then kicking the body into the open pit. She saw her father and mother disappear into the ditch. Then the Germans approached her grand-mother, who was holding two little girls in her arms, comforting them and pointing to heaven where they would soon meet all their beloved ones. In a moment all three were shot. "Then I saw my sister embrace a girlfriend; the two of them tried to cover their nakedness with each other's bodies, pleading with a uniformed SS man to spare their young lives. In reply they were both shot and went down. As I stood there paralyzed with horror, my little daughter Malka was wrung from my arms and killed."

At that particular moment, she said, she felt nothing more. The German who shot her missed his aim, and the bullet merely grazed her head. She only felt a booted leg kicking her into the ditch to bleed to death or die of suffocation. By some miracle she did not die and alone escaped from the pit, was found by partisans, and survived.

How many of those people in Pinsk had Golda known, or had her parents known? Had her family not emigrated to America, she would have been in that pit.

She tried to tell some of this to a British official she liked. "I could see in his worried, rather kind blue eyes that he thought I had gone quite mad." Then he gently told her, "You mustn't believe everything you hear. . . ."

They were not the only ones who didn't believe. Golda sometimes found it difficult to make her own people believe what she knew.

"It's bad enough that the rest of the world doesn't and won't help us, but our own people, some of them, just don't understand what is at stake." Even *Davar*, the highly respected daily Hebrew newspaper, was skeptical about the early news of horror from concentration camps. Printing an account of the reported killing of 242,000 Jews on the Russian front in 1942, *Davar* put the story in the lower left-hand corner of their front page with the disclaimer that it should be taken with reservation.

It printed similar reservations about the first news of the Nazi gas chambers. The tragedy was simply too enormous for almost anybody to believe.

What depressed Golda was the constant debating in committees about everything, almost to an infinity. Arguing seemed to be a national sport, and the answer to everything was "Why?" What made the debating so difficult was that every person seemed perfectly capable of giving both sides of an issue with equal logic and passion. After a convincing argument, the same person would say, "But on the other hand, under circumstances, the opposite is true. . . . Many things that aren't the same are equally right and many things that are wrong at one time are right at another . . ." All this was part of traditional training in the Talmud.

Golda found too many peers to be abstract visionaries and philosophers. Her own pragmatic mind had always been oriented toward results and responsibility. She found it hard to understand how people could believe in something and not try to implement it.

It was a tense time for Golda: the nerve-racking relations with the British, where she was always the angry suitor; her complex love life, full of jealousy and conflict; her marvelous energy suddenly drained by frequent illness; the daily conflict with small bureaucratic minds as she tried to get things done.

Berl Katznelson had set forth the new policy on illegal immigration: "From now on, not the pioneer but the refugee will lead us." Golda tried to control her emotions on most issues but not on the refugees. Whenever Golda wanted action, she always found it in the home or office of Eliahu Golomb. He looked more like a scholar than what he was—commander-in-chief of the Haganah. He was a small man who spoke softly, and the most expressive parts of his face were his "rather beautiful eyes." A friend of Berl's, a high school classmate of Moshe Sharett (who became his brother-in-law), Golomb had come to Palestine from Russia in 1909, "a very persuasive man with definite ideas." Out of his Rothschild Avenue apartment, or office in room 17, "people would go on their various missions." Golda regarded Golomb as "one of the real founders" of the future state. "I don't think the light was ever turned off in Eliahu's home during the entire war." Nor was the room ever empty.

One of the regulars in the room, a right hand to Golomb, was Dov

Hos,* who was also Golomb's brother-in-law. Golda had worked with Hos in England, and worked with him more intimately later. Not physically imposing, he still had "tremendous charm." "Everyone who saw him for the first time fell in love with him." Neither Golomb nor Hos would live long enough to see the state of Israel established.

These were men Golda trusted, respected, loved. To such men, her loyalty was complete. "But God forbid if she didn't like you. She could be intensely vindictive. And she remembered. She never missed anything anybody ever said or did." "She had no side, absolutely no side. She was always natural, always herself." People knew what she felt, when she felt it, "and she was not magnanimous." This meant she made enemies.

In a complaint to the Secretariat of the Vaad Hapoel, Golda angrily reported, "I have a feeling that my brother-in-law Korengold was let out of work because he is my brother-in-law. . . . I can't accept the fact that my sister's family has to suffer because I am a member of the Secretariat." She insisted she wasn't applying pressure because "I don't have a right to." Until they proved to her that Korengold's job didn't suit him, she said, she could only interpret it that he was fired because of her. If this was so, "it isn't possible to continue on my job."

Writing to Remez about how difficult and complicated things had become in other areas, she repeated that she couldn't work under the current conditions and asked him to help her find a way.

There was a party with cakes, an event in those days of rationing when one needed special permits to get eggs. Everybody at the party seemed to be having a good time except Golda. "Golda obviously had offended a large number of people by something she had said or done, and nobody now remembers what it was . . ."

Golda sat in an easy chair at the edge of the room, almost like a pariah. Everybody was laughing and joking, "but no one spoke to Golda,

*Dov Hos (1894–1940) came to Palestine from Russia in 1906, became a protégé of Berl Katznelson, and helped initiate military training among Jews for future events. He had been part of the Jewish Legion, helped pioneer aviation in Palestine, was one of the founders of the Public Works Office of the Histadrut, served as deputy mayor of Tel Aviv. Golda knew him best when he was Yishuv representative to Great Britain. Golda succeeded him as political head of the Histadrut when Hos was killed in an auto accident.

no one! Everybody ignored her as if she wasn't there, just passed her by. I have no idea why, or what it was. But I've never seen her so cowed."

Remez entered the room, and he was the only one who went to her, *"the only one!"*

It would never happen again. Never again would she be ignored anywhere. Never again would she be so cowed.

14

The date was September 1943. The court trial in Palestine concerned two young Palestinian Jews accused of stealing arms from the British army in order to turn them over to the Haganah. Golda's testimony was memorable in its simplicity, clarity, dignity.

There were many questions, some of them patronizing:

Q. You are a nice, peaceful, law-abiding lady, are you not?
A. I think I am.
Q. And you have always been so?
A. I have never been accused of anything.

The judge then asked a policeman to show Golda a photograph and asked, "Do you know this man?"

"I was horrified," said Golda afterward, recalling that she had seen that man almost every day outside her office. Golda debated within herself: "Should I know him or shouldn't I know him? And I decided according to what my mother always used to say: when you say no, you never regret it. So I said, 'No.'"

Golda felt the judge was "bursting with hatred" when he read a speech and asked if she had made that speech.

"And I said 'Yes, and I think it's quite good.'"

It was a speech in which she had said, "If a Jew who is armed in self-defense is a criminal, then all Jews in Palestine are criminals.... If a Jew or Jewess who uses arms to defend himself against firearms is a criminal, then many new prisons will be needed."

Then, after further questions:

> President of the Court: I ask you to limit yourself only to what concerns this case, or otherwise we'll soon be back to a period of two thousand years ago.
>
> A: If the question had been solved two thousand years ago ...
>
> President of the Court: Keep quiet!
>
> A: I object to being addressed in that manner!
>
> President of the Court: You should know how to conduct yourself in Court.
>
> A: I beg your pardon if I interrupted you, but you should not address me in that manner!

With this single appearance in court, Golda enlarged her national celebrity. Before that, she was an intimate of the élite, well known to the various secondary layers of leaders, the concentric circles of power, and moderately recognized among the people. But now, suddenly, she was their daring voice, speaking up without fear to the all-powerful British. People saw her not only as a pillar of strength but as a pillar of fire.

"... you should not address me in that manner! ..."

The people reveled in it. Suddenly, she was their Deborah, the biblical prophetess, the proclaimed mother of ancient Israel, who led the war of liberation from the oppression of Jabin, king of Canaan, and promised her people, "I will deliver him unto thy hand." Newspapers headlined the story, featured her picture. Her father proudly toured his neighborhood, saying, "See, look what my Golda did ..."

Golda was not exultant. Her own personal life was in turmoil. Remez had broken with her, probably because of her relationship with Aranne. Golda was distraught, not willing to give him up, not ready for a choice. Her letters spoke of anguish and yearning and personal pain. He had become a stranger, she said, and left her with a terrible loneliness. She longed for the strength of his look and the touch of his hands. She begged him not to harden toward her. She reaffirmed her own great love for him. She knew she had hurt him and begged his forgiveness. She had thanked God for their relationship and she didn't want their closeness to stop.

Her depression was eased by her children. Her pride was great when Menachem performed in a solo cello concert and when she saw in Sarah a future kibbutznik pioneer.

"I stopped my studies at the age of seventeen, in 1943, not only me, but my whole youth group—we were all in the same class in school. We had a very heated argument with our teachers. They didn't want to accept it because it was a young school with not many classes and it was a blow for the school to have a whole class leaving. But we felt that since the older people had to go into the army, the seventeen-year-olds should stop their studies and go to the agricultural settlements to replace those who were mobilized.

"That was my decision," Sarah said firmly. "Mother had nothing to do with it." Her aunt Shana, her father, and others in the family tried to persuade her to postpone her decision another year until graduation. Sarah's reply was that she felt that what her group was doing was more important than finishing high school.

"Mother asked only one question of us: 'Are you going to the settlements because you want to fulfill a national mission or simply because you don't want to study?' " Convinced of her daughter's sincerity, Golda gave her blessing. Sarah was doing what she would have done.

The plan for the group was to spend a year in an agricultural workshop, another year at the large kibbutz near Haifa called Yagur. Then she and her group would go to the Negev to join a new kibbutz called Revivim.

At eighteen, soon after leaving school, Sarah had the right to vote in Histadrut elections for the first time. "Mother was interested to know how I would vote." What convinced Sarah to vote for Mapai—her mother's political party—was a pamphlet by Berl Katznelson.

The death of Berl Katznelson in August 1944 was a shock to the entire country. The day he died suddenly of a stroke was a day nobody seemed to forget. If Palestine was a sea of sand, Berl had been the rock. What Berl said, what Berl wanted, what Berl advised—on any issue—had been a matter of keen meaning for everyone. And now, almost everybody seemed to remember exactly what they were doing the time they heard the news. Golda was on a bus coming home from the Habimah Theater. She remembered afterward how many people were whispering in groups, but she didn't hear what they said. A stunned group of friends awaited her at home with the details. Her grief was as deep as it was private and she seemed to retreat within herself. "There was nothing to say . . ."

He had meant too much for her to put in words. Berl had been her teacher, her Socrates, the wise man in her life. He had plucked her out of a kibbutz, given her a direction, and smoothed her road. She would side with Berl against anybody, against Ben-Gurion on partition, even against Remez on isolated issues. Berl had been her final word on anything or anybody.

His was a "serenity charged with anxiety, this unrest restrained by a faith which nothing could shake, this firmness which was so compelling because one was always aware of the gentleness from which it was issued." Golda often repeated quotes from Berl: "A nation must discover in itself its strength and its dignity if it is to achieve its true destiny." The challenge for his Mapai Labor Party, he said, "does not mean only the demolition of present evils, but the construction of a better society."

There were those who said he died not of a stroke but of a broken heart because the unity of his labor movement had been smashed into splinters. Berl had pointed to a massive wall and said grimly, "You see this strong wall? Although it understands nothing, it too will disintegrate, it too will split. Disintegration has a logic of its own."

When Ben-Gurion heard about Katznelson, "he sat up, staring ahead with a frozen glance. Suddenly his face twisted into a terrible grimace and he fell on the bed. . . .

"He covered himself up with a sheet, wrapping it around his head, and uttered sighs and groans like a wounded beast . . . it was awful," said David Hacohen. "I have never seen anyone so shaken. He rolled around banging his head on the mattress. His mouth uttered incoherent words: 'Berl, without Berl, how is it possible without Berl . . . Oh, Berl, how will I live without you . . .' "

Later, when he went to see the body, Ben-Gurion asked to be left alone. As they left, others heard him talking to the corpse: "How can you do this, Berl, how can you leave us? . . ." As he emerged, he told his son, "He was the only true friend I had."

Berl's Zionist dreams had penetrated the power circles of the world. Several months later a frail President Franklin D. Roosevelt told Marshal Stalin at Yalta that he was a Zionist, and asked Stalin if he was one. Stalin said he was, in principle, "but there were difficulties." After Yalta, Roosevelt met with King Ibn Saud of Saudi Arabia and asked him to sanction the admission of more Jews into Palestine, indicating it was such a small percentage of the total population of the Middle East. "He was shocked when Ibn Saud said no." The king said the Jews made the deserts bloom only because of American money, that the Palestine army of Jews was fighting Arabs, not Germans, and that Arabs would take up arms before yielding further. According to his close friend, Harry Hopkins, who was there, the seriously ill President seemed not to comprehend fully what Ibn Saud was saying because he brought up the subject several times more "and each time the king was more emphatic." The President still gave him a present of an airplane.

Harry Hopkins admitted even more puzzlement at the President's press conference afterward when FDR said "that he had learned more from Ibn Saud about Palestine in five minutes than he had learned in a lifetime." "The only thing he learned," said Hopkins, "was that Arabs don't want any more Jews in Palestine."

"I honored him, but also a little bit suspected him," recalled the president of the Zionist Organization of America, Rabbi Israel Goldstein. "I was never sure just where we stood with him. We were getting words of friendliness, but nothing that we could really put our fingers on."

A secret note FDR had sent to Ibn Saud revealed his promise: "I will not undertake in my role as head of the Executive Branch in this administration any action likely to be hostile to the Arab people."

Although Prime Minister Winston Churchill had specific reservations about how many Jews Palestine could absorb, he continued to be a strong Zionist supporter, and took pleasure in telling Weizmann that through his efforts a 5,000-man Jewish brigade within the British army had been formed. Weizmann was delighted but many Palestinian Jews were not. Instead of fighting elsewhere in the world, they felt Jews should stay in Palestine to fight the Nazis if they came. "B-G said that was crazy, to sit on our borders and wait," Golda recalled. "He said we must fight the Nazis wherever they were." Golda then smiled. "On major problems, as a rule, B-G was not wrong."

Partition was still a lingering question, and Churchill set up a committee to try to propose final plans. Ben-Gurion saw this as progress; the Irgun Zvai Leumi did not.

Also known as the IZL, the name Irgun, in Hebrew, meant "national military organization." It had several thousand members, mostly young, trained for small, commando-type raids, and pledged to constant attack on British police posts and army installations. Its leader, Menachem Begin, was a bland, balding man with horn-rimmed glasses. Ben-Gurion derided Begin as a "bespectacled petty Polish solicitor," but he was a man of much mystery.

A visiting journalist was told he could interview Begin only in a pitch-dark room. Trying to get a glimpse of Begin's face, the journalist puffed hard on a succession of cigarettes to create some light. It didn't work, and Begin was amused. He was not often amused. Begin didn't see himself as a terrorist. "We fought to right the greatest wrong done in history to any people. . . . We fought to bring the Jewish people back to their ancient country and to build a home for homeless people. . . . We were aware of all the dangers and . . . used two words which all freedom fighters had used throughout history: 'Liberty or death.' "

The appeal of the Irgun, particularly to young Jews, was heightened by the fact that they believed in a policy of action and revenge. Nor would they compromise on partition—they wanted *all* of Palestine.

More extreme than the Irgun were the Lohamei Herut Israel (Fighters for the Freedom of Israel). Known as the Lehi, or the Sternists, their organizer was Avraham Stern, a young poet who had also written a Hebrew manual on the use of the revolver. A handsome intellectual with the code name of Yair ("The Illuminator"), Stern was caught and killed by the British in 1942. He left behind this verse:

> We will wrestle with God and with death . . .
> We will welcome him. Let our blood
> Be a red carpet in the streets,
> And on this carpet our brains will be like white lilies . . .
> We are men without names, without kin
> Who forever face terror and death
> In days that are red with carnage and blood
> In nights that are black with despair.

With fewer than a thousand members, the Sternists—among them Yitzhak Shamir—concentrated on the assassination of British leaders. Two Sternists killed former colonial secretary Lord Moyne in Cairo at the end of 1944, shortly after Moyne had reluctantly agreed to partition. This caused even Churchill, in a bitter address to the House of Commons, to say, "If terrorism continues, many persons like myself will have to reconsider the position that we have maintained so consistently and so long in the past." Weizmann promised Churchill that terrorism would be rooted out. A furious Ben-Gurion threatened to crush all terrorists. Said Golda, "We were against personal terror for the sake of terror, either against the Arabs or the British, for moral reasons because we felt it was wrong and because we were also convinced it could only boomerang against us—which it usually did."

To counteract the personal terrorism of the Irgun and Sternists, a small, secret group of the Haganah and Jewish Agency leaders organized Sezon. The word meant "hunting season." Golda refused to discuss it, even years later, referring to it as "dynamite, real dynamite," something that might tear apart the Jewish community. In its hunting season, Sezon kidnapped members and several leaders of the Irgun or Sternists and handed them over to the British. Their idea was to nip any attempted assassination or terrorism before it happened. In learning of a proposed terrorist operation, Sezon might share it with British Intelligence, then alert the Irgun or Sternists that the British now knew about the proposed action—with the hope that they would call it off. It was like walking a tightrope over a burning fire, and sometimes it worked and sometimes it didn't.

"I don't think it was possible to destroy terrorism," Golda added, "as long as immigration was not permitted. . . . If it had not been for the Haganah, probably most of the Jews would have been with the Irgun. The idea of not doing anything was unthinkable."

Refugees were always uppermost in her mind. "There is no Zionism save the rescue of the Jews," Golda said repeatedly.

Roosevelt and the U.S. State Department refused to follow up on Ben-Gurion's plea to accept a Nazi Gestapo offer of refugees for money, "blood for goods."

Eleanor Roosevelt was later asked by an Israeli friend, Moshe Kol, how her husband had really felt about the Holocaust. "Please, Moshe," she replied, "I don't want to talk about it. . . . It's too unpleasant for me to talk about." Kol inferred from that, that she had tried to get President Roosevelt to do more things about getting Jews out of Germany—obviously without success.

With all the emerging horror of the Holocaust, the British belatedly loosened their limit of 1,500 visas a month for refugee Jews into Palestine in 1944. When Dr. Weizmann proposed that the British bomb the gas chambers of the Auschwitz concentration camp, Churchill told his Defense Ministry, "Get anything out of the air force you can and invoke my name if necessary." British military leaders, strongly supported by the U.S. War Department, ruled out the mission. Randolph Churchill later quoted his father as saying that he now tried to avoid Weizmann: "Whenever I see him, I can't sleep at night . . ."

The British military had ruled out any bombing of concentration camps, or the railroad connections to them, as a low priority, claiming they had too many more important things to bomb.

Golda mournfully recalled a poem by Bialik about the Kishinev pogrom: ". . . the senseless living and the senseless dying . . ."

And another verse:

I grieve for you, my children, my heart is sad for you,
Your dead are vainly dead and neither I nor you
Know why you died or wherefore, nor for whom
Even as was your life, so senseless was your doom.

The unspeakable horror modified the thinking, imposing patterns of behavior on Jews everywhere in a way that the outside world could not comprehend. It heightened anger, bitterness, and the need for action.

Despite the nonviolent pleas of Weizmann, Golda agreed with Ben-Gurion that violence was now justifiable in obtaining the release of refugee Jews. She was no longer concerned about whether their methods were legal or illegal. "If I felt it was the right thing to do, I was for it." This feeling stamped everything Golda ever did.

She finally accepted partition plans as being "right," mainly because no matter how small the created state, it would be free to open the door to all refugees. She knew the terror they had come from, she had seen them kiss the ground when they got off the ships, she had watched the sheer joy on their faces when they burned their identity cards in a traditional bonfire on arrival so that each could claim, "I am a Jew from the Land of Israel . . ."

One of the countless stories told was of a camp at Przemysl in Poland where the Nazi SS built a bonfire and made the arriving Jews undress, surrender their jewelry. Then the officers shot men and women, "often not fatally, and threw them alive in the fire. Children were grabbed by an arm or leg, their heads smashed against a wall, and they were thrown into the flames. . . . By this method, 900 people were murdered . . . their ashes later sifted for any remaining gold."

Aharon Remez, who had been an RAF pilot and later visited some of the concentration camps, angrily described it to Golda:

"In one of the sheds, I saw people who were already candidates for the crematoria ... only skin and bone, with no muscles and no complexion, no sign that the body had any life whatsoever, except for the eyes. One of the things that I'll never forget is the light in the eyes of people who sometimes could not even talk."

The burning memory for a young reporter at Buchenwald—more than the huge piles of naked bodies, or even the huge stack of children's shoes in the crematorium—was this lone, gaunt man, all bones, naked except for a rag wrapped around his middle, surrounded by a fence of barbed wire, his gaping eyes filled with the madness of the place.

American troops had flushed through Germany, crushing the arrogant Nazi dream of an empire that Hitler had boasted would last a thousand years. The world war was over in 1945, but not for the Jews.

One might have thought that the civilized world would have swept up these pitiful survivors of the concentration camps, embraced them and absorbed them as a symbol of victory. Instead, they were simply transferred from the death camps to other camps for Displaced Persons. The cots were cleaner, the food better, but the barbed wire was the same, and so was the hopelessness. And there they stayed, month after month after month, stretching into years, "despised and rejected," and then almost forgotten by the so-called civilized world.

Golda was one of the lonely voices begging the British to relax their immigration quotas and permit these refugee Jews to pour into Palestine, promising: we will feed them, we will house them, we will give them new lives. But Bevin and the British remained inflexible.

Golda later said, "Look, I was against partition in 1937, when Ben-Gurion was for it. When war came with all its horrors, I often said to myself, thank God it wasn't because of my vote that the partition was not implemented. But supposing we had, in '37, a little tiny country of our own with free immigration, we surely would have saved some of the six million Jews. ...

"Here were the British who we thought were responsible more than anyone else for the destruction of Hitler. So we were full of admiration for them. But then having finished the war, having conquered the Nazis, it seemed that they had to conquer us, to send destroyers to stop Jews coming to these shores, the same destroyers that had fought the Nazi submarines. It seemed like an impossible world. You didn't understand what was happening. Our young men had fought with the British, been in the same POW camps with the British, and then suddenly they turned on us."

Then Golda added bitterly, "The gentlemen of England really have some strange and peculiar ideas." But she had no illusions about what the British would do. "Britain will under no circumstances decide to go with us against the Arabs." The British, she said, had decided that "the Arabs can create trouble, and therefore you have to give in." Then she added defiantly, "Very well, *we'll* create trouble!"

Golda accented *this* vigorously to a British audience.

"We will not permit you to reduce our members by even one child of the few Jewish children that are still left. . . . We do not want pity. We demand the rights of a people to live. . . . We will not become reconciled to the fact that the only difference between the Hitler regime and the regime in the liberated countries is that now our children are permitted to cry. True, the democratic countries do not kill Jewish children for the crime of crying, but we will not consent that this be the only right granted to the children."

"You can't swing a cat," commented a British observer on what he called an overcrowded Palestine.

"Who wants to swing a cat?" mocked Golda. Of course Palestine was small, she added, but there was plenty of uncultivated, unsettled space for more people. "Every Jew that comes to Palestine, in his suitcase there is absorptive capacity for a few more Jews." Then she added, "Britain is trying to prevent the growth and expansion of the Jewish community, but it should remember that Jews were here two thousand years before the British came."

Golda and the Yishuv did not want to believe that the British would actually open fire on unarmed people trying to help a small group of survivors from Hitler's death camps. They did not want to acknowledge that hate and violence engendered hate and violence.

The violence intensified when the British began executing more Jews. A high school boy putting up anti-British posters was shot and wounded in the hip, sent to jail, and tied to his bed without getting any medical attention. When a prison chaplain, a rabbi, intervened, he was told, "Rabbis should be concerned with the souls of the prisoners, not with their bodies. Mind your own business."

The boy's leg was later amputated and he died soon after.

The Haganah coordinated an attack on British rail traffic with the Irgun and Sternists but broke with them after an Irgun attack killed some British soldiers. The Irgun and Sternist members refused to accept Haganah discipline, insisting that only force could bring on Jewish statehood. Golda sensed how popular the extremists were, particularly with young people frustrated by the British juggernaut.

The British caught two Irgun saboteurs and sentenced them to be hanged. One of the condemned young men declared proudly, "You cannot destroy us with the gallows." Golda's comment then was that she felt the young men had done what they did "with pure hearts and believed that their action would hasten redemption. But I do not believe they brought us statehood."

What worried Golda was world reaction to Irgun extremism, the negative feeling of Jews all over the world. British High Commissioner Cunningham discussed this with Golda, whom he highly regarded. "He asked me why we weren't cooperating in finding the terrorists. I reminded him that a captain of an 'illegal' immigrant ship had been shot in Haifa a few days earlier. I said, 'After that, do you really expect us to cooperate with you?'" To another similar query for cooperation, she declared angrily, "We cannot make informers of 600,000 Jews, each one watching his neighbor or friend."

But the Irgun and Sternists were watching Golda. They resented and suspected her, particularly since she was the Yishuv liaison with the British. "There were pretty nasty slogans against me," recalled Golda, "saying that I was selling out to the British, and that I was a traitor. I remember once walking to the bus station and Berl Repetur came up to me and said, 'What are you doing walking alone?' People were nervous. I remember once I went with my older sister to the theater and all of a sudden leaflets were thrown down from the balcony . . . against me. I don't believe that they would have assassinated me. I was never afraid, but it wasn't pleasant."

Despite Golda's unwillingness for wholesale cooperation with the British, there was the highly selective, supersecret cooperation of the Sezon. Golda never ever admitted any involvement in it.

Marie Syrkin arrived in Palestine in the fall of 1945. It had been six years since she had seen Golda in Geneva, but there was no needed bridge between the two old friends. Marie got a room in the same cluster of Histadrut apartments, across an inner courtyard from Golda. When the British later imposed a curfew forbidding anyone on the streets after certain hours, Marie or Golda could simply cross the inner courtyard to be with the other.

The curfew was a kind of enforced rest for Golda, and she needed it. She had had the adoring attention of Leah Biskin, who still lived with her. Leah was never abrasive, always agreeable, ever attentive. Marie made Golda's blood circulate, her brain work, her ideas sparkle. Marie was a woman with her own mind, never afraid to argue or disagree. Golda needed that, too.

As the two of them sat there discussing everything in the world, "the phone was always, always ringing," the world refusing to let Golda alone. "She would never tell me what any of the calls were about."

Marie marveled at the skillful way Golda turned the worn part of a skirt so that it was on the inside, a skill she had learned in her Denver days. "Golda still had one blouse and one skirt which she washed and ironed every day. She was contemptuous of females like myself who couldn't iron or cook or bake or wash dishes. She used to tell me, 'You intellectuals think it's beneath you.'" Once asked her favorite hobby, she replied, smiling, "Washing dishes."

Golda soon gave Marie a personal focus in the Yishuv struggle, told her of a secret radio station being set up to bypass British censorship. Marie took over the broadcasts and had to move constantly so she wouldn't be caught. With her amazing discipline, Golda never asked Marie about it. This was a time when no one "chattered or confided."

Golda's unheated four-room apartment on the third floor was often bitterly cold in the winter, despite small electric heaters. But the women wore layers of warm clothing while Marie often warmed the room by reading selections from Shakespeare, or Walt Whitman. Menachem remembered that, just as he remembered their warm laughter. He also recalled his mother asking Marie to put down on paper a clarification of her own ideas on the problems they discussed.

Marie worried about Golda's health. "Several times when I was with her, she would suddenly pass out and then have to lie prostrate on the living room couch. The pain from gallstones was sometimes bad enough for her to need morphine injections. And those unpredictable massive migraine headaches were always with her. I remember once the doctor told her, 'You're sick, Golda, you can't go to Jerusalem to see the high commissioner tomorrow morning.' But she went anyway."

"I always try to convince my friends that I am lazy by nature, that I don't like to work," said Golda, "but I never had the chance to prove it. I am lazy, but I have a sense of duty which stifles my laziness."

In their long hours together, Marie Syrkin gradually sensed that Golda was entertaining a suicidal impulse. In time, she felt convinced of it. Part of it, surely, came from a tired body and a tired mind. Part of it may well have been from her own growing despair, a despair she admitted to no one else, a despair about the future of her people in a world that seemed stacked against them. There were other things. The death of her gentle father had been a large loss—he had flowered in his pride of her. Her love life, often traumatic, was now in disarray, and she was often lonely. But what gnawed at her most was her mother's senility. She was terrified that she, too, might soon suffer the same mindlessness, that it was perhaps genetic. She had no fear of danger or death, she told Marie, but she could not tolerate the thought of losing her mind.

"I remember that her doctor told her that her body could not stand her pace of work. The doctor warned that if she didn't ease up, it could prove fatal. I'll never forget her reply: 'A lot of us die around fifty.'" Golda was then forty-eight.

Golda was in a meeting one morning when she suddenly felt this "terrible tiredness," then suddenly her left foot seemed paralyzed and her head started spinning. The next thing she knew she was on a stretcher. Again, her main concern was that something might be affecting her brain.

She reached out for Remez. She and Remez had patched their differences but still had not quelled their occasional need to seek elsewhere. Still, Remez was the one to whom she wrote from Beilinson Hospital telling him of her current lack of confidence in her strength, and how the doctors had marveled at the miracle that she did not have further complications, and that they now wanted to punish her with a lot of rest.

Tests showed her mind was fine, feeling returned to her foot, but doctors warned her to stop smoking, and persuaded her to go to the Monte Carlo Hotel in Cyprus for a rest. She actually did stop smoking, but not for long. She was too highly charged to really rest anywhere.

"I don't know. Perhaps I don't rest enough," she once said when asked about her faults. "This kind of work demands rest. Certain people say—I don't know whether it's true or not—that I do too much myself. My way of working dictates that I know everything. I delegate authority to people to get things done, but I want to know what they are doing. . . . I want to know everything, even the details . . . exactly what the problems are. I find myself saying, 'You decide. You do it.' But I want to know."

Her brain was always buzzing with things she wanted to do, things she felt she could do better and more quickly than most other people. As for smoking, the habit was too ingrained and was now part of her restlessness.

Perhaps it was this restlessness, too, that made her search for others to fill out her private life. Remez seemed to be abroad more than usual and her work no longer permitted her to accompany him often. Her intimacy with Aranne was more sporadic, but now another man came into her life.

Her relationship with this man was most remarkable because he and Golda were on opposite political poles. Remez, Shazar, Aranne were all of a like mind with Golda on issues, but this man was in direct conflict with her. Such critics were generally anathema to Golda. She was impatient with anyone who could not see things as she saw them, especially when she was certain she was right. Yet this man disagreed with her violently on basic issues.

Nothing was more basic to either of them than politics. Mapai was the traditional center party, the Establishment party for statehood, and Golda had never deviated from it. Party principles were her bible. Mapam was a party that had split from Mapai, a party far to the left of it. This man was one of the founders of that party. Mapai wanted a state for the Jews; Mapam wanted a binational state with the Arabs. Mapai felt closely tied with the United States; Mapam regarded Soviet Russia as "a second homeland."

It seemed inconceivable that Golda could even befriend such a man, much less love him. Yet she surely did. Asked by a mutual friend, "Who did Golda love *most* as a *man*?" Golda's closest companion answered without hesitation: "Yaacov Hazan."

Meeting Hazan, one sensed how handsome he must have been in his earlier years, this straight, big, broad-shouldered man full of twinkles and small smiles. He had this impressive head with thick unruly hair, penetrating eyes that gave him a tremendous dignity. Golda respected this dignity in him, as well as his stubborn strength that defied her mainly because she knew that underneath were absolute honesty and love.

With Remez and Shazar, Golda was younger and junior; with Aranne, Golda was the loving eminence; but with Hazan, it was an affair of equals. Their early sparring was angry and respectful, but their relationship soon deepened.

"What can you say about your intimate relations with Golda?" an interviewer asked.

Smiling enigmatically, clearly not offended, Hazan replied, "I will not discuss my intimate relations with Golda."

He beamed with an obvious pride when he was told that Golda's closest companion had said that Golda loved him most as a man. Flushing a little, Hazan even asked for a copy of the tape that recorded it. Despite this he had no compunction in describing himself as "a sane Zionist" and Golda and her friends as the impractical ones, "the Messianics." He did not deny that he had some political impact on her. "I felt Golda had a lot of dictatorial qualities, and I told her often that she had to have more democratic methods, and I think I convinced her." He did not quickly admit that Golda had an even greater impact on him, later pulling his party into a coalition government.

What was important to Golda about Hazan was not that he was married, or a year younger, but that he was an action man. Hazan not only had worked on a kibbutz but helped found the central kibbutz organization. The very few who knew about Golda's intimacy with Hazan had no doubts about its depth, or that it lasted until her death.

Did Golda talk about Hazan, or any of her other men, with anyone? "Never, never!" Golda insisted.

Golda's children were still in residence, but not for long. Menachem had been made a member of the Palestine Philharmonic Orchestra in 1943, its youngest member. A friend recalled going to a Jerusalem concert hall to hear Menachem in a recital. "It was freezing in that hall, and we all sat there in our overcoats and there was Golda, beaming with pride." Menachem quit the orchestra to join the Jewish Settlement Police, complete with khakis, puttees, and a raised, flat-topped hat. Such police were primarily trained as guards for prisoners of war, arsenals, and warehouses. They were all taught to use a rifle. Most of them were secretly also members of the Haganah.

Sarah's life was even more exciting, a life Menachem secretly envied. She was practicing to be a pioneer, learning how to plant, fight, survive. Her peer group of high school classmates not only went through a grueling training program in a northern kibbutz, learning exactly what to expect, but all of them became part of the Palmach. As an elite Palmachian, trained in guerrilla warfare, Sarah also became an expert radio operator. Set up in 1941, Palmach units were flexible reserve fighting forces, available to go anywhere immediately.

Sarah's group was scheduled to settle on Revivim, the most isolated kibbutz in the most southern part of the desolate Negev, a place of heat and loneliness. The only way to get there was to travel a single, potholed road that disappeared into nothing, then follow the ruts of earlier cars if you could see them in the thick, blinding dust.

"I really thought I would die," said Golda when she saw the site. It was an acre of scorching sand, and almost nothing else—no grass, no trees, no birds. A watchtower to scan for unfriendly Arabs, a protective wall, and behind it some tents. Water from the well was too salty to drink. Summer weather was blazing heat; winter meant fierce cold.

Stronger than Golda's shock was her pride. "There's *nothing* there!" she almost exulted to her friends. Forever after, Golda proudly referred—always almost beaming—to "my daughter in the kibbutz!" Menachem remembered that their mother never told Sarah how proud she was of her. It was something felt by both of them, but never expressed. Between mother and daughter there was an emotional gap but also a gap of non-intrusive privacy. They simply did not confide intimate, personal things to each other. Nor did they ask questions.

The year 1945 changed the world. The war was over, the atomic bomb born. Hitler was dead and so were 35 million others, including six million Jews. President Roosevelt was also dead and the new president, Truman, was still an unknown quantity. So was the new president of France, Charles de Gaulle. A general election in Great Britain replaced Winston Churchill with a Labour government.

Churchill had been a special friend. "This is a country," he had said of Palestine, "where the Jews have great historic traditions, and you cannot brush that aside as though it were absolutely nothing." But even

Churchill had been unable to revoke the restrictions on immigration. With a new Labour government of friendly socialists, Golda now hoped that the restrictions would finally be lifted.

She did not take into account the mind of a beefy man with a bulldog face, the new British foreign minister, Ernest Bevin. Bevin had been a trade-union leader, a member of Churchill's war cabinet. With the Palestine question now transferred from the Colonial Office to his Foreign Office, Bevin intensified his basic policy: since the vast majority of the Middle East was Arab, nothing should be done against the Arab will, and therefore there should be no Jewish state in Palestine. As for the immigration problem, he proposed an Anglo-American commission to study it.

The commission started with a contemptuous remark by Bevin publicly warning the Jews that they should not "push to the head of the queue." Indeed the question was raised as to whether the displaced Jews of Europe *"really* want to go to Palestine."

Really want to go?

A United Nations team of investigators came to probe that question at a Displaced Persons camp near Munich. Ruth Tropin, then an official of UNRRA (United Nations Relief and Rehabilitation Administration), recalled that the group queried a ninety-nine-year-old Jewish woman, who replied, firmly, "I want to go to Palestine." They asked her why. She looked at them with surprise, "Because I want to start a new life."

Another visitor wanted to interview some of the children: a teenager who had witnessed his mother being shot by a German soldier, after which the boy found a wagon to cart away his mother's body so he could bury her; a young girl who had been shot and thrown into a burial pit with others, and somehow survived and escaped; another girl, slightly older, who had helped blow up a Nazi train. They were all children who never opened a package until they were told to, who regarded a forest not as a place to play but as a place to hide.

The visitor wanted to know where the other children were.

"Taking a walk," was the laconic reply.

They were taking a walk to Palestine, guided, illegally, by men and women from the Haganah.

The commission headed from Europe to Palestine with its chairman, Herbert Morrison, warning of Muslim opposition to any relaxation of immigration restrictions. Some released statistics indicated that the flow was really a trickle, that only 13,100 refugees had been legally permitted to enter Palestine in 1945, 1,500 *less* than the previous year. And a news item described a DP camp in Austria where Jewish women survivors behind barbed wire, demanding to be allowed to go to Palestine, were stripped and searched by Austrian guards.

Golda viewed the arriving commission with few expectations—there had been so many commissions who knew little and cared less. But when she was asked to testify before the commission in a courtroom-like setting on March 25, 1946, the mood suddenly became tense.

"One felt that all the commission members, without exception, were hanging onto every word she uttered. In the beginning it was her personality, her commanding presence, and also that certain femininity of which she was not devoid. But once she had begun to speak, it was what she said and how she said it that mattered. It was clear-cut, lucid, precise, and based on knowledge of facts, rather than on emotions or opinions. She definitely stole the show."

"She's handsome in her own way," described an observer, "broad, steady in appearance, with rather heavy features and a general air of quiet self-assurance, but without the fussiness or bustle which often surrounds political women . . . and commands unanimous respect. She is always neatly dressed, without pretense to elegance, and gives the general impression of firmness, quiet efficiency, strength, and repose. One cannot help thinking that, once the strength has been set in motion and has gathered speed, its impact must be definitely felt by the object at which it is directed."

The committee felt the full impact of Golda's replies:

". . . There is not a Jew . . . not a settlement that would not throw its doors open and fill their houses and their settlements to capacity. If it is tents, it is tents; if it means barracks, it is barracks . . . every house would be filled to capacity in order to bring Jews into the country. . . . Otherwise our life here, too, becomes senseless. . . ."

Q: Your organization is in favor of large-scale immigration?
A: Unlimited.
Q: At once and unlimited?
A: Unlimited immigration.
Q: And at once?
A: Yes.

David Remez offered poetic support for Golda. Speaking to assembled Jewish leaders, he talked about the "mute wall" the British had built against immigration, how "we beat our heads against this wall. . . . The world is paving its way toward its future. Shall there be a future for all except the Jewish people? Why?" Then he added defiantly, "The cry of the homeless will be answered."

Golda now found a dramatic way to answer that cry: a hunger strike.

In April 1946 more than a thousand refugees intercepted on two ships near Italy—the *Dov Hos* and the *Eliyahu Golomb**—had announced to the world that they would sink their ships and kill themselves if they couldn't come to Palestine. In the meantime they would refuse all food.

Feeling their anger and their desperation, an indignant Golda proposed that the leaders of the Yishuv must do more than send telegrams of pious platitudes. They must participate in a show of solidarity, they must prove to the world how deep was their shared grief.

Pushed by Remez, the proposal passed. The only requirement: each participant in the fast needed a medical certificate of good health. Golda's doctor refused the certificate. An adamant Golda then insisted that if her doctor continued this refusal, she would fast alone at home without medical supervision. Her doctor knew his patient, realized she would do exactly what she said, and reluctantly gave her the certificate. The heavyset Shazar, who had also been in poor health, had even greater trouble finding a willing doctor and settled for a friendly gynecologist.

There were thirteen of them, including three women, each of them representing a specific community group. They simply set up cots in their offices in the Jewish National Council Building in Jerusalem. "Thank God they let us smoke cigarettes," said Golda. Their only other sustenance was conversation and a glass of tea without sugar twice a day. Among Palestinian Jews, conversation was often more sustaining than food. There is no available record of the conversation, but it is easily imagined, knowing the quality of the people and their intelligent mocking wit, particularly that of the three men Golda had loved so well: Remez, Shazar, and Aranne.

They were permitted limited visitors at certain hours. Sarah and

*Golomb had died in 1945, Hos in 1940.

Menachem came. "We were worried," said Menachem, who knew how ill their mother had been. David Ben-Gurion also came. He had called the whole idea theatrical nonsense, but now he admitted that he was very moved.

The drama caught the people and crowds came to their courtyard, praying for their success. "We will not touch food until the Jews are brought here, or we will all die!" Golda told them.

Talking to her privately, a senior British official asked, "Do you think for a moment that His Majesty's Government will change its policy because *you* are not going to eat?"

"No, I have no such illusions. If the death of six million didn't change government policy, I don't expect my not eating will do so. But it will, at least, be a mark of solidarity."

The Rabbinate was aghast. It was Passover season, and the fast was a desecration to the holiday—food *must* be eaten, a service *must* be held. So intense was rabbinical pressure that the thirteen finally compromised, each of them eating a tiny piece of matzo the size of an olive. Shazar was very weak but insisted on conducting the Passover service. Devout Jews, who normally went to the Wailing Wall for their holiday prayers, now came to the courtyard.

With the flair and fervor everybody expected of him, Shazar said:

"In every generation, men have risen up to destroy us, but the Holy One, blessed be He, always delivers us from their hands." Shazar then led the group in singing the Hasidic songs associated with the Seder, and afterward all the people joined in to sing the "Hatikvah," which would one day become the national anthem of the new country. "Our spirits are high!" Remez told everyone.

An appeal came from the negotiators at the *Dov Hos*, asking them to stop their hunger strike. They would only stop, replied Golda, when guarantee came of the release of the ships and the people.

After 104 hours of the fast, the guarantee finally came that the ships would sail for Palestine.

"Our fast is at an end," fifty-nine-year-old Remez told the people. "The refugees will come. We shall receive them in our midst. The minor affliction which we have undergone has earned us recompense in the wide support of the Yishuv. We have been able to look into the hearts of the people of Jerusalem.... In imposing this fast on ourselves we did not delude ourselves that this is the end of the struggle."

The thirteen who ate their first meal of milk, matzo, and white cheese knew that their struggle was just beginning.

The hunger strike had received world publicity and twanged an international conscience. The Anglo-American report on Palestine in May 1946 recommended an immediate entry of 100,000 Jews. The United States government agreed.

Speaking to the Sixth Conference of the Histadrut in Palestine, still introduced as "Goldie Meyerson," Golda sharply pointed her remarks on the report to the visiting representatives of the British Labour Party: "The 100,000 certificates for Jewish immigration into Palestine that are demanded of you are the test of your sincerity—whether you remain true to your declarations and promises of the past, or whether, at the very beginning of your term in office, you bow to the heritage of those whom you replaced in office. I do not believe that a Labour government can be faithful to part of its program while reneging on the rest."

Bevin, who had proposed the Anglo-American commission, refused a month later to abide by its decision. To agree, he said, would result in Arab riots and it would take a British army division to quell them.

Golda was both bitter and defiant. "For over twenty years, British Labour supported the Jewish Labor movement in Palestine. . . . Who could have dreamed that this covenant . . . would be broken?" Then she added, "You will not frighten us. We do not want to fight you. We want to build. We want to enable the small remnant of European Jewry to come to Palestine in peace. But should you persist in preventing us from doing this . . . Bevin will also have to send a division to fight us. . . . We have no alternative."

That phrase became Golda's personal banner which she repeated again and again: *"We have no alternative!"*

Ben-Gurion added his own emphasis: "We must be strong. Everything depends on us!"

Reaction in the United States was mixed. An article in the *New York Post* concluded: "It would be better for the United States to have Palestine reopened to the Jews than to have millions of them coming over here after the war as unassimilated refugees." British ambassador Lord Halifax reported his own view of the American attitude: "The average citizen does not want them [the Jews] in the United States and salves his conscience by advocating their admission to Palestine."

Palestine then was a place of uneasy peace. People in cities lived their daily lives, but death was no longer unexpected. British troops made their presence increasingly felt and seen. Once, Golda remembered, when police started searching her neighborhood, "there was a nice Jewish family living across the street and I knew the police wouldn't think of searching their house so I went across and asked if we could leave some arms with them and I got a terrible shock when they said, 'Oh, but we're opposed to arms.' " Subterfuge and sabotage were a way of life. Arab snipers were everywhere. All travel was hazardous.

In a desperate gesture of defiance, the Haganah on the midnight of June 16 simultaneously blew up all the bridges on the frontiers of the country, temporarily isolating the British. "If British troops come searching in kibbutzim for arms—arms we need to fight the Arabs—then Jews have the right to retaliate," Golda warned. "If fighting for the right of Jews to enter the Land of Israel means terrorism, then we are all terrorists. . . . Those who were killed in the gas chambers by Hitler were the last Jews to die without defending themselves." Then she added prophetically, "This is going to become an independent state. . . . There may be a lot of blood that's going to flow, but this is what's going to happen."

In Palestine, the war was not over—it was barely beginning.

15

Black Saturday, June 29, 1946, was the day British Foreign Secretary Ernest Bevin declared war on the Jews.

Palestine was already an armed camp with 100,000 British troops fenced off behind barbed wire with sandbagged machine-gun positions, now given the name of "Bevingrad." But on that day, the troops closed the borders, imposed a general curfew, and launched Operation Broadside, backed by tanks and armored cars. Their objective: arrest Jewish leaders all over the country. Secret documents later revealed that the British planned to paralyze the Yishuv, undermine the unity of the resistance, and leave the country leaderless. They hoped that some moderate leaders would then take over and cooperate more fully with the British.

Before the day was done, they had arrested 2,738, killed three, wounded dozens more, tortured many, and created chaos.

"I can ... sweep the whole lot into the Mediterranean," boasted the commanding officer. "I've got the force to do it."

Golda had her own reaction:

"I was always aware of the terrific power opposing us. I didn't go into the struggle with any easy feeling, without sweat."

"I remember they broke into the offices of the Vaad Hapoel and broke all the doors and broke all the furniture," added Golda. "They

265

didn't have to break the doors. They could have walked in. . . . It was terrible to see. I remember the shock I got when I went to Yagur kibbutz afterward. The British had found some 'slicks'—caches of Haganah arms—and they occupied that place for a week. They really destroyed it. I went into a room and there were photographs of children with the eyes poked out by pins. It was better doing it to a picture than doing it to a child, but it was a horrible sight."

Yagur kibbutzniks also told of the British soldiers spraying hot oil on them to force them into barbed-wire enclosures. Golda later commented bitterly that she had never seen a pogrom but this is what she imagined a pogrom to be.

At Degania kibbutz, a British soldier was beating a fourteen-year-old boy when he was told, "Don't you realize you are beating a survivor of Hitler's extermination camps?" Replied the soldier, "If Hitler had finished the job, I would not have to do it."

Churchill later denounced it as "Bevin's dirty war."

"As perfect an example of the absolute police state as is found anywhere on earth," reported the *New York Herald Tribune*, ". . . utterly tyrannical."

Golda knew the British had sometimes acted like that in India and Ireland, but she said she didn't think they would dare use such brutal police methods against the Jews, not after the mass extermination of six million. "They won't dare . . ."

Many Jews fought back, particularly on the kibbutzim. One angry woman threw boiling water on British soldiers trying to arrest her. But not all the British were brutal, or even harsh. Months afterward, a British officer sought out Golda to apologize for their actions. "We hated to do it but we had our orders."

Such was the frenzied chaos of the day that nobody knew who was arrested and who was next. The British had specific lists of people. One Jewish leader marched up and down a main street almost pleading to be arrested and he was politely told to go home. Ben-Gurion, in Paris, was alerted to stay there. Haganah commander Moshe Sneh got an early warning, and disappeared. Irgun and Sternist members were untouched because the British didn't know where to find them. Among those caught and jailed were Remez and Sharett, listed by the British as VIJs (Very Important Jews).

Friends urged Golda to go into hiding, but she refused. "If they want me, they know where I am." Ben-Gurion's wife, Paula, who clearly never liked Golda, called her repeatedly that day, asking disappointedly, "They didn't come to take you yet?" Golda broke off one telephone conversation, saying she had to hang up because she heard policemen coming up the stairs. But they were coming for her neighbor.

"I don't know why they didn't arrest me," Golda later reflected. "Maybe they didn't have women at Latrun [a heavily fortified jail near Jerusalem]. Maybe I wasn't important enough. I was very annoyed."

Golda's friends deplored with her the fact that she had not been arrested that day, called it "the worst thing the Mandate ever did to her." More than that, it was the worst thing the British authorities did to themselves.

Golda promptly complained to the British high commissioner about the mass arrests. "I knew him well," she said, "and we had become good friends." Sir Alan Cunningham, the sixth and last of the British high commissioners under the Mandate since 1920, had a distinguished army record in Africa and Egypt with the reputation of honesty. He was later criticized by his superiors for not using enough military measures to crush terrorism. Cunningham had warned the British Colonial Office of the urgency for a political settlement: "Time is running out."

Cunningham had a high regard for Golda. In their frequent meetings, when Golda wondered aloud what good she was doing, he reassured her, "You are doing very well, Mrs. Meyerson."

Who was to lead the Yishuv, the Jewish community? With Ben-Gurion in Paris the leader next in line was the political head of the Jewish Agency. Originally considered equivalent to a ministry of foreign affairs, the Political Department now had responsibility for almost everything. The highly effective Moshe Sharett had practically created the job, and it seemed inconceivable that anybody could replace him.

Marie Syrkin was present at a meeting of American Jewish leaders considering the question, "So who's going to stand up to the British?"

"Why not Golda?" asked Marie.

"Golda?" said one of the men, slightly sneering. "A lovely lady, a good speaker, but are you kidding? A woman?"

"I wanted to choke him," said Syrkin.

The strongest opposition to Golda came from Orthodox Jews. Their daily newspaper, *Hatzofeh*, wrote: "It is difficult for a people whose religion assigns women a place of honor in the home to accept the idea of a woman at the head of a political department. With all due respect to women of good sense and diligence, a woman should not be placed at the helm of one of our central political bodies."

Nevertheless, Golda *was* selected.

Remez, Shazar, Aranne all vigorously supported her, but she already had the strong approval of the majority of the Jewish Agency Executive. Most important of all, Ben-Gurion absolutely agreed, and called her to Paris. Ben-Gurion reportedly had once said of Golda: "Good politician, but not much intellect, not much vision." Some said that Golda lost favor in Ben-Gurion's eyes when she became too important, that Ben-Gurion saw himself on a mountaintop of supreme power and didn't want his peers to get too close, rejected them when they did. At this time, though, there is no question that Ben-Gurion greatly respected Golda, asked her advice often, and listened to it attentively. At this pivotal time in Yishuv history, he trusted her intuition, her practical mind, her clear vision of right and wrong—all this with dedicated obstinacy.

Ben-Gurion knew that the Yishuv needed someone like this, more than ever before in its history. This was not the time for the Talmudic examination of every side of every question, arguing every issue into infinity. This was the time for immediate, pressing, crucial decisions; this was the time for Golda.

Golda went into immediate action. First she made an announcement: "What we want is complete independence. What happened during the war and after, proved that if we had been independent we might have rescued hundreds of thousands of Jews in Europe. We were the best possible, the only friends of the British in the Middle East, but British policy has put us in an impossible position. With the detention of our leaders and thousands of other Jews who are accused of no crime, we have reached the limit. Something of that friendship may yet be preserved, but only if we are liberated from British rule and every other foreign control, be it in the form of a Mandate or a Trusteeship."

She then went to see the British high commissioner, trying to persuade him to release the VIJs imprisoned at Latrun. "You English with your moral power, your moral strength, should set an example for everybody." Regarding the arrest of Moshe Sharett, she insisted, "If he is guilty, then I am equally guilty."

"Perhaps you should be arrested, too?" Cunningham suggested.

"Perhaps."

"She found herself facing a lot of factual material, specific details—the raw material of decision-making—that she didn't know about. She wasn't sure of herself then," said Gershon Avner, then a tall young man from Oxford University who became her press officer, "and she would take a great deal more advice than she would later. In those early days, she was less intolerant of dissenting opinions, especially on immediate political questions. Not basic principles, but tactical questions, especially in dealing with the British, and especially in her contacts with the high commissioner. She'd contact Ben-Gurion in Paris and Remez in prison, or telephone various people in Tel Aviv. She wasn't sure of her judgment yet. She grew into this."

Golda's contact with Remez at Latrun was a daily contact via the milkman. The heavily fortified Latrun, on the historical crossroads to ancient Jerusalem, had a barbed-wire camp where detainees were often kept months without trial, with a special-treatment section for the VIJs.

"We had two Palmach people who were policemen inside Latrun. Nobody knew that. The prison commandant, a British assistant superintendent, received an amount of money from me once or twice a month. Plus presents. Nobody knew that either," said the Haganah intelligence chief. As the British later discovered, "They used money, drink, women—whatever they thought was a man's weak point."

And, then, of course, there was the milkman.

"I brought our leaders in the Latrun their milk and their daily food. Our food boxes had double walls, and inside the walls were official letters. They would eat their food, read their letters, write their replies, put them back inside the double walls, and I would take the boxes back to Tel Aviv. It was a kind of post office, more or less a daily contact.

"Golda once asked me to get a special message to Moshe Sharett and get his verbal answer that same day. The question was whether to make the release of Latrun prisoners a condition of whether or not to attend the roundtable conference in London. It was Yom Kippur and I had to make an excuse about Sharett requiring fresh milk that day. I did get to see him and his answer was 'No condition.' Golda sent a courier with that message to London that same day."

Golda had a more personal courier for her more personal notes to Remez: his son, Aharon.

Aharon had volunteered for the Royal Air Force and returned to Palestine, still wearing his uniform. Visiting his father at Latrun, he discovered that the British officer in charge of the prison was a wartime buddy. Aharon's friend not only gave him freedom of the prison, but assembled Remez and other leaders for a party, complete with whiskey. Aharon afterward carried almost daily notes "in little folded-up papers" between his father and Golda. On these intimate private notes, Golda used a personal code name, "Ruth." Years after Remez died, Golda asked his son to return these notes to her. Aharon Remez remembered how she had blushed when she had asked for them. The leaders then all had code names. Golda's official code name was "Zahava." *Zahav* is the Hebrew word for "gold." Another gold code name was "Pazzit," part of which also means gold in Hebrew.

The British had collected masses of documents in their Black Saturday sweep, "but I can only think of five men in the whole British detective force who spoke Hebrew." They had the same problem in eavesdropping by hidden microphone on the men in prison, when they found the translation difficulty "soul-destroying."

One of the fifty-nine women prisoners in Latrun B was an important Haganah intelligence agent, and there was worry that she might be made to talk. "We found someone who looked very much like her, who pretended she was a nurse, and they switched clothes. We then got our girl out of the country."

Golda's door was always open. An American visitor remembered, "Some of those Jewish Agency people were able, but timid, but not Golda. She was a doer, a real eager-beaver, a pusher right from the start. Maybe Ben-Gurion was the guiding genius, but she was the real activist."

"I remember I needed Golda's decision on something," recalled an intelligence chief. "She was in a room with her legs in bowls of water, changing one leg from hot water to cold water to circulate the blood."

Golda no longer had any private time, not even to soak her feet. Her job consumed her. If she wasn't negotiating with the British, she was negotiating with the Irgun or the Sternists. Or she was planning the next illegal arrival of refugees at a secret beach. Or worrying about food rations for the people, or jobs, or arms, or housing, or world opinion, or Arab massacres, or isolated kibbutzim, or the price of eggs. Remez, Sharett, and others in Latrun sent her a stream of advice. Ben-Gurion in Paris offered all kinds of ideas, but she was the one in command, she was the one who finally decided, she was the one who gave the orders for any action. Golda was the Jewish mother of a Jewish people, who now looked to her for everything, for solutions and for strength.

She had little time for lovers now. Remez was in prison. Aranne and Shazar and Hazan were as consumed as she was. There was little time for romance or laughter. There was also little time for her children. She seldom saw Sarah. "Travel to Revivim was not easy. The trip took hours and hours and hours. Besides, Mother had no time then. Just some letters." Menachem also saw little of his mother. He was lonely. Even when he met girls, he wondered whether "they liked me for myself or because I am Golda's son." He was miserable with the Settlement Police and finally prevailed on his mother to send him to New York to study at the Manhattan School of Music.

Dr. Chaim Weizmann was still the elder statesman of the Yishuv. Weizmann was still strongly opposed to violence, still felt he could settle anything with his British friends by negotiation.

But thousands of Jews had been picked up, and Golda protested:

"I said to Weizmann, 'Look, something has to be done. The Yishuv just can't pass this over as if nothing happened.' Many of them had been tortured and beaten in battles in various kibbutzim. The Haganah ordered everybody to refuse to give fingerprints, to avoid identification, and many of our people were beaten when they refused. I also told Weizmann that if we didn't do something positive, the Irgun and Lehi would. And if they did something, it would be something much more serious than we planned."

The stubborn old man insisted that any reaction would spell the doom of Zionism, that he never before had interfered with their affairs, "but I need this right and demand that you cease all activities."

Equally stubborn, Golda instead proposed a campaign of civil disobedience to the British. In prison, Remez was of a like mind. He had written her, "I use the afternoon or evening for reading Gandhi." Weizmann reluctantly agreed but only if he received assurance that they would suspend all violence until an international conference in August.

Golda informed Weizmann that the ultimate decision on any violent action rested with a group of five called "X." She was not one of the five, but she was privy to their decisions and she knew they had decided "to do something soon." She contacted one of the five, Levi Eshkol, who had cast the critical vote in favor of action. Eshkol was a mild-looking pragmatic man who had helped found the first kibbutz. His life was integrated into every phase of Yishuv history, and he would one day be prime minister. Listening to Golda about Weizmann's agreement on civil disobedience, Eshkol said he would change his vote at the next meeting of "X."

There were others who still wanted "to spill a lot of blood" before the British Parliament reconvened in several weeks, and Golda kept busy containing them, saying, "Look, I'm among the activists, but I need a long time till I decide that we need a lot of bloodshed."

Her civil disobedience plans collapsed when Weizmann suddenly withdrew his support. Weizmann's advisers persuaded him to change his mind. "I was very angry," said Golda.

"To us you are the leader of the Jews, the president of the Zionist organization, and your task is to break through the gates of Palestine," a Young Pioneer leader had once told Weizmann. "If you cannot, then kindly step down and we will break through by our own powers."

At that time Weizmann embraced the young man, told him, "Please break through and I will go with you."

This time he was not ready to go.

Golda knew now that the Irgun *was* ready to go—but in a different direction.

The Irgun believed in "an eye for an eye." They wanted the most dramatic reaction to Black Saturday. Why not sabotage the King David Hotel, which housed British administrative headquarters? They informed the "X" committee only that their objective was "an important government building." Their proposal was that this would "humiliate the British, not kill them." "X" agreed, the Haganah agreed, and, reportedly, even Ben-Gurion agreed.

"We did not imagine that even one life would be lost," Irgun leader Menachem Begin afterward insisted.

The Irgun plan was to give the British thirty minutes to evacuate the hotel before the blast—they had planted a high explosive in the hotel basement. Begin claimed that they made three telephone calls, warning, "This is the Irgun! We have placed explosives in the hotel. Clear out! This is a warning!"

Nobody cleared out. The explosion on July 22, 1946, destroyed five floors of the southern wing of the hotel, killed ninety-one people—British, Arabs, Jews—and wounded hundreds of others.

A furious Ben-Gurion promised to punish the Irgun. A grim Golda emphasized, "We never cooperated with the Irgun in any operation aimed at human life.... I can testify to solemn discussion, in the heat of the struggle, on the nature of justified force ... the determination that resistance not degenerate into terrorism."

The shocked British reacted with fury. The British cabinet seriously considered stopping all immigration. In the House of Commons, even Churchill felt compelled to warn, "It is perfectly clear that Jewish warfare directed against the British in Palestine will, if protracted, automatically release us from all obligations to persevere, as well as destroy the inclination to make further efforts in British hearts." For the first time now, he flatly said, "The idea that the Jewish problem could be solved or even helped by a vast dumping of the Jews of Europe into Palestine is really too silly to consume our time in the House this afternoon." He was still, however, a partisan of the Jewish Homeland, and he added, "We must not be in a hurry to turn aside from large causes which we have carried far."

A British Foreign Office confidential note had already been sent to the Control Office for Germany and Austria:

"We must prevent German JEWS from emigrating to PALESTINE."

In Palestine, the military command was brutally curt, forbidding any further fraternization with the Jews "in order to punish Jews in the way the race dislikes more than any other, by striking at their pockets and showing contempt for them."

Golda was philosophical about the British. "I suppose people felt that if it had been any other army, it could have been worse. The British had an empire, and always had trouble somewhere in their empire, and knew how to handle it. But if it had been the French, I think they would have killed all of us."

"They came from different places—India, Gold Coast, Nigeria, Malaya—and they had never met natives of our sort," explained a Palestinian Jew trying to sum up the psychological problem of the British forces in Palestine. "They couldn't come to terms with us."

Golda tried to explain to British officials that the Jews needed arms for self-defense against the Arabs. The British did not seem to understand the growing intensity of hate, accelerated by such incidents as an Arab roasting alive a one-year-old girl in front of her Jewish mother. Was such an outrage any different from a Nazi skinning a tattooed Jew and using his skin as a lampshade? Thirty miles east of Gaza, in the desert area of Ruhama, an isolated Jewish village had been twice destroyed by Arabs. "Taking away [their] arms means an invitation to destroy Ruhama a third time."

But the British interest in Arab massacres of Jews had further decreased. In the same way, there seemed to be a greater number of lighter sentences at the Nuremberg trials in Germany, at a quicker pace, "because we don't want war-crimes trials to become a universal bore."

Golda understood the boredom of the British. It was not difficult to understand that the British here were tired of this hate and danger they could not fully comprehend. They were tired of playing policemen for unappreciative people, being the bully boys and feeling the bitter resentment. They were tired of being away from their families and not being permitted to be part of any local families. They could hardly wait to go home.

Could Golda ever explain to them that that was all her people wanted—to go home, to live the peaceful life, to die in their beds? That was not, of course, what Golda herself wanted. She was doing what she most wanted to do—every day fresh adventures, critical crises, excitement, enormous decisions, hot confrontations, everything in high gear, danger, life and death, the tingle of great expectations. This was her life, the life she relished.

Terrorism intensified in the coming months in 1946. "Our cooperation with the government now consists in our putting forward demands and the government refusing them. Whatever we do will entail sacrifices." When Golda told this at a committee meeting, she was also angered at the passive reaction of the British to Arab attacks. Golda expected little from the British. She knew the British sided with the Arabs and Arab oil and that Bevin was an enemy of the Jews. But she had expected more from British High Commissioner Cunningham and some of his senior associates, whom she had regarded as sympathetic. She had hoped for more of an evenhanded fairness, the realization that the extremists represented only a small minority of the Yishuv.

As political head, Golda's dilemma was that the combined Jewish force, including the extremists, compared to the British "like a weed waving in front of a cannon." She knew the extremists had lost world Jewish support but she could only try to dissuade them from being too extreme, persuading them to delay and minimize. In this she was not successful, especially after British soldiers disarmed some members of Haganah and handed them over to Arab mobs who brutally murdered them.

When the British caught and flogged Sternists, the Sternists retaliated by catching and flogging British soldiers. When the British hanged two Sternists, the Sternists hanged two British soldiers.

"The incident was terrible and I don't want to talk about it," said Golda afterward. "They degrade the moral stature of every Jew."

The Irgun and Sternists became a force beyond control in 1946, not only raiding British arsenals but even Haganah arsenals. Before the end of the next year they had completed some sixty operations of all kinds. Golda learned they were going to dynamite some railroads just about the time of a Zionist congress in London. When she tried to get them to delay it, their reaction was "Nothing doing!"

What concerned Golda was not the violence but the killing. "We were against personal terror. We never accepted the reasoning that these killings were useful because they brought us attention."

"Look, I believe you're going to have a Jewish state," British High Commissioner Cunningham once told her, "but you are going to have a lot of trouble with these people."

"I said I know, but we'll take care of it."

She never stopped trying. "She got angry with me," said Dr. Ariyeh Altman, "because she felt I had the influence to intervene and stop some terrorist actions, and wouldn't do it."

Irgun leader Menachem Begin was not a man easily influenced. Polite, precise, more gracious than angry, except when stirred, he became irate when an interviewer compared his terrorism with Arab terrorism.

"We fought to save our people. They fight to destroy a people," he insisted.

Golda believed that, too. Her prime argument was that Jewish terrorism hurt their cause in the eyes of the world. Begin was not interested in the world view; Golda, as head of the Political Department, now had to be.

There were few problems that did not pass onto Golda's desk. The British had arrested a young man for a terrorist action, and Golda discovered that he was absolutely innocent. She went to Cunningham, telling him what she knew, and pleaded for his life. "He believed what I said to him and saved the boy's life for me."

Golda returned the favor. She learned the Irgun planned an action at a concert hall to protest a British killing aboard a refugee ship at Haifa. The orchestra that night would set the mood by refusing to play "God Save the King." That would be the signal for further action. Golda learned that Cunningham planned to attend that concert to hear some favorite music. She persuaded him not to go. "I cannot take responsibility for what might happen."

Many years later, when Golda was in Britain negotiating for some British tanks, she received a letter in longhand which read, "This will sound to you like a voice from another world. . . . While you were in London, I followed your every word and I agreed with every word you said. . . . Don't budge an inch from anywhere." It was signed "Cunningham" and Golda admitted, "You know, I was so excited."

Golda frequently accused the British of "malevolent neutrality," blatantly siding with the Arabs. She protested that they seldom searched the Arabs for weapons, but constantly stopped and searched the Jews, even confiscating knives longer than four inches.

"Look," a British officer told her, "if you know of places where Arabs have arms, you tell me and I'll get after them."

"So I gave him very clear, definite information," said Golda, "and he never did anything about it." Meanwhile, warned by British friends, the Arabs moved their guns elsewhere.

It was a trying time for Golda because friends and enemies were often blurred. She had to know which British officers she could trust, and how much. Some seemed wholly understanding, some partly sympathetic, a great many more were unpredictable. The general axiom was to trust no one absolutely, and generally suspect everyone among the British.

Golda regarded High Commissioner Cunningham and his subordinate, John Shaw, the chief secretary to the government of Palestine, as friendly and largely sympathetic. She vividly recalled Shaw's reaction when she detailed the deplorable conditions aboard another ship filled with refugees, intercepted by the British. She remembered how Shaw "sat there with his head in his hands and said that the only way a person can be here in government is just to sit in the office and not to see anything and not to hear anything."

But Golda hated Shaw's successor, Henry Gurney. In time, she denounced him as "a bastard, an anti-Semite to the nth degree." One of his small tricks, she noted, was to summon her to the King David headquarters, not during the safe hours of the day, but in the dangerous hours of the evening when the streets were deserted and the Arab snipers were busy. Golda always worried about her driver. "We would never figure out whether it was safer for him to wait for me outside or else risk driving back to the Agency and then come back for me."

When the war was still going on, Golda had gone to Gurney pleading for a ship to save some 4,000 children in Hungary.

"Mrs. Meyerson, don't you know there's a war on?"

"All right, but if they were British children, wouldn't you have a ship?"

Golda afterward admitted, "I still say to his credit that he didn't answer and he didn't lie."

But the conversation she could not forgive or forget was when he told her, "Mrs. Meyerson, if this is how the Jews are being treated by the Nazis, there must be a reason for it."

"I got up and walked out and never came to see him again."

This same official later queried one of Golda's compatriots, "Oh, why does Mrs. Meyerson not come and see me? She knows how much I think of her."

"After what you said to her?"

"But she knows I did not mean *her* ..."

In August 1946, the British government decreed that all illegal immigrants caught in Palestine waters would be sent to camps in Cyprus or elsewhere. The "elsewhere" meant displaced-persons camps, mostly in Germany, where so many thousands of Jewish refugees were still waiting painfully for the world's conscience to reach out to them.

Cyprus had some of the look of a concentration camp, complete with barbed wire and watchtower. Most of the housing was simply tents on the sand. At one time, the population of refugees reached 40,000 waiting for their British entry permits.

There was great concern about the health of the children in the camp. Golda was determined to try to get them out first.

"Imagine the moral force of a woman who feels she has the right to ask people who have been in detention camps for more than a year to give up their chance to go to Palestine and let the children go first," said Marie Syrkin. "And there was another catch: the children couldn't go alone—their parents had to go with them. I remember I later met a couple who had to wait three more years in that Cyprus camp because a more recently arrived couple with a child had gone ahead of them. It was an overwhelming sacrifice. I could no more have asked people to do that than stand on my head. I wouldn't feel I had the moral right. But Golda was convinced the thing had to be done."

And she did it.

First, she needed permission from the British camp officer. His opposition melted when he received a cable from the British high commissioner. "Mrs. Meyerson is a very formidable person. Watch out!"

To the people of the camp to whom she made her plea, she promised, "I promise you that every one of you will be freed to come into a Jewish state."

Years later, people walked up to her in Israel saying that they were the ones in Cyprus who heard her make that promise.

One of those in the camp then was a young woman who had served as a radio operator on a captured Haganah ship—and later became Golda's daughter-in-law. But Golda recalled her most moving moment in that Cyprus camp—two small children presented her with a bouquet of paper flowers. What hurt her was that they probably never had known what real flowers looked like.

"She had this gift of propaganda, and I use this word unashamedly," said Gershon Avner. "She was developing something that became central in her life, a capacity to explain Jews to non-Jews, and she could do this better than almost anyone. She could do it in a time when most of them knew nothing at all about the problems in Palestine. And she could do it in a talk of three-quarters of an hour. I used to sit with her at press conferences and marvel how she was able to do this. In those days there was a crisis every day and the journalists pulled no punches at the press conferences. But she could handle them, all of them."

Watching all this from abroad, Ben-Gurion was restlessly unhappy. His cure for restlessness was to bury himself in the books of a library. He did this on a visit to New York, where many Jewish leaders still regarded him "as more of a machine politician." In Paris, he was befriended by an interesting man from Vietnam named Ho Chi Minh, staying at the same hotel. Ho Chi Minh offered Ben-Gurion and his people sanctuary in his country—as soon as he took control.

But Ben-Gurion wanted only one sanctuary. He even decided to make a secret trip to Palestine for a meeting of the Jewish Agency Executive,

They gave her jobs of greater responsibility, and her door was always open to everyone, especially young people.

She firmly believed women could do any work that men could— and proved it.

Golda coped easily with people in power, even American senators (here with Senator Owen Brewster of Maine).

The British controlled Palestine, restricted immigration, and Golda was put
in charge of finding jobs and homes for "illegal" immigrants

...including the first group of Holocaust survivors.

She later became political head of Jerusalem during the siege by Arabs. The
world did not protest when the Arabs shelled the city

...the destruction and drama were constant.

These were some of the most important men in Golda's life, the pioneering giants of her country: Zalman Shazar, who later became President of Israel

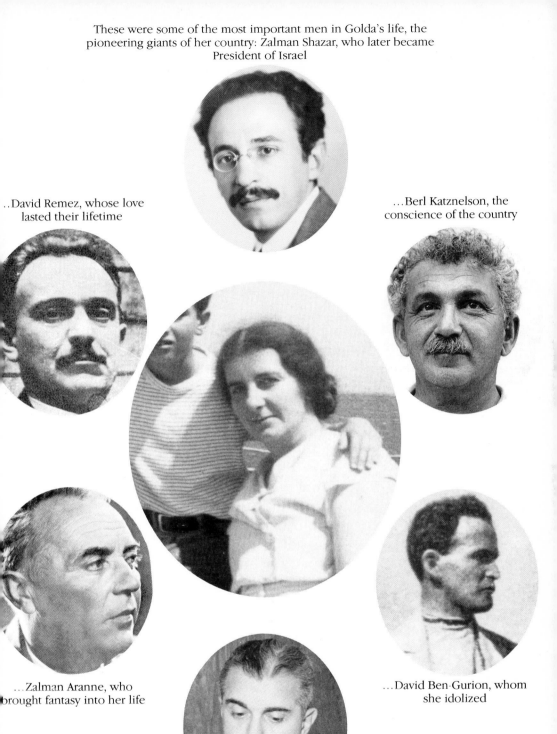

..David Remez, whose love lasted their lifetime

...Berl Katznelson, the conscience of the country

...Zalman Aranne, who brought fantasy into her life

...David Ben-Gurion, whom she idolized

...Henry Montor, her American dynamo.

The British Mandate finally came to an end

...and they now had their own army

...and Golda signed the
Declaration of
Independence

...and everyone celebrated
the birth of their new
nation

...but they still had a war to fight, and Golda's dramatic future was just
beginning.

but Golda persuaded him that it was too dangerous. Instead, she said, they would all come to him in Paris.

Some of their news was good. Since August 1945, some sixty-four ships had left ports in France, Italy, Greece, Bulgaria, Yugoslavia, and Romania with 73,000 refugees headed for Palestine. Some of the news was bitter. Anti-Semitism in Poland had not died with the extermination of four million Jews; the Polish town of Kielce, where there were only a hundred Jewish survivors, had recently suffered a local pogrom that killed forty-six. Some of the news was exciting. On the next holy day of Yom Kippur, the start of the new year, eleven forbidden Jewish settlements would be set up in a single night in the Negev. In the event of a future partition, Yishuv boundaries would automatically be enlarged.

The British news was bad. Foreign Minister Bevin had proposed an "independent unitary state" in Palestine "incorporating as much as possible of the Arab plan," with the Jews as a minority and immigration cut drastically. All this now appeared in a top-secret memorandum to the cabinet. Any encouragement of Jewish settlement or their aspirations for a separate state "would offend the Arabs." This he did not want to do, Bevin explained in another top-secret memorandum, because of "the vital importance to Great Britain and the British Empire of the oil resources of this area."

Bevin smirkingly described Jewish refugees as "the scum of the earth," and added, "Zionism and anti-Semitism are two sides of the same coin." Golda countered, "I don't know whether Bevin was a little insane, or just anti-Semitic, or both." Then she added, more quietly, "I had no doubt that if we gave in to Bevin, we were finished."

Golda and the furious Ben-Gurion journeyed to London to discuss this with Weizmann. The elderly Weizmann, who had lost a son in World War II, had still not lost all his faith in Britain. He seemed ready for any compromise, and called Golda and Ben-Gurion "irresponsible." "I lost my temper," said Golda, "something I very rarely do. I got up and walked out of the room."

All over the world, the seventy-two-year-old Dr. Chaim Weizmann was regarded as "the king of the Jews." Golda defied him again in December 1946 at the twenty-second Zionist Congress, held in Basel, Switzerland. Ailing, almost blind now, Weizmann still valiantly insisted on a halt of all Jewish violence in Palestine, calling it "a cancer on the body politic." The scene, as described by Golda, was "like the gathering of a terribly bereaved family mourning the death of multitudes." "Zion shall be redeemed through righteousness, and not by any other means," Weizmann told them.

But these were delegates who still recalled the faces of their murdered compatriots, who felt the pressure of hundreds of thousands of Jews sweating and rotting in DP camps behind barbed wire. They were tired of waiting for "righteousness"; they wanted action.

Speaking in her fluent Yiddish, Golda described the current action, and promised them more. And she gave them hope. She told them about the children born in Palestine, the *sabras*, how they risked their lives to rescue the refugees from the ships: "sixteen- and eighteen-year-old Palestinian girls and boys carried the survivors on their backs ..." In these *sabras* was their future, Golda declared proudly.

The Congress defeated the Weizmann proposal for nonviolence, and it was a long time before Weizmann forgave Golda.

Returning to Paris with Ben-Gurion, Golda was depressed. It took the Congress to dramatize again how many of her old friends were now dead. "We were all staying at the same hotel," said David Ginsburg, "and the chef there had a reputation, but I had the feeling that she didn't even know what she was eating, or even that she *was* eating. She was talking about the people she had known who had died in concentration camps, and there were tears in her eyes. . . .

"B-G would turn to her and discuss some subject and ask, 'Well, what do you think should be done?' and Golda would answer with an action program, one, two, three, four. It was clearly not a relationship of senior to junior, but here Golda was an equal partner with views of her own. I had the strong feeling that this woman in her black, drab clothes was a woman of power, of force, a woman in full command. And, yet, an odd combination of emotion and toughness. She was so dynamic! I had never known a woman like that!"

"Dynamic" was a good word for her. Behind her look of outward calm was a coiled electricity probing for a connection. This was not a style or a pattern, not something she developed or learned. This was simply the way she was, the way she had been all her life, the way she always would be. Many people saw Golda as a simple cut—the toughness. But behind that toughness, always, was emotion, warm and flowing, however private. To those who did not know her well, the combination of toughness and emotion seemed odd, almost contradictory, but that was Golda.

While mourning for her dead French friends, Golda made moves to help the living. Some 200 Jewish children, survivors of camps, were waiting in an orphanage in Toulouse, and Golda hurried there to arrange for their transportation to Palestine. The seamstress at the orphanage was another Jewish survivor, and Golda tried to fill her with the pride that she would one day carry a Jewish passport.

"No," declared the woman. "I do not want to go there. I am not a Zionist. I am a Communist."

Golda bristled. "What is a Communist? Sharing? Here are my clothes. Take what you want."

The seamstress was not converted. But Golda seldom suffered such defeats.

She was more successful in France arranging for future arms shipments. Ben-Gurion had told a group of Jewish leaders in New York the month before that their current battle against the British would not decide anything. "We will have to fight a war the Arabs will force on us."

What primarily interested Paris reporters was the current violence against the British. Jews would fight to defend themselves, Golda told them. Jews wanted peace and quiet, "but not the peace and quiet of a cemetery."

In the interval between Paris and Basel, Golda had gone back to Tel Aviv to celebrate the release of Remez and the other Yishuv leaders from Latrun prison. Golda had been counting the time: four months and seven days.

Side by side at Beth Haam Hall, Golda and Remez spoke to the thousands of people about their continued defiance of the British and the fresh urgency for a Jewish state. Remez returned with Golda to her apartment that night.

"We were sitting on the porch facing the sea," Golda recalled, "and he said, 'Ben-Gurion and you are destroying the last hope of the Jewish people.' Still full of the Gandhi civil disobedience he had studied, he now felt more than ever that counterviolence was not the answer, but that reason would right everything.

"I wasn't angry at him for saying that, but I answered, 'Look, you are afraid and I am afraid. But which way is more dangerous, yours or mine? Yours won't amount to anything, which will really bring us to destruction. My way means people's lives, but one thing I am sure of —we can't forfeit things necessary to our existence for the promise that if we'll be in trouble we can get help from the outside.' "

How Golda had grown! She had confronted the "king of the Jews" at Basel, conferred with Ben-Gurion as an equal, and now here she was disputing with her teacher, guide, and lover.

But the two still enjoyed each other.

"Look, I never pray to live long," Golda told Remez, "but I want to live long enough to see the day when a Britisher will come to the consulate of a Jewish state and ask for a visa."

And they laughed when Remez replied, "No, you don't want to live *long*!" indicating how remote that day was.

How implausible it seemed! The enormous force of the British. The overwhelming superiority of the Arabs. The implacable Bevin. The unconcerned world. And somewhere inside all this, like a gnawing nucleus, a small, battered people yearning to breathe free.

"I was never able to explain rationally why I believed that we would win," Golda reminisced.

A close friend described this "peculiar streak" in Golda, that "if you believe in something, you should go and try to accomplish it."

With so many poets for lovers, perhaps Golda knew Goethe's lines:

Whatever you can do,
or dream you can,
Begin it!
For boldness has genius, power and
magic in it.

With Moshe Sharett out of jail at the end of 1946, he was due to resume his post as political head of the Jewish Agency, thereby releasing Golda for a needed rest. It never happened. The Yishuv needed someone to argue their case for statehood before the world at the United Nations. Sharett went, and Golda stayed on as political head. Ben-Gurion had returned from Paris, still responsible for major policy. Golda was, as ever, intensely loyal to B-G, but no longer his clone.

Golda was now her own force, fit to face confrontation with a fresh

British ultimatum: you have seven days to express cooperation with us in putting down terrorism.

"We were astounded. . . . The Yishuv cannot under pressure of threats yield to the government's demands. . . . The keys to sincere cooperation are in the hands of the government—immigration, settlement, liberty, and independence."

The British did not know that the Vaad Leumi, the national committee, in January had seen Golda—with Remez's support—already declaring that representatives of all Jewish groups unanimously condemned the dangerous political and moral consequences of terrorism. They could make their own private condemnation of extremists, but they still refused to cooperate with the British. Jews were no longer a cringing people under a colonial oppressor; they were speedily emerging with the sense, and the dignity, of a nation.

Golda felt this keenly. If this land was going to give birth to a new nation, and Ben-Gurion was the father, then Goldie Mabovich Meyerson was unquestionably its mother.

Expectancy was in the air. After so much frustration, Bevin and the British were fed up with their Mandate in Palestine. A year earlier, Golda had told an international labor convention that the British should return their Mandate to the United Nations—and the British delegation had walked out in protest. In the course of the year there had been too much death and too much danger—and expense—even for the British, and they were now mulling over their next move.

Into Golda's open-door office one day, a feisty, twenty-year-old woman entered with a gift of lives. Her name was Geula Dagan, and her father had been an adviser on Jewish affairs to the British. She herself worked for the British Information Office, planted there by Haganah intelligence. Her gift was the information that the British now had specific plans to pull out of Palestine. Her British boss had told her of the planned pullout and offered her a job in Jordan, warning her she would be killed if she stayed behind because the Arabs were preparing to massacre all the Jews as soon as the British left.

Geula had little concept of the impact of her report, "but Golda asked *me* a bunch of questions, then took me to a big meeting with the Yishuv leaders where she told everybody what I had said while I sat on the stage slightly awestruck."

Geula's report meant peace and war and statehood: an eventual peace with Britain, the coming war with the Arabs, and the looming promise of statehood. The smell of this promise reached the isolated settlements, which were wondering whether they would become power pawns in any partition plan. Since there was no such plan yet, no isolated settlement knew its future—would it become a part of a Jewish state or a minority in an Arab one? Nahariyah did not plan to wait.

Founded by German immigrants in 1934, on the coast of western Galilee, Nahariyah was part of a compact with ten other settlements, some 2,400 people completely surrounded by Arabs. They demanded Golda's presence. Arriving by motorboat, Golda found an angry populace. They warned that they planned to set up their own ministate and to fight to the death rather than belong to the Arabs. Golda applauded their courage, urged them to "shout, but shout quietly." Their shouts should be loud enough to reach Yishuv leaders, but not the world. She promised her full support.

She could not promise more because nobody knew more. The Palestinian problem had moved to the world stage at the United Nations. The problems of partition now rested with the newly created United Nations Special Committee on Palestine, soon to be known by its initials as UNSCOP, a committee of eleven with a Swedish supreme court judge as its chairman. In the coming months, they would journey through Europe and then to Palestine before making their report.

While relinquishing the problem of partition to the UN in May 1947, the British still maintained control of Palestine and strictly regulated the immigration quotas. They had not yet set their own date of departure. Meanwhile, at the UN, Arabs and Jews presented their case to the world. "Why should we suffer the crimes of Hitler?" complained the Arabs. And the Jews replied, "Immigrant Jews were brought to Jewish settlements, not Arab areas." To the world democracies, the Jews added forcefully, "We were your allies in the war . . . the Jewish people belong in this society of nations."

". . . This is the first time that representatives of ours have appeared in the United Nations forum to defend our rights," Golda told a workers' council in Tel Aviv. "The Messiah hasn't come, the Day of Redemption isn't here yet . . . but it is a victory . . . Jews speaking for themselves. . . .

". . . We have had our fill of ridicule and contempt for this hard and thankless task of ours . . . explaining our cause over and over again . . . to outsiders who would never understand. . . .

"... Let us have the courage ... if we prepare for the worst then there is some hope that it won't come to the worst."

Newspaper headlines around the world featured a new, bitter drama in July 1947 with the story of the *Exodus*. A former Mississippi River steamer, it now had a new name, *Exodus Europe 1947*, and an old cargo, 4,500 lost people reaching for a root. Among them were hundreds of children and some 400 pregnant women, defiant and determined that their babies must be born in Palestine. British Foreign Secretary Ernest Bevin was equally determined that they would not.

Bevin's orders were clear. Four destroyers of the Royal Navy intercepted the *Exodus* in Palestine waters. When its embittered passengers refused to surrender, boarding parties killed three and used tear gas to subdue the rest. Bevin now ordered these survivors of death camps to be transferred to prison ships in Haifa harbor and taken to France. Four members of UNSCOP witnessed the transfer as British soldiers used "rifle butts, hose pipes, and tear gas, locking these battered men, women, and children in cages below decks." The UNSCOP members were "pale with shock." Abba Eban, who was with them, noted, "I could see that they were preoccupied with one point alone: if this was the only way that the British Mandate could continue, it would be better not to continue it at all."

The battered people were not yet beaten. In France they refused to disembark, and the French refused to force them. Golda had already intervened with the French consul, and a French minister named François Mitterand echoed the government insistence that the French would not intervene. The French distributed notices aboard the *Exodus* in three languages telling the people they need not leave the ship unless they wanted to. Reporter Paul S. Green of the Overseas News Agency described the daily trips of Haganah representatives in small boats going alongside the *Exodus* urging passengers to hold out against the British, one of them yelling through a megaphone, "None but the dead will land here!" One dead baby was later carried ashore. Another enterprising reporter, Ariyeh Gelblum of *Haaretz*, slipped in among the waiters delivering food on board, and wrote a vivid account of the British brutality and the refugee bravery. For nineteen days, the lost people suffered the summer heat without adequate food, with constant danger of disease. As world opinion heated up, with public demonstrations everywhere, the British conscience squirmed and the government requested the help of the Jewish Agency in persuading the passengers to leave the ship.

Golda refused. The Jewish Agency, she said, "would never lend itself, even under cruel menace, to prevent Jews from reaching their national home." She added her voice to the message sent to the refugees: "All of you will yet come to us," and quoted Deuteronomy: "If any of thine be driven out onto the outmost parts of heaven, from thence will the Lord, thy God, gather thee, and from thence will fetch thee."

An embittered Bevin held the final, dirty card. He ordered the ship back to Germany and its cargo back to the camps. The survivors would have to survive more barbed wire. Many of the desolate mothers would not see their babies born in Palestine. On that day of disembarkation, September 9, 1947, Golda declared a day of mourning, the Zionist flags draped in black. The mourning was not for the Jews, she shouted to the crowd, "but for the vanished justice and morality of Great Britain."

Golda made the *Exodus* her private mission, as many did. Each *Exodus* passenger, scattered in various camps, received a priority certificate on departing "illegal" ships. All were helped to escape, either singly or in small groups, and within the year they had reached their root, their home in Palestine.

"What was Bevin thinking?" asked Golda, calling it "the acme of brutality." "There doesn't seem to be a limit to hate and meanness," Remez wrote Golda. "Where do these people get their strength? It seems that suffering also doesn't have its limits."

"... To Britain we must say: it is a great illusion to believe us weak," Golda declared in a speech in Tel Aviv. "Let Great Britain with her mighty fleet and her many guns and planes know that this people is not so weak, and that its strength will yet stand it in good stead." Golda promised they would fight back, that the British would need more troops to quell them.

The nonviolent Remez wrote Golda: "... I read what you said at Tel Aviv ... about the stages including war. Perhaps there is still a glimmer of hope that we won't lose this stage. ... We will be put before a hard decision. Matters are still in the making and we won't know them until they're formally suggested, which isn't far away." If the mind of Remez was evolving toward the need for conflict, some of the influence of Golda must be counted. In the early years, the influence was always Remez on Golda; in the final years, they influenced each other.

The Royal Navy at Haifa still lit the harbor with searchlights every night searching for still more "illegal" ships, and depth charges rocked the city. British police vehicles still patrolled the streets at all hours, loudspeakers blaring warnings to wandering Jews. The world compassion for the *Exodus* did not penetrate the British military mind and Ernest Bevin had learned little. British soldiers, however, did not try to stop Golda and the thousands of people who followed the funeral, to the Haifa cemetery, of the three Jews killed on the *Exodus*, the first of the passengers to arrive in Palestine.

"The fact that the marine who killed the refugee used the Union Jack instead of the swastika didn't alter the fact that another Hebrew was killed in cold blood for no other reason than that he is a Hebrew." And in the United States, in a pageant on Broadway, "A Flag Is Born" by Ben Hecht, a character said: "The English have put a fence around the Holy Land. But there are three things they cannot keep out—the wind, the rain and the Jew . . ."

Golda went to Vienna to check on the surviving Jewish community. David Ginsburg, then with the American Embassy, working on the Austrian State treaty, lunched with her.

"I think she was wearing the same black dress she wore two years before," said Ginsburg. "Maybe she had a little gray in her hair, a few more lines on her face. There wasn't much laughter in her then. She had gone to see some of the concentration camps and she was terribly hard hit. But she didn't talk about it that much. This was not a person who spilled her soul. She never sought solace in solace. But there was such a feeling of overwhelming sadness in her. Still, she had this sense of command. Whoever she met, man or woman, automatically accepted her authority. And you never thought of her particularly as a woman or a man—she was a person."

Golda seldom saw Sarah during 1947. "The people at the kibbutz treated me even more nicely because my mother was already famous," said Sarah. She had been trained as a radio operator. "It was really our only connection with the world." As the most isolated settlement in the Negev, Revivim was expected to feel the first brunt of an Arab war. "It was a hard life, simple life. We lived in tents, and they used to fall down in the winter—on us, sometimes. And there were sandstorms. And it was very cold in the winter. It was sometimes terrible. We tried growing vegetables. We had some dates and palm trees. Nobody in his right mind would drink water from our well. Our social life was even more simple. People can be very lonely . . ."

When Golda did manage to get there, "she liked it very much. She used to meet everybody and people liked her. They all wanted to hear what she had to say." Sarah had matured, establishing herself as an individual. At one kibbutz meeting when Golda had talked for a long time, Sarah suddenly bristled and said, "Let them hear what I think for once." Golda retold that story many times, always with a point of pride.

Golda's pride in Sarah was enormous—but she kept it to herself, never told Sarah. She did tell it to Oriana Fallaci: "I'll tell you who I like: my daughter. Sarah is so good, so intelligent, so intellectually honest! When she believes in something, she goes all the way. When she thinks something, she says it without mincing words. And she never gives in to others, to the majority. I really can't say the same for myself. When you're doing the job I'm doing, you always have to stoop to compromises, you can never let yourself remain one hundred percent faithful to your ideas. . . ."

Golda moved again to Jerusalem in September 1947, and she and Remez saw more of each other. Earlier that year, they had even made a trip to Paris together. Jerusalem then was "a wonderful, dirty city with a domed skyline, many beggars, and little water." Water was a major problem. Even at the rebuilt and posh King David Hotel, water was used for washing hands, then reused for washing floors.

"Golda was the most capable woman I ever met," said Albert Spencer, secretary of the British War Economic Advisory Council. "Like our Mr. Churchill, she saw a simple solution to any problem. . . . If there was a shortage of timber, she knew where there was timber available in Syria. When we couldn't get meat, she would inform the Council that there were cattle walking across the desert near Baghdad. She *knew* these things."

She also knew that Jerusalem was a besieged city. She knew what horrors awaited the people there once the inevitable war came with the Arabs. UNSCOP delegates were still collecting evidence all over the country. Testifying about the Jewish plight, Weizmann told them, "They are a people and they lack the props of a people. They are a disembodied ghost." But it was a ghost, he said, which had "not disappeared through-out centuries, thousands of years of martyrdom and wandering." Responding to the question "Why Palestine?" Weizmann mentioned Moses, who "chose to stop here," and then added, "We are an ancient people with an old history and you cannot deny your history and begin afresh." Finally he asked UNSCOP to make their decision quickly, "Do not let it drag on. Do not prolong our agony. It has lasted long enough and cost a great deal of blood . . ."

Golda was "horrified" at how little the eleven UNSCOP members knew about the history of Palestine and Zionism. Golda offered her own short course:

"A little bit of history. Before the First World War, there wasn't one independent Arab country in the area. What was called Palestine was referred to by many Arabs as Southern Syria. The League of Nations gave the Mandate over Palestine to Great Britain. And what was Palestine then? It was all the area between the Mediterranean and the Iraq border. One high commissioner, one set of laws. This was Palestine. Then Churchill divided Palestine and made the Jordan River the dividing line, creating Transjordan east of the river.

"So Palestine was partitioned. . . . And we never had one single day of peace. That is a fact."

Another fact of another partition was now emerging at the United Nations. UNSCOP outlined the creation of two separate and independent states: an Arab state to contain 725,000 Arabs and 10,000 Jews, and a Jewish state to contain 498,000 Jews and 407,000 Arabs. The city of Jerusalem and its surrounding area, with 105,000 Arabs and 100,000 Jews, would be under international trusteeship. The Negev was to be Jewish, western Galilee was to be part of the Arab state, but eastern Galilee, including Nahariyah, was in Jewish control. The plan also obliged the British to leave Palestine within eight months.

Golda reluctantly accepted partition. She thought painfully of the people in those Jewish settlements who would become part of the Arab state. Beba Idelson's daughter was in such a settlement, determined to fight rather than be Arab-controlled. "You are responsible that I lost my home!" she wrote bitterly to her mother. "If I am killed, they will let you know."

The UN debate done, the General Assembly of the United Nations voted on the UNSCOP partition plan on November 29, 1947. The six Arab nations had already vetoed the proposal because they denied the right of Jews even to have a ministate.

It was past midnight in Palestine when the United Nations vote began.

Cafés were bright with people, everybody's radio blaring loudly. After two thousand years, would they *really* have a state? Few people slept as the count began.

Golda always hated to be alone. But who could she share this with? Her son was in the United States, her daughter on a kibbutz, her lovers and her *chaverim* with their own families. Yet perhaps, for one of the few times in her life, she preferred to be alone at this historic moment, a kind of culmination of her life. So she settled herself in her apartment with her usual pot of coffee, her endless cigarettes, and a notepad to mark the votes.

The final vote was thirty-three in favor, thirteen against, and ten abstentions. The United States and the Soviet Union voted in favor, and Great Britain abstained.

"We all jumped for joy," said Golda. She hurried to the Jewish Agency building, past the people singing and dancing in the streets. A wine company had brought barrels of wine for the street crowd. Perfect strangers became kissing kinsmen.

Weizmann was in America and Ben-Gurion wouldn't make a speech, so once again Golda became the spokesman of a people:

"I went upstairs to my office . . . there was a balcony . . . I came out and I was looking very, very sad because the Arabs had rejected it [partition] and we expected that there would be war . . ."

Still fresh in her mind, however, was her extraordinary interview with Emir Abdullah ibn Hussein, first king of the Hashemite Kingdom of Transjordan earlier that month. Ben-Gurion had sent her to see him to learn where he stood on peace and war, and the creation of a Jewish state. They had met at a private house near the Naharayim power station close to the bridge that crossed the Jordan River.

"When I was told of this interview, I thought the Israelis had made a mistake by being represented by a woman," said the British high commissioner in Jordan. "Although he respected the opposite sex, King Abdullah was a conservative. In his eyes, women could not be the equal of men, particularly in politics. In addition, Golda had little experience in negotiating with the Arabs. It is regrettable that this mission was not entrusted to someone like Sharett who knew the Arab language and the Arab mentality."

Sharett had been unavailable because he was busy representing the Zionist cause at the United Nations.

"I really took a liking to him," Golda said afterward about Abdullah. "He was a very, very charming person, very gentle and very nice. They say he wrote poetry." The king could not have seemed more cooperative. He shared the Jewish hate of the grand mufti, demeaned the military power of the other Arab states, and promised not to join them in any attack on the Jews.

Golda knew the scope of King Abdullah's power. His British-trained Arab Legion had 15,000 men and 400 tanks, the strongest Arab military force. Remembering all this as she stood on the balcony in the square, her voice choking with emotion, she aimed some of her words at the Arabs:

"... The partition plan is a compromise—not what you wanted, not what we wanted ... but let us now live in friendship and peace together...."

But her core words were for the exultant Jews:

"For two thousand years we have waited.... We always believed it would come.... Now we shall have a free Jewish state.... It surpasses human words...."

Overcome by emotion, she then cut short her speech, saying only, almost shouting, "Jews ... *mazel tov*! ..."

The human electricity lasted all night, people dancing and drinking and singing until dawn.

Watching the street scene in Jerusalem, an Arab woman bitterly told an American correspondent, "Let them dance now; they will all soon be dead anyhow!"

16

Clark, you just don't understand this. It's a question of arithmetic. There are 45 million Arabs and 350,000 Jews, and the 45 million Arabs are going to push the 350,000 Jews right into the ocean. That's all there is to it.

—Secretary of Defense James Forrestal to Clark Clifford

Why are there so many stones in Jerusalem?

"Because each arriving Jew drops a heavy stone from his heart."

In late 1947, the Jews again picked up their heavy stones. Jerusalem was a city holding its breath, waiting. No Jewish target in Palestine was more vulnerable, more susceptible to strangling.

Only a month after the UN partition vote, Jerusalem in mid-December 1947 was a paralyzed place isolated behind a curtain of fear. The Arabs had refused to accept the UN internationalization of the city. Their immediate reaction to the partition vote was to loot, burn, destroy, often in full view of the British police. That December Ben-Gurion visited Golda and they watched an Arab mob in action from her office window.

An angry Golda went to the office of the British high commissioner to confront his top official, the chief secretary. She produced photographs of the Arab looting showing a British police officer watching the scene with his arms folded. The chief secretary dryly admitted that the photographs seemed to show that the British police did nothing to stop the riots, and promised an inquiry. Nothing happened. It was later revealed that the British police had not seized any Arabs during those riots but had arrested sixteen Haganah men for carrying guns.

Two young Jewish women arrested for carrying arms were sentenced to three years in prison. In a letter to the *Palestine Post*, a non-Jew wrote:

> As a spectator on the sidelines and a countryman of neither side, may I, through the courtesy of your columns, express my tremendous admiration of the fortitude, courage, and restraint of the members of the Haganah under provocation as galling as it is criminal, with little or no help from those quarters from which it could have been expected in view of repeated official statements on the subject of law and order?
>
> I can never hope to witness again, anywhere else in the world, a better discipline, a greater courage, or a more admirable spirit than that which has been displayed by the Jewish people as a whole ever since Partition was approved by the UN.

Golda asked the direct question of the high commissioner: why should British police penalize the Jews because the Arabs would not agree to set up their provisional government under the United Nations plan? She described his vague answer as "dusty."

Due to leave on May 15, the British were determined to minimize their own casualties and largely stayed behind the sandbagged, barbed-wire area of "Bevingrad" that included the police headquarters, post office, telephone exchanges, hospital, and broadcasting studios. Aside from the insane asylum, these were the only places where Jews and Arabs were still in close contact, although people who were friends now averted their eyes. There was little question of the British partiality. Jews with guns were arrested—more than fifty in two months—"but we didn't mind the Arabs moving around with grenades all over their chests and cartridge belts hanging from their shoulders, just as long as they didn't bother us."

The presence of the British police prevented open war, but terrorism flourished. Jerusalem was a city of neighborhoods sitting on hills, and some areas were mixed, but not for long. Most Arabs had already moved out of Jewish areas just as Jews had moved out of Arab areas. To hurry them along, houses were blown up. Crossing from one area to another "was like crossing between two foreign countries."

Most people stayed inside, their doors locked, venturing outside only when necessary. When they did, they walked quickly, their eyes searching everywhere, their ears tuned for sniper fire. A sixteen-year-old Arab boy recalled buying a pistol and firing it from his window toward the adjoining Jewish neighborhood until he heard the voice of a woman he recognized, a woman for whom he had lit the lamps every Sabbath:

"Do not shoot," she cried. "Are we not neighbors since many years?"

The agony of Jerusalem was Golda's agony. Ben-Gurion had given her complete command of the city with all its awesome responsibility.

"Everybody went to Golda for everything, even my wife, who wanted money for a scientific unit that was building weapons," recalled Chaim Herzog. Herzog, who later became president of the country, never forgot a speech Golda made after a concert "and imbued the people with a certain spirit. She had a way of stirring up pep in people." He also never forgot an explosion under Golda's office window. An American consular car had been parked there. "When a guard checked it, it blew up the whole front of the building. If Golda had been in her office then, she would have been killed."

Golda's responsibility included military decisions, and the military position was precarious. In the Old City, the Holy City, surrounded by its ancient stone wall and seven gates, the only lifeline for the 2,000 Orthodox Jews living in the Jewish Quarter was the number 2 bus. It passed through the Jaffa Gate for the dangerous five-minute ride past Arab crowds into the Jewish area of New Jerusalem. Once that lifeline was cut, Golda knew that the Jews there were under siege. Most of the Orthodox were so religious that they refused to fight. They depended on a small force of 150 young Palmach who were armed with fourteen working rifles, three submachine guns, and twenty-five pistols.

To protect the 100,000 Jews in New Jerusalem, Golda had a force of 500 trained Haganah soldiers, all available at instant alert, women as well as men. The code name for the Jerusalem Haganah was "the Aunt," and it collected its own blankets and clothes from the community, had meal tickets at local restaurants for its recruits, and maintained a tough training program for future fighters among the young boys and girls. It specialized in guerrilla fighting at night, which the Arabs feared.

If the handful of Orthodox Jews in the Old City depended on the number 2 bus for their lifeline, the 100,000 Jews in New Jerusalem represented a small island surrounded by a sea of Arabs, completely isolated, connected to Tel Aviv by a skinny string of twisting road under constant fire from snipers.

Arab snipers had a favorite deathtrap on that road, a place called Bab el Wad where they hid in the flanking pine forest ready to ambush. Israeli "sardine-tin" buses—ineffectively reinforced with thin metal—were forced at that point to travel in slow, low gear, and Arab guns were always waiting.

Convoy driver Yona Golani admitted afterward, "I would become so frightened that the sweat would pour from my head down my neck. When you know they could shoot at you from both sides, you'd hear a sort of echo inside, plucking at your nerves. It was also a horrible sight to see the car in front of you hit a mine and blow up. . . . You can cry, but you have to go on. The convoy must get through . . ."

When a convoy did get through, the children would rush out of their homes "and kiss us, crying. . . . We would stand and weep with them."*

Golda traveled that road twice a week to report to Ben-Gurion in Tel Aviv.

During an Arab attack, Zeev Sherf asked Golda what she was doing.

"Covering my eyes. I'm not really afraid to die, you know. Everyone dies. But how will I live if I'm blinded? How will I work? What will I do without eyesight?"

She had some close calls. She was on a bus on that road with two dozen other people, and sat next to Hans Beyth, head of Youth Aliyah. His was the job of greeting newly arrived orphans at Haifa and assigning them to homes around the country. He had told Golda that morning how his wife had berated him for making the dangerous journey. "Why are you going?" she had asked him. "People there are getting killed all the time. You could make your own children orphans."

As the bus approached the curve, the Arab ambush began. Beyth had a pistol and fired back. Before he could fire again, another shot killed him. He fell on Golda's lap.

Many years later, when Golda was dying, a young doctor came to examine her. She noticed his name and asked if he was related to Hans Beyth.

"He was my father," said the young doctor, "and I've wanted to ask you more about how he died."

---

*On April 17, 300 trucks traveling bumper to bumper for six miles carried 1,000 tons of supplies to Jerusalem. Their cargo included 180,000 eggs, 470 cases of tinned milk, and 156 tons of flour. Even though the convoy arrived on Sabbath, religious Jews left their synagogues still in their prayer shawls and proceeded to begin their duties of checking and distributing food and supplies.

Golda replied softly, "He died in my arms."

"The only privilege that we enjoyed due to the Arabs," said Golda, "was that the British never searched an Arab woman, and since they were evenhanded they wouldn't search a Jewish woman either. So we would start out with a convoy of buses and the boys of the Haganah in the bus with Sten guns. Then in the distance we would see a check post so the bus would stop and the Sten guns would be broken up into parts. No matter how hot it would be, the women would be there with coats and would take the Sten guns under their coats. And that's what was done and then we'd pass the check post and you'd put the Sten guns together again because five minutes after that you were liable to have Arabs shoot at you."

Golda once traveled with a convoy of 170 vehicles when they were stopped unexpectedly by British armored cars at a crossroads. Rivka Yisraeli recalled that it happened so suddenly that there was not enough time to take apart all their guns and hide them. Golda offered to put some grenades and small guns in her purse. Other women stuffed parts in their brassieres or between their thighs. Golda asked Rivka if she was afraid; she said no, but she was worried about her parents. A passing British officer noticed part of a Sten gun sticking out of Rivka's coat and arrested her.

"Where are you taking her?" asked Golda.

The officer mentioned a nearby hostile Arab village, and Golda worried what would happen to Rivka there, all alone.

"Arrest me, too," Golda told him.

The bewildered officer consulted his superior, who recognized Golda, apologized to her, and offered her a glass of wine and a personal escort for the rest of her trip.

The British even returned the gun to Security Chief Chaim Herzog "and apologized for taking it. They understood that Golda had to be protected." Golda afterward brought Rivka to a Vaad Hapoel meeting to tell the story and show the gun.

The story proved Golda's power, even among the British. That power meant nothing to the Arabs when Golda's driver once took a wrong turn, arriving in a hostile village. They fortunately raced away before being recognized.

"We will strangle Jerusalem," promised Abdul Kader Husseini, the Arab planning officer on Jerusalem. "We must make the Jews live hell."

The hell started when the Arabs sabotaged the only three pipelines bringing water to the city. Golda detailed her deputy, Dov Joseph, to search for available cisterns. A tenacious Canadian, Joseph had first seen Jerusalem in 1919 when he was a sergeant in the Jewish Legion. Joseph discovered some 2,000 cisterns and filled them with 22 million gallons of water as soon as the British repaired the pipes. Water-ration cards were issued and water was delivered on fixed schedules in water carts to different parts of the city. Joseph also had taken an inventory of all available food, and the location of warehouses to store it.

The terrorism intensified throughout December 1947. Snipers killed at random: people hurrying home from work in early dusk; women waiting in line for their daily water ration of half a pail; children coming from school. Other murders were more plotted: Israel Schreiber, kidnapped and killed, his body dumped in a burlap bag near the Damascus Gate; a crippled newsdealer shot to death by an Arab customer; a *Palestine Post* columnist, Robert Stern, murdered after writing his last column saying he wanted his readers to contribute to the zoo if he was killed. Even his funeral convoy to the Mount of Olives cemetery was machine-gunned en route.

The Jews had their own snipers, their own assassins who believed in "an eye for an eye," and they had commando squads of Haganah forces infiltrating into Arab hideouts on sudden raids, usually at night. "Go in fast . . . blow up some houses . . . kill some people and get out."

In the first two weeks after the partition announcement, ninety-three Arabs, eighty-four Jews, and seven British soldiers were killed in Jerusalem.

If the Arabs felt that the surrounded, outnumbered, besieged Jews of Jerusalem would panic and run, they were wrong. "We live in a very dangerous part of the world but we intend to stay here," Golda had once said.

"She always managed to cheer up the rest of us when we felt low."

"The fact that the Jews have survived . . . is due to one thing," Golda insisted, "something which many in the non-Jewish world have never understood. We are *am k'shey-oreff* [a stiff-necked people]. We are a people which does not bow, a people which stands erect to face its tragedies. If we are criticized because we do not bow, because we cannot compromise on the question 'To be or not to be,' it is because we have decided that, come what may, we are and we *will* be." Golda later amplified that statement: "We intend to remain alive. Our neighbors want to see us dead. This is not a question that leaves much room for compromise."

In deciding things, Golda said, "I tried to differentiate between the basic and the essential and things that one can fight and argue about. But ideas, hopes, and ideologies were not then things that one burned up his house for."

To keep going, Golda trained herself to get along with no more than four hours' sleep for days at a time, then perhaps sleep for fourteen hours. Part of her secret, something she considered "my strongest point," was her added ability to fall asleep anywhere anytime for a short, refreshing nap.

The British were not concerned with the Battle of the Roads, except to search Jewish convoys and protect their own trade. British industry badly needed phosphate and so the British provided an armed convoy for their phosphate trucks. On her trips to report to B-G in Tel Aviv, Golda sometimes rode with the trucks to the north shore of the Dead Sea. "Then I would board the small plane we called a Primus and fly to Tel Aviv."

She did this once to supervise the wedding of her nephew, Shana's son Yona. Shana had gone to New York months before for special surgery, a colostomy.

"I mean, Golda did everything at that wedding," remembered Yona. "My grandfather was dead but she even sent a car to bring my grandmother. That was the first day the Arabs had blocked the Jaffa road, and so a lot of guests couldn't come. But Golda made all the arrangements, did it all." "As if she doesn't have enough to do running the government," her sister Clara commented, "she also sort of runs the whole family."

Golda afterward wired her niece, Judy Bauman, Yona's sister, in Brooklyn, New York, that the wedding had gone off "beautifully." She also had told Judy that she was very concerned about Menachem in New York and asked Judy to watch out for him. Menachem had lived with Judy and her husband for several months before moving to an apartment near the Manhattan School of Music.

Golda had a greater, more immediate worry: guns. She pleaded with Ben-Gurion—who made all major military decisions—to send more arms to Jerusalem.

Ben-Gurion did not need to be reminded of Jerusalem's pitifully absurd arms inventory: 500 rifles, 400 Sten guns, twenty-eight machine guns, and some mortars to confront the whole Arab Legion and the hordes of Jerusalem Arabs. What he told Golda was that the total Haganah arsenal included only 10,000 rifles, 19,000 Sten guns, and sixty-six mortars. "We didn't even have enough bullets." The quartermaster general had come to him before Golda and said, "I can't go on like this. People are getting killed because they don't have things to protect themselves. We are short of arms, equipment, short of everything . . ."

"There was no doubt that Ben-Gurion was the strongest and the bravest," declared Golda, "but . . . he called me in once and said, 'Golda, I'm going mad. I can't sleep nights. I have taken a survey and I know exactly what the Haganah has and what it doesn't have. We are facing a war—what is to become of us?'

"Why did he call me? I say that even Ben-Gurion, who wasn't a man for socializing, had to talk to someone about what bothered him and he chose me because he knew that he could tell me and I wouldn't despair." Ben-Gurion knew this well, and said it often:

"She had faith when others wavered. She believed in the absolute justice of our cause when others doubted."

With all his doubts, and occasional fears, few had a clearer vision than Ben-Gurion. He was the one, the year before, who had asked fund-raiser Henry Montor in New York to prepare a list of thirty Americans "who will be prepared to do whatever we need so that we will be ready to defend ourselves when war breaks out." B-G told these thirty men of his certainty of an Arab attack as soon as the British pulled out, told them that it would be a war of survival. These thirty helped raise the initial money to buy and move the vital weapons the Haganah needed. "They really saved us," recalled Golda.

The power center in Jewish Palestine started concentrating after the partition announcement. David Ben-Gurion was chairman of the Jewish Agency and David Remez the chairman of the Vaad Leumi. The Agency had been the shadow government responsible for everything from immigration to British contact; the Vaad Leumi represented all the various Jewish groups in the country. Together they had supervised the Haganah defense force. Together they now created a Committee of Thirteen to run the Yishuv until it became a state. Golda was one of the thirteen.

They met in a simple room around a simple table in the Jewish Agency building in the heart of Tel Aviv. Agency treasurer Eliezer Kaplan had just returned from the United States with discouraging news. American Jews, he told them, were tired of giving and giving and giving. It was unrealistic to expect any more massive sums in fund-raising. They would be lucky to get a fraction of the millions they needed for arms. He summed it up as the mission impossible.

Ben-Gurion, like Golda, refused to admit that anything was impossible. "This is the time for the United States," he said defiantly; he himself would go to America and raise the money. The mood in the room dampened. Nobody questioned Ben-Gurion's enthusiasm, but all of them realized that it was not matched by his fluency in English. Word had come back from the United States that Ben-Gurion was often difficult to understand. But who could tell him this? Who would beard the lion?

Golda alone voiced her protest.

"What you can do here, I cannot do," she told him, "but what you can do in the United States, I can also do."

Ben-Gurion tried to brush her aside, saying curtly, "I need you here." Golda insisted on a vote. The men around the table in this unadorned room, tired and harassed, seemed to catch her spirit. Defying B-G, whom they called "The Old Man," always involved a tinge of danger. But now they looked at Golda, and at one another, and voted. They all voted with Golda.

Brusquely, the Old Man insisted she leave the next morning.

That night the quartermaster general came to see her to emphasize their needs. "I told her ... how we needed even the simple things, something for the soldiers to cover their heads in the cold. . . . I remember her face listening to all this, and I will never forget the seriousness of how she took it . . ."

Just before she left, Ben-Gurion paid her a visit at her hotel. He seemed almost embarrassed when he gave her the list of some books he wanted her to buy for him while she was in the United States.

Golda was worried. This would be her first trip to the United States in ten years. This time she would not be talking to Pioneer Women, ardent Zionists who believed what she believed. "I was terribly afraid of going to those people who didn't know me from Adam." She regarded Henry Montor as one of "those people"; she knew him only as "a great power who did great things." She even asked Kaplan "to write to Montor that my visit was the decision of the Jewish Agency, asking him to be helpful." It would have surprised her to learn then that Montor already knew all about her, and preferred her to Ben-Gurion because "she had the American label, the American touch, the American identity."

"I came to New York on a Friday night toward the end of January 1948 during one of the worst blizzards (almost twenty-eight inches) New York ever knew." The story that Golda later added was that all she had in her purse was a ten-dollar bill—this woman who had come to ask for millions. She hadn't even had time to go to Jerusalem to get some clothes.

Her son, Menachem, and sister Shana met her at the airport. At customs, they asked Golda if she had any other relatives living in the United States. "I told them I had a sister but I couldn't tell them her address. They became suspicious. How could a woman have a sister and not know where the sister lived? How could I explain that I didn't know her address because I never answered her letters? Finally one of the officials looked up her name in the phonebook and let me in."

Golda and Clara hardly knew each other. Clara's personal life had become tragic. Her only son had died of pneumonia the year before Golda arrived. Her husband had been seriously ill, and their marriage stayed sour. By dedicated devotion, Clara had created for herself a secure place in her community, particularly in social welfare and interfaith relationships. She had a reputation for intensity, hard work, and honesty. Some saw her as loud, dictatorial, blunt, but those who knew her best knew the warmth within her. It was as if she had thrown all of herself into her career because there was nothing much left in her marriage. Golda later said of Clara's marriage: "Clara was very, very brave. She really sacrificed herself . . . for nothing, because she really got nothing in return. I don't know how my sister did it. She really was a hero."

But that Friday night, meeting at the airport, Golda and Clara were strangers trying to reach each other from opposite ends of a long bridge. Montor's assistant was also there. Montor, he said, was at a meeting in Chicago of the Council of Jewish Federations, the leaders of organized Jewry in the United States. Montor, then executive director of the United Jewish Appeal, had felt that there was no need for Golda to join him at the meeting, since the Council was anti-Zionist. Clara protested. She knew about that meeting. Maybe they weren't Zionists but they were all multimillionaires. She strongly urged Golda to go. It was curious that Clara, however anti-Zionist, would still be concerned with the success of the fund-raising, and the survival of the Israeli dream.

Clara went back to Bridgeport that night, Menachem to his Manhattan apartment, and Golda went with Shana to Judy's apartment near the Brooklyn Navy Yard. "We only had a one-bedroom apartment," said Judy, "but we had a lot of couches." Judy and her husband gave up their double bed to Golda and Shana, and the two sisters spent the long night talking.

"Up to that point, I had no itinerary," said Golda. "When I got up in the morning, I decided maybe the Chicago meeting was a good idea." She called Montor's assistant and told him. "Look," he said, "I'm not directing this thing. They have their own agenda, but I'll talk to them." He soon called her back, "Okay, they're preparing to let you speak but how do you propose to get to Chicago?" The blizzard had closed the airport, but Golda went there anyway, and waited. There was finally a short break in the weather and Golda's plane took off. "I think our plane was the only one that left that day."

It was one of the most important plane trips Golda ever took. It was, in fact, a turning point in her life. In retrospect, her speech was surely the most critical one she ever made. The birth of a country depended on it.

Her audience were the VIJs of America, some 800 of them, in the former Chicago Athletic Club. All of them were community leaders and very rich, but also very cynical. They had been giving a lot of money to a lot of worthy causes for a long time. They had heard all kinds of emotional pleas and it would take much to move them now, particularly on a Sunday afternoon after a long business session—and most particularly since they had little interest in Zionism and even less in Palestine. Palestine was not on their agenda, and never had been. The only reason they were listening to Golda was as a courtesy to Henry Montor, who had described her as "perhaps the most powerful Jewish woman in the world today."

"I admit I was shaking," remembered Golda. "This was an audience I didn't know. I had no idea what was going to happen." When reporters once asked for an advance copy of her speech, she had told them, "Gentlemen, I have no idea what I'm going to say until I get on that platform and I see the people I'm talking to."

What they saw this day was a woman in a simple blue dress, her hair in a bun. If she was afraid, she did not show it. She spoke, as always, without notes. She seemed neither overawed nor condescending. She spoke almost without emotion for thirty-five minutes, never raising her voice. The normal din of the dense crowd was absent.

What she said was this:

We must ask the Jews the world over merely to see us as the front line and do for us what the United States did for England when England was in the front line in the World War. All we ask of Jews the world over, and mainly of the Jews in the United States, is to give us the possibility to go on with the struggle. . . .

I want you to believe me when I speak before you today that I came on this special mission to the United States today not to save seven hundred thousand Jews. The Jewish people have lost during the last few years six million Jews, and it would be audacity on our part to worry the Jewish people throughout the world because a few hundred thousand more Jews were in danger.

That is not the problem. The problem is that if these seven hundred thousand Jews can remain alive, then the Jewish people as such are alive and Jewish independence is assured. If these seven hundred thousand people are killed off, then at any rate for many, many centuries we are through with this dream of a Jewish people and a Jewish home. . . .

My friends, we are at war. There is not a Jew in the country that does not believe that in the end we will be victorious. The spirit of the country is such—we have known Arab riots since 1921 and '29 and '36 when for four years we had Arab riots. We know what happened to Jews in Europe during this war. Every Jew in the country knows that within a few months a Jewish state in Palestine will be established. We have to pay for it. We knew that we would pay for it. We knew that the price we would have to pay was the best of our people. There are a little over three hundred killed now. There will be more. There is no doubt that there will be more. But there is no doubt that the spirit of our young people is such that no matter how many Arabs come into the country, the spirit of our young people will not falter.

The spirit is there. This spirit alone cannot face rifles and machine guns. Rifles and machine guns without spirit are not worth very much. But spirit without these in time can be broken with the body.

The problem is time. The time factor is the most important factor now in this issue. Millions that we get within three or four months will mean very little in deciding the issue now. The problem is what we can get immediately. And, my friends, when I say immediately, it does not mean next month. It does not mean two months from now. It means now. . . .

I have come to the United States, and I hope you will understand me if I say that it was not an easy matter for any of us to leave home at present —to my sorrow I am not in the front line. I am not with my daughter in the Negev, nor with other sons and daughters in the trenches. But I have a job to do.

I have come here to try to impress Jews in the United States with this fact, that within a very short period, a couple of weeks, we must have in cash between twenty-five and thirty million dollars. Not that we need this money to use during these weeks, but if we have twenty-five or thirty million dollars *in the next two or three weeks* we can establish ourselves. Of that we are convinced, and you must have faith; we are convinced that we can carry on. . . .

We are not a better breed; we are not the best Jews of the Jewish people. It so happened that we are there and you are here. I am certain that if you were there and we were here, you would be doing what we are doing there, and you would ask us who are here to do what you will have to do. . . .

You cannot decide whether we should fight or not. We will. No white flag of the Jewish community in Palestine will be raised for the Mufti. That decision is taken. Nobody can change that. You can only decide one thing: whether we shall be victorious in this fight or whether the Mufti will be victorious in this fight. That decision American Jews can take. It has to be taken quickly, within hours, within days. . . . The time is now. . . .

The audience saw her "just like a woman out of the Bible . . . so plain, so strong, so old-fashioned . . . we had never seen anyone like her." "She had all the elements of courage and danger and passion." "Remember, we had dozens and dozens of Jews there who did not know where they stood. They were angry at Hitler, but they were not for any Jewish independent state . . . then Golda made this magnificent speech."

The response was electric. This cynical, sophisticated, partly hostile audience stood up cheering, applauding, crying. More than that, they pledged $25 million. One speech in a day resulted in three times as much money as Agency treasurer Kaplan felt was possible only after a prolonged national campaign.

Montor was stunned. Never before in his professional fund-raising life had he ever witnessed anything like this. He had heard many more speakers far more brilliant and equally sincere. But Golda was unique. What came through so clearly was her shining spirit, her sense of dedication that pierced like a searchlight. Montor knew that most people give money because they're fired by a purpose. Golda's fire was a furnace. This woman was magnificent.

There and then began the relationship of Golda and Henry Montor. The two shared an enormous excitement. They held in their hands the fate of a people in an unborn country. Golda marveled at the way Montor could organize anything, almost instantly. He had an air of absolute authority. Like Remez and Shazar, he was a dynamo creating his own electricity. Like them, too, he was married, but on a loose string.

Montor was a handsome man of medium height with big black eyes and coal-black curly hair. His mother had died in childbirth, and Henry Montor was brought from Canada to the United States as a boy. He had described his childhood as "very sad." With a scholarship at Hebrew Union College to become a rabbi, he grew a beard down to his chest, graduated with a brilliant scholastic record. Then he changed his mind, refused to be ordained as a rabbi, and decided to go to New York and be a writer. He shaved off his beard, settled for a mustache, and tried to get the curls out of his hair. He married the only woman enrolled at his school training to be a rabbi. When Montor applied for a job on the magazine *New Palestine*, he was asked, "Do you want the job because you're a Zionist, or because you need the job?" "I don't give a damn about Zionism," Montor replied, and still got the job.

"Montor was the kind of person who never did or felt anything halfway. Whether emotionally or intellectually, he was the kind of man who was a thousand percent." "Montor had a one-track mind—Jews in Palestine. He was a real Jekyll-and-Hyde—sweetest guy you ever saw, but if you rubbed him wrong, look out!" Other people saw Montor as a man with a hard shell, almost a brusqueness, "who picked up enemies on every hand by a sort of natural antiaffinity." "A very strange man in many ways, but a genius who could sense history at the right moment, a genius in propaganda ... some people *look* like a success; he didn't. But there was no fund-raiser like him or ever will be."

"He could do the work of a half dozen people—a half dozen secretaries, a half dozen executives, a half dozen typists—I think he was one of the world's fastest typists. He had great imagination, great vision, and incredible energy. He wanted to push harder and harder. He would come in Monday morning with a briefcase—almost a suitcase—full of

Dictaphone rolls, some thirty or forty, and every secretary there would groan. His output was enormous. He was really outstanding."

At nearly fifty "hardly a spring chicken," Golda was described by Montor's assistant then as "a very attractive, very striking woman." Except for her hair, she had little vanity about her clothes or appearance. But she still could be coquettish with men—she always would be.

Montor had "a distaste for pious phrases, and this did not endear him to the Zionist regulars." It endeared him to Golda. The two also shared an intense energy. "Montor was mad," remarked Golda. "I've never seen anybody who worked like he did. His ability to work was limitless." His passion also impressed her. He once got so angry at a meeting that he banged his hand hard on the podium and broke his little finger. "That was his war wound—the evidence of his passion, determination, or whatever you want to call it. . . . Montor wasn't asking them or cajoling them, but he *demanded*! He would say, 'You are not doing us a favor. This is *your* business!' "

Montor had an equally passionate partner in Golda. "Take her away from me," one wealthy Jew complained. "What crazy person is this?"

Together they formed a dynamic force. For the next several months, January through March, Golda and Montor crisscrossed the country, stopping at more than twenty cities for one-night appearances. With his card-catalog brain, Montor knew just how much they could ask from whom. "It was incredible," Golda remembered, "the way he knew every prominent Jew, what his problems were, and how much he should give."

Montor was seven years younger than Golda, but their mutual attraction was quick and strong. What tied them tightly was the tension and electricity of their constant togetherness, the pull of their mutual need. If they could not share the same memories, they still could reminisce about the same people, even laugh at the same jokes. With the enormity of their daily emotional drain, they reached to each other for some release in laughter, and maybe love, to recharge their batteries.

Montor listened attentively as Golda made a different but equally emotional speech at the United Nations at the end of January.

"Why is our buying arms for the Jewish community in Palestine so terribly illegal when it is perfectly legal for Iraq or Syria to buy arms from Great Britain?"

She flatly accused the British of supplying arms to the Arabs because "peace and good relations with the Arabs must be had at all costs, and if it costs a lot of Jewish bloodshed and chaos in the country ... well, then let's have it that way."

The British should withdraw their navy from Palestinian territorial waters and they should permit arms to reach the beleaguered Jews. If the United Nations truly wanted to help, she added, they should send an international force to buffer the Arab aggression. Nor did she have kind words for the United States. The United States had not spoken up at UN debates "in support of moral or spiritual rights of Jews ... not one sympathetic word.... The U.S.A. meekly bowed to Arab threats in order to gain what it hopes may be strategic or economic advantages in Arab countries."

She added a postscript at a press conference afterward:

"There can be peace in Palestine in five minutes. It depends entirely upon the attackers. The minute the attackers stop there will be peace in Palestine. But as long as they go on, there will have to be war and we will have to fight back."

The United States in 1948 had an air of prosperity. Women's fashions featured the "New Look," more than a million World War II veterans were enrolled in colleges under the GI Bill, and an increasing number of people reported seeing "flying saucers." Babe Ruth had died, heavyweight champion Joe Louis had retired, and the long-playing record had been invented. A favorite song that year would be "All I Want for Christmas Is My Two Front Teeth."

Traveling through the country on their frenetic schedule, Golda and Montor were joined by two of the "Three Musketeers." That's what Golda called them; three young millionaires in their late thirties, all fervent admirers of Golda ever since they had heard her Chicago speech. Sam Rothberg had made his fortune in manufacturing, and Julian Venezky was a noted lawyer. Rothberg and Venezky were from Peoria, Illinois. Joining them later was Lou Boyar, a real estate tycoon from Chicago and Los Angeles. These three would become an integral part of her life, her American arms. They would support her, defend her, love her.

"I was the advance man," proclaimed Sam Rothberg, a tall, broadshouldered, impressive-looking man. "I'd go into a community first to check the leadership. If the leadership didn't meet the standard, I'd destroy the leadership, because most people followed the leaders. I used to break tables—dishes used to fly. I'd scare the hell out of people. I'd really tell them what I thought of them. I'd say, 'There are 5,000 Jewish communities in the United States. But as of tonight, there are only 4,999.' If there was a rabbi sitting at the table, I'd ask him to stand up and say Kaddish, a prayer for the dead community. Then I'd get up and walk around the block a couple times to cool off. I remember once when I came back to the meeting, a woman came over to me and said, 'I want to kiss your hand ... this community needed a shaking up ...' At any rate it became a good community." Nobody was more effective in this than Sam Rothberg.

"They had to change off," said Golda, smiling. "They couldn't take the schedule." When they did work, the Musketeers worked day and night.

"Montor would travel with Golda; and Sam and I, and later Lou, would be the advance men, traveling ahead of them all the time," recalled Julian Venezky. Venezky earlier had helped raise money for the Haganah, and afterward recruited Rothberg. "In most of the towns, we usually found someone who had heard Golda in Chicago and had stirred up everybody about her before we came. Sometimes, if the city was big enough, Sam and I would work together. He did more than I on that trip. Who converted me to Zionism? Hitler converted me."

Not all American Jews believed. Some of the more cynical told Golda, "No war was ever won on donations." Her reply: "We are a special case." In St. Louis, one man reacted, "Golda made a very nice speech, but she talked a lot of nonsense. How can a group of people so outnumbered have a state in a gulf of hatred?"

Golda's blurred memory of the trip was "going from town to town, mostly by train, and I remember very many rooms ..." The Musketeers would go into a community and "tear the house down if they weren't getting the contributions they thought they should be getting. They used to terrorize the Jewish community." It was soon said of them that they could get water out of a stone.

Golda always gave the greatest credit to Montor, who was "fantastic and gave his heart and soul ... played an enormous part in waking American Jewry to go way beyond what they dreamed they could do or should do." Montor was a driven man. His assistant, Meyer Steinglass, told how he would get out of bed in the morning, wherever he was, and head straight for the telephone or the typewriter while he was still absolutely nude.

Montor kept Golda going by having her speak to small groups at breakfast, larger groups at lunch, massive meetings at dinner. And the money mounted. If Montor knew how much each Jew should give, Golda knew exactly how much arms and equipment that money would buy.

Various Haganah agents scouring Europe had contacted her about a dozen fighter planes for sale in Czechoslovakia, large amounts of captured German equipment in France, and unlimited amounts of available ammunition. Reporting all this in her speeches, Golda told about the discouraged arms agent saying he was going home because he had no money.

"Money is not any of your business," she told him. "You stay there." And when another agent told Golda he could buy tanks but needed ten million dollars, Golda wired him, "Okay, you stay and I'll get you the ten million dollars."

"I had a lot of *chutzpah*," Golda told her audience. "Where was I going to get ten million dollars? But we got it, and the American Jews saved us."

"Golda goes from strength to strength and million to million."

Some of the money bought needed clothing for the soldiers. In jesting gratitude, soldiers referred to their Haganah hallmark, a woolen balaclava cap, as "Golda's stocking."

Golda could reach her audience by keeping her stories intimate. "I remember before I left home," she would say. "I sat around for hours with the people in the Haganah asking them, 'Tell me, what have we got?' One of them who was responsible for Haifa said, 'You know, we had four machine guns. Three were taken away by the British yesterday. We have one left.'"

Golda would then sum it up: "Believe me, my friends, that's all we ask of you—to share in this responsibility with everything that it implies—difficulties, problems, hardships, but also joy—a lot of joy!" The essence of her proposal was: give us the money for the weapons and the tools, and we will create a nation. She never let them forget that she had American roots, too. "See, you don't have to be anybody to be somebody. Look at me! I came from nowhere, from Russia to Wisconsin ... my husband a sign painter ... who would have thought?

Join me, come, you and I, shoulder to shoulder . . . we need you and you need us."

The country they were creating, she said, her eyes shining, was going to be different, more exciting and better than they had ever known, and they could be part of it. Then she added, "The country cannot be established by speeches and by resolutions and by applause . . ."

"It was marvelous to watch her pulling out of an audience the noblest in them, the highest moral level, without degrading them, without making them wallow in guilt."

Always at her side, Montor advised her, suggested how she might improve a speech, told her what she might expect from the audience. If anybody suggested to Montor that Golda was "making a pitch," Montor "would bounce right off the wall. He hated that phrase." With Montor as a tough critic, Golda was developing her own speechmaking style.

"No, I can't prepare a speech. What I say depends on the audience. I always like the chairman to talk a little longer while I look around and feel whether this is a good audience or not a good audience." Nor did she believe in tears. "Tears don't have to be elicited from anyone in our movement."

Golda changed Montor, too. Originally a non-Zionist, he was now a fervent follower. Palestine took precedence over everything in his mind. But he had a limited picture of how many immigrants the country could or should absorb: "30,000 or 60,000 a year may be possible . . ." Golda opened his eyes to the absolute necessity of unlimited immigration, and persuaded him that this was an attainable goal.

Others besides Montor used Golda as a fund-raising lever. Zionist leader Dr. Israel Goldstein took Golda with him to see David Dubinsky, the energetic head of the International Ladies' Garment Workers Union in New York City. Dubinsky had arranged for the ILGWU to loan the Jewish Agency a million dollars for a year. The year had expired and Dubinsky nervously awaited Goldstein's arrival. If the loan went down the drain, Dubinsky was in dire trouble. Instead, Goldstein told him, "David, we owe you money and we've come to pay you." Dubinsky pushed all the buttons and as his assistants streamed in, he shouted, "I told you it would be all right. Where's the photographer?" After the presentation of the million-dollar check, and after everyone else had left, Golda then told her Jerusalem story and walked out with another ILGWU loan for a half-million dollars.

Trying to explain Golda, Goldstein said, "She had a goodly measure of the 'Yiddishe mama' in her, yet few could excel her in strength of character. She was at once logical and intuitive. . . . With almost unerring instinct, she went to the heart of a problem." The secret of her power, he said, was in her moral force. "It shines through her."

As an afterthought, he added, "She loved to be loved. Who doesn't? With Golda, however, this was more than usually the case."

Golda was sick with exhaustion when she got back to New York. She had worn out the men with her, propelled by her fierce determination, but suddenly she herself was at low ebb. She wrote Remez of her relentless schedule, calling for eight cities in ten days, and of Montor's talking about still another trip that month for ten days. He had made her promise she would do it, and now she wondered if she could.

Remez wrote from Tel Aviv:

Golda:
1. Alive.
2. Hope to keep going despite all.
3. There was a big meeting at Tirat Zvi. There was an attack with guns, grenades for a close assault and were completely destroyed. Also a lot of arms. The Arab press is deceiving or deceived and is telling wild tales. We need comfort. . . .

Golda needed comfort, too. She found none with sister Clara in Bridgeport. Clara's husband, Fred, greeted her with sarcasm and cynicism about Zionism, and Golda found herself in argument when she wanted quiet. Shana, recuperating from surgery, also needed Golda's compassion. Menachem was continuing his music studies in New York, and they went to occasional concerts and shows. Then there was Montor, now always available.

Remez telephoned her with encouragement, and she wrote him afterward that it was wonderful to hear his voice. She hadn't known what to say because she worried about who might be listening, but their talk had made her very happy although she felt mixed up.

What mixed her up? Montor? Another note from Remez filled her in on some of the new interparty politics. Remez reported that some visiting Americans she had sent over for his supervision "are enthused and it's good that they came." His more personal note was that he hoped to see her at the Zionist congress in Europe, that he was longing to see her. She quickly replied that she did, indeed, hope to see him there, that she, too, was longing to see him.

But Golda now found somebody else in America to enrich her life, a great new friend, Eleanor Roosevelt. "Henry Morgenthau brought a Mrs. Meyerson from Palestine to breakfast," Mrs. Roosevelt wrote, "a woman of great strength and calm and for me she symbolizes the best spirit of Palestine. Evidently at last we mean to follow through on a policy of aid to the Jewish state. The British role seems to me quite stupid, no more greedy and self-interested than ours has been but at last we seem to be doing better."

Golda adored Eleanor Roosevelt, this "First Lady of the World" who had served as the ears, legs, and conscience of her husband. Golda saw her as a role model, a woman fourteen years older who had made her own imprint on history with the strength of her character. When her husband died, the new President, Harry S Truman, promptly appointed Mrs. Roosevelt as the United States representative to the United Nations. She had made her greatest contribution as chairman of the Human Rights Commission, and even the Russians shied away from debating her. "Her interest is human beings, her hobby is human beings, her preoccupation is human beings, and her every thought is for human beings . . ."

Inspiring to Golda was Mrs. Roosevelt's unending dedication. "Think of it! I am over sixty, which means I only have fifteen years left of useful public service!" Impressive to Golda was that this widow of a President was not consigned to any public scrap heap. The political boss of New York had offered her the Democratic nomination for the United States Senate. President Truman had stated publicly that he would be happy to have her as his running mate in the 1948 election.

Mrs. Roosevelt afterward praised Golda's probing mind, and added that Golda was "a woman one cannot help but deeply respect and deeply love." Golda did not need to convince Mrs. Roosevelt about Zionism, because Mrs. R. was already convinced. She had written, "There was a lump in almost everybody's throat, I think, at the thought of a new nation being born, and one whose people had suffered greatly."

But the sympathies of the new President Truman were still a Zionist question mark, just as President Roosevelt's had been. Truman made it plain that he did not want to confer with anyone from the Middle East because of his need to walk the diplomatic tightrope in this time of tension. Truman was fully aware of the State Department's pro-Arab bias, and confided to his diary:

"Like most of the British diplomats, some of our diplomats also thought that the Arabs, on account of their numbers, and because of the fact that they controlled such immense oil resources, should be appeased. . . . The Department of State's specialists on the Near East were, almost without exception, unfriendly to the idea of a Jewish state. . . . I am sorry to say that there were some among them who were also inclined to be anti-Semitic. . . ."

The Jews felt an urgent need to present their case to the President in the spring of 1948, and to get his views. They prevailed on their ailing elder statesman, Chaim Weizmann, to make the attempt. Golda visited Weizmann and his wife when they were at the Waldorf-Astoria Hotel in New York. It was her way of apologizing for the rift between them, expressing the hope for acceptance and amends. She told them what she told everybody else, that if the Jews got the arms they needed they could "beat the Arabs hollow." She described to them how "the Arab soldiers sit in their armored tanks and shoot from a long range; but if we get near them and shoot at them, they run away."

Golda was aware of the preparations for the possible presidential interview. Sharett had written a memo for Weizmann: "Informal. 'We are reluctant to impose our problem on you. It involves not only our survival and independence, but the overall question of peace. I am sure that something can be worked out (favorite phrase of the President) to prevent more suffering for our people.' Then practical proposals of help, but stressing the determination of the Jews to take care of themselves."

There was to be none of the frustrated anger of the Palestine Appeal chairman, Abba Hillel Silver, who had declared to Roosevelt that the Jews had had enough Rosh Hashanah (New Year's) greetings from the President and it was now time to get something more meaningful from him in reference to "our hopes and aspirations."

Weizmann's primary hope for access to President Truman lay with a former Missouri haberdasher named Eddie Jacobson. Jacobson had been Truman's partner in a Kansas City men's clothing store long before Truman went into politics. Truman had written of Jacobson, "In all my years in Washington he had never asked for anything for himself. . . . it would be hard to find a truer friend."

Truman than described in his diary a Jacobson visit at the Oval Office in the White House: "Great tears were running down his cheeks and I took one look at him, and I said, 'Eddie, you sonofabitch, you promised me you wouldn't say a word about what's going on over there.' And he said, 'Mr. President, I haven't said a word, but every time I think of the homeless Jews, homeless for thousands of years, I start crying. I can't help it. . . .

" 'Harry, all your life you have had a hero. You are perhaps the best-read man in America on the life of Andrew Jackson. I remember when we had our store together that you were always reading books and papers and pamphlets on this great American. . . . Well, Harry, I too have a hero, a man I never met but who is, I think, the greatest Jew who ever lived. I too have studied his past and I agree with you, as you have always told me, that he is a gentleman and a great statesman as well. I am talking about Chaim Weizmann.

" 'He is a very sick man, almost broken in health, but he has traveled thousands and thousands of miles just to see you and plead the cause of my people. Now you refuse to see him . . . it doesn't sound like you, Harry.' "

When Jacobson left, Truman called the State Department to inform them that he planned to see Weizmann.

"Well, you should have heard the carrying on," Truman recalled. "The first thing they said, Israel wasn't even a country yet and didn't have a flag or anything. 'What are we going to use for a flag?' "

The State Department worried more about Arab oil than it did about an Israeli flag. Detailing this influence for a report Golda read, Eliahu Elath* noted, "The oil companies have in the past been pro-Arab and will remain pro-Arab because it is within Arab territory that oil is found."

Elath had another interesting report for Golda to read, a conversation with General Dwight D. Eisenhower—out of the army but not yet in politics. Sought as a U.S. presidential candidate, he instead chose to become president of Columbia University. But the political bug had

---

*Eliahu Elath (Epstein) (1903–   ), born in Russia, where he was an active Zionist before he came to Palestine in 1924. Worked as a laborer in settlements, became an Arabist and director of the Middle East section of the Jewish Agency Political Department (1934–45), then head of Agency's Political Department in Washington D.C. (1945–48), and later ambassador in Washington, ambassador in London, and president of Hebrew University.

bitten, and Eisenhower now wanted to know more about the issues, including the Middle East. Eisenhower's questions were pointed: Was the Arab threat of violence just a bluff? Could partition be implemented without a UN international force? How did he explain British behavior in the area?

No, the Arab threat was not a bluff. The British-trained Arab Legion force was poised at the border for full-scale invasion as soon as the British ended their Mandate on May 15. Yes, partition could be implemented without the UN. "We would be proud if we could show that not a single non-Jew had to lose his life to establish a Jewish state." Explain British behavior? They were playing the numbers: there were so many more Arabs than Jews, and the Arabs had the oil. "They would not mind sacrificing us if there was the slightest chance of their receiving in exchange more cooperation from the Arabs." Elath told of a remark by the British consul in Jordan to BBC correspondent Richard Williams about the Arab Legion invasion: "You know that Amman will not take any action until they get orders from London."

To all this, Eisenhower offered his own memory of the Tunisian Arab, ". . . who would never lift a finger to do any kind of work, much less sacrifice his life." Eisenhower reacted more sorrowfully to an Elath statement about Jewish children in Europe being born behind barbed wire because of the international political indecision on Palestine immigration.

"His face took a tense look," Elath reported. "After a pause, he said, 'Yes, I have seen a lot of the Jewish tragedy in Europe. It was horrible.' "

But Eisenhower was no Truman when it came to Zionism. Truman had said fervently, "I surely wish God Almighty would give the Children of Israel an Isaiah."

Golda was no Isaiah, but more and more she was becoming a primary Israeli voice to the American people. Her sisters were incredulous at her *chutzpah*. Having recovered her strength, Golda made a speech at a large meeting in New York in which she said, "If you side with us, I'm sure we'll win." Clara was indignant afterward. "How can you promise that?" Golda told another audience, "You have a choice either to meet in Madison Square Garden to rejoice in the establishment of a Jewish state or to meet in Madison Square Garden at another memorial meeting for the Jews in Palestine who are gone." Shana was aghast. "My sister wanted to choke me," Golda later commented. "She couldn't understand how I could talk like that."

Shana never relinquished the role of Golda's sharpest critic, and Clara was never hesitant about challenging Golda. Golda's growing fame was a point of pride with them, but never inhibited them in their intimacy.

Grouping around Golda now was a nucleus of strong supporters. Montor was an anchor, but Rabbi Stephen S. Wise was a linchpin. He had formed the Federation of American Zionists when Golda was born. He had given the Movement a voice and a dignity and a strength. No man was a more symbolic leader of American Jewry. In 1948, he would live only another year.

"I don't know how many times he came to my meetings. Not that he spoke at any of them. He would just come and sit down on the stage. And I felt that he, more I believe than any other Zionist leader at that time, wanted personally to be an example to any group of Jews that this is something that has to be done." In his honor, Golda used his first name, Stephen, as a code name for each million-dollar contribution to Palestine.

To collect her final "Stephens," Montor prevailed on Golda to go to Miami. Golda was not amused by the statement, "If Miami exists, who needs Tel Aviv?" Nor did she enjoy the Miami definition of an American Zionist: "someone who tells somebody else to go to Palestine."

Still, Miami meant money and money meant guns and guns meant lives.

"I remember coming down to the patio which was so beautiful and seeing the people there dressed with all that beauty . . . this I couldn't take," Golda recalled. "I was sure that they couldn't care less. I was sure that when I began talking, they'd walk out of the room. Before I went in to dinner, I drank black coffee and smoked my cigarettes, tears coming out of my eyes. I thought, How can I, in this beautiful atmosphere, tell what's happening at home? So I said to Montor that I was sure that when I got up and talked, they'd all walk out. But believe me, God, we ended that day in Miami with four or five million dollars."

She had told them in intimate terms about her own personal odyssey from pogroms to the present, then added: "As it now stands, unless we get sufficient funds, we will be heroes, but we may be dead heroes." She then explained, "We're trying to do something that no other nation has had to do before: fight a war, make preparations for absorption of large numbers of immigrants, and make preparations for setting up a state."

Her remarkable tour was now over, almost three months of it. Returning home in mid-March, she had much to contemplate. This was to be a pattern of her life, migrating between the opulence of a generous America and the pioneer struggle for her people's survival. The contrast between the two worlds would always be part of her existence. Her basic alliance was clear, but these two worlds would always share in her senses and her thoughts. She now had fervent admirers in both worlds, and she would find few friends more loyal than her new Three Musketeers.

The fifty million dollars, "fifty Stephens," she had raised was three times the entire oil revenue of Saudi Arabia for 1947. Part of that money was transferred from the Chase Manhattan Bank via a Swiss bank to the Znostenska Bank in Prague. Part of it enabled Ehud Avriel in room 121 of the Hotel Aleron in Prague to pay for 25,000 rifles, 300 machine guns, 5,000 Bren guns, and fifty million cartridges.

When Golda finally returned to Palestine, David Ben-Gurion met her at the airport and told her, and the world, "Someday, when history will be written, it will be said that there was a Jewish woman who got the money which made the state possible."

And she also brought Ben-Gurion the books he wanted.

17

If you will it, it is no fairy tale.
—Herzl

Golda had left Jerusalem in January 1948 when she could still say of it, "There is a light within this city." She returned in mid-March; the lights were dimmer and she found a city under siege. The siege officially began on March 20 when the first convoy failed to get through.

The British had three brigades in Jerusalem but no longer made any pretense of either policing the city or keeping open the thirty-nine miles of vital road to Tel Aviv to protect convoys. Their single gesture was a daily patrol of two armored cars. "You'd boom down in the morning and boom back. You'd do the same thing before nightfall."

Arabs along the route knew this and reported the size and progress of all convoys so that Arab leaders could prepare the proper ambush. The results were devastating, the roadsides soon littered with burned-out Jewish vehicles. "On both sides of the road, our dead are piled up."

Terrorism also intensified within Jerusalem. Arabs hired British deserters, still in uniform, and used British army trucks filled with dynamite to blow up the headquarters of the *Palestine Post* as well as the Atlantic Hotel area on Ben-Yehuda Street, a favorite Jewish promenade of out-door cafés. The Ben-Yehuda blast killed forty-seven, wounded 130. Arabs hoped to convince the 100,000 Jerusalem Jews that their cause was hopeless, that they were completely surrounded, under siege, and would soon starve, and therefore should flee the city as soon as they could.

Since they were ending their Mandate on May 15, the British were determined not to endanger their soldiers. British High Commissioner Cunningham attempted to persuade the church officials to help create a local police force of some 3,000. When he failed, British Foreign Secretary Bevin proposed the complete evacuation of Jerusalem. Evacuation would have meant an Arab takeover of the city. Cunningham refused, and stopped the order by threatening to resign.

"You will hang onto Jerusalem with your teeth," Ben-Gurion ordered Golda and her deputy, Dov Joseph. They had enough flour to supply six slices of bread for each person, enough margarine for five days, macaroni for four days. The weekly ration was soon cut to three ounces each of dried fish, lentils, macaroni, and beans, and one and a half ounces of margarine.

"My son and I sometimes lived on a single slice of bread and four olives a day with some occasional vine leaves we picked," remembered Golda's old friend Regina, who then worked at the Jewish Agency. So-called spinach blintzes were made with leaves instead of cheese. Since there was so little rationed kerosene for cooking, some women added their children's urine to the kerosene. Friendly Arabs sometimes bartered a few vegetables and an occasional lamb. One egg was worth seven olives.

Dov Joseph itemized the city supply of twenty-one basic commodities and organized a community kitchen to provide 5,000 meals a day for vital workers, ensuring each of them at least two nutritious meals a week. Twenty-nine bakeries were consolidated into five to save fuel, but the bread was still gray. People cooked in their backyards over campfires.

"What did we do?" Golda recalled. "Water was rationed to practically a few drops a day. We were even short of medicine." Jerusalem's 2,000 infants got their milk powder via the only lifeline left, a tiny "Primus plane." They named it that because it looked as fragile and unstable as their three-legged Primus kerosene stove. The makeshift airstrip was cut out of the wadi floor next to the Monastery of the Cross where the Israelis would one day house their parliament.

Morale was Golda's greatest challenge. People were fearful of the unknown, and the weighty odds against them. She went everywhere making short, spirited speeches. A major problem was coping with the many fanatical sects of Orthodox Jews. Most of them "wanted to live for God, not die for a Jewish state." One such sect even ignored snipers and artillery bursts to parade with signs protesting immodesty in dress. Others, solely concerned with God and prayer, openly proposed surrender to the Arabs.

With Dov Joseph, Golda organized work details for cleaning streets, digging underground cellars to connect houses, placing strategic tank traps along expected routes, organizing makeshift hospitals in various areas for future emergency. The Haganah had requisitioned all private cars and there was no gasoline.

"We didn't go to work, we *crawled* to work," said Regina. "Stooping, then running, because they were now shelling all the time. People timed the Arab artillery patterns so they knew how many minutes they had between shell bursts to race down the streets."

The United Nations resolution of 1947 had internationalized Jerusalem, promising free access to all religious places. An embittered Golda now cabled the UN "family of nations" protesting the Arab shelling of Jerusalem: DOES WORLD INTEND REMAINING SILENT?

"What happened to this holy city?" Golda asked. "Not one single power in the world to whom the city is holy—not one—lifted a finger to defend it from the shells. . . . I didn't hear at that time that acquisition of territory by force is inadmissible. . . . The only people who could not go to their holy places were the Jews. Who worried about it? Did anybody say: 'But in this place there is the Mosque, there are Christian holy places, there are also Jewish holy places; how is it that Jews are not allowed to go to their holy places?' Did it give anybody sleepless nights? Are Jewish holy places less holy than Moslem holy places?"

The British were in command but not in control. Golda tried to get their military protection for Orthodox Jews who wanted to pray at the Wailing Wall. The Wailing Wall was the physical dividing line where Arabs and Jews rubbed against each other. The British refused. The Old City of Jerusalem, surrounded by its ancient stone wall, was divided into enclaves of Christians, Moslems, Armenians, Jews, among others. The small concentrated area of Jews, with its twisted cobblestoned streets, with its twenty-seven synagogues, was isolated and vulnerable, surrounded by Arabs.

"If you can't face death, you can run," Jews were told. "But remember, if you run, you can't run just a mile. You must run a thousand miles."

"Ben-Gurion sat in Tel Aviv, and there was no contact at all," recalled

Golda, "and so I had to take responsibility to decide on defense actions within Jerusalem. When I would decide on some action or other, I would wait all night for the explosion."

Haganah commando units would infiltrate behind an Arab head-quarters in some nearby village and attack from the front and rear at the same time, creating panic, making their kill, then disappearing. The plan was to encourage further Arab withdrawal from the Jerusalem perimeter, and it sometimes worked.

One of the bitter battles within Jerusalem was for control of the French monastery, San Simon, which served as an Iraqi fortress and observation post of the area. It took a force of 150 Haganah to do this. Their main weapon was a single machine gun, a water-cooled Schwatzlöser with 800 rounds of ammunition. The area was littered with hand grenades that the retreating Iraqi soldiers had thrown without pulling the pins. The Haganah collected them to use again.

Golda quickly came to visit this key conquest and saw a combat sergeant, a Mem-Kaf, of the Moriah Brigade, leaning against a wall with an American comic book he had found on the floor.

"Can you understand what you're reading?" Golda asked him in Hebrew.

"Of course," said the sergeant. "I'm an American."

"Ah, then you must be one of the fifty American students at Hebrew University who enlisted. What's your name?"

"Daniel Spicehandler."

She had started to walk away, then stopped and smiled. "Give my regards to your father," she said.

His father was Abraham Spicehandler, a man she knew well in New York, a prominent Zionist leader, the founder of *Hadoar*, the first weekly Hebrew magazine. The Spicehandlers spoke only Hebrew at home. Daniel's older brother Ezra, a rabbi, was then fighting on the front near Mount Scopus as a machine gunner "because I'm too fat to run."

Daniel's young pregnant wife, Louise, was also playing her part in Jerusalem. She was an information coordinator for Israeli intelligence with those Jerusalem Jews still working for the British. She also acted as an intermediary with those British soldiers volunteering to sell in-formation. One such soldier knew the exact time when the British would evacuate a key headquarters building. It was vital because that building commanded clear observation of the surrounding area, and it was critical for the Jews to take possession before the Arabs did. Louise had her own daily trauma when she went to work. She lived on a street adjoining the boundary of the Arab quarter and the entrance to her apartment building was subject to constant sniper fire.

Jerusalem Jews had no heavy artillery, no tanks, no planes. The total Israeli air force at that time consisted of seven single-engine planes that could cruise only at eighty miles an hour, and one plane that had two engines.

The city was slowly starving. Hundreds of workers and engineers, with bulldozers, were cutting through rock on a narrow strip of mountainous area to create an alternative "Burma Road." Supplies were brought from Tel Aviv by trucks, jeeps, and oxcarts to a steep rocky drop of 400 feet, where they were piled on the backs of hundreds of boys and girls who would bring them to Jerusalem in the dark silence of night.

People also flowed back and forth over this route, and one of them was David Remez. His presence was a great gift to Golda. The daily tension with a thousand dramatic decisions was often unbearable. Golda needed the warmth and wisdom of somebody with whom she felt safe. Remez supplied both.

"And my father was a listener," noted Aharon Remez. "He would listen, pick up the right points, and react. In a human, patient, but very selective way, he would detect problems. I think Golda learned his way of weighing things, his way of thinking." Remez also observed that Golda was "more dependent on feedback, more volatile than my father."

Almost equally important for Golda was Remez's gift of laughter. "He was always joking! So witty! And such fun! He was so brilliant and so full of life!"

Most of Golda's decisions were black-and-white, but some of them were black with mystery and intrigue.

"Golda and Remez knocked on my door at three o'clock in the morning," said Shlomo Zalman Shragai, "and told me they wanted me to go to London within the next two hours." They told him, "You must pass on a document which we have just received." They even told him where to hide it, inside a prayer shawl, in the tefillin. (Tefillin are two small black-leather boxes containing scriptural passages worn on the hand and head during prayer by Orthodox Jews.) The document was to be delivered to the Jewish Agency in London, then passed on to Moshe Sharett at the United Nations. Shragai never learned what the message was.

So great did the crisis grow in Jerusalem that Golda and Remez journeyed to Tel Aviv to present the desperate picture to Ben-Gurion. The main road to Jerusalem must be reopened. The people needed food and guns or they could not survive. Ben-Gurion needed little convincing. While they were in his office, he called in the heads of the various sectors and said, "Take everything you have, all the ammunition, and take almost all your men, and break through the road to Jerusalem. . . . We must save Jerusalem. . . . The fall of Jewish Jerusalem might prove to be a death blow to the entire Jewish cause. The Arabs understand this very well. . . . We have to keep pouring in reinforcements and to ask the commanders to find the best men and dispatch them now, tonight."

It was a daring move. The code name for the plan was "Nachshon," the same code name she and Remez had used for the start of the Jewish navy, the name of the first Hebrew to accept the challenge of Moses to plunge into the Red Sea during the exodus from Egypt. Nachshon assembled a task force of 1,500 from all over the country, the largest single Israeli force collected in one place up to that time. The danger was that it left many settlements stripped of fighters and vulnerable. But the prize was worth the price. "The Jewish state without Jerusalem—it's like a body without a head."

"Salvation comes from the sky!" Aharon Remez had told this to Golda and Ben-Gurion, trying to dramatize the need for planes. The British had handed over one of their small airfields to the Arabs, who had abandoned it. Remez moved in with a small force, renovated the dilapidated facilities, filled the runway potholes, making it usable. Part of the small miracle in timing was the delivery, just at that vital time, of the first planeload of arms from Czechoslovakia—bought with Golda's fund-raising money. Another delivery of guns came by ship camouflaged under tons of onions brought in "right under the noses of the British." Some of this was flown to the Remez airstrip near the Nachshon front even before the grease had been removed from the guns. "When the shipment arrived, the Nachshon commander kissed each one of the 140 new machine guns."

Before the battle could begin, Kastel had to be captured. This Arab village, once the site of a Roman fortress, sat near the summit of a 2,500-foot peak, the last hilltop bastion dominating the Jerusalem road. On a dark, rainy night, a Harel Palmach brigade of 180 surrounded it, drove out the Arabs. A smaller Haganah force of seventy relieved them, dug in outside the village awaiting counterattack. It soon came. The first attack by 400 Arabs drove the Haganah from their trenches to the quarries. A second reinforced Arab attack drove them back to the edge of town. Arab women had moved up to feed their men. Arab messengers were scouring nearby villages to buy more ammunition. "I pay cash!" The Haganah meanwhile converted each house into a strongpoint. By the third attack, the Arab force was stronger than ever. "It was a terrible battle!" The turning point came when the Haganah seriously wounded the Arab commander.

The Arabs have a mystique about the men who lead them in battle. When their commander was strapped on a mule and evacuated, the heart seemed to go out of their fight and most of the Arabs wandered off the battlefield, back to their villages.

D-Day for Nachshon was the night of April 5. The objective for the three 500-man battalions was to seize all the villages and strategic heights overlooking the road above Bab el Wad. So fierce was the fighting, so great the need for reinforcements, that newly arrived refugees, fresh off the ship, were rushed directly to the battlefield in requisitioned trucks, many of these men without any military training at all, most of them still wearing the clothes of their DP camps.

By midnight, Nachshon controlled Bab el Wad gorge and all the flanking hills. Word came to start the first convoy. Sixty trucks, waiting bumper to bumper, started moving, filled with food, arriving just in time for the Passover holidays. On the front bumper of Harry Jaffe's blue Ford truck were the words from the biblical pledge, "If I forget thee, O Jerusalem ..." The full phrase added the words, "... let my right hand wither."

In Jerusalem, women rushed forward to kiss the truck drivers, children brought flowers and everyone cheered and cried. Golda and Dov Joseph had estimated that the city needed 3,000 tons of food to withstand further siege, and the next convoy of 300 trucks stretched out for fifteen miles. Golda and Remez were in Tel Aviv, again reporting to Ben-Gurion, at the time one of the convoys arrived in the outskirts.

"Two of us were secret couriers, picking up things to bring back to

Tel Aviv. We walked for hours that night and we were very, very tired, and we stopped at a small coffeehouse just outside Tel Aviv. It was a place where everybody came. It was almost morning. The door was open and the place was empty except for Golda and Remez. They were waiting all night for news about the convoy. We didn't know they would be there. We sat down and Golda and Remez went to get us some coffee and bread. You could see on their faces how much they cared about us, about everything that was happening. To me, they seemed like one person. This picture is still vivid in my mind."

Jews were killing Arabs and Arabs were killing Jews, but both groups were still ambivalent toward each other. A sixth-grade textbook for Arab children declared, "Rise in vengeance! Crush the heads of the marauders! Make out of Palestine a fatherland for the Arabs and a graveyard for the Jews!" But there were also many like Jamil Hamid, who told of his own family's relations with Jews. "To me, to all members of my family, the Jews were friendly . . . I never felt the mistrust. We played football. We would take them to our fields, give them presents—grapes, melons, eggs. They used to stay at our house. We used to stay at their houses." He remembered as a boy spending Friday nights with a Jewish friend. "I remember Shabbat evening. I loved to see them lighting the candles, praying in a language which I didn't understand. I used to go back to my mother and father and ask, 'Why don't we have that?' To this very day I have a weakness for candles. I buy them frequently. When I have guests for dinner, I put a candle on the table and light it."

These were the Arabs to whom the Haganah appealed in posters and leaflets:

For two days running, order in the country has been broken in various places by shooting, arson, and murder by incited Arabs.

We know that the overwhelming majority of the Arab population has no desire to disrupt security, but the influence of these provocateurs who began the attacks seems to us to be on the increase.

So far we have exercised restraint, for we want peace, neighborly relations, quiet work, and happiness for both Arabs and Jews. However, we serve grave warning: If strife and bloodshed continue, we shall be compelled to take severe measures against the rioters and those responsible for the disturbance of the peace.

Pay attention to our call for peace!

Pay attention to our warning!

A mass migration of Arabs in Palestine could cause havoc, since Arabs provided so much of the work force in industry and farming. Conscious of this, the grand mufti urged all Arabs in Palestine's Jewish areas to leave their homes immediately and head for the nearest Arab territory. Unless they did, he warned them, they might be killed by the heavy bombing and intense shelling of the Arab invasion forces when the British left on May 15. What he promised them was that they could return a few days after that and profit from whatever loot they found in the empty Jewish homes—by then, he told them, all the Jews would be dead.

Local Arab leaders were among the first to leave, followed by those Arabs with the most money. In Haifa, some 30,000 Arabs had already left within the past four months, and 70,000 more were preparing to go. Some farmers were waiting until they picked and sold their spring citrus crops.

"I want you to go to Haifa immediately," Ben-Gurion told Golda, "and try to persuade those Arabs at the port to return home. You must convince them that they have nothing to fear."

Ben-Gurion and Golda were both of mixed minds about Arabs. Both worried about remaining Arabs serving as a fifth column for invading Arab armies. Ben-Gurion, however, stressed repeatedly that those Arabs staying behind in Jewish areas would enjoy the same civic and political equality as their Jewish neighbors, with access to the same public services on the same terms as any Jew.

Golda similarly had said at different times:

"We are absolutely opposed to hurting Arabs just because they were Arabs.... It would be more than foolish to expect that we could live here in comfort and in peace and not do everything for the Arab minority.... We realize that it is essential that we live on the basis of peace with our surrounding neighbors.... We have no desire to be a master race and have people of a much lower standard among us.... We shall have to show the world how we are making up for our suffering, not by emulating what was done to us.... We cannot do otherwise ... we must be completely different."

Golda had pamphlets circulated through Arab areas, posters put on walls. "Do not fear. For years we lived together in security and in mutual understanding and brotherhood. Thanks to this, our city flourished and developed for the good of both Jewish and Arab residents.... By moving out, you will be overtaken by poverty and humiliation. But in this city, yours and ours, Haifa, the gates are open for work, for life, for peace, for you and your families."

Golda then went to the remaining Arab leaders, saying, "Look, we are preparing legislation to safeguard your rights." Some who were tempted to stay felt that if they did they would be regarded as traitors by the conquering Arabs. Besides, the British already had provided trucks and ships to ease their way. "I sat near the beach and pleaded with them to return to their homes," said Golda. "They would not listen."

Haifa suddenly had become "a dead city . . . a corpse city . . . a horrifying and fantastic sight." Of an Arab majority population of 100,000, only a few thousand Arabs remained.

"I have failed in my job," Golda said afterward. Failure did not come easily to Golda, who always felt that common sense and commitment could resolve most problems.

Ben-Gurion sent Moshe Dayan—one of his bright young men—to Haifa while Golda was still there, to help secure the almost empty city. It was part of a strategy called "Plan D," a program to secure all areas assigned to the new Jewish state, and to position defenders in Jewish areas outside proposed borders. This meant the confiscation of all equipment in the deserted city that might have military use. Dayan and Golda viewed such confiscation as reparation for Arab terrorism, but others regarded it as "a deplorable act of appropriation."

Taking with one hand, the Yishuv gave with the other. A meeting at Golda's Tel Aviv apartment with the Jewish Agency Executive passed a proclamation promising "full and equal citizenship and due representation in all its bodies and institutions" to all Arabs remaining in Jewish areas. Golda carefully pointed out that these were rights that Arabs did not have in any Arab state.

The Irgun and Sternists did not agree. Fresh in their minds was the long list of Arab killing, looting, rape, and mutilation of bodies. Typical Arab mutilation was performed on the body of an American volunteer, a company commander, Captain Noam Grossman. Grossman's penis and testicles were cut off and stuffed into his mouth, his head hacked off his body and so bloodied as to be unrecognizable, and the rest of him similarly slashed so as to make him completely unidentifiable. Grossman's friend Daniel Spicehandler was able to make a positive identification only because Grossman always wore a Boy Scout belt, and the belt was still there.

The Irgun and Sternists decided to destroy the village of Deir Yassin as their own dramatic gesture for reprisal. This small Arab village in the hills on the outskirts of Jerusalem had never been regarded by the Haganah as any immediate military threat, but the Irgun-Sternists did not consult the Haganah about their objectives.

The leader of the attacking force of 120, Ben Zion Cohen, freely admitted, "The majority was for liquidation of all the men in the village and any other force that opposed us, whether it be old people, women, or children." Afterward, though, they insisted that they had broadcast warnings in Arabic to the villagers from a loudspeaker on a vehicle at the edge of town, urging them to evacuate before the battle. Later observers reported that the vehicle had broken down and the warning was never delivered.

The battle had been bitter, launched at dawn on April 9. It lasted two days, with heavy house-to-house fighting. In the frenzy, the attackers killed 245 villagers, "lined men, women, and children up against the wall and shot them."

"It was a massacre in hot blood," a Haganah intelligence officer, Meir Pa'il, who witnessed the scene as an observer, later reported. "It was not preplanned. It was an outburst from below with no one to control it. Groups of men went from house to house looting and shooting, shooting and looting. You could hear the cries from within the houses of Arab women, Arab elders, Arab kids. I tried to find the commanders but I did not succeed. I tried to shout and to hold them, but they took no notice. Their eyes were glazed. It was as if they were drugged, mentally poisoned, in ecstasy."

Some differed with this assessment. Sent into Deir Yassin with a Haganah infantry unit to relieve the Irgun, Daniel Spicehandler recalled "hearing loudspeakers warning women and children to go to the edges of the village" before the attack. Inside the village, he saw "maybe some fifty dead . . . among them women and older people who didn't listen to the warnings. So far as I saw, there was no rape or looting." Spicehandler, however, did consider offensive the fact that the Irgun paraded packs of village prisoners (blindfolded, with their hands tied behind their backs) in trucks through the streets of Jerusalem.

Others obviously witnessed much more offensive things, so offensive that the chief rabbi of Jerusalem "took the extraordinary step of ex-communicating the participants in the attack."

Irgun leader Menachem Begin sent a congratulatory telegram to the attacking force: "on this splendid act of conquest . . . you have made history."

The history made sent a shudder through the civilized world. The world might have expected such actions from those Arabs who preached death and hate and slaughter in the name of Allah, but the Jews were expected to adhere to a higher standard—perhaps it was a double standard—of pride in and duty toward their biblical roots of honor and decency. It seemed impossible for many Jews to believe that Jewish soldiers could murder, loot, and rape. It had seemed equally impossible in World War II to believe that some American soldiers cut off ears and noses of Japanese soldiers as souvenirs, and even chopped off fingers to get rings and pulled gold teeth from dead men.

The Jewish Agency called Deir Yassin "a barbaric act." The chief rabbinate expressed "shame and sorrow." Ben-Gurion sent a letter of apology to King Abdullah. But from then on, the Arabs used Deir Yassin as a clarion cry for all their terrorism. "In order to justify supporting terrorists," Golda remarked, "you must picture the object of your hate as something very terrible."

Deir Yassin had a double edge. In their radio reports, Arab leaders dramatized the gruesome details and heightened the panic among those Arabs undecided about exodus, which now swelled into a stampede. "This Arab propaganda was worth a half dozen battalions to the forces of Israel," noted Irgun leader Menachem Begin, citing Arab villages that afterward evacuated overnight. By mid-May some 550,000 Arabs had fled from Jewish areas, more than two-thirds of them to the Arab areas of Palestine, the West Bank, and the Gaza strip.

"The phenomenon of peasants fleeing from their land is without parallel," warned Mapam leader Yaacov Hazan. "We will pay a harsh political and moral price for what is being done." He rejected the idea that an Israeli army was bound to act like all armies. "Poison is being injected into our lives and it won't stop with the end of the war."

Some disagreed. "If the command believes that by destruction, mur-der, and human suffering they will reach their desired end more quickly,

I wouldn't stand in their way," wrote Ezra Danin. "There is no alternative but to swim with the tide, even if, at times, it is foul and defiling."

Ben-Gurion would be forced to make his own "defiling" decisions. On the question of what to do with 50,000 Arabs in two hostile areas near Tel Aviv, a danger to the military supply route, "Ben-Gurion waved his hand in a gesture of 'Drive them out!' " It meant a forced march of ten miles to an Arab Legion outpost, and some old people and children died en route.

Elder statesman Weizmann saw the flight of the Arabs from Jewish areas as "a marvelous simplification of the problem." Ben-Gurion recorded in his diary, "We can afford civic and human equality to every Arab who remains, but it is not our task to worry about the return of the Arabs." He later put it more sharply: "If we win, we shall not annihilate the Egyptian or the Syrian people, but if we fail, and fall to defeat, they will exterminate us; because of this ... their return must be prevented at all costs."

Many Arabs afterward had qualms about their hurried exodus. Some of their complaints later appeared in Arab newspapers. In one of them, *Falastin*, there was this: "We left our homeland relying on the false promises of cheating military officers of the Arab countries. They promised that our exile would last not more than two weeks and would be a kind of hike, that at the end of this period, we would return. We are your victims, you Arab leaders."

A woman from the Arab village of Bassa in northern Israel was asked by a reporter if she wished she had stayed behind.

"Oh, of course, yes." And whom did she blame? "Not the Jews," she said, and not her own Palestinian people, but the Arabs, by which she meant the larger Arab world, the Arab leaders, who had told her people to leave and had never helped enough to regain the land. "The blood of my son is equal to all the Arab governments," she declared bitterly.

Arab leaders also changed their minds. The prime minister of Syria, Khaled al-Azm, freely admitted that "we ourselves are the ones who encouraged them to leave." But the unexpectedly massive migration created so many major problems of food and housing for surrounding Arab areas that Arab leaders began broadcasting appeals for remaining Arabs to stay where they were. For most Arabs, the broadcasts came too late to still the panic and stop the flight. Only 150,000 Arabs had stayed in place, most of them fearful and reluctant.

Deir Yassin would one day become the site of an Israeli mental institution, but on April 13, 1948, its name was a battle cry.

Just four days after Deir Yassin, a convoy of seventy-seven Jewish doctors and nurses was en route through an Arab area of Jerusalem to the nearby Hadassah hospital on Mount Scopus. Then, as now, the Hadassah hospital provided equal treatment for Jews and Arabs. Even King Abdullah's grandson had been born there—he later became King Hussein of Jordan.

British forces were responsible for keeping that road open, and they informed the convoy that "the way is clear." They were wrong. The Arabs had prepared an ambush and were waiting. When the leading convoy car exploded a mine, the Arabs opened fire on the stalled vehicles, throwing grenades and Molotov cocktails.

"The attack took place less than two hundred yards from the British military post responsible for the safety of the road .... The soldiers watched the attack but did nothing . . . the attack lasted seven hours . . . most of the passengers who had not already been killed were burned alive." So completely had the flames consumed the bodies that twenty-four of them would never be identified.

The resulting bitterness increased Jewish attacks on British soldiers. The Irgun often took a British hostage when the British had taken an Irgun member. If the British killed the Irgun, the Irgun killed the British hostage. Elie Wiesel's novella "Dawn" describes the feelings of a young Jewish terrorist ordered to kill a British hostage as a reprisal. The young terrorist, a Buchenwald survivor, haunted by the ghosts of his past, previously had believed "the mission of the Jews was to represent the trembling of history, rather than the wind which made it tremble." But he kills the hostage, as ordered, and realizes "there is night now and there will be night tomorrow and the day the week the century after."

On that same day, April 13, in Tel Aviv, another hospital admitted an emergency patient named Goldie Meyerson. Doctors diagnosed her condition as a mild heart attack and sent this report to Ben-Gurion and Remez:

1. There is no danger to her life.
2. The attack that she had was the result of physical and emotional exertion beyond her strength due to tension at work.

3. In order to prevent worsening the situation and to strengthen her working ability in the future, it is necessary for her to rest at least three weeks in a very quiet place.

There was no quiet place and there was little rest. Ben-Gurion soon had an urgent mission for Golda. B-G felt that the time had come for Golda to pay another visit to King Abdullah of Transjordan. Much had happened in the six months since her first meeting with the king. Word had reached Ben-Gurion from Paris of a secret agreement in which the British had promised Abdullah the crown of Palestine after the expected quick defeat of the Jews in the coming war with the Arabs. Intercepted intelligence also revealed: "Saudi Arabia, Syria, and Egypt have decided (1) Abdullah will enter [Palestine] to fight the Jews, (2) they will assassinate him, and (3) they will set up a Mufti government."

The king seemed reluctant to meet Golda again. Ezra Danin, a bulky, curly-haired Israeli who knew Abdullah well, finally maneuvered a meeting. This time, though, they would have to go to Amman, capital of Transjordan, with Danin as Golda's interpreter. When Danin discussed the danger, Golda told him, "I would walk to hell if there was a chance of saving one Jewish soldier's life by my action."

Esther Herlitz, a fresh graduate of a newly organized diplomatic training school, and former British officer, assembled Golda's Arab costume and refreshed her on the proper courtesies to "Your Majesty." Their code name for Abdullah was "the friend."

"I ordered a plane put at her disposal," noted Ben-Gurion, "but as luck would have it, the plane broke down."

"It was not a happy mission," recalled Golda. "We knew pretty well what was happening . . . there was practically no hope by that time. For several months we were getting intelligence information that he had practically joined the Arab League and was cooperating with them. But we still had to know definitely. If Jordan kept out of the war, then the Iraqis would have to go around Syria instead of having a shortcut. I wasn't looking at it as some heroic act . . . what had to be done had to be done and that was it. . . . But I wasn't afraid . . . I don't think I ever worried about being in danger."

The danger was obvious. They changed cars at the border and were stopped ten times at checkpoints by security guards demanding identification. Golda sat in the backseat, looking like any heavily veiled Arab wife.

Abdullah met Golda at the ornate stone house of one of his rich friends. They sat on a low sofa in front of a coffee table inlaid with mother-of-pearl near a black-tiled fireplace in a lime-green room. Abdullah looked like a warrior king with his long, white robes and his flowing white headdress. He was a slight man whose short beard and exuberant mustache heightened an impressive dignity.

Golda felt that he seemed "very depressed, troubled, nervous" and later added the adjectives "frightened and haggard." For all his charm, Abdullah was obviously not happy in dealing again on a political level with a woman. Arab women kept their faces covered and their mouths shut, and belonged in his harem for his pleasure. Golda, however, spoke with determination. If she sometimes expressed herself with more force than she felt, her resilient strength came from her pride in being the delegate of an ancient people soon to be a new nation.

She reminded Abdullah first about his promise that he would never join the other Arab states in a war against the Jews. She did not need to add that a Bedouin never went back on his word, a king always kept his promise, and a king would never retract a promise to a woman.

"He appeared weary when he replied, 'Then I was one. Now I am one of five . . .' "

He bristled, obviously resenting being put in an impossible position, "the alternative of submitting to the ultimatum from the lips of a woman, or going to war."

He then tried flattery, praising the Jewish transformation of the desert "into a Paradise," insisting that "Divine Providence has brought you back here . . . only with your help and guidance will the Semites be able to revive their ancient glory." Then he offered a proposal: if the Jews would not declare a state, if they would stop immigration, he would take over all of Palestine, including what he called "the Jewish republic." If they merged with him, he would give the Jews proper representation in his parliament.

The thought later went through Golda's mind: "Abdullah wants to sit on the throne of David . . ."

Golda flatly rejected the proposal, and the king then had a question: "Why are the Jews in such a hurry to have a state?"

"We have been waiting for two thousand years. Is that hurrying?"

Now Abdullah's voice became hard. Unless the Jews allowed themselves to be absorbed into his kingdom, he warned her, war was inevitable.

Golda somehow managed to retain some defiance in her voice as she told him, "If Your Majesty has turned his back on our original understanding and wants war instead, there will be war. Despite our handicaps, I believe that we will win. We will meet again after the war, and after there is a Jewish state."

Reflecting afterward on her prediction of victory, she commented, "That was the sheerest audacity on my part because I knew we *had* to win." She was not so certain that they truly could.

She said good-bye to the small man in the opulent house, wondering whether he had sealed the fate of her people. If she had come to him with hope, she left with fear.

It was two o'clock in the morning when they drove away in the king's car. The chauffeur left them on a hill, about two miles from the border. He was afraid to take them any farther, he claimed, "because the Arab Legion is already there." As they stood on the hilltop in the dark before dawn, Golda could see "the Mufrak camp where the Iraqi army was massed with their heavy equipment and extensive field artillery." Golda's mood was fearful as she and Danin slowly groped their way toward the border. A Haganah reconnaissance scout had been sent to search for them, and he found them. His name, he said softly, was Abraham Baskal. Golda grasped his hand warmly, saying, "I *am* glad to meet you, Abraham!" Years later, he came out of a crowd to greet Golda, and reminded her, "I am the one who led you over the hills . . ."

Esther Herlitz was waiting in Tel Aviv to interview Golda on her return, for the report. Herlitz was disappointed. She was expecting Golda to dress up her story as the great adventure.

"You'd think she'd be very excited or emotional when she told me the story," remembered Herlitz, "but she wasn't. She was very factual. 'We went . . . we came . . . he said . . . and then I said . . .' The most important thing he said to her was, 'The Arab world is going to declare war on you and I can't stop it.' The thing that impressed me in hearing her report was that Golda could have been so bitter so many times, but she never showed it."

The time clock was ticking when Golda arrived on May 11, 1948, in the middle of a Tel Aviv meeting of the Council of Thirteen. The triumph of statehood and the tragedy of war would happen within four days. The Council, also known as the National Administration Executive, now ran the war. A larger group of thirty-seven controlled everything else, and was scheduled to become the provisional parliament when the British Mandate ended within four days. Golda belonged to both groups.

Three of the Thirteen were elsewhere in the country, so Golda joined the others sitting around a square table. She passed Ben-Gurion a hurried note with her bleak news about Abdullah. Ben-Gurion had received other grim news that morning from Moshe Sharett. Sharett had just returned from the United States with a warning from Secretary of State George Marshall. The Americans were edging away from their support of partition; they now wanted the Jews to postpone their declaration of statehood and instead accept an American truce proposal. Otherwise, Marshall warned, the Arabs would annihilate them "and you cannot count on any help from us."

Sharett had agreed with Marshall and planned to say so in his report. Ben-Gurion, however, persuaded him not to do this "for the sake of your future." Another persuasive voice was the surprisingly strong statement from Dr. Weizmann. Long known as a patient compromiser, Weizmann now vigorously advised Sharett, "Declare a state! What are you waiting for? Don't let them discourage you! Either a state is established now or, God forbid, it will never be established!"

Golda's presence proved pivotal. The American truce offer seemed tempting. It might stretch out the peace, postpone the war. But Weizmann's warning was apt. If they postponed statehood now, it might never happen. Golda agreed with Weizmann and refused to be intimidated by the United States. "We refuse absolutely to be the one people in the world which consents to having its fate decided by others." In a final show of hands, the truce plan lost by a single vote. One vote— Golda's vote, or any other single vote—had determined the birth of a country.

While the leaders argued, the battlefronts were already burning. The date was May 12, and Ben-Gurion asked his military chiefs for an assessment. Their honesty was absolute. The Haganah chief of operations, a twenty-eight-year-old former archaeologist named Yigael Yadin, was a brilliant, birdlike man. "To be very frank, I would say that they [the Arabs] have a considerable advantage." Acting Commander-in-Chief Israel Galili, short, pudgy and ten years older, added reflectively, "The situation will be very grave ... the best we can tell you is that we have a fifty-fifty chance."

In the midst of all this came the renewed peace offer from King Abdullah, the hard news of an intensified Arab Legion attack on Kfar Etzion, and the advance of the Egyptians into the Negev. The British were leaving in three days. What should be done? Any delay only created a vacuum. A vote was necessary on whether the declaration of statehood should be made before or after the British departure. Votes were also necessary on the name of the state and on its symbol.

Golda scurried from meeting to meeting, from vote to vote. Should their symbol be a lion, according to the Bible ("Judah is a lion's whelp") or a menorah? They decided on a menorah, representing the light of Zion. And what of the name? "Judea" and "Zion" were discarded in favor of "Israel." And, now, most important of all: when?

The final vote decided that they would proclaim their state of Israel within two days, on Friday, May 14, 1948, the day before the British left. On the Hebrew calendar it was the fifth of Iyar, in the year 5708.

Golda now got some unhappy news from Ben-Gurion. The British high commissioner had specifically requested her presence at his farewell ceremony in Jerusalem. She would have to miss the ceremony of statehood in Jerusalem. She would not now be able to sign the Declaration of Independence.

"So on the thirteenth of May I got into a Piper Cub back to Jerusalem. Then the Piper motor started funny tricks ... this motor was going as though it was going to jump out at any moment. The pilot said, 'I can't make it, we have to go back.' Down deep in my heart I wasn't so sorry.... I saw this poor pilot very tense looking, but at moments of this kind, when I know I can't do anything, I am very relaxed, very quiet. He was looking out of the window to see which was the best Arab village for a forced landing." The pilot managed to get to Tel Aviv. "When we reached the airfield, he didn't make any turns, he went right down, boom, boom, boom. So that's why ... I participated in the meeting the next day on the Declaration of the State."

Another version of the incident noted that Golda's pilot, a South African volunteer, "wanted to find a 'friendly' Arab village to make a forced landing, but Golda explained that there were no such 'friendly spots' in existence on the Arab side in those days." With a defective propeller, the pilot didn't dare risk a flight over the Judean hills and barely managed to effect a forced landing in Tel Aviv "with the last efforts of the expiring engine."

Sir Alan Gordon Cunningham was disappointed at Golda's absence. As friendly enemies, they had respected each other. Golda later had her own regrets at not saying good-bye to him.

Golda never forgot Cunningham's thoughtfulness in suggesting that she take her daughter out of the kibbutz in the Negev before the Egyptian army rolled over it, "as they surely would." She had thanked him for his consideration but had replied, "All the boys and girls in these settlements have mothers. If all of them take their children home, then who will stop the Egyptians?"

The high commissioner reviewed the guard of honor at Government House in Jerusalem at 8:00 A.M., May 14, and made a simple farewell statement about his "great sadness." He had hoped to leave behind him a secure peace instead of the bedlam of war. Then he entered his black limousine for the airport, flew to Haifa, reviewed another guard of honor, and got in a motorboat heading for a British battleship in the harbor. Strict on protocol, he would wait there until midnight—the dated end of thirty years of British rule in Palestine. Meanwhile, at the King David Hotel in Jerusalem, the British Union Jack had been hauled down from the flagpole.

Several hours before the Independence Day ceremony, Golda returned to her room by the sea and washed her hair. Once again, at an eventful time, she was alone. Sarah was at her kibbutz in the Negev, probably with a rifle in her hand, searching the area for the expected Egyptians. Menachem was at the Manhattan School of Music, but would probably head home soon to be part of the war. Her lovers and friends were with their families. As she dried her hair and brushed it, she had time to consider the excitement and the loneliness of her life.

A phone call snapped her out of her reverie to say that a car was soon coming for her. It was time to dress. She never had a problem with this, since she never had much to choose from. The invitation had suggested "dark, festive clothes," and so she wore "her best black dress."

Only two hundred people had been invited to the ceremony, mostly those older pioneers who had earned their way in. "It was hush-hush, nobody was supposed to know where we were going to meet." The place picked was the Tel Aviv Art Museum on Rothschild Boulevard, once the home of the city's first mayor. It needed to be small enough so that it could be completely secured. If it wasn't, a single bomb could wipe out the entire Jewish leadership.

How silly to think that secret could be kept. When Golda arrived, the entire area was mobbed with thousands of people. This was the birth of their nation and they would not be denied. And who could deny them?

"And of course the place was packed." It was so packed that the radio technicians were forced to work in the toilet. The heat on that May day inside the hall was intense, made hotter by the constant flashing of photographers' lights.

The tension was palpable. Golda recalled Franklin D. Roosevelt's phrase "rendezvous with destiny," and she saw it all as a fusion of past and present, joy and dread, vision and reality. She took her seat at a T-shaped table in front of the auditorium under an enormous picture of Theodor Herzl. In 1897, Herzl had prophesied the birth of a Jewish state "certainly in fifty" years. He was exactly right.

Golda sat among the Jewish leaders—twenty-three men and one other woman*—who would sign the document that day. Most of the thirteen others who would sign it later were then in Jerusalem. They were all members of the provisional parliament. Wearing an unaccustomed tie and jacket, David Ben-Gurion rapped his gavel sharply as the clock struck four. The stillness became absolute. That was the moment when the orchestra in the gallery was scheduled to play the national anthem; but they, too, must have been mesmerized by the magic of the moment because nothing happened. Almost spontaneously, the entire audience stood up to sing the "Hatikvah" with the words "To be in a free nation in our own land ..." They sang with full fervor and many eyes were wet, including Golda's.

"I shall now read the scroll of independence," Ben-Gurion quietly declared. In the rush of time, the artist had decorated the heavy parchment, but had not had time to inscribe the words. Ben-Gurion read from several pages of typed text fastened onto the blank parchment.

The audience gave a profound, audible sigh when he described an

*The other woman was Rachel Cohen (Kagan), at that time chairman of the Women's International Zionist Organization. Born in Russia in 1888, she had come to Palestine in 1919 and became director of the Social Welfare Department of the Vaad Leumi. She later was elected to the first Knesset. She was an ardent feminist.

exiled people never ceasing to hope and pray for their return. There was a shine of pride on their faces when he declared, "They reclaimed the wilderness, revived their language, built cities and villages. . . . They sought peace yet were prepared to defend themselves." Then came a sentence that tore down the barbed wires of the world: "The state of Israel will be open to the immigration of Jews from all countries of their dispersion." The applause rose like a storm.

It took seventeen minutes to read the 979 words, and then something wonderful happened. An elderly man with a trembling voice unexpectedly stood up to recite the traditional Hebrew prayer of thanksgiving. He was Rabbi Fishman-Maimon. The silence was again golden as he intoned, "Blessed be Thou, O Lord, our God, King of the Universe, who has kept us alive and sustained us and brought us to this day. Amen."

"It was a prayer that I had heard often," Golda recalled, "but it had never held such meaning for me as it did that day."

The time came for the members of the provisional parliament to sign the scroll, and they did it in alphabetical order. As she waited her turn, Golda reminisced to herself:

"From my childhood in America, I learned about the Declaration of Independence and the geniuses who signed it. I couldn't imagine these were real people doing something real. And here I am signing it, actually signing a Declaration of Independence. I didn't think it was due me, that I, Goldie Mabovich Meyerson, deserved it, that I had lived to see the day. My hands shook. We had done it. We had brought the Jewish state into existence. Whatever price any of us would have to pay for it, we had re-created the Jewish national home. The long exile was over. Now we were a nation like other nations, masters—for the first time in twenty centuries—of our own destiny."

Moshe Sharett held flat the slippery parchment so that Golda could sign her name.

"All I can recall about my actual signing of the proclamation is that I was crying openly, not able even to wipe the tears from my face. . . . David Pincus asked why I was crying and I said, one, because of the honor, and two, because there are people missing here, Berl, Eliyahu, Dov, and others who had more of a right to be here and sign. . . . I wept almost beyond control . . ."

Sharett, who had seemed so calm when he wrote his name, later told

Golda that "he felt as though he were standing on a cliff with a gale blowing up all around him and nothing to hold onto except his determination not to be blown over into the raging sea below." David Remez also used a similar phrase: "Today Israel pulls itself into the sea which is the state of Israel."

"It had taken thirty-two minutes to proclaim the independence of a people who for 1,887 years had been at the servitude of other nations."

"The state of Israel has arisen!" Ben-Gurion declared. "The meeting has ended!"

With the words of the "Hatikvah" still ringing in their ears, the people embraced one another, laughed, cried, cheered, danced, clapped, a scene of ineffable joy, irradiated faces, kissing and hugging, shaded with an air of almost disbelief.

If it was the "happiest moment" of Golda's life, it was also a moment filled with fear. Golda could only see the expected 60,000 casualties, one out of every ten Jews.

Like Ben-Gurion, Golda felt she could not "be among the dancers," that she was "like someone in mourning at a wedding." That Friday night, she went downstairs to the dining room of the small hotel where she was staying and "there were people there singing and celebrating." She thought how lucky they were that "they didn't know . . . what's in store for us . . ."

Golda's mind was in Jerusalem, where the battle had been bitter for five days and nights. She knew the teenagers were being sent into battle as reinforcements because there was nobody else. "I didn't have the heart to put them in to fight," Palmach leader Yitzhak Rabin recalled, "but we lost so many men and so I had to." He remembered a pause in the battle when some of them grouped around an ancient radio to listen to Ben-Gurion's proclamation of independence, and a tired young soldier said, "Hey, guys, turn it off. I'm dying for some sleep. We can hear the fine words tomorrow." Somebody got up and turned it off.

Some friends came to be with Golda, and they opened a bottle of wine and toasted the new state. They could not hear it, but somewhere at sea the last British ship was leaving the coastal area promptly at midnight and the band was playing "Auld Lang Syne." A few minutes after midnight, the phone started ringing and Golda finally answered it. "Golda? Are you listening? Truman has recognized us! . . ."

She felt a special pride then that some of her roots were American, that the United States had been the first country. Guatemala was next. She had known its ambassador to the UN. And the Soviet Union gave its recognition shortly afterward. In this time of danger, it was an exultant moment to know that the two greatest powers in the world officially approved the birth of their new nation.

Golda slept little that night. "At five o'clock in the morning I saw four Egyptian planes ... and soon I heard the bombing. A little later, I watched the first boatload of Jewish immigrants enter the port of Tel Aviv ... coming in freely to a free Israel." The first visa went to a survivor of the Buchenwald concentration camp and it said simply, "The right to settle in Israel is hereby given."

"Nothing ever would be the same again," Golda realized. The whole world also seemed to watch and wonder what would happen next on this small piece of land in the Middle East.

The *New York Post* editorialized:

"Imagine an area of 8,000 square miles in all. Make it 270 miles long and seventy miles wide at its widest; border it on three sides with enemy nations, their armies totaling between 70,000 and 80,000 troops; place within it 600,000 people from more than fifty nations, whose last experience with self-rule dates back 1,887 years; sever its sea and air communications; besiege one-sixth of its number in a land-bound enclave; sack its former government; give it a name; declare it independent—and you have the state of Israel, one minute past midnight, May 15, 1948."

World Jewry was full of pride and questions, but the Arab world had no doubt about the quick outcome. "This will not be a war with the Jews," the Egyptians announced. "It will be a parade. Within two weeks we will be in Tel Aviv ..." It would not only be a parade, proclaimed the secretary-general of the Arab League, as the five Arab armies advanced into Israel on all fronts. "There will be a war of extermination which will be spoken of like the Mongolian massacres and the Crusades."

"With 50 million Arabs, what does it matter if we lose ten million to kill all the Jews?" said Ibn Saud, king of Saudi Arabia. "The price is worth it."

The Arab strategy was simple. The Egyptian navy would sail in and destroy Tel Aviv. King Abdullah and his Arab Legion would capture Jerusalem, then advance to encircle Tel Aviv, helped by the Egyptian army sweeping from the south. Striking from the center, the Iraqis would cut the country in half. Syrians and Lebanese, moving from the north, would wipe out Haifa. It would all be over in ten days.

Golda knew that the total Israeli force was 30,574, that it might take a miracle to beat the combined armies of five Arab countries. But as one old man said to a visiting American, "In Israel, the man who does not believe in miracles is not a realist."

This was a people with their backs to the wall, only there wasn't any wall—simply the sea. This was not a new people coming to a new country; this was an old people coming home. For nearly two thousand years they had scattered around the world, and now still had the tenacity to come back. "I don't think anyone can rationally explain it," Golda once said. Almost defiantly, she had added, "We would not ask for a state if we did not think we could defend ourselves. . . . Those who were killed in the gas chambers were the last Jews to die without defending themselves. . . . I didn't know how we would make it . . . I only knew one thing, that we must. . . . We had a secret weapon: 'No alternative!' " (*Ain lanu derech acheret.*)

The Jews had no alternative when they had defended their sovereign rights nearly nineteen hundred years before against the invading Roman forces at Batrar. They had no alternative that week when thirty-five young men fought back against hundreds of Arabs at an outpost outside Jerusalem. "They fought to the very end. The last one killed was fighting when he was wounded . . . when he had no more ammunition left, he was killed with a stone in his hand."

Golda spent part of the next day in the so-called Red House, now a faded pink stucco on Hayarkon Street, overlooking the sea, the nerve center for the war. The need for decisions was constant and critical:

Our casualties are heavy against the Syrians and Lebanese in the north. Where are our replacements? Can you find an expert to repair the defective firing pins on our new machine guns? . . . We have shot down an Egyptian plane. Do you want to interrogate the pilot? . . . We cannot hold Naharyim. We blew up the two bridges across the Jordan but the Iraqis have put up a temporary bridge and are bringing over armored cars. What help can you send us? . . . Our first four artillery pieces have arrived, 65mm guns without any gun sights. Where shall we send them? . . . The Egyptians have captured the strategic police fortress in the northern Negev. What do we have to fight their tanks? . . . What is our strategy?

Shall we defend static positions or hit hard at the enemy?... We have to abandon the potash works near the Dead Sea.... The defenders in the Old City in Jerusalem can no longer hold out.... The Arab Legion has cut the road to Mount Scopus.... Our road to Jerusalem is blocked again.... What shall we do?... What shall we do?... What shall we do?...

These were days of dramatic decisions. For Golda, the years of power were yet to begin.

Notes

In the following notes, the page on which each entry appears or begins is found preceding that entry.

Chapter 1

p. 1   *"the licentious freethinker":* Yehoshua Gottlieb, "The Legend of Pinsk," in Dr. Wolf Zeev Rabinowitsch, ed., *History of the Jews at Pinsk, 1506–1941* (Tel Aviv–Haifa Association of the Jews of Pinsk in Israel, 1973), pp. 110–12.

p. 1   *the Russians still ruled:* Gottlieb, "The Legend of Pinsk."

p. 2   *"innocent and confiding":* Peggy Mann, interview with Clara Stern (Golda's sister), Bridgeport, Connecticut.

p. 2   *"a man's head":* Shana Korngold, *Zichronot* (*Memories*) (Tel Aviv: Id-press, 1968). These memoirs of Golda's sister were originally published in Yiddish and then translated into Hebrew. There is no official English translation.

p. 2   *"very sociable":* Richard Yaffe, "Golda, a Mother Who Gave Israel All Her Strength," New York: *Jewish Week–American Examiner*, December 17, 1978.

p. 3   *"profaned by the presence of Jews"* ... *assigned inn: Encyclopaedia Judaica,* Vol. 10 (1972), Vol. 10, p. 994.

p. 3   *even a Jewish theater:* Simon Dubnow, *History of the Jews in Russia and Poland,* Vol. 3 (New York: Ktav Publishing House, 1975).

p. 3   *"... obtain them at all":* Michael Davitt, *Within the Pale* (Philadelphia: Jewish Publication Society of America, 1903).

p. 3   *"... another son":* Korngold, *Zichronot.*

p. 4   *"... what he left me!"* Ibid.

p. 4 *letting Goldie suck on it:* Ibid.

p. 4 *"Death to the Jews!":* Yigal Lossin, *Pillar of Fire* (Jerusalem: Shikmona Publishing Co., Ltd., 1983). Herzl witnessed the scene in the courtyard of the military school where Dreyfus was degraded and condemned to ten years' imprisonment.

p. 5 *"Distress binds us together":* Ze'ev Chafets, *Heroes and Hustlers, Hard Hats and Holy Men* (New York: William Morrow and Co., 1987).

p. 5 *". . . that was a red-letter day":* Radio interview in Israel in Hebrew, 1969. Reprinted in translation in Marie Syrkin, ed., *A Land of Our Own, an Oral Autobiography by Golda Meir* (New York: G. P. Putnam's Sons, 1973).

p. 5 *". . . an added spoonful of chicken fat":* Charlotte Baum, Paula Hyman, and Sonya Michel, *The Jewish Woman in America* (New York: Dial Press, 1976).

p. 5 *". . . a little too empty inside":* Israel Shenker, "Golda Meir, 80, Dies in Jerusalem," *The New York Times* (Biographical Service), December 1978.

p. 6 *"Hunger is his name":* Poem by Mekrossov, quoted in Joseph J. Cohen, *The House Stood Forlorn* (Paris: Imp. Les Editions Polyglottes, 1954).

p. 6 *"spilled his priceless blood":* Martin Gilbert, *Exile and Return: The Struggle for a Jewish Homeland* (Philadelphia: J. B. Lippincott Company, 1978).

p. 6 *". . . will later devour":* Reprinted in undated clipping on Auschwitz in *The New York Times.*

p. 6 *". . . punishment on the Jews":* Shamai Korngold, quoted by Peggy Mann in her book *Golda, The Life of Israel's Prime Minister* (New York: Coward, McCann, 1971).

p. 6 *". . . have some fun with the Jews":* "The Diabolical Massacre of Jews in Kishinev," *The Commercial Advertiser*, May 23, 1903.

p. 7 *". . . melt away like salt on the water":* Sholem Aleichem, *The Adventures of Menachem-Mendl* (New York: G. P. Putnam's Sons, 1969).

p. 7 *". . . to me and my family":* Stephen Klaidman, "Golda Meir: She Lived for Israel," *Washington Post*, December 9, 1978.

p. 7 *". . . and leave them alone":* David M. Brownstone, Irene M. Franck, and Douglass L. Brownstone, *Island of Hope, Island of Tears* (New York: Rawson Wade Publishers, 1979).

p. 7 *". . . drunk-crazed rioters":* "The Diabolical Massacre of Jews in Kishinev."

p. 7 *". . . nails being driven in":* Kenneth Harris interview with Golda Meir, *The Observer* (London); reprinted in the *Washington Post*, January 17, 1971.

p. 7 *". . . and how angry":* Klaidman, "Golda Meir . . ."

p. 7 *". . . similar experience":* Current Biography, 1970.

p.   8   *"the same story"*: Edwin Newman interview with Golda Meir on "Speaking Freely," December 31, 1972.

p.   8   *"I ... plead guilty"*: *The New York Times* (Biographical Service), December 1978.

p.   8   *"... all a lie!"*: Louis Greenberg, *The Jews in Russia*, Vol. 2, *The Struggle for Emancipation* (New York: Schocken Books, 1976).

p.   8   *"... flee at once to our room"*: Korngold, *Zichronot*.

p.   8   *"... what's the difference ..."*: Ibid.

p.   8   *"... combed her hair"*: Ibid.

p.   8   *"... very seriously"*: Ibid.

p.   9   *"... going to America"*: Ibid.

p.   9   *"... that he has no home"*: Dubnow, *History of the Jews in Russia and Poland*.

p.   9   *"... tin pots" ... "just like the millionaires"*: Rose Pesotta, *Days of Our Lives* (Boston: Excelsior Publishers, 1958).

p.   9   *for the United States:* On May 12, 1882, the *Jewish Chronicle* in London reprinted an article by Laurence Oliphant, a non-Jewish Englishman, advising all Jews to choose Palestine instead of the United States, where "Judaism, scattered and dispersed in all parts, threatens to disappear." (See Gilbert, *Exile and Return*.)

p.   9   *recorded a diarist:* Dubnow, *History of the Jews in Russia and Poland*.

p.   9   *"... I want my family alive"*: Brownstone et al., *Island of Hope, Island of Tears*.

p.   9   *"... not just the forest"*: Carole Malkin, *The Journeys of David Toback: As Retold to His Granddaughter* (New York: Schocken Books, 1981).

p.   9   *"... heads held high"*: Marie Trommer, *America in My Russian Childhood* (Brooklyn: privately printed, 1941).

p.   9   *"... do not know or care"*: Dubnow, *History of the Jews in Russia and Poland*.

p. 10   *"... the better"*: Mann interview with Clara Stern.

p. 10   *"... would gobble them up"*: Malkin, *The Journeys of David Toback*.

p. 10   *"... scraps of food to them"*: *People*, December 23, 1985, p. 133. Some 40 percent of Americans claim an ancestor who immigrated past the Statue of Liberty.

p. 10   *"... my child won't get through"*: Fannie Kligerman, quoted in Brownstone et al., *Island of Hope, Island of Tears*.

p. 10   *"... through Ellis Island"*: English inscription recalled by Ida Mouradjian, who saw it in 1922 when she arrived from Turkey. See Brownstone et al., *Island of Hope, Island of Tears*.

p. 11   *one of them said:* Review of Marie Syrkin's book, *Way of Valor*, in *Pioneer Woman*, January 1956.

p. 12   *read underground newspapers:* Korngold, *Zichronot*.

p. 12   *"... fell in love"*: Ibid.

p. 12   *"... my poor mother ..."*: Mann interview with Clara Stern.

p. 12 *"... really mattered to her"*: Ibid.

p. 12 *"... a little arithmetic"*: Yaffe, "Golda ..."

p. 13 *bought the notebook anyway ... jumping off the roof:* Korngold, *Zichronot.*

p. 13 *"... and I'll never return"*: Ibid.

p. 13 *"... meant the most to me."*: Golda Meir, *My Life* (New York: G. P. Putnam's Sons, 1975).

p. 14 *"... watching the show"*: Mann, *Golda.*

p. 14 *looted and destroyed: Encyclopaedia Judaica*, Vol. 10.

p. 14 *"... taken official action"*: Davitt, *Within the Pale*, quoting from an article on Roosevelt and the Jews in the *Daily Press.*

p. 14 *"... fast for the little children"*: Mann interview with Clara Stern.

p. 15 *raced away:* Korngold, *Zichronot.*

p. 15 *killing hundreds:* Greenberg, *The Jews in Russia.*

p. 15 *"... slogans, and laugh"*: Korngold, *Zichronot.*

p. 15 *"... through with them"*: Harris interview with Golda.

p. 15 *disperse immigrant Jews around the country:* John Livingston, "The Industrial Removal Office, the Galveston Project, and the Denver Jewish Community" in *American Jewish Historical Quarterly*, Vol. 68, no. 4 (June 1979). This original proposal for dispersion was reportedly made by a New York banker, Jacob Schiff, in 1906.

p. 16 *"... like going to the moon"*: Meir, *My Life.*

p. 16 *disinfected with kerosene:* Malkin, *The Journeys of David Toback.*

p. 16 *weren't healthy enough:* Pesotta, *Days of Our Lives.*

p. 16 *"... chalk on a blackboard"*: Abraham Cahan, *Grandma Never Lived in America: The New Journalism of Abraham Cahan*, ed. Moses Rischin (Bloomington: Indiana University Press, 1985). Cahan's phrase "the language of birds" was a quote from Turgenev.

p. 17 *caul in which he was born:* Interview with my father.

p. 17 *could only listen:* Pesotta, *Days of Our Lives.*

p. 17 *"... pretend to be other people"*: Meir, *My Life.*

p. 17 *caused a good laugh:* Korngold, *Zichronot.*

p. 17 *he was a cheat:* Ibid.

p. 17 *Golda recorded:* Ibid.

p. 18 *"... will be killed"*: Edith La Zebnik, *Such a Life* (New York: William Morrow and Co., 1978).

p. 18 *... their ragged children:* Malkin, *The Journeys of David Toback.*

p. 18 *"... confusion of sound"*: Mary Antin, *From Plotzk to Boston* (Boston: W. B. Clarke Co., 1899).

p. 18 *"as though we were cattle"*: Meir, *My Life.*

p. 19 *"... like a ballerina"*: La Zebnik, *Such a Life.*

p. 19 *"... herring and seasickness"*: Mary Zuk, quoted in Brownstone et al., *Island of Hope, Island of Tears.*

p. 19 *"... staring at the sea for hours"*: Meir, *My Life.*

p. 19 *". . . riches of America"*: Ibid.

p. 19 *". . . hello, here we are . . ."*: La Zebnik, *Such a Life*.

Chapter 2

p. 21 *". . . without his beard"*: Korngold, *Zichronot*.

p. 22 *". . . beer so brown . . ."*: Isaac Levitats, *The Story of the Milwaukee Jewish Community* (Milwaukee: Bureau of Jewish Education, 1954).

p. 22 *". . . so good after that"*: Rinna Samuel, interview with Golda Meir, July 24, 1973, Revivim, Israel. Part of a series of interviews filed at the Lavon Institute for Labour Research, Tel Aviv.

p. 22 *"a lovely person"*: Interview with Regina Hamburger Medzini, Jerusalem.

p. 22 *". . . a stranger to her"*: Korngold, *Zichronot*.

p. 22 *". . . in a kind of trance"*: Meir, *My Life*.

p. 23 *". . . they don't have to live in this world"*: Meriel McCooey, "The Making of Golda Meir," *Sunday Times Magazine* (London), April 18, 1971.

p. 23 *". . . that way, too"*: Mann interview with Clara Stern.

p. 23 *". . . and I did"*: Ibid.

p. 23 *. . . a grocery store*: Ibid.

p. 23 *". . . fruit stand outside"*: Ibid.

p. 23 *". . . across the street"*: Ibid.

p. 24 *"but on my own"*: Korngold, *Zichronot*.

p. 24 *". . . a day later"*: Linda Maiman, "Golda's Milwaukee," *Milwaukee Journal*, October 31, 1976.

p. 24 *". . . I really don't think so"*: Interview with Regina Hamburger Medzini.

p. 24 *"laughter in her"*: Quoted in Sidney Fields, "Only Human," *New York Daily Mirror*, December 30, 1956.

p. 24 *the same classes*: Interview with Regina Hamburger Medzini.

p. 24 *". . . on the kitchen table"*: Mann interview with Clara Stern.

p. 25 *". . . terror of Pinsk and Kiev"*: Oriana Fallaci, interview with Golda Meir, *London Daily Mail*, February 12, 1974.

p. 25 *". . . went into convulsions"*: Beatrice Berger interview with Clara Stern, Bridgeport, Connecticut.

p. 25 *". . . with a high fever"*: Oriana Fallaci, *Interview with History* (New York: Liveright & Co., 1976).

p. 25 *". . . massacre the Jews . . ."*: Ibid.

p. 25 *renamed her "Clara"*: Clara's Hebrew name was Sapora and she discovered in Israel another Clara whose Hebrew name was Sapora. She then told Beatrice Berger in Bridgeport, "And I thought the Irish principal had just thought this up."

p. 26 *". . . everyone spoiled her"*: Korngold, *Zichronot*.

p. 26 *". . . 'Excuse my back' "*: Berger interview with Clara Stern.

p. 26 *". . . of this and that"*: Interview with Regina Hamburger Medzini.

p. 26   *". . . Wound round each other?"*: Quoted in interview with Sadie Ot-
        tenstein, Milwaukee, Wisconsin.

p. 26   *". . . valued citizens"*: Quoted in Levitats, *The Story of the Milwaukee
        Jewish Community*. The only date given for the *Sentinel* story is
        1898; the title is "Into the City's Ghetto."

p. 27   *". . . but no paupers"*: January 11, 1905, from the Lizzie Kander Papers,
        University Archives, Golda Meir Library, University of Wisconsin,
        Milwaukee.

p. 27   *". . . of female German Jews"*: Letter to the editor by M. Altman, *Mil-
        waukee Sentinel*, undated clipping.

p. 27   *". . . out of the window"*: Interview with Sadie Ottenstein.

p. 27   *". . . stand them up"*: Mann interview with Clara Stern.

p. 27   *their final word*: Interview with Robert A. Hess by Robert W. Sherman,
        Wisconsin Jewish Archives, February 3, 1965, pp. 5, 6, and 8 of
        transcript.

p. 28   *". . . much bread or butter"*: Ibid., p. 5.

p. 28   *any immigrating relatives*: Interview with Dorothy Weingrod, Mil-
        waukee, Wisconsin.

p. 28   *"spoke pieces"*: *The Settlement*, Milwaukee, Wisconsin, January 1, 1905.

p. 28   *". . . Income: $413.95"*: Kander Papers.

p. 28   *the owner's daughter*: Interview with Morris Silber, Jewish Home for
        the Aged, Milwaukee, Wisconsin.

p. 29   *". . . and her parents"*: Korngold, *Zichronot*.

p. 29   *"and none of them married a doctor"*: Berger interview with Clara
        Stern.

p. 29   *". . . everyone runs home"*: Korngold, *Zichronot*.

p. 29   *". . . pain in the neck"*: Berger interview with Clara Stern.

p. 29   *". . . typical Jewish mother . . ."*: Ibid.

p. 29   *". . . heavy price for it"*: Korngold, *Zichronot*.

p. 30   *". . . second mother to Goldie"*: Berger interview with Clara Stern.

p. 30   *". . . if I died"*: Mann interview with Clara Stern.

p. 31   *". . . and he would be right"*: Korngold, *Zichronot*.

p. 31   *". . . among our people"*: Report in *The Settlement*, March 27, 1910, by
        Lizzie B. Kander, president.

p. 31   *". . . None may pay to enter"*: Allen D. Breck, *The Centennial History
        of the Jews of Colorado 1859–1959* (Denver: Hirschfield Press,
        1960).

p. 31   *came too late*: *Denver Municipal Facts*, 1912.

p. 31   . . . DEPORT PAUPER HEALTH SEEKERS: Ida Libert Uchill, *Pioneers, Peddlers
        and Tsadikim* (Denver: Sage Books, 1957).

p. 31   *". . . send a few dollars"*: Korngold, *Zichronot*.

p. 31   *". . . by the cough"*: Ibid.

p. 32   *". . . your lovingly sister"*: Meir, *My Life*.

p. 32   *". . . used them as doilies"*: Mann interview with Clara Stern.

p. 32   "*. . . gives her for school money*": Korngold, *Zichronot*.

p. 32   "*. . . money from mother's till*": In other interviews, Golda confessed that she took money for stamps more often.

p. 32   "*. . . too poor to pay for books*": Berger interview with Clara Stern.

p. 32   "*I was indignant!*": Harris interview with Golda.

p. 33   *. . . she admitted:* Berger interview with Clara Stern.

p. 33   "*. . . Think what that means . . .*": Meir, *My Life*.

p. 34   "*. . . he was so immaculate*": Mann interview with Clara Stern.

p. 34   "*. . . don't see any harm in it*": Meir, *My Life*.

p. 34   "*. . . at ten cents an hour*": Interview with Regina Hamburger Medzini.

p. 35   *. . . said Goldie:* Meir, *My Life*.

p. 35   "*. . . pick up every penny*": Interview with Regina Hamburger Medzini.

p. 35   "*. . . shorter one, but together*": Korngold, *Zichronot*.

p. 35   "*. . . take a stand*": Berger interview with Clara Stern.

p. 35   *known as "Jennie"*: Shana had signed herself as "Jennie" at the Jewish Consumptive Relief Society on September 5, 1908. Shana's daughter, Judy, also recalled that her mother similarly gave her name as "Jennie" on their passport.

p. 36   "*. . . saw red spots on the snow.*": Korngold, *Zichronot*.

p. 36   "*. . . it is enough for me*": Meir, *My Life*.

p. 36   "*. . . too honest to succeed*": Mann interview with Clara Stern.

p. 36   "*. . . made a trail behind him*": Ibid.

p. 36   "*. . . kiss the child*": Korngold, *Zichronot*.

p. 37   *Morris was "Moshe"*: On Golda's wedding certificate, however, Morris was listed as "Moses."

p. 37   *indicated that she was "talkative"*: Article by Seth King on Golda's return to her school in Milwaukee, *The New York Times*, October 3, 1969.

p. 37   "*. . . for men only*": Golda, quoted in article by Jonathan Broder in the *Chicago Tribune*, undated.

p. 37   "*. . . marry, while quite young*": Kander Papers.

p. 37   "*. . . where the big clash came*": Interview with Golda Meir on the BBC television program "Panorama," August 9, 1971.

p. 38   "*. . . parents and their children*": *Jewish Courier*, September 21, 1916.

p. 38   "*. . . willing to wait a few more years*": Mann interview with Clara Stern.

p. 39   "*. . . bring you good results. Be brave*": Marie Syrkin, *Golda Meir, Israel's Leader* (New York: G. P. Putnam's Sons, 1969), p. 29.

p. 39   *Sara Feder:* She later became one of the leaders of Labor Zionism in the United States.

p. 39   "*. . . just to remind her*": Interview with Regina Hamburger Medzini.

p. 39   "*. . . stroked her face and kissed her*": Meir, *My Life*.

p. 40   "*. . . never let Goldie forget that*": Interview with Regina Hamburger Medzini.

p. 40   "*. . . I can't get at . . .*": Ibid.

Chapter 3

p. 41   "...night without sleeping.": Korngold, Zichronot.

p. 41   "... sense of direction": Ibid.

p. 41   "... on her own feet": Ibid.

p. 42   "... ten o'clock at night": Interview with Irene Kahn Morgan, who lived next door to Shana at 1604 Julian Street, Denver, when Golda stayed there.

p. 42   shimmering among the small boats: Denver City Directory, 1914. Also notes of Polly Wilson Kemp, Denver, and article by Bette D. Peters, "Denver City Park," Colorado University at Denver Historical Studies, Vol. 2, no. 2 (1985).

p. 42   shopping for the homebound people: Intermountain Jewish News, June 28, 1985.

p. 42   along with everyone else: They were primarily of German origin. Exhibition notes by Mrs. Belle Marcus from photo collection of Ira M. Beck Memorial Archives, Rocky Mountain Jewish Historical Society, project of Center for Judaic Studies, University of Denver.

p. 43   something you could "feel": Interview with Rudy Boscoe in article by Stacey Burling, Rocky Mountain News, July 5, 1985.

p. 43   ... on the way to the synagogue: Rocky Mountain Jewish Historical Notes, Vol. 3, no. 4 (January 1981); Marjorie Hornbein, Jewish Life Near the South Platte.

p. 43   when Goldie came there: American Jewish Historical Quarterly, Vol. 68, no.4 (June 1979).

p. 43   "... nobody had any money": Interview with Michael Licht by Joni H. Blackman, Denver Post, July 5, 1985.

p. 43   bloomers made out of flour sacks: Intermountain Jewish News, June 28, 1985.

p. 43   "... next-door neighbor said 'Gezundheit' ": Interview with Joe Kuner, Rocky Mountain News, July 5, 1985.

p. 43   "... stronger than iron": Korngold, Zichronot.

p. 43   "Little by little, she recovered": Ibid.

p. 44   at North Side High School: Ruth Eloise Wiberg, Rediscovering Northwest Denver (Boulder, Colo.: Pruett Publishing Co., 1976). The school was built in 1911. North Side High School records show that Golda was fourteen years and nine months old when she registered on February 17, 1913. Golda entered as a freshman, completed her sophomore year, and had some credits toward her junior year when she left on June 5, 1914.

p. 44   and very few Jews: Notes of Ida Libert Uchill, Denver.

p. 44   "... WOW! WOW! WOW!": Interview with Polly Wilson Kemp, who supplied her notes of interviews with alumni of North Side High School.

p. 44 *"... Cleaning and Pressing Works"*: The 1914 *City Directory* lists the address as 1823 Glenarm Place. In the Denver city directories from 1909 to 1918, he is listed as Samuel Korengold. The spelling varies on different documents.

p. 44 *stockings below the knee:* Polly Wilson Kemp, "Golda in Denver," *Denver Post*, December 10, 1978.

p. 44 *haven for all the* catootnicks: The word "catootnick" comes from the Yiddish word "catooteh" or "katatah," which means "in a prayer, to be safe from calamity." Especially referred to nonconformists. From an interview with Mike Zelinger, currently writing book on the Jewish West Side of Denver. Zelinger quotes Rabbi Eiseman's father as his source.

p. 45 *"... rarely turned down"*: Meir, *My Life.*

p. 45 *"way over my head"*: Ibid.

p. 45 *"... the most sense to me"*: Ibid.

p. 45 *"... leave us in peace"*: Gilbert, *Exile and Return*, p. 49.

p. 45 *legally secured homeland:* Ibid.

p. 45 *"... everyone will know it"*: Ibid.

p. 45 *"... finally find his Zion"*: Simon Wolf in *The Jewish American*, August 28, 1903.

p. 45 *fit for Jews to die in:* Uchill, *Pioneers, Peddlers and Tsadikim.* Quotes article by Rabbi Friedman in *Jewish Daily News* (undated). Until 1912, Rabbi Friedman was "the sole voice of the Jewish community."

p. 46 *the future was a challenge:* Article in *Rocky Mountain News*, August 9, 1981, claims Golda told Denver reporters that the Korngold home was where she heard political discussions that committed her to the idea of a Jewish state.

p. 46 *"... books and dry subjects"*: Interview with Regina Hamburger Medzini.

p. 46 *"Goldie was vivid"*: Interview with Minnie Willens by Polly Wilson Kemp, "Golda in Denver," *Denver Post*, December 10, 1978. Their school was twenty blocks away.

p. 46 *"... solid 14-karat-gold watch"*: Invitation found in Shana's house to East Side affair at East Denver Town Hall, February 15, 1913.

p. 47 *"... once called her a lemon"*: Interview with Regina Hamburger Medzini.

p. 47 *"... have stayed in Milwaukee"*: Meir, *My Life.*

p. 47 *"... taking nothing else with me"*: Notes of Polly Wilson Kemp.

p. 47 *"... carries out her decision"*: Korngold, *Zichronot.*

p. 48 *"... was in the last stages"*: Leonard Wolf, *The Passion of Israel* (Boston: Little, Brown & Company, 1970).

p. 48 *"a castle in the air"*: The school yearbook had a section called "High School Dictionary."

p. 49 "... *'Stay away* ...": Interview with Golda's niece, Judy Bauman, Baltimore, Maryland.

p. 49 "... *life really opened up for me*": Notes of Polly Wilson Kemp.

p. 50 "*Kol Nidre*": *Denver Municipal Facts*, January-August 1913, June 1914.

p. 50 "... *in Philadelphia and Chicago*": Ibid.

p. 50 "... *spring and summer of 1914*": Notes of Polly Wilson Kemp.

p. 50 *from Broadway to Cherokee Street: Denver Municipal Facts*, July 13, 1913.

p. 51 "... *and the Book of Job*": The Dickinson Branch Library in West Colfax, surrounded by a Jewish neighborhood, had the highest book circulation of all the city's branch libraries. When the Jews moved out of the area, the library closed in 1954 and was replaced by a bookmobile.

p. 51 *The Woman of Today: History of the Denver Theater, 1901–1915*, dissertation by Earle D. Winters, University of Denver, August 24, 1957. Also, John Livingston, "Yiddishkeit Along the Platte in the Jazz Age," *Rocky Mountain Jewish Historical Notes*, Vol. 3, no. 4 (April 1980).

p. 51 "... *its lodestar to you*": Rachel Bluwstein's poem "To You."

p. 51 "... *never soft or clinging*": Private interview.

p. 51 "... *he has a beautiful soul*": Interview with Regina Hamburger Medzini.

p. 52 "... *be spick-and-span*": Wolf, *The Passion of Israel*.

p. 52 "... *clean and perfectly sanitary*": Thursday was women's day at the *shvitz*. Interview with Mike Zelinger. Zelinger had interviewed a person who gave Golda a ride to Cook's.

p. 52 *one of Goldie's close friends*: Interview with Ida Libert Uchill.

p. 53 "*blissful happiness*": Interview with Regina Hamburger Medzini.

Chapter 4

p. 55 "... *with our troubles*": Interview with Sadie Ottenstein.

p. 55 "... *if I hadn't met her*": Interview with Regina Hamburger Medzini.

p. 56 "... *as second-best pupil*": Ibid.

p. 56 "*a voracious reader*": Ibid.

p. 56 "... *to distract us*": Ibid.

p. 56 "... *vibrant and attractive*": Ibid.

p. 56 "... *qualities which I lack*": Syrkin, *Golda Meir*.

p. 56 "... *people will be helped*": Untitled poem recited by Sadie Ottenstein in an interview, Milwaukee, Wisconsin.

p. 57 "... *escape from your conscience?*": Syrkin, *Golda Meir*.

p. 57 "... *in her footsteps*": Interview with Regina Hamburger Medzini.

p. 57 "... *among royalty either*": Meir, *My Life*.

p. 57 *"... only American in the family"*: Berger interview with Clara Stern.

p. 57 *"... never came back to our section"*: Mann interview with Clara Stern.

p. 58 *"... I could hate her"*: Berger interview with Clara Stern.

p. 58 *"... dared to put on lipstick"*: Interview with Sadie Ottenstein.

p. 58 *"... confided in Regina, but not me"*: Mann interview with Clara Stern.

p. 58 *"... honor bright"*: Berger interview with Clara Stern.

p. 59 *"... smiling Goldie you were heretofore"*: Meir, *My Life*.

p. 59 *"... join our movement"*: Isadore Tuchman, quoted in McCooey, "The Making of Golda Meir."

p. 60 *"... not be a parlor Zionist"*: Samuel interview with Golda, August 9, 1974.

p. 60 *"... teacher since I was eight"*: Samuel interview with Golda, April 29, 1973.

p. 60 *"... tried to teach me Yiddish and failed"*: Ruth Shapiro, quoted in Maiman, "Golda's Milwaukee."

p. 61 *"... out would come more wine"*: Interview with Sadie Ottenstein.

p. 61 *"... very tight, close group"*: Interview with Aviva Passow, Jerusalem.

p. 61 *"... home of a Hebrew poet"*: Ephraim Lisitsky, who operated a small Hebrew school and kept a collection of Yiddish, Hebrew, and Russian books.

p. 62 *"add to your fame"*: Poem entitled "My Motherland."

p. 62 *"... get her up in the morning"*: Julie Nixon Eisenhower, *Special People* (New York: Simon and Schuster, 1977).

p. 62 *"... pioneers in Palestine"*: Kemp, "Golda in Denver."

p. 63 *"... go forth to the fray"*: This was the anthem of the pro-Zion Shevua, solemnly sung in Yiddish with raised clenched fist.

p. 63 *... I did not go*: Syrkin, *Golda Meir*.

p. 63 *"... among the nations of the world"*: *Milwaukee Journal*, December 21, 1914. Brandeis was then honorary chairman of the Provisional Committee for General Zionist Affairs.

p. 64 *"... I am reading Job with Goldie"*: Syrkin, *Golda Meir*.

p. 65 *"... her enjoyment of life"*: *The Tattler*, North Division High School, Milwaukee, Wisconsin, Vol. 8, September 1915–June 1916.

p. 65 *"... 'I might just do that.'"*: Louise G. Born, quoted in McCooey, "The Making of Golda Meir."

p. 65 *"... what a tongue!"*: Syrkin, *Golda Meir*.

p. 65 *"... best I ever made in my life"*: Meir, *My Life*.

p. 66 *"... reservoir of energy"*: Louis J. Swichkow, *Memoirs of a Milwaukee Labor Zionist* (The Diaspora Research Institute, Tel Aviv University, 1975).

p. 66 *"... right word at the right occasion"*: Interview with Regina Hamburger Medzini.

p. 66 *"... she had a lot of it"*: Dorothy Weingrod, quoted in Eileen Ogintz,

"Milwaukee Firebrand," *Milwaukee Journal*, December 10, 1978.

p. 66 *". . . which I cannot bear"*: Meir, *My Life*.

p. 66 *". . . live it all over again"*: Interview with Sadie Ottenstein.

p. 66 *". . . the Palestine homeland"*: Ibid.

p. 66 *". . . we sang with a holy feeling"*: Ibid.

p. 67 *". . . as it begins, in faith"*: *The Echo*, Vol. 3, no. 5 (January 1917), published by State Normal School for Teachers, Milwaukee, Wisconsin.

p. 67 *". . . of the church and shot"*: Syrkin, *Golda Meir*.

p. 68 *against these pogroms:* The march occurred on May 22, 1919.

p. 68 *". . . your privilege"*: Mann interview with Clara Stern.

p. 69 *". . . am glad to have her"*: Unidentified library supervisor, quoted in Maiman, "Golda's Milwaukee."

p. 69 *". . . a dollar a dinner"*: Interview with Sadie Ottenstein.

p. 69 *". . . alive in Palestine"*: Quoted by Max Shulman, chairman, Provisional Executive Committee for General Zionist Affairs, Chicago, September 15, 1916. See Saffro Papers, University Archives, Golda Meir Library, University of Wisconsin, Milwaukee.

p. 69 *"We wanted to earn it"*: Harry Chemerow, quoted in the *Wisconsin Jewish Chronicle*, April 21, 1977.

p. 69 *". . . good to die for our Palestine"*: *Milwaukee Journal*, July 10, 1921.

p. 69 *". . . I was heartbroken"*: Samuel interview with Golda, August 9, 1974.

p. 70 *and homemade cookies:* Ibid.

p. 70 *". . . went where Goldie went"*: Mrs. Isadore Tuchman, quoted in Maiman, "Golda's Milwaukee."

p. 70 *". . . could tell that right away"*: Louise G. Born, quoted in Maiman, "Golda's Milwaukee."

p. 70 *". . . loved Goldie so much"*: Interview with Sadie Ottenstein.

p. 70 *". . . in love with Morris"*: Samuel interview with Golda, July 23, 1974.

p. 71 *". . . my first opera album"*: Interview with Sadie Ottenstein.

p. 71 *". . . revive it, and live in it"*: Michael Bar-Zohar, *Ben-Gurion* (New York: Adama Books, 1977).

p. 71 *return with them:* Shabtai Teveth, *Ben-Gurion: The Burning Ground, 1886–1948* (Boston: Houghton Mifflin, 1987).

p. 72 *". . . our ancient ancestral land!"*: Lossin, *Pillar of Fire*.

p. 72 *". . . have him as a guest"*: Samuel interview with Golda, July 10, 1973.

p. 72 *". . . beg you to come with me"*: Meir, *My Life*.

p. 73 *". . . You are a good motor"*: Interview with Regina Hamburger Medzini.

p. 73 *". . . in the small town of Milwaukee"*: Interview with Judy Gottlieb, Tel Aviv.

p. 73 *". . . will of my own!"*: "Panorama" interview.

p. 73 *". . . the more it suffers"*: Syrkin, *Golda Meir*.

Chapter 5

p. 75 *"We went to this place ..."*: Interview with Judy Gottlieb.

p. 75 *the break with Morris:* Ibid.

p. 76 *" 'I'm perfectly against it' "*: Ibid.

p. 76 *"... and take a walk"*: Ibid.

p. 76 *"... for about six months"*: Interview with Esther Zackler, Tel Aviv.

p. 76 *"... so vivid in my mind"*: Interview with Judy Bauman.

p. 77 *"... $480 per year"*: *Proceedings of the Board of Directors of the Chicago Public Library*, July 10, 1916, to June 24, 1918, Vol. 21 (Chicago Public Library, 1918), p. 261.

p. 77 *"... she loved to sleep"*: Interview with Judy Gottlieb.

p. 77 *adaptation of* Hamlet: Anthony E. Netboy, *A Boy's Life in the Chicago Ghetto* (Jacksonville, Oregon: privately printed, 1980).

p. 77 ... *"We want no Jews"*: *Jewish Daily Courier*, April 27, 1917.

p. 77 *twice the city average:* R. C. Longworth, "The American Milestone," *Chicago Tribune*, November 17, 1985.

p. 77 *editorialized a local paper:* Quoted by Jacob G. Grossberg (no paper mentioned) in Hyman Meltes, *The History of the Jews in Chicago* (Jewish Historical Society of Illinois, 1924).

p. 77 *even a synagogue for politicians:* Melvin G. Holli and Peter d'A. Jones, eds., *Ethnic Chicago* (Grand Rapids, Mich.: William B. Eerdmans Publishing Co., 1984). That area constituted the Twenty-fourth Ward, the strongest Democratic ward in the city.

p. 77 *"... and tact of Lord Chesterfield"*: Philip Bregstone, *Chicago and Its Jews*, privately printed, 1933 (New York Public Library, 1933).

p. 78 *"... young Zionist we should be"*: Private interview.

p. 78 *"... wants no separate residents"*: Rabbi Tobias Schamasaizer, Chicago, in *The Sentinel*, August 3, 1917.

p. 78 *"... still dreams of the new youth"*: *Chicago Daily Jewish Courier*, August 24, 1916.

p. 79 *"... what was going on"*: Interview with Judy Gottlieb.

p. 79 *"... How can you describe happiness?"*: Celina Sokolow, London, quoted in Lossin, *Pillar of Fire*.

p. 80 *"... to Zion! Let us go!"*: Dan Leon and Yehuda Amin, eds. "Chaim Weizmann: Statesman of the Jewish Renaissance" in *Confrontation* Series 3 (Jerusalem: The Zionist Library, 1974).

p. 80 *"... London was just a swamp"*: Lossin, *Pillar of Fire*.

p. 80 *"... or America is American"*: Leon and Amin, eds. "Chaim Weizmann."

p. 80 *"... Help us and it will help you"*: Ibid.

p. 80 *"... But he couldn't, so he came"*: Harris interview with Golda.

p. 81 *"... under the chuppa, so what?"*: Samuel interview with Golda, May 29, 1973.

p. 81 *"... plainest of the plain"*: Interview with Sadie Ottenstein.

p. 81   *made an emotional speech:* Interview with Regina Hamburger Medzini.

p. 81   "*. . . left foot from their right foot":* Interview with Sadie Ottenstein.

p. 82   *didn't list any occupation:* Goldie Mabowehz gave her address as 950 Tenth Street; age last birthday, nineteen.

p. 82   *"Because I loved him":* Samuel interview with Golda, July 23, 1974.

p. 82   "*. . . poetry, music, books, ideas":* Harris interview with Golda.

p. 82   *. . . the last years before she died:* Interview with Marie Syrkin, Santa Monica, California.

p. 82   "*. . . till the day he died":* Fallaci, *Interview with History.*

p. 83   "*. . . was a very impractical man":* Mann interview with Clara Stern.

p. 83   "*. . . a crazy thing to do then":* Samuel interview with Golda, August 9, 1974.

p. 83   "*. . . leaves a new husband and goes on the road?":* Ibid.

p. 83   "*. . . on all fours if they told her to":* Interview with Sadie Ottenstein.

p. 84   "*. . . didn't smoke at that time, thank God!":* Samuel interview with Golda, May 29, 1973.

p. 84   "*. . . the woman of the house":* Samuel interview with Golda, August 9, 1974.

p. 84   "*. . . slept in the same bed":* Interview with Claire Greenberg, Chicago.

p. 84   "*. . . then you don't go":* Samuel interview with Golda, August 9, 1974.

p. 84   "*. . . on his way to work":* Ibid.

p. 84   "*. . . resort to oratory":* This was part of a paper written by Mrs. Alice Lerman for History 590 on December 9, 1974, at the University of Wisconsin, Milwaukee. Her paper, "Golda Meir and Poale Zion in Milwaukee," included this section written by Moshe Dickstein for the *Canadian Jewish Chronicle,* Montreal, April 6, 1951, p. 12.

p. 85   "*. . . but he was a tailor":* Interview with Marie Syrkin.

p. 85   "*. . . your family a few months later":* Ibid.

p. 85   "*. . . wouldn't shake hands with him":* Samuel interview with Golda, May 29, 1973.

p. 85   *"I long for you":* Syrkin, *Golda Meir.*

p. 85   "*. . . a very private kind of person":* Mann interview with Clara Stern.

p. 85   "*. . . was okay with her":* Maiman, "Golda's Milwaukee."

p. 86   "*. . . friends for fifty years":* Interview with Sadie Ottenstein.

p. 86   "*. . . I'll speak to them outside":* Louis Perchonok, quoted in Louis J. Swichkow, *Memoirs of a Milwaukee Labor Zionist* (The Diaspora Research Institute, Tel Aviv University, 1975).

p. 86   *"Speak as long as you wish!":* Ibid.

p. 86   *"Jewish people, where are you?":* Chaim Weizmann, July 1920, quoted in Lossin, *Pillar of Fire,* p. 85.

p. 86   *". . . leader told them to do so":* Isaac Bashevis Singer, quoted in Lossin, *Pillar of Fire*, p. 107.

p. 86   *". . . almost a sin toward the Movement":* Golda Meir, speech at memorial service for Avivah Zuckerman, June 19, 1977, Jerusalem.

p. 87   *". . . was more than the average girl":* Bill Marten, interview with Isadore Tuchman, February 21, 1962, State Historical Society of Wisconsin, Madison.

p. 87   *". . . with huge man-sized handkerchiefs":* McCooey, "The Making of Golda Meir."

p. 87   *". . . unique woman leader": Canadian Jewish Chronicle*, April 6, 1951, p. 12.

p. 87   *Goldie wrote her friend Regina:* Interview with Regina Hamburger Medzini.

p. 87   *". . . one could have died happy":* Meir, *My Life*, p. 68.

p. 87   *". . . We had a really good time":* Samuel interview with Golda, May 29, 1973.

p. 88   *". . . find your own self":* Syrkin, *Golda Meir*.

p. 88   *". . . that was the difference":* Interview with Sadie Ottenstein.

p. 88   *". . . gone alone, but heartbroken":* Harris interview with Golda.

p. 88   *". . . couldn't* imagine *letting them build it alone!":* David Hartman, interview with Golda Meir on "Good Morning, America," June 17, 1976.

Chapter 6

p. 90   *". . . final horror of the Civil War":* Henry James, quoted by William Irwin in his *Highlights of Manhattan* (New York and London: The Century Co., 1927).

p. 90   *". . . might have finished as head librarian":* Interview with Ruth Shapiro, Milwaukee, who worked with Golda at the library. Quoted in McCooey, "The Making of Golda Meir."

p. 90   *". . . guzzled it by the quart":* Clara Stern, quoted in McCooey, "The Making of Golda Meir."

p. 90   *she did a good job:* Pinchas Caruso, quoted in interview with Menachem Jacobi, executive director of the Labor Zionist Alliance.

p. 91   *gathering place for writers and musicians:* Interview with Dr. Jacob Katzman, New York City.

p. 91   *". . . Goodmans were all heart":* Interview with Nomi Zuckerman, Jerusalem.

p. 91   *". . . and always talking":* Interview with Judith Goodman Lautt, Baldwin, New York.

p. 92   *". . . wax hot under the collar":* Interview with Dr. Jacob Katzman.

p. 92   *". . . stand on the corners and sell newspapers":* Samuel interview with Golda, May 29, 1973.

p. 92 "*. . . with this family*": Golda Meir speech at Zuckerman service.

p. 92 "*. . . that I cannot forget*": Ibid.

p. 92 "*. . . That was it! Finished!*": Interview with Nomi Zuckerman.

p. 92 "*. . . didn't lose weight on her marvelous diet*": Interview with Judith Goodman Lautt.

p. 92 *Baruch's daughter Nomi*: Interview with Nomi Zuckerman.

p. 93 "*. . . involved and complicated*": Golda Meir speech at Zuckerman memorial service.

p. 93 "*. . . supposed to go with Goldie*": Interview with Judy Gottlieb.

p. 93 "*. . . all these literary lights*": Interview with Regina Hamburger Medzini.

p. 93 "*. . . didn't have time*": Ibid.

p. 95 "*a very simple woman*": Interview with Sarah Rehabi (Golda's daughter), Tel Aviv.

p. 95 "*. . . rebel against God*": Interview with Regina Hamburger Medzini.

p. 96 "*. . . to see each other again*": Interview with Sadie Ottenstein.

p. 97 "*. . . sorry but it was too late*": Korngold, *Zichronot*.

p. 97 "*I am going*": Ibid.

p. 97 "*I must go*": Ibid.

p. 98 "*. . . to take her place*": Bill Marten interview with Morris Weingrod, State Historical Society of Wisconsin, Madison, February 20, 1962.

p. 98 "*. . . decide again to go*": Interview with Regina Hamburger Medzini.

p. 98 "*. . . that anybody could do*": "Panorama" interview.

p. 98 "*. . . I loved America*": Maiman, "Golda's Milwaukee."

p. 98 "*. . . security for my own people*": Harris interview with Golda.

p. 98 *lost world of fragments*: Lesley Hazleton, *Jerusalem, Jerusalem*, (Boston: Atlantic Monthly Press, 1986).

p. 98 "*. . . be prepared for it*": McCooey, "The Making of Golda Meir."

p. 99 "*. . . desert or the wilderness*": Samuel interview with Golda, May 29, 1973.

p. 99 "*. . . whose feet are whose*": Interview with Nomi Zuckerman.

p. 99 "*We had a great time!*": Interview with Judy Bauman.

p. 100 "*. . . What would we fight about?*": Interview with Regina Hamburger Medzini.

p. 100 "*. . . at that age, you're romantic*": Ibid.

p. 100 "*. . . prepared anything for us*": Samuel interview with Golda, May 29, 1973.

p. 100 "*. . . some felt like joining them*": Isaac Hamlin, Wisconsin Historical Society, Madison.

p. 101 "*. . . she wouldn't budge*": Samuel interview with Golda, May 29, 1973.

p. 101 "*. . . next day we were still there*": Interview with Regina Hamburger Medzini.

p. 101 "*. . . never in better singing voice*": Ibid.

p. 101 "*. . . showed us a good time*": Ibid.

p. 102 "*. . . about two dollars*": Ibid.

p. 103   *"... things like that"*: Ibid.
p. 103   *" a chaos and a mishmash"*: Korngold, *Zichronot.*
p. 103   *"... right on the spot"*: Ibid.
p. 103   *"... enter Eretz Yisroel"*: Ibid.
p. 103   *"... wait for baggage; I won't"*: Interview with Regina Hamburger Medzini.
p. 103   *"... to what do I lead them?"*: Korngold, *Zichronot.*
p. 104   *"...foundations with their backs"*: Meir, *My Life.*
p. 104   *"... dedicated, austere, and determined"*: Ibid.
p. 104   *"... sneered at us aboard ship"*: Interview with Regina Hamburger Medzini.
p. 104   *"... excitement and uncertainty"*: Syrkin, *Golda Meir.*
p. 105   *"... pioneer or not!"*: Meir, *My Life.*
p. 105   *"... on the train, of course"*: Interview with Regina Hamburger Medzini.
p. 105   *"... nice English policeman"*: Ibid.
p. 105   *"... Pocahontas reunion"*: Ibid.
p. 106   *"... hot, heavy air"*: Korngold, *Zichronot.*
p. 106   *"... coming to another planet"*: Interview with Regina Hamburger Medzini.

Chapter 7

p. 107   *"... Now we can go back—it's enough"*: Syrkin, ed., *A Land of Our Own.*
p. 107   *"... wanted to go back home"*: Interview with Judy Bauman.
p. 108   *"I will live!"*: The man who asked the question was the noted Hebrew poet Chaim Bialik.
p. 108   *"... suspicion of its neighbors"*: Korngold, *Zichronot.*
p. 108   *"... wounding hundreds more"*: Lossin, *Pillar of Fire.*
p. 108   *"... Jews on horseback"*: Millicent Fawcett, *Easter in Palestine, 1921 to 1922* (London: T. Fisher Unwin, Ltd., 1926).
p. 108   *"... or two hundred more"*: Sophie Irene Loeb, *Palestine Awake: The Rebirth of a Nation* (New York and London: The Century Co., 1926).
p. 109   *"... our children in such filth!"*: Korngold, *Zichronot.*
p. 109   *first day in Palestine*: Regina's husband, Yossel, also lost a pair of pants and put this ad in the local paper: "Either the thief should return my pants or come and get my jacket, too."
p. 109   *"... must have fallen in by accident"*: Korngold, *Zichronot.*
p. 109   *"of all the horrors"*: Samuel interview with Golda, May 29, 1973.
p. 109   *shared by forty or fifty people*: Samuel interview with Golda, May 29, 1973. The rent was three and a half pounds a month (equivalent to eighteen dollars).

p. 109   *". . . everything will be all right here"*: Meir, *My Life.*

p. 110   *". . . came home and cried"*: Samuel interview with Golda, May 29, 1973.

p. 110   *". . . in the land of the Jews?"*: Korngold, *Zichronot.*

p. 110   *nothing to wait for*: Syrkin, *Golda Meir.*

p. 110   *". . . in a Hebrew village"*: Amos Elon, *The Israelis, Founders and Sons* (Tel Aviv: Adam, 1981).

p. 111   *". . . listening to his report"*: Samuel interview with Golda, May 29, 1973.

p. 111   *". . . a foot in each country"*: Eliahu Agress, *Golda Meir, Portrait of a Prime Minister* (New York: Sabra Books, 1969).

p. 111   *". . . build things up by yourself"*: Yehuda Wertman quoted in Lossin, *Pillar of Fire*, p. 121.

p. 111   *". . . beloved, blessed land of mine"*: Letter from Jessie Sampter in Jerusalem to an American friend, May 25, 1921, quoted in Bertha Badt-Strauss, *White Fire: The Life and Works of Jessie Sampter* (New York: Reconstructionist Press, 1956).

p. 112   *". . . with nothing to do"*: Edwin Samuel, son of the first British high commissioner in Palestine, Herbert Samuel.

p. 112   *". . . I like walking barefoot . . ."*: Yehuda Wertman, who arrived in Palestine, like Golda, with the Third Aliyah.

p. 112   *". . . you would rather not know"*: Hazleton, *Jerusalem, Jerusalem.*

p. 112   *". . . We thought we were already free"*: Shmuel Ben-Ze'ev, quoted in Lossin, *Pillar of Fire*, p. 91.

p. 113   *". . . one Palestine complete"*: Rt. Hon. Viscount Herbert Samuel, *Memoirs* (London: Cresset Press, 1945).

p. 113   *". . . not a house, not a tree"*: John Bowle, *Viscount Samuel, A Biography* (London: Victor Gollancz, Ltd., 1957).

p. 113   *". . . at home with the Arab landowners"*: Ibid.

p. 114   *". . . you have contact with it"*: The Wailing Wall was so named because it was said to be made of tears. One legend has it that the wall survived the Roman destruction of the Second Temple because the Archangel Gabriel saw the temple in flames, came down to earth, sat on the western part of the Temple's retaining wall, and wept. Where his tears fell, the stone ceased to crumble, and instead hardened. Small pieces of paper with prayers written on them were pushed in between the stones by the faithful and were regularly collected by rabbis, then buried. Only when the Wall was in Jewish control was it renamed the Western Wall, because there was supposedly no more cause for tears. It has recently been said of the Wall that if the Jews are indeed a "stiff-necked people"—as a prophet reportedly called them—"it seems appropriate that such a people should choose to worship at a wall, knocking their heads against stone."

p. 114   *"the baggage came"*: Syrkin, *Golda Meir.*

p. 114   *"... and they listened to records"*: Samuel interview with Golda, May 29, 1973.

p. 114   *"... stacks of his records"*: Interview with Gideon Meir, San Francisco, California.

p. 114   *shuffling gait of the old ghetto:* Joseph Krimsky, *Revisits and Revisions* (New York: Bloch Publishing Co., 1924).

p. 114   *"... housewives, chauffeurs, shopkeepers"*: Milton J. Goell, *Tramping Through Palestine: Impressions of an American Student in Israel-Land* (New York: Kensington Press, 1926), p. 38.

p. 115   *"... would never understand Hebrew"*: Samuel interview with Golda, May 29, 1973.

p. 115   *"... some letters the other day"*: Ibid.

p. 115   *"You're bigger than a fly!"*: Interview with Judy Bauman.

p. 115   *"... not to teach English"*: Mann, *Golda*.

Chapter 8

p. 117   *"... and why do they stay?"*: Jessie Sampter poem from her book *The Emek*, 1925. Reprinted in Badt-Strauss, *White Fire*.

p. 117   *"... and they wanted single girls"*: Golda Meir, "My First Days in Kibbutz Merhavia," *Jewish Affairs*, December 1970. Johannesburg, South Africa.

p. 117   *"... all about American girls"*: Ibid.

p. 118   *"... and to draw upon the earth"*: Elon, *The Israelis*.

p. 118   *"... society, and nature"*: Melford E. Spiro, *Kibbutz: Venture in Utopia* (Cambridge: Harvard University Press, 1956).

p. 118   *"That is not Zionism"*: Interview with Golda Meir, on "Issues and Answers," September 21, 1970.

p. 118   *"... should do things for them," said Golda:* Conversation with Golda Meir, "Eternal Light" radio program, New York City, June 1, 1969.

p. 118   *"... will be an honor"*: Rinna Samuel interview with Golda, Jerusalem, July 16, 1973. Lavon Institute.

p. 119   *and long benches:* Joseph Raphael Blasi, *The Communal Experience of the Kibbutz* (New Brunswick, N.J.: Transaction Books, 1986).

p. 119   *named Franz Oppenheimer:* Oppenheimer gradually alienated himself from the Zionist movement in 1913 because he opposed nationalism. The original settlement at Merhavia in 1911 was based on his idea. It proved unsuccessful, but laid the foundation for future settlements.

p. 119   *"... under a cloudless sky"*: Samuel, *Memoirs*.

p. 119   *"... potshots at us from time to time"*: Meir, "My First Days in Kibbutz Merhavia."

p. 119   *... as a holy mountain: Encyclopaedia Judaica*, Vol. 15 (1972), p. 693.

p. 120 *"... can't stay in Merhavia"*: Meir, "My First Days in Kibbutz Merhavia."
p. 120 *"... have been a block square"*: Interview with Judy Bauman.
p. 120 *"... soil to put seedlings in"*: Rinna Samuel, interview with Golda, Lavon Institute, May 29, 1973.
p. 120 *"... suffice to stand the test"*: S. B. Jaffe, quoted in Chaim Gvati, *One Hundred Years of Settlement: The Story of Jewish Settlement in the Land of Israel* (Jerusalem: Keter Publishing House, 1985).
p. 120 *"... revitalizing such soil"*: Rahel Yanait Ben-Zvi, quoted in Lossin, *Pillar of Fire.*
p. 120 *"... he can overcome hardship"*: Spiro, *Kibbutz.*
p. 120 *"... but for life itself"*: Aaron David Gordon, quoted in Lossin, *Pillar of Fire.*
p. 120 *"... such an elated experience"*: Spiro, *Kibbutz.*
p. 120 *"... best of all possible worlds"*: Nathan Zach, quoted in Amia Lieblich, *Kibbutz Makom* (New York: Pantheon Books, 1981).
p. 121 *"... let alone swallow"*: Golda Meir, in Syrkin, ed., *A Land of Our Own.*
p. 121 *"Nobody owed me anything"*: Samuel interview with Golda, July 16, 1973.
p. 121 *"... especially if you had a fever"*: Ibid., May 29, 1973.
p. 121 *"... because of the snipers"*: Meir, "My First Days in Kibbutz Merhavia," *Midstream*, May 1970.
p. 121 *"... forget their past"*: Dan Vittorio Segre, *Memoirs of a Fortunate Jew: An Italian Story* (Bethesda, Md.: Adler and Adler, 1987).
p. 122 *"... as quickly as possible"*: Ibid.
p. 122 *"... but we wouldn't agree to that"*: Shenker, "Golda Meir, 80, Dies in Jerusalem."
p. 122 *"... someone else might wear them"*: Yehuda Wertman, quoted in Lossin, *Pillar of Fire.*
p. 122 ... *exchange information, solve problems:* Yonina Garber-Talmon, *Family and Community in the Kibbutz* (Cambridge: Harvard University Press, 1972).
p. 122 *"... and the boys too"*: Meir, "My First Days in Kibbutz Merhavia," New York: *Midstream*, May 1970.
p. 122 *"... the water practically boiled"*: An account of an experience in Degania Kibbutz told to Sana Hasan, author of *Enemy in the Promised Land: An Egyptian Woman's Journey into Israel* (New York: Pantheon Books, 1986).
p. 123 *"... were viewed with scorn"*: Garber-Talmon, *Family and Community in the Kibbutz.*
p. 123 *"... because he is a human being"*: Samuel interview with Golda, May 29, 1973.
p. 123 *"... real activity of mind"*: Report by Sir Herbert Samuel in Fawcett, *Easter in Palestine, 1921 to 1922.*
p. 123 *wrote one kibbutznik:* Joseph Raphael Blasi, *The Communal Future:*

The Kibbutz and the Utopian Dilemma (Norwood, Pa.: Norwood Editions, 1980).

p. 124 *". . . talked about was more work":* Interview with Judy Bauman.

p. 124 *". . . and the plan is worked":* Sir Ronald Storrs, governor of Jerusalem, Jaffa and the federal district of Palestine, quoted in Loeb, *Palestine Awake.*

p. 124 *". . . It was very special":* Lossin, *Pillar of Fire.*

p. 124 *". . . felt absolutely fulfilled":* Meir, *My Life.*

p. 124 *". . . bourgeois marriage":* Spiro, *Kibbutz.*

p. 124 *". . . norms of Eastern Europe":* Lesley Hazleton, *Israeli Women: The Reality Behind the Myth* (New York: Simon and Schuster, 1977). Spiro also notes in his book *Kibbutz* about some kibbutzim experimenting with polygamy and polyandry.

p. 124 *". . . as lifelong fidelity":* Garber-Talmon, *Family and Community in the Kibbutz.*

p. 125 *". . . woman's weakness and instability":* Hazleton, *Israeli Women.*

p. 125 *". . . not part of this freedom":* Blasi, *The Communal Future.*

p. 125 *. . . at Merhavia as "discreet":* Meir, *My Life.*

p. 125 *". . . business of those concerned":* Sternman, quoted in Hazleton, *Israeli Women.*

p. 125 *. . . that they were in love:* Spiro, *Kibbutz.*

p. 125 *". . . not on display":* Samuel interview with Golda, July 16, 1973.

p. 125 *". . . in nonessentials—liberty":* Blasi, *The Communal Future.* Yonima Garber-Talmon also observed in *Family and Community in the Kibbutz* that "formal wedding was usually deferred until after the birth of the first child" to legitimize it. Spiro added that it was taboo for a woman to refer to her mate as "my husband (*baali*)."

p. 125 *". . . a target for Arab snipers":* Harris interview with Golda.

p. 126 *". . . smiling his enchanting smile":* Yaël Dayan, ed., *Pioneers in Israel* (Cleveland and New York: World Publishing Co., 1961).

p. 126 *". . . week in advance," Golda recalled:* Meir, "My First Days in Kibbutz Merhavia," *Jewish Affairs.*

p. 126 *". . . into a fit of depression":* Ibid., *Midstream.*

p. 126 *". . . they are your family":* Ibid.

p. 126 *". . . bought Quaker Oats":* Kibbutzniks called the cereal "Kwoker."

p. 126 *". . . bits of hard-boiled eggs":* Meir, *My Life.*

p. 126 *". . . because it was so bad":* Interview with Celia Stern, outside of Tel Aviv.

p. 126 *". . . at the expense of my work":* Samuel interview with Golda, May 29, 1973.

p. 127 *. . . as "bourgeois weakness":* Syrkin, ed., *A Land of Our Own.*

p. 127 *. . . "gave us a bad name":* Meir, "My First Days in Kibbutz Merhavia," *Midstream.*

p. 127 *. . . lessons to the owner's daughter:* The grocer was named Blumenfield and came from Germany. Golda gave his daughter lessons several times a week, after her work. In lieu of payment, Blumenfield gave her a monthly credit of three pounds in his store. With this, she bought "all our luxuries." This included potatoes, salt, Quaker Oats, "and sometimes even raisins for our cookies."

p. 127 *"... but I refused to give in"*: Meir, "My First Days in Kibbutz Merhavia," *Midstream*.

p. 127 *"... bake her own* challeh*"*: Ibid., *Jewish Affairs*.

p. 127 *"... who would have to be fed"*: Ibid.

p. 128 *"... even one chicken (or living mouse)"*: Syrkin, ed., *A Land of Our Own* p. 41.

p. 128 *"... filled with dead ducks"*: Meir, "My First Days in Kibbutz Merhavia," *Midstream*.

p. 128 *"... exquisite taste of that lemonade"*: Ibid.

p. 129 *"... but not for the* barhash*"*: Ibid.

p. 129 ... *"so many men worked in the kitchen"*: Korngold, *Zichronot*.

p. 129 *"... going to come and fight"*: Interview with Judy Bauman.

p. 129 ... *firewood on their heads*: Segre, *Memoirs of a Fortunate Jew*.

p. 130 *"So did Goldie!"*: Interview with Judy Bauman.

p. 130 *"... struggling all alone"*: Meir, *My Life*.

p. 130 *"... as productive as the cow"*: Mann, *Golda*.

p. 131 *"... thousands of miles away"*: Goell, *Tramping Through Palestine*.

p. 131 *"... would return without Golda"*: Interview with Marie Syrkin.

p. 131 *"... drive and talent and* mazel*"*: Interview with Regina Hamburger Medzini.

p. 131 *"... that's* mazel*"*: Interview with Mike Green, Westport, Connecticut.

p. 131 *"... thought I would never understand Hebrew"*: Samuel interview with Golda, May 29, 1973.

p. 132 *"... who shed light on America"*: Interview with Regina Hamburger Medzini.

p. 132 *"... had not even arisen yet"*: Meir, *My Life*.

p. 132 *"... with somebody through the country"*: Samuel interview with Golda, May 29, 1973.

p. 133 *"... within Constantinople"*: Ibid.

p. 133 *"... but we were not enemies"*: Interview with Shirley Shapiro, Jerusalem.

p. 133 *"... had never lived anywhere else"*: Samuel interview with Golda, May 29, 1973.

p. 133 *"... always, telling us things"*: Syrkin, *Golda Meir*.

p. 133 *became chronically ill*: Samuel interview with Golda, May 29, 1973.

p. 133 *"... a tragedy, a great tragedy"*: Fallaci, *Interview with History*.

p. 134 *"... taking us as members"*: Meir, "My First Days in Kibbutz Merhavia," *Jewish Affairs*.

Chapter 9

p. 135   *". . . showing, that's a man":* Yehuda Wertman, quoted in Lossin, *Pillar of Fire.*

p. 136   *flowered within the next few years:* Interview with Aharon Remez, Jerusalem.

p. 136   *"Jew! Speak Hebrew!":* Ziona Rabau, Tel Aviv, quoted in Lossin, *Pillar of Fire.*

p. 136   *"Tel Aviv was built on sand":* Thomas L. Friedman, *The New York Times,* July 21, 1987.

p. 137   *". . . never allowed any germs in the house":* Interview with David and Aviva Passow, Jerusalem.

p. 137   *". . . tribute to their relationship":* Ibid.

p. 137   *". . . don't know how many friends he had":* Ibid.

p. 137   *". . . look what man is doing to it!":* Berger interview with Clara Stern.

p. 137   *". . . about a free, workers' Palestine":* Syrkin, *Golda Meir.*

p. 137   *". . . to have a child":* Harris interview with Golda.

p. 138   *". . . the place where I am now":* Jacques Derrida, quoted in Mishkenot Sha'ananim Newsletter, No. 7, December 1986.

p. 138   *". . . directions at the same time":* Loeb, *Palestine Awake.*

p. 138   *". . . I have a dream!":* Lossin, *Pillar of Fire,* p. 135.

p. 139   *". . . the worst in my life":* Harris interview with Golda.

p. 139   *". . . sad there, really sad":* Interview with Judy Bauman.

p. 139   *". . . you received one lirah's":* Gideon Lev-Ari, interview with Golda, "On Occasion of Fifty Years of Her Aliyah," Lavon Institute, 1971.

p. 139   *"She was desperate":* Interview with Judy Bauman.

p. 140   *neighbor who lived above them:* Interview with Faigel Berkenblitt, suburbs of Tel Aviv.

p. 140   *". . . live here and, yes, suffer":* Golda Meir, "Letter to America"—letter to Shamai in Nachman Tamir, ed., *Golda, Articles in Her Memory* (Jerusalem: Am Oved, 1981).

p. 140   *". . . almost put that thing around his neck":* Interview with Judy Bauman.

p. 140   *". . . women have compared with men":* Fallaci, *Interview with History.*

p. 140   *the doctor told Morris:* Mann, *Golda.*

p. 140   *". . . retold that story a hundred times":* Private interview.

p. 141   *". . . never should have children":* Interview with Regina Hamburger Medzini.

p. 141   *". . . who thought it was not necessary":* Meir, "My First Days in Kibbutz Merhavia," *Midstream.*

p. 141   *. . . Golda's "brandy babies":* Mann, *Golda.*

p. 142   *". . . without a night-watch girl":* Meir, "My First Days in Kibbutz Merhavia," *Midstream.*

p. 142   *". . . loved so much as the kibbutz life":* Fallaci, *Interview with History.*

p. 142   *". . . of public life . . . to private life":* Harris interview with Golda.

p. 143   *And Goldie cried:* Interview with Judy Gottlieb.

p. 143   *". . . and made little curtains":* Interview with Faigel Berkenblitt.

p. 143   *". . . who was a pain in the neck":* Interview with Judy Bauman.

p. 144   *". . . oil lamp in the window":* Lev-Ari interview with Golda.

p. 144   *". . . whatever needed washing":* Wolf, *The Passion of Israel.*

p. 144   *". . . quite advanced educational views":* Interview with Sarah Rehabi, Tel Aviv.

p. 144   *". . . made him very unhappy":* Wolf, *The Passion of Israel.*

p. 144   *"It isn't working out":* Interview with Regina Hamburger Medzini.

p. 144   *". . . how these two people found love":* Interview with Faigel Berkenblitt.

p. 145   *"It all just happened":* Eisenhower, *Special People.*

Chapter 10

p. 147   *". . . sometimes in Jerusalem": Jewish Frontier,* December 1984.

p. 148   *". . . loved to make fudge":* Interview with Judy Bauman.

p. 148   *"The Heart, by D'Amicis":* Interview with Sarah Rehabi.

p. 148   *"Your heart is rent":* Fallaci, *Interview with History.*

p. 148   *". . . something different there":* Marlin Levin, "The Many-Sided Golda Meir," *Life* magazine, November 4, 1963.

p. 149   *". . . wasn't always around":* Berger interview with Clara Stern.

p. 149   *". . . would have remained outside":* Interview with Sarah Rehabi.

p. 149   *". . . meetings of all kinds":* Interview with Drora Volcani, Rehovot, Israel.

p. 150   *". . . lift our hands to vote":* Interview with Sarah Rehabi.

p. 150   *". . . vote of confidence I ever got":* Samuel interview with Golda, August 9, 1974.

p. 150   *". . . life of a democracy," said Menachem:* Menachem Meir, *My Mother, Golda Meir* (New York: Arbor House, 1983).

p. 150   *"It ate her up":* Interview with Judy Gottlieb.

p. 150   *". . . to enjoy herself":* Interview with Masha Rabinovich, Tel Aviv.

p. 150   *". . . for such a woman there is no rest":* Syrkin, ed., *A Land of Our Own.*

p. 150   *". . . hovering over them":* Ibid.

p. 151   *". . . don't fill up my life":* Rachel Katznelson Shazar, ed., *Plough Women: Records of the Pioneer Women of Palestine* (New York: Herzl Press, 1975, in conjunction with *The Pioneer Woman*). Originally printed by Council of Women Workers of Palestine, 1928, from essay by Golda Meir called "Borrowed Mothers."

p. 151   *". . . remained with them but couldn't":* Levin, "The Many-Sided Golda Meir."

p. 151   *". . . a lot on my account":* Fallaci, *Interview with History.*

p. 151 *"... you'll never be lonesome"*: Mann, *Golda*.

p. 151 *"... born a generation later"*: Interview with Marie Syrkin.

p. 152 *"... had never heard before"*: Samuel interview with Golda, July 16, 1973.

p. 152 *named Jean Jaurès:* Shazar had heard Jaurès address French International Congress in Basel, Switzerland, January 1913.

p. 153 *"Fought the battle of the Lord"*: Shazar wrote a description of Jaurès's performance in *Kochvei Boker* (Tel Aviv: Am Oved, 1950). Quoted in "Shazar, the Zionist Socialist Who Remained an Ardent Hassid," *Jerusalem Post*, October 6, 1944.

p. 153 *"In a tumult of desire"*: Zalman Shazar, *Poems* (South Brunswick, N.J.: A.S. Barnes & Co., 1974).

p. 153 *"... hear what he had to say"*: Interview with Shulamit Nardi, Jerusalem.

p. 153 *"... wanted to do everything"*: Ibid.

p. 153 *"... make here a pogrom"*: Sulamith Ish-Kishor, *Zalman Shazar, President of the People.* Pamphlet (New York: Jewish National Fund, 1966).

p. 153 *Shazar's closest associates:* Private interview.

p. 153 *"... teachers of the new generations"*: Samuel interview with Golda, July 16, 1973.

p. 154 *"... out of this world"*: Interview with Shulamit Nardi.

p. 154 *"... lithe as a gazelle"*: Zalman Shazar, *Morning Stars* (Philadelphia: Jewish Publication Society of America, 1967).

p. 154 *"... trunk of a carob tree"*: Ibid.

p. 154 *"... childhood of our people"*: Ibid.

p. 155 *"We are a people"*: Philip Gillon, "A Birthday Portrait of President Zalman Shazar," *Jerusalem Post*, November 11, 1969.

p. 155 *"... no airs about him of any kind"*: Samuel interview with Golda, July 16, 1973.

p. 155 *... called her "ugly"*: Private interview.

p. 000 *... the book,* The Ploughwoman: Rachel Shazar, ed., *Plough Women*.

p. 155 *"... get started with her"*: Private interview.

p. 156 *"... this is what she wanted"*: Private interview.

p. 156 *"... only woman I ever really loved"*: Ibid.

p. 156 *"... my basic interest in life"*: Samuel interview with Golda, July 16, 1973.

p. 156 *"... more important than women's rights"*: Ibid.

p. 156 *"... woman in the labor movement"*: Interview with Rivka Idelson, Tel Aviv.

p. 156 *"... didn't step on one another"*: Ibid.

p. 156 *"... gave her much strength"*: Nachman Tamir interview with Rina Dotan, Jerusalem.

p. 156 *". . . perceived as 'sexually tinged' ":* "Women of 42 Nations Set Leadership Roles," *The New York Times,* n.d.

p. 157 *". . . that kind of nonsense":* Fallaci, *Interview with History.*

p. 157 *". . . more or less true, I guess":* Private interview.

p. 157 *". . . been good to me," Golda reminisced:* Fallaci, *Interview with History.*

p. 157 *". . . what else can you ask of fortune?":* Ibid.

p. 157 *". . . better at her job than a man":* Ibid.

p. 157 *". . . unfair deal as an illogical one":* Harris interview with Golda.

p. 157 *". . . so that she be so modest":* Raphael Patai, *The Seed of Abraham: Jews and Arabs in Contact and Conflict* (Salt Lake City: University of Utah Press, 1986).

p. 157 *a man who worked with her:* Interview with Dr. Jacob Katzman.

p. 158 *". . . couldn't say no to Goldie":* Ibid.

p. 158 *involved much explanation:* Lavon Institute interview with Golda.

p. 158 *". . . was not secretary of the Histadrut":* Ibid.

p. 158 *". . . had beaten him over the head":* Meir, *My Life.*

p. 159 *". . . younger than my brother":* Interview with Yona Kama, Avigdor, Israel.

p. 159 *". . . youngster, tagging along":* Samuel interview with Golda, July 16, 1973.

p. 159 *". . . lighting a spark":* Interview with Sara Erez, Tel Aviv.

p. 159 *". . . drank in what he said":* Ibid.

p. 160 *". . . as if I had been in a confessional":* Ibid.

p. 160 *". . . his light on that one spot":* Robert St. John, *Ben-Gurion: A Biography* (Garden City, N.Y.: Doubleday, 1971).

p. 160 *". . . achieve its true destiny":* Ibid.

p. 160 *". . . no one left the room":* Ibid.

p. 160 *". . . loved him for that":* Meir, *My Life.*

p. 161 *". . . had a very fertile mind":* Interview with Bert Goldstein, Tel Aviv.

p. 161 *prominent Zionist leader:* Dr. Israel Goldstein had been president of the Zionist Organization of America and the Jewish National Fund. He and his wife had settled in Jerusalem in 1961.

p. 161 *". . . combination of logic and emotion":* Interview with Bert Goldstein.

p. 161 *". . . couldn't hold against her tears":* Interview with Rivka Idelson.

p. 161 *". . . cry like a high school girl":* Interview with Shulamit Nardi.

p. 161 *one hundred most important leaders:* Interview with Gershon Avner, Jerusalem.

p. 161 *who worked with her at that time:* Ibid.

p. 161 *". . . respected by everyone":* Ibid.

p. 161 *said a younger friend:* Interview with Aviva Passow, Jerusalem.

p. 161 *". . . to that image, or even try":* Ibid.

p. 162 *". . . for her, The Mattress":* Private interview.

p. 162 *daughter of an old friend:* Private interview.

p. 162 *". . . and for the same reason":* Private interview.

p. 162 *". . . people let people live":* Interview with Rivka Idelson.

p. 163 *". . . walls imagine is happening":* Lesley Hazleton, *Israeli Women.*

p. 163 *". . . and I am one of them":* Samuel interview with Golda, July 16, 1973.

p. 163 *"Never! Never!":* Ibid.

p. 163 *". . . won't give it to me," she replied simply:* Interview with Regina Hamburger Medzini.

p. 163 *". . . a male community all-male dominated":* Interview with Rivka Idelson.

p. 163 *". . . I'd clear out quickly":* Interview with Regina Hamburger Medzini.

p. 164 *". . . the style of their life":* Interview with Marie Syrkin.

p. 164 *". . . do it just for ourselves":* Samuel interview with Golda, July 16, 1973.

p. 164 *Shazar's longtime personal friend:* Private interview.

p. 164 *". . . no kibbutz quickie":* Private interview.

p. 165 *"Should we rejoice in this?":* Korngold, *Zichronot.*

p. 165 *". . . in one house or the other":* Interview with Yona Kama.

p. 165 *". . . what we want and what we are":* Meir, *My Life,* p. 118.

p. 166 *". . . always a lot of anxiety about her":* Mann interview with Clara Stern.

p. 166 *guessing how late their mother would be:* Interview with Sarah Rehabi.

p. 166 *". . . that I neglected them":* "Panorama" interview.

p. 166 *". . . she was always there":* Interview with Sarah Rehabi.

p. 166 *". . . For such a mother, it was worth it":* Ibid.

p. 166 *". . . want us to know what it was":* Ibid.

p. 167 *"I should throw the paper":* Lavon Institute interview with Golda.

p. 167 *". . . just opening the door and saying he is here":* Ibid.

p. 167 *". . . Crash on Black Thursday":* October 24, 1929. It was the most spectacular market drop up to that time.

p. 167 *". . . didn't know what happened to me":* Samuel interview with Golda, August 9, 1974.

p. 167 *". . . when Shmarya is sitting there":* Ibid. Golda first heard Shmarya Levin speak in Milwaukee, and later said of him: "He was so wise, but you know there is wisdom that is cold. The man has a good head but his wisdom was so warm and sparkling, and a sense of humor which was fantastic."

p. 167 *. . . as "a firebrand":* Interview with Arthur Goldberg, Washington, D.C.

p. 168 *". . . knew very little about each other":* Samuel interview with Golda, August 9, 1974.

p. 168 *"Life is too big for letters":* Badt-Strauss, *White Fire.*

p. 168 *". . . were prepared to save us":* Lossin, *Pillar of Fire.*

p. 168 *anti-Zionist colonial secretary:* Bar-Zohar, *Ben-Gurion.* Colonial Secretary Lord Passfield had assured the grand mufti, Haj Amin, on May 1, 1930, that there was no intention of allowing them to be dispossessed. Passfield then urged the British Cabinet to note that the Arabs were a larger growing force than the Jews (Gilbert, *Exile and Return*). Passfield not only limited the amount of land that could be sold to the Jews, but also limited the number of immigrants (Dan Kurzman, *Ben-Gurion, Prophet of Fire* [New York: Simon and Schuster, 1983]).

p. 169   *"Perhaps you understand me now?"*: Syrkin, *Golda Meir*.

p. 169   "*. . . chasing out the Arabs"*: Report to the Histadrut, July 11, 1930.

p. 169   "*. . . hard not to be pessimistic"*: Ibid.

p. 170   "*. . . what is going to happen"*: Samuel interview with Golda, June 18, 1973.

p. 170   "*. . . what it was all about, and I did"*: Ibid.

p. 170   "*. . . never saw such sad eyes"*: Ibid.

p. 170   *"Weizmann and Shertok, but you!"*: Ibid.

p. 171   *"We must resist!"*: Kurzman, *Ben-Gurion, p. 175*.

p. 171   "*. . . you have become a nation"*: Lossin, *Pillar of Fire*.

p. 171   "*. . . all you're getting is a rented flat"*: Meir, *My Life*.

p. 173   "*. . . because I have no home"*: Remez Papers, private collection of Aharon Remez, Jerusalem.

Chapter 11

p. 175   "*. . . this is meat and this is soup"*: Interview with Sarah Rehabi.

p. 175   "*. . . oh, she suffered"*: Samuel interview with Golda, July 24, 1973.

p. 176   *"Gusta has a remez"*: Private interview.

p. 176   "*. . . otherwise I wouldn't have gone"*: Samuel interview with Golda, July 24, 1973.

p. 176   *in New York at the same time:* Private interview.

p. 177   *"You better go finish it."*: Interview with Sara Erez.

p. 177   *. . . considered it "madness"*: Meir, *My Life*.

p. 177   "*. . . she had to reassure me"*: Ibid.

p. 177   "*. . . for hours," Menachem remembered:* Meir, *My Mother, Golda Meir*.

p. 177   "*. . . so Mother slept on a cot"*: Peggy Mann interview with Menachem Meir, June 1970.

p. 178   "*. . . as though they were on their own"*: Samuel interview with Golda, July 24, 1973.

p. 178   "*. . . eat good nourishing food"*: Interview with Judith Goodman Lautt.

p. 178   "*. . . treatment could have killed her"*: Samuel interview with Golda, July 24, 1973. Sarah's illness was diagnosed as chronic glomerulonephritis.

p. 178   *. . . her fear of the unknown:* Dr. Bettie Youngs, *Stress in Children: How to Recognize, Avoid and Overcome It* (New York: Arbor House, 1985).

p. 179   *"One woman gave her a doll"*: Interview with Sonia Lehr, New York City.

p. 179 "*. . . picked up English, snap, just like that*": Interview with Judith Goodman Lautt.

p. 179 "*. . . teach you whole words, using cards*": Interview with Sarah Rehabi.

p. 179 "*. . . sort of very shy of each other*": Interview with Judith Goodman
Lautt.

p. 180 "*But he did go home*": Ibid.

p. 180 "*. . . don't remember if she spoke English*": Interview with Sarah Rehabi.

p. 180 "*. . . everything back home was good*": Samuel interview with Golda,
July 24, 1973.

p. 180 *. . . to save it for the next day:* Interview with Judith Goodman Lautt.

p. 180 "*. . . would marry when they returned home*": Private interview.

p. 181 *And she took it*": Interview with Dr. Jacob Katzman.

p. 182 "*. . . pointing to his watch*": Ibid.

p. 182 "*. . . yes, who liked the ladies*": Ibid.

p. 182 "*. . . don't think Golda had tangents*": Ibid.

p. 183 "*. . . very quiet, withdrawn*": Ibid.

p. 184 "*. . . softness and selfishness*": Nick Mandelkern, "*The Story of Pioneer
Women,*" Part 2, *The Pioneer Woman,* November 1980.

p. 184 "*. . . who gave it imagination*": Ibid.

p. 184 *. . . Golda was one of the sparks:* Ibid, Part 1, September 1980.

p. 184 '*Yiddish! Yiddish!*'": Zelda Lemberger quoted in *The Pioneer Woman,*
January/February 1981.

p. 184 "*. . . sex roles had not yet arrived*": Mandelkern, "The Story of Pioneer
Women," Part 4, *The Pioneer Woman,* March/April 1981.

p. 185 "*. . . development of civilization*": 1929 issue of *The Pioneer Woman*
quoted in Mandelkern, "The Story of Pioneer Women," Part 3,
The Pioneer Woman, January/February 1981.

p. 185 "*. . . blindly stuck to it*": Interview with Dr. Jacob Katzman.

p. 185 "*. . . smell of toil and sweat*": Unpublished essay in the Golda Meir file
of *The Pioneer Woman.*

p. 185 "*. . . for the ecstasy of creation*": *The Pioneer Woman,* June 1934.

p. 185 "*. . . in a Bronx warehouse*": Essay by Dvorah Rothbard, Golda Meir
file in *The Pioneer Woman.*

p. 185 "*. . . songs from the Yishuv*": Ibid.

p. 185 "*. . . wee hours of the morning*": Mandelkern, "The Story of Pioneer
Women," Part 2.

p. 185 "*. . . really built us spiritually*": Nick Mandelkern, "A Talk with Dvorah
Rothbard," *The Pioneer Woman,* November/December 1984.

p. 186 "*. . . way of reaching you directly*": Interview with Esther Zackler, Tel
Aviv.

p. 186 *via Lithuania and London:* Interview with Sonia Schelpark, Tel Aviv.

p. 186 "*. . . younger than Golda*": Interview with Dr. Jacob Katzman.

p. 186 "*. . . curt and rather cold*": Interview with Sonia Schelpark.

p. 187 "*. . . with Leah from New York*": Interview with Sarah Rehabi.

p. 187 "... *work as hard as men on farms*": Meir, *My Mother, Golda Meir.*

p. 187 "... *she and Golda shared a room*": Interview with Judith Goodman Lautt.

p. 187 "... *we saw so little of her*": Interview with Sarah Rehabi.

p. 187 "... *because it was too expensive*": Samuel interview with Golda, August 9, 1974.

p. 187 "... *stay home and talk to me*": Interview with Dr. Jacob Katzman.

p. 187 ... "*and idolized her*": Ibid.

p. 188 "*She was beautiful*": Ibid.

p. 188 "... *young people to tears*": Interview with David Breslau, Jerusalem.

p. 188 "... *only when I was sick*": Samuel interview with Golda, July 24, 1973.

p. 188 "... *never have seen a jail or policeman*": *Chicago Tribune*, February 20, 1929.

p. 189 "... *that grows from within*": Golda Meir's speech at the convention of The Pioneer Women of America, 1932.

p. 189 "*Goldie Meyerson Clubs*": Essay by Dvorah Rothbard.

p. 189 ... "*Over my dead body*": Michael Levanthol, Jerusalem, letter to the editor, *Hadassah* magazine, April 1988.

p. 189 "... *to walk again*": Debs Myers, describing the funeral train of Pres. Franklin D. Roosevelt in *Yank, the Army Weekly.*

p. 189 *for a group in Columbia, Missouri, to donate $45*": "Quota and Dues" (from October 1933 to July 1, 1934), *The Pioneer Woman*, June 1934.

p. 189 "*Never!*" *said Golda indignantly*: Samuel interview with Golda, August 9, 1974.

p. 190 "... *never live it down*": Golda quoted by Anne Melman, St. Louis, Missouri.

p. 190 *answered firmly, "No, never!*": Samuel interview with Golda, July 16, 1973.

p. 190 "... *organizing into a group*": Cyrile Eisenberg quoted in *The Pioneer Woman*, December 1933.

p. 191 "... *and just be Pioneer Women*": Mandelkern, "A Talk with Dvorah Rothbard."

p. 191 "... *you are only a* woman": Samuel interview with Golda, August 9, 1974.

p. 191 ... "*wept and we all wept*": Ibid.

p. 191 "... *always enough to cry about*": Shenker, "Golda Meir, 80, Dies in Jerusalem."

p. 192 "... *paraded back to the hotel*": Essay by Dvorah Rothbard.

p. 192 "... *rather smitten with her*": Interview with Meyer Steinglass, New York City.

p. 192 "... *taking care of the house*": Interview with Judith Goodman Lautt.

p. 193 "... *a pianist, really very good*": Interview with Sarah Rehabi.

p. 193 "... *she could wear her new dress*": Interview with Marie Syrkin.

p. 194   *". . . simply knew what to do"*: Ibid.

p. 194   *"Let us march!"*: Ibid.

p. 194   *". . . translated my poetry into Hebrew"*: Ibid.

p. 195   *". . . aprons, towels, dolls, tablecloths"*: Interview with Dr. Jacob Katzman.

p. 195   *". . . among those society dames"*: Ibid.

p. 195   *"I was the first"*: Golda was quoting Joseph Baratz. Of the original ten members of Degania, two died of malaria and one was killed by an Arab.

p. 196   *". . . she was so remarkable even then"*: Interview with Faigel Berkenblitt.

p. 196   *". . . shall never forget her"*: "Bronx English-Speaking Club Gives Farewell Party," *The Pioneer Woman*, June 1934.

p. 196   *". . . leading them in Hebrew and Jewish songs"*: Meir, *My Mother, Golda Meir*.

Chapter 12

p. 197   *". . . wasn't going to marry anyone"*: Interview with Regina Hamburger Medzini.

p. 197   *". . . but she was never there"*: Interview with Nomi Zuckerman.

p. 197   *". . . there has to be a clash"*: Fallaci, *Interview with History*.

p. 198   *". . . vacant housing for me"*: Samuel interview with Golda, May 29, 1973.

p. 198   *". . . would confide in each other"*: Interview with Rivka Idelson.

p. 198   *". . . almost too cloying"*: Private interview.

p. 198   *". . . was very handy"*: Interview with Regina Hamburger Medzini.

p. 199   *"It was so sad"*: Private interview.

p. 199   *". . . that made it easier for Mother"*: Interview with Sarah Rehabi.

p. 199   *". . . but we did it on the sly"*: Ibid.

p. 199   *". . . bicycle to do it"*: Interview with Ben Rabinovich, Tel Aviv.

p. 199   *". . . emotions battened down, hard"*: Private interview.

p. 200   *". . . please leave me alone"*: Private interview.

p. 200   *"Papa, I knew!"*: Mann, *Golda*.

p. 200   *". . . big enough to carry it himself"*: Samuel interview with Golda, July 24, 1973.

p. 200   *". . . difficult to pay the fees"*: Interview with Sarah Rehabi.

p. 200   *". . . these were only nightmares"*: Remez Papers.

p. 201   *". . . the Great Unifier, and he was"*: Interview with Aharon Remez.

p. 201   *"This is the time of youth"*: Excerpt from Arbor Day speech, delivered at the laying of the cornerstone for a youth hostel, quoted in "David Remez, a Man of Books and Words," *Jerusalem Post*, May 21, 1951.

p. 201   *". . . the heart of her forefather"*: Ibid.

p. 201 *". . . a romantic way with words"*: Private interview.

p. 202 *"I will accept the verdict"*: Remez Papers.

p. 202 *". . . it was very serious"*: Private interview.

p. 202 *noted a mutual friend*: Private interview.

p. 202 *". . . flame that was in Golda"*: Interview with Nomi Zuckerman.

p. 202 *". . . had great dignity"*: Private interview.

p. 202 *". . . let's forget them"*: Interview with Aharon Remez.

p. 202 *". . . his advice and guidance"*: Meir, *My Life*.

p. 203 *"Without Remez, she didn't move"*: Interview with Sara Erez.

p. 203 *". . . and she needed him"*: Ibid.

p. 203 *"He was my real compass"*: Interview with Aharon Remez.

p. 203 . . . *"and for a long time"*: Private interview.

p. 203 *". . . compact, concentrated group"*: Interview with Sara Erez.

p. 203 *". . . gave me plenty to do"*: Harris interview with Golda.

p. 204 *". . . didn't understand a word he said"*: Interview with Sarah Rehabi.

p. 204 *". . . and that is all"*: Ibid.

p. 204 *". . . consider him very sad"*: Interview with Rivka Idelson.

p. 204 *"So she had that"*: Interview with Dr. Jacob Katzman.

p. 205 *". . . work on the soil"*: Meir, *My Life*.

p. 205 . . . *"speaking over the chicken"*: Interview with Esther Zackler.

p. 206 *". . . most of her love affairs"*: Interview with Rivka Idelson.

p. 206 *"I just loved it!"*: Lavon Institute interview with Golda, June 18, 1974.

p. 206 *". . . loved him very much"*: Private interview.

p. 206 *". . . more important than she was"*: Interview with Geula Dagan, Jerusalem.

p. 207 *"And then wept"*: Interview with Rivka Idelson.

p. 207 *". . . ever been in such a contraption"*: On that same trip she met Bronislaw Huberman, who told of his plans to start the first symphony orchestra in Palestine, made up mostly of Jewish refugee musicians from Germany.

p. 207 *". . . that you don't know these things!"*: Private interview.

p. 207 *"And a good manager"*: Private interview.

p. 207 *". . . very kind, and beautiful"*: Interview with Sara Erez.

p. 207 *". . . enormous personal magic"*: *Maariv*, Weekend Supplement, February 26, 1988.

p. 207 *". . . they should not break up marriages"*: Private interview.

p. 208 *". . . and everybody knew"*: Private interview.

p. 208 . . . *from their private homes*: Ibid.

p. 208 *". . . washed one and wore the other"*: Interview with Sarah Rehabi.

p. 208 *". . . sixty-five piasters for a blouse"*: A piaster was then worth five cents. Samuel interview with Golda, July 23, 1974.

p. 208 *". . . that anyone could imagine"*: Ibid.

p. 208 *". . . only sleep with Jews"*: Lossin, *Pillar of Fire*.

p. 209 *23 percent of Western Palestine*: Joan Peters, *From Time Immemorial*:

The Origins of the Arab-Jewish Conflict Over Palestine (New York: Harper & Row, 1984).

p. 209 *". . . never come home again"*: Meir, *My Life*.

p. 209 *". . . kill the Jews"*: Shalom Fixman, quoted in Lossin, *Pillar of Fire*.

p. 209 *". . . a change from Hell to Heaven"*: Gilbert, *Exile and Return*.

p. 210 *". . . bear their fate or they will not"*: Official report of the Twentieth Zionist Congress, Zurich, August 3–17, 1937. Reprinted in *The New Judea*, August/September 1937.

p. 210 *". . . sat too long at English feasts"*: Norman Rose, *Chaim Weizmann: A Biography* (London: Weidenfeld & Nicolson, Ltd., 1987).

p. 210 *". . . primary need for the family"*: Martin Gilbert, *Sir Horace Rumbold: Portrait of a Diplomat, 1839–1941* (London: Heinemann, 1973).

p. 210 *former attorney general of Palestine*: His name was Musa Alami. St. John, *Ben-Gurion*.

p. 211 *". . . what our decision was"*: Meir, *My Mother, Golda Meir*.

p. 211 *". . . to help as much as I could"*: Interview with Nomi Zuckerman.

p. 211 *. . . same thing some years before*: Ibid.

p. 211 *in the Russian compound*: The school was initiated by an American, Horace Kallen.

p. 212 *". . . too unconcerned with selling"*: Interview with Nomi Zuckerman.

p. 212 *". . . stayed for two weeks"*: Interview with Judy Gottlieb.

p. 212 *". . . leaving my father. Why? Why?"*: Private interview.

p. 212 *. . . "against the workers"*: Syrkin, *Golda Meir*.

p. 212 *". . . sadistic streak in her"*: Ibid.

p. 212 *". . . something that is impossible"*: "Panorama" interview.

p. 212 *". . . to pay doles for our poor"*: Syrkin, *Golda Meir*.

p. 213 *. . . "as strong as iron"*: Ibid.

p. 213 *". . . popularizer of the party viewpoint"*: Ibid.

p. 213 *". . . a moral license to do it"*: Interview with Aharon Remez.

p. 213 *". . . and we went to hers"*: Ibid.

p. 213 *". . . to Paris, obviously ill"*: Ibid.

p. 213 *". . . eyes filled with tears"*: Private interview.

p. 213 *". . . out to its purest form"*: Interview with Aharon Remez.

p. 213 *". . . every sentence like a diamond"*: Interview with Rivka Idelson.

p. 214 *"Golda could do this too"*: Interview with Aharon Remez.

p. 214 *". . . she had with any men"*: Interview with Nomi Zuckerman.

p. 214 *". . . too much guilt, and it showed"*: Ibid.

p. 214 *". . . and the children resented it"*: Private interview.

p. 214 *". . . break my heart"*: Interview with Nomi Zuckerman.

p. 214 Oxford English Dictionary *"that thick"*: Ibid.

p. 214 *". . . all loved him dearly"*: Ibid.

p. 215 *". . . hospital as a dietician"*: Interview with Judy Bauman.

p. 215 *". . . saying, 'I'm hungry' "*: Ibid.

p. 216 *". . . adamant about that"*: Interview with Sarah Rehabi.

p. 216 *". . . bravura as a performer":* Interview with Nomi Zuckerman.
p. 216 *insisted a family friend:* Private interview.
p. 216 *"He suffered deeply":* Ibid.
p. 216 *". . . resented me for quite a few years":* Samuel interview with Golda, July 23, 1974.
p. 216 *"It was my fault":* Ibid.
p. 216 *". . . regret that we parted":* Ibid.
p. 216 *". . . like looking at somebody else":* Interview with Rebecca Shulman, New York City.
p. 216 *". . . because of his active love life":* Interview with David Passow.
p. 217 *". . . always either black or white":* Ibid.
p. 217 *". . . rage, frustration and horror":* Meir, *My Life.*
p. 218 *". . . see others who were weaker victimized":* Eisenhower, *Special People.*
p. 218 *". . . can't depend on others":* Ibid.
p. 218 *". . . but Goldie was fabulous":* Eliahu Stern interview with Arieh Tartakower, Hebrew University of Jerusalem, Institute of Contemporary Jewry, Department of Oral History, April 12, 1971.
p. 218 *". . . could ever obtain in their hour of need":* Lossin, *Pillar of Fire.*
p. 218 *". . . paid for it dearly":* Fallaci, *Interview with History.*
p. 218 *". . . met him coming and going":* Interview with Nomi Zuckerman.
p. 219 *". . . those that won't let them in":* Leon and Amin, eds. "Chaim Weizmann."
p. 219 *". . . safe for the Jewish people":* Article by Golda Meyerson in *D'Var HaPoelet* of the Histadrut, May 3, 1939.
p. 219 *". . . but not the shame":* Syrkin, *Golda Meir.*
p. 220 *". . . road back to their Homeland":* Mann, *Golda.*
p. 220 *". . . he didn't like crowds":* Interview with Sarah Rehabi.
p. 220 *". . . come home at once":* Meir, *My Mother, Golda Meir.*
p. 220 *". . . as if there were no war":* Bar-Zohar, *Ben-Gurion.*
p. 220 *". . . not so simple to implement":* "Golda Remembers Battle with the British," *Jerusalem Post,* September 12, 1975.

Chapter 13

p. 221 *. . . because the Arabs would not like it:* Official minutes of Colonial Office meeting taken by Lucy Baggalay, in Gilbert, *Exile and Return.*
p. 222 *". . . part of a group":* Lev-Ari interview with Golda, 1971. Lavon Institute.
p. 222 *". . . was done by Jewish workers":* Transcript of Anglo-American Committee of Inquiry Hearings in Jerusalem, March 25, 1946.
p. 222 *". . . including the Arab workers":* Interview with Yitzhak Eylam, Jerusalem.
p. 223 *". . . invented the post for her":* Interview with Shulamit Nardi.

p. 223   *"... knew nothing about us":* Interview with Gershon Avner.

p. 223   *"... come to Palestine":* Chaim Weizmann, quoted in Shmuel Katz, "Certified Sanity," *Jerusalem Post*, August 10, 1984.

p. 224   *far outweighed the tactical advantages:* Teddy Kollek, *For Jerusalem, a Life* (Jerusalem, Tel Aviv, and Haifa: Steimatzky's Agency Ltd., 1978).

p. 224   *"... to fight against Hitler":* Samuel interview with Golda, August 4, 1974.

p. 224   *... were discharged:* Gilbert, *Exile and Return.*

p. 224   *"... under the noses of the British":* Interview with Sarah Rehabi.

p. 224   *"... dying to say something":* Meir, *My Life.*

p. 225   *... "hunched over, brooding":* Interview with Morton Klein, Philadelphia.

p. 226   *"... you could smell the love":* Private interview.

p. 226   *the need for his strength:* Private collection.

p. 227   *"... until she died":* Interview with Sara Erez.

p. 227   *"They found ways":* Private interview.

p. 227   *"... to do something at night":* Private interview.

p. 227   *... between her husband and Golda: Maariv*, Weekend Supplement, February 26, 1988.

p. 227   *... "even though I knew":* Interview with Regina Hamburger Medzini.

p. 227   *... "long-lasting relationships":* Interview with Marie Syrkin.

p. 227   *"You have to get used to it":* Bar-Zohar, *Ben-Gurion.*

p. 227   *"... the opposite is also possible":* Ibid.

p. 227   *... finally replied, "I think so":* Claude Lanzmann interview with Golda, Paris, *Elle* magazine.

p. 227   *"... never knew which day":* Interview with Eliezar Shmueli, Jerusalem.

p. 227   *"... almost a romantic adolescent":* Ibid.

p. 227   *"... nobody else in the room":* Ibid.

p. 228   *"... shocked by it than I was":* Private interview.

p. 228   *"... your soul is darker than dark":* Interview with Masha Rabinovich, Tel Aviv.

p. 228   *originally Ziama Ahronowitz:* Mitchell Cohen, *Zion and State: Nation, Class and the Shaping of Modern Israel* (Oxford and New York: Basil Blackwell Ltd., 1987).

p. 229   *"... can't forget it":* Interview with Rivka Idelson.

p. 229   *"Always defiant":* Ibid.

p. 230   *"... but are alone":* Ibid.

p. 230   *"... to say she would be late":* Interview with Regina Hamburger Medzini.

p. 230   *"... but we were chaverot":* Interview with Masha Rabinovich.

p. 230   *"... we also cried together":* Ibid.

p. 231   *"... in so-called men's jobs":* Samuel interview with Golda, July 16, 1973.

p. 231   *"... better than all the men":* Ibid.

p. 232   *... experiencing a terrible tiredness:* Interview with Aharon Remez.

p. 232   *"... a nation on the march":* Brochure about 1939 World's Fair in New York. In the Jewish-Palestine pavilion, one exhibit was called "The Holy Land of Yesterday," and another, "Tel Aviv, the Wonder City of Tomorrow." Mayor Fiorello LaGuardia and Chaim Weizmann were both present at the dedication.

p. 232   *newly arrived Italian-Jewish refugee:* Dan Vittorio Segre, who later wrote a book about his experiences. (See *Memoirs of a Fortunate Jew.*)

p. 233   *"... and hopes were here":* Ibid.

p. 233   *"... many languages at night":* Ibid.

p. 233   *"... as if they were an independent nation":* Nicholas William Bethell, *The Palestine Triangle: Palestine's Struggle Between the British, the Jews and the Arabs, 1935–1948* (London: André Deutsch Ltd., 1979). Bethell quotes Robert Scott, a senior political officer with the Secretariat, listing a series of British complaints in a document dated October 1941.

p. 235   *"... to be mad, but it helps":* Elon, *The Israelis.*

p. 235   *"... live our lives with them":* Interview with Golda, Hebrew University Archives, June 10, 1975.

p. 235   *"... better off with the mother they had":* Interview with Marie Syrkin.

p. 235   *"... what do they* feel *toward me?":* "Panorama" interview.

p. 235   *"... always brought us presents":* Interview with Sarah Rehabi.

p. 235   *"... spoke up about it":* Interview with Nomi Zuckerman.

p. 236   *"We have no alternative":* Interview with Marie Syrkin.

p. 236   *"... one more* dunam *of land":* Lossin, *Pillar of Fire.*

p. 236   *"... no use to us in the present war":* Gilbert, *Exile and Return.*

p. 236   *"... into the camp's electric fence":* Ibid.

p. 236   *"... are not unlimited supplies":* Ibid.

p. 236   *"... there are now far too many":* Ibid.

p. 236   *"... and longing for them":* Bethell, *The Palestine Triangle.*

p. 236   *"We never forget":* Leon and Amin, eds. "Chaim Weizmann."

p. 236   *"... which they cannot enter":* Ibid.

p. 237   *"... to help organize the drop":* Interview with Arthur Goldberg.

p. 237   *"... much too valuable here":* Meir, *My Life.*

p. 237   *tortured, and executed in Budapest:* Gilbert, *Exile and Return.*

p. 237   *"... had been given fresh meaning":* Speech by Golda Meyerson to the Council Meeting of the General Federation of Jewish Labor, July 3, 1946.

p. 238   *"... shame and anti-Semitism":* Letter by Czeslaw Milosz, Nobel Prize poet, in *The New York Times,* July 26, 1987.

p. 238   *"... while the human was a dwarf":* Cyprian Norwid, an eighteenth-century poet, quoted in *The New York Times,* July 26, 1987.

p. 238   *"... with their own underwear":* Gilbert, *Exile and Return.*

p. 238   *killed in a field outside of town:* "By the end of 1941, one SS group was able to report ... a total of 56,696 executions. ... In two days, at Kiev (where Golda was born), 33,771 Jews were killed. Within a year of the German invasion of Russia, 1,400,000 Jews were killed." Gilbert, *Exile and Return.*

p. 239   *"... found by partisans and survived":* Ibid.

p. 239   *"... mustn't believe everything you hear":* Meir, *My Life.*

p. 240   *"... the refugee will lead us":* Gilbert, *Sir Horace Rumbold.*

p. 240   *"... during the entire war":* Ibid.

p. 241   *"... fell in love with him":* Ibid.

p. 241   *"... anybody ever said or did":* Interview with Nomi Zuckerman.

p. 241   *"... always natural, always herself":* Interview with Zena Harman, Jerusalem.

p. 241   *"... nobody now remembers what it was":* Interview with Nomi Zuckerman.

p. 242   ... *"the only one!":* Ibid.

Chapter 14

p. 243   *two young Palestine Jews:* Lieb Sirkin and Abraham Richlin.

p. 243   *"... So I said, 'No' ":* Samuel interview with Golda, August 4, 1973.

p. 244   *of Jabin, king of Canaan:* In that war, the Israelites first succeeded in overcoming the Canaanite chariots (Judges, 4:24).

p. 244   *"... deliver him unto thy hand":* Scholars place the period at about 1200–1125 B.C.E. Deborah was one of the seven prophetesses of the Bible. "She dispensed justice in the open air under a palm tree to avoid being alone in her home." (*Encyclopaedia Judaica*, Vol. 5.)

p. 244   *"... what my Golda did":* Meir, *My Life.*

p. 245   *"... because you didn't want to study":* Interview with Sarah Rehabi.

p. 245   *"... know how I would vote":* Ibid.

p. 246   *"... achieve its true destiny":* Ibid.

p. 246   *"... construction of a better society":* Ibid.

p. 246   *"... has a logic of its own":* Ibid.

p. 246   *"... was awful":* David Hacohen was one of the founders and directors of the Solel Boneh. During World War II, he was Haganah liaison officer to the British army. From 1943, he was a member of the Knesset and became a prominent leader of the Mapai Party.

p. 246   *"... only true friend I had":* Bar-Zohar, *Ben-Gurion.*

p. 247   *"... Ibn Saud said no":* Robert E. Sherwood, *Roosevelt and Hopkins: An Intimate History* (New York: Harper & Brothers, 1948).

p. 247   ... *still gave him a present of an airplane:* James MacGregor Burns, *Roosevelt, the Soldier of Freedom, 1940–1945* (New York: Harcourt Brace Jovanovich, 1970).

p. 247   "... *learned in a lifetime*": Ibid.

p. 247   "... *than he had learned in a lifetime*": What FDR actually said in an address to Congress on the Yalta Conference, March 1, 1945, was "... I learned more about that whole problem—the Moslem problem, the Jewish problem—by talking with Ibn Saud for five minutes, than I could have learned in the exchange of two or three dozen letters." *The Public Papers and Addresses of Franklin D. Roosevelt*, 1944–45 Volume (New York: Harper & Brothers, 1950).

p. 247   "... *don't want any more Jews in Palestine*": Sherwood, *Roosevelt and Hopkins*.

p. 247   "... *could really put our fingers on*": Lossin, *Pillar of Fire*.

p. 247   "... *as a rule B-G was not wrong*": Samuel interview with Golda, July 10, 1974.

p. 248   *"Liberty or death"*: Lossin, *Pillar of Fire*.

p. 248   "... *so consistently and so long in the past*": Gilbert, *Exile and Return*.

p. 248   "... *will be like white lilies*": Abraham Stern, shot by British police in 1942, was quoted in Hasan, *Enemy in the Promised Land*.

p. 249   "... *which it usually did*": Samuel interview with Golda, August 4, 1974.

p. 249   "... *not doing anything was unthinkable*": Interview with Golda, May 24, 1977.

p. 250   "... *can't sleep at night*": Lucy Davidowicz, *The Jewish Presence* (San Diego, Calif.: Harcourt Brace Jovanovich, 1978).

p. 250   "... *so senseless was your doom*": Anglo-American Committee of Inquiry Hearings in Jerusalem, March 25, 1946.

p. 250   "... *right thing to do, I was for it*": Interview with Marie Syrkin.

p. 250   "... *a Jew from the Land of Israel*": Lossin, *Pillar of Fire*.

p. 250   "... *sifted for any remaining gold*": Siegfried Kellerman, quoted in *The New York Times*, November 23, 1987.

p. 251   "... *sometimes could not even talk*": Lossin, *Pillar of Fire*.

p. 251   "... *some of the six million Jews*": Lavon Institute interview with Golda, August 7, 1973.

p. 252   "... *suddenly they turned on us*": Interview with Golda, n.d.

p. 252   "... *we'll create trouble*": Ibid.

p. 252   "... *granted to the children*": Address by Goldie Meyerson, at the Sixth Conference of the Histadrut in Palestine, entitled, "To the British Labour Government." Reprinted in *The Pioneer Woman*, November 1945.

p. 252   "... *swing a cat*": Newman interview with Golda.

p. 252   "... *years before the British came*": Speech by Golda, May 2, 1940, quoted in a transcript of testimony at the Sirkin-Richlin arms trial, September 1943.

p. 253   "... *watching his neighbor or friend*": Syrkin, *Golda Meir*.

p. 253 *". . . but it wasn't pleasant":* Samuel interview with Golda, July 23, 1974.
p. 254 *". . . any of the calls were about":* Interview with Marie Syrkin.
p. 254 *"Washing dishes":* Ibid.
p. 254 *. . . "chattered or confided":* Ibid.
p. 255 *"But she went anyway":* Ibid.
p. 255 *". . . stifles my laziness":* Lanzmann interview with Golda.
p. 255 *". . . punish her with a lot of rest":* Remez Papers.
p. 256 *". . . But I want to know.":* Lanzmann interview with Golda.
p. 256 *. . . without hesitation, "Yaacov Hazan":* Private interview.
p. 257 *". . . intimate relations with Golda":* Interview with Yaacov Hazan, Tel Aviv.
p. 257 *. . . "the Messianics":* Ibid.
p. 257 *". . . and I think I convinced her":* Ibid.
p. 257 *"Never, never!":* Samuel interview with Golda, July 16, 1973.
p. 257 *". . . beaming with pride":* Interview with Nomi Zuckerman.
p. 258 *". . . as though it were absolutely nothing":* Gilbert, *Exile and Return*.
p. 259 *". . . push to the head of the queue":* Ibid.
p. 259 *. . . "really want to go to Palestine":* Interview with Ruth Tropin, Harrison, New York.
p. 259 *". . . I want to go to Palestine":* Ibid.
p. 259 *". . . to start a new life":* Ibid.
p. 259 *". . . men and women from the Haganah":* Ibid.
p. 260 *. . . immigration restrictions:* Ibid.
p. 260 *". . . definitely stole the show":* Interview with Dr. Jacob Katzman.
p. 260 *". . . object at which it is directed":* *The Pioneer Woman*, March 1947.
p. 261 *". . . cry of the homeless will be answered":* *Jerusalem Post*, April 14, 1946.
p. 262 *". . . a senior British official":* Henry Gurney.
p. 262 *". . . be a mark of solidarity":* Meir, *My Life*.
p. 262 *". . . this is the end of the struggle":* *Jerusalem Post*, April 17, 1946.
p. 263 *". . . while reneging on the rest":* *The Pioneer Woman*, November 1945.
p. 263 *"We have no alternative":* Ibid.
p. 263 *". . . the* New York Post*":* December 19, 1944, quoted in Bethell, *The Palestine Triangle*.
p. 264 *". . . this is what's going to happen":* Interview with Oscar Dystel, Oral History Research Library, Columbia University, October 23, 1984.

Chapter 15

p. 265 *". . . got the force to do it":* Bethell, *The Palestine Triangle*.
p. 265 *". . . easy feeling, without sweat":* Lev-Ari interview with Golda, 1971.
p. 266 *". . . it was a horrible sight":* Samuel interview with Golda, August 4, 1973.

p. 266   *into barbed-wire enclosures:* Jewish Agency—Paris file, morning-afternoon session Mrs. Goldie Meyerson, August 2, 1946.

p. 266   *". . . would not have had to do it":* Ibid.

p. 266   *"They won't dare":* Speech at 58th Council Meeting of General Federation of Jewish Labor, July 3, 1946.

p. 266   *". . . but we had our orders":* Samuel interview with Golda, August 8, 1973.

p. 267   *". . . they know where I am":* Syrkin, *Golda Meir.*

p. 267   *". . . coming for her neighbor":* New York World Telegram, June 23, 1956.

p. 267   *". . . was very annoyed":* Abraham Rabinovich in article in *Newsday*, December 9, 1978.

p. 267   *". . . doing very well, Mrs. Meyerson":* Ibid.

p. 267   *". . . wanted to choke him":* Interview with Marie Syrkin.

p. 268   *". . . of our central political bodies":* The Pioneer Woman, March 1947.

p. 268   *". . . set an example for everybody":* Interview with Berl Repetur, Tel Aviv.

p. 268   *"Perhaps":* Syrkin, *Golda Meir.*

p. 269   *"She grew into this":* Interview with Gershon Avner.

p. 269   *". . . was a man's weak point":* C. A. Waide, quoted in Bethell, *The Palestine Triangle.*

p. 269   *". . . to London that same day":* Interview with Uri Meretz, Jerusalem.

p. 270   *". . . detective force who spoke Hebrew":* Bethell, *The Palestine Triangle.*

p. 270   *. . . "soul-destroying":* Ibid.

p. 270   *". . . girl out of the country":* Interview with Uri Meretz.

p. 270   *". . . she was the real activist":* Interview with Robert Nathan, Washington D.C.

p. 270   *recalled an intelligence chief:* Interview with Uri Meretz.

p. 271   *"Just some letters":* Interview with Sarah Rehabi.

p. 271   *". . . as if nothing happened":* Samuel interview with Golda, August 4, 1973.

p. 271   *". . . more serious than we planned":* Ibid.

p. 271   *". . . for reading Gandhi":* Remez Papers.

p. 272   *British administration headquarters:* The southern wing of the hotel housed the headquarters, with the Military Police and Special Investigations Branch in an annex. The operation was called *Malonchik*—the Hebrew word for hotel.

p. 272   *". . . humiliate the British, not kill them":* Dr. Moshe Sneh, who had been chief of the Haganah, later charged that David Ben-Gurion had approved the destruction of the King David, sending orders from London. *The New York Times*, February 16, 1973.

p. 272   *Begin afterward insisted:* Lossin, *Pillar of Fire.*

p. 272   *"This is a warning!":* Ibid., quote by Adina Nisan of the Irgun.

p. 273   *". . . further efforts in British hearts":* Gilbert, *Exile and Return.*

p. 273   *". . . emigrating to* PALESTINE*":* Ibid.

p. 273   *". . . would have killed all of us":* Samuel interview with Golda, August 4, 1973.

p. 273   *". . . couldn't come to terms with us":* Bethell, *The Palestine Triangle*.

p. 274   *". . . destroy Ruhama a third time":* Syrkin, *Golda Meir*.

p. 274   *". . . to become a universal bore":* Gilbert, *Exile and Return*.

p. 274   *". . . will entail sacrifices":* Minutes of Jewish Agency meeting, August 14, 1946, Jewish Agency archives, Jerusalem.

p. 275   *". . . because they brought us attention":* Samuel interview with Golda, August 4, 1973.

p. 275   *". . . but we'll take care of it":* Samuel interview with Golda, June 18, 1973.

p. 275   *". . . and wouldn't do it":* Natan Cohen interview with Dr. Arieh Altman, Hebrew University of Jerusalem, Institute of Contemporary Jewry, Department of Oral History, December 25, 1966.

p. 275   *". . . destroy a people":* Wolf, *The Passion of Israel*.

p. 276   *". . . saved the boy's life for me":* Samuel interview with Golda, June 18, 1973.

p. 276   *". . . responsibility for what might happen":* Ibid.

p. 276   *". . . never did anything about it":* Ibid.

p. 277   *". . . and not to hear anything":* Ibid.

p. 277   *". . . to the nth degree":* Ibid.

p. 277   *". . . and then come back for me":* Ibid.

p. 277   *". . . wouldn't you have a ship?":* Ibid.

p. 277   *". . . never came to see him again":* Ibid.

p. 277   *". . . she knows I did not mean* her*":* Ibid.

p. 278   *". . . the thing that had to be done":* Interview with Marie Syrkin.

p. 278   *". . . freed to come into a Jewish state":* Ibid.

p. 278   *". . . she could handle them, all of them":* Interview with Gershon Avner.

p. 279   *memorandum to the Cabinet:* January 7, 1947. It was entitled "Middle East Oil," and illustrated with charts and statistics the vital importance of the area's oil resources to Great Britain. Its authors were Ernest Bevin, foreign secretary; and Emanuel Shinwell, the minister of fuel and power. In Gilbert, *Exile and Return*.

p. 279   *top-secret memorandum:* January 14, 1947, ibid. It was a warning against partition by Bevin.

p. 279   *". . . anti-Semitic, or both":* Meir, *My Life*.

p. 279   *". . . walked out of the room":* Ibid.

p. 280   *". . . the death of multitudes":* Ibid.

p. 280   *". . . survivors on their backs":* Speech, in Yiddish, to 22nd Zionist Congress in Basel, December 1946. Reprinted in Syrkin, ed., *A Land of Our Own*.

p. 280   *". . . never known a woman like that!":* Interview with David Ginsburg, Washington, D.C.

p. 281 *"Take what you want!"*: Robin Ostow, "Voice from the East," *Jerusalem Post*, December 9, 1986.

p. 281 *"... the Arabs will force on us"*: Interview with Golda Meir.

p. 281 *"... peace and quiet of a cemetery"*: *The New York Times*, September 2, 1936.

p. 282 *"... can get help from the outside"*: Samuel interview with Golda, August 4, 1973.

p. 282 *"... you don't want to live long"*: Ibid.

p. 282 *A close friend*: Interview with Aharon Remez.

p. 283 *"... on the stage slightly awestruck"*: Interview with Geula Dagan.

p. 284 *"... suffer the crimes of Hitler"*: Dr. Fadel al-Jamal, in an address to a Special Session of the United Nations, May 8, 1947.

p. 284 *"... society of nations"*: Rabbi Hillel Silver, in a U.N. speech.

p. 285 *"... won't come to the worst"*: Speech at Workers' Council, Tel Aviv, October 21, 1947.

p. 285 *"... not to continue it at all"*: Abba Eban, *An Autobiography* (New York: Random House, 1977).

p. 285 *intervened with the French consul*: The French consul was René Neville.

p. 286 *"... from thence will fetch thee"*: Syrkin, *Golda Meir*.

p. 286 *"... justice and morality of Great Britain"*: Terence Prittie, *Eshkol: The Man and the Nation* (New York: Pitman, 1969).

p. 286 *"... doesn't have its limits"*: Remez Papers.

p. 286 *"... stand it in good stead"*: Gilbert, *Exile and Return*.

p. 286 *"... which isn't far away"*: Remez Papers.

p. 287 *"... that he is a Hebrew"*: Lossin, *Pillar of Fire*.

p. 287 *"... she was a person"*: Interview with David Ginsburg.

p. 288 *"People can be very lonely"*: Interview with Sarah Rehabi.

p. 288 *"... what I think for once"*: Interview with Nomi Zuckerman.

p. 288 *"... faithful to your ideas"*: Fallaci, *Interview with History*.

p. 288 *"... many beggars, and little water"*: "Jerusalem After 31 years," *Jerusalem Post*, June 18, 1978.

p. 288 *"She knew these things"*: Ibid. Spencer first came to Palestine in 1943 to serve as a policeman in Petah Tikva; he was Jerusalem town clerk from 1946 to 1947.

p. 288 *"... years of martyrdom and wandering"*: Gilbert, *Exile and Return*.

p. 289 *"... cost a great deal of blood"*: Ibid.

p. 289 *"That is a fact"*: Elsviers magazine interview December 23, 1972.

p. 289 *"... they will let you know"*: Interview with Rivka Idelson.

p. 290 *"... expected that there would be war"*: "Panorama" interview.

p. 290 *"... and the Arab mentality"*: Jacques Derogy and Hesi Carmel, *The Untold History of Israel* (New York: Grove Press, 1979).

p. 291 *"Jews ... mazel tov"*: Kurzman, *Ben-Gurion*.

p. 291 *"... will all soon be dead anyhow"*: Syrkin, *Golda Meir*.

Chapter 16

p. 293   *Forrestal to Clark Clifford:* Quoted in Lossin, *Pillar of Fire.*

p. 294   *". . . like crossing between two foreign countries":* Larry Collins and Dominique Lapierre, *O Jerusalem!* (New York: Simon and Schuster, 1972).

p. 295   *". . . neighbors since many years":* Ibid.

p. 295   *". . . stirring pep in people":* Interview with Pres. Chaim Herzog, Jerusalem.

p. 295   *". . . she would have been killed":* Ibid.

p. 296   *". . . convoy must get through":* Lossin, *Pillar of Fire.*

p. 296   *". . . stand and weep with them":* Ibid.

p. 296   *". . . make your own children orphans":* Interview with Dr. Yoram Beyth, Jerusalem.

p. 297   *". . . died in my arms":* Ibid.

p. 297   *". . . have Arabs shoot at you":* Interview with Golda, January 19, 1971, United Jewish Appeal.

p. 297   *". . . that Golda had to be protected":* Interview with Pres. Chaim Herzog.

p. 297   *". . . planning officer on Jerusalem":* Son of Mussa Kazem, founder of the Palestine Arab National Movement. Yigael Yadin, Haganah chief operations officer, called him, "the most dangerous enemy during the War of Independence."

p. 297   *". . . make the Jews live hell":* Collins and Lapierre, *O Jerusalem!*

p. 298   *had once said:* McCooey, "The Making of Golda Meir."

p. 299   *". . . one burned up his house for":* Samuel interview with Golda, June 18, 1973.

p. 299   *. . . "my strongest point":* Eisenhower, *Special People.*

p. 299   *". . . made all the arrangements, did it all":* Interview with Yona Kama.

p. 299   *". . . sort of runs the whole family":* Mann interview with Clara Stern.

p. 299   *. . . watch out for him:* Telegram sent to 201 Clinton Avenue, September 18, 1947.

p. 300   *". . . short of everything":* Geraldine Stern interview with Gen. Joseph Avidar, Elmer Winter Tapes, University of Wisconsin Archives, Milwaukee.

p. 300   *". . . when others doubted":* Mark Segal, "Golda at 80" in "News and Views," June, July, and August 1978. Published by World Zionist Organization of South Africa.

p. 300   *". . . really saved us":* Interview with Jeff Hodes, Hebrew University of Jerusalem, Institute of Contemporary Jewry, Department of Oral History, June 8, 1975.

p. 301   *"I can also do":* Syrkin, *Golda Meir.*

p. 301   "... of how she took it": Stern interview with Gen. Joseph Avidar.

p. 301   "... who did great things": Interview with Jeff Hodes.

p. 302   "... New York ever knew": Ibid.

p. 302   "... and let me in": Harry Golden, *The Israelis: Portrait of a People* (New York: G. P. Putnam's Sons, 1971).

p. 302   "... really was a hero": Samuel interview with Golda, August 9, 1974.

p. 303   ... spent the long night talking: Interview with Judy Bauman.

p. 303   "... propose to get to Chicago?": Interview with Meyer Steinglass.

p. 303   "... only one that left that day": Interview with Jeff Hodes.

p. 305   "... the time is now": Golda Meyerson, a Report from Palestine by the Head of the Political Department, Jewish Agency for Palestine, to Council of Jewish Federation and Welfare Funds, Chicago, January 21, 1948.

p. 306   "... who was a thousand percent": Interview with Meyer Steinglass.

p. 306   "... rubbed him wrong, look out!": Interview with Julian Venezky, New York City.

p. 306   "... by a sort of natural antiaffinity": Ibid.

p. 306   "... a genius in propaganda": Quote from interview with Charles Rottenberg, Hebrew University of Jerusalem, Institute of Contemporary Jewry, Department of Oral History.

p. 307   ... "very attractive, very striking woman": Interview with Meyer Steinglass.

p. 307   "This is your business!": Samuel interview with Golda, August 9, 1974.

p. 307   "What crazy person is this?": Interview with Nomi Zuckerman.

p. 307   "... and how much he should give": Samuel interview with Golda, August 9, 1974.

p. 307   "... buy arms from Great Britain?": Statement of Mrs. Golda Meyerson, United Nations, Lake Success, N.Y., January 26, 1948.

p. 308   "... then let's have it that way": Ibid.

p. 308   "... advantages in Arab countries": Ibid.

p. 309   "... it became a good community": Interview with Sam Rothberg, Jerusalem.

p. 309   "... couldn't take the schedule": Interview with Jeff Hodes, Shulamit Nardi, and Menachem Kaufman, Hebrew University of Jerusalem, Institute of Contemporary Jewry, Oral History Department, June 8, 1975.

p. 309   "Hitler converted me": Interview with Julian Venezky.

p. 309   "... in a gulf of hatred": Neil Reisner, "Awed Onlooker Remembers a Visit by Golda Meir," *Los Angeles Times*, December 13, 1978.

p. 309   "... very many rooms": Ibid.

p. 309   "... terrorize the Jewish community": Interview with Jeff Hodes, Shulamit Nardi, and Menahem Kaufman.

p. 309   "... they could do or should do": Samuel interview with Golda, August 9, 1974.

p. 310 *"... get you the ten million dollars":* United Jewish Appeal interview with Golda, January 19, 1971.

p. 310 *"... and the American Jews saved us":* Ibid.

p. 310 *"Golda's stocking":* Zeev Sharef, *Three Days* (London: W. H. Allen, 1962).

p. 310 *"We have one left":* Reisner, *Los Angeles Times*, December 13, 1978.

p. 310 *"... but also joy—a lot of joy!":* Mann, *Golda*.

p. 311 *"... and by applause":* Ibid.

p. 311 *"... always enough to cry about":* Shenker, "Golda Meir, 80, Dies in Jerusalem."

p. 312 *"... than is usually the case":* Dr. Israel Goldstein, *My World as a Jew: The Memoirs of Israel Goldstein* (New York: Herzl Press, 1984).

p. 312 *"... it's good that they came":* Remez Papers.

p. 313 *"... seem to be doing better":* Joseph P. Lash, *Eleanor: The Years Alone* (New York: W. W. Norton and Company, 1972).

p. 313 *"... deeply respect and deeply love":* Eleanor Roosevelt foreword in Henry M. Christman, ed., *This Is Our Strength: Selected Papers of Golda Meir* (New York: The Macmillan Company, 1962).

p. 313 *"... people had suffered greatly":* Letter from Eleanor Roosevelt to Miss Berg, April 25, 1950, in Lash, *Eleanor*.

p. 314 *"... inclined to be anti-Semitic":* Harry S. Truman, *Memoirs: Years of Trial and Hope, 1946–1952*, Vol. 2 (Garden City, N.Y.: Doubleday & Co., 1956).

p. 314 *"... shoot at them, they run away":* Vera Weizmann, *The Impossible Takes Longer*, the memoirs of Vera Weizmann as told to David Tutaev (London: Hamish Hamilton Ltd., 1967).

p. 314 *"... take care of themselves":* Secret memorandum, Moshe Shertok (Sharett), re talk with B.H. in Washington, March 11, 1948, Foreign Office Papers, File 2513/2.

p. 314 ... *"our hopes and aspirations":* Menachem Kaufman interview with Dr. Israel Goldstein, May 6, 1975, United Jewish Appeal.

p. 314 *"... hard to find a truer friend":* Truman, *Memoirs*.

p. 315 *"... I can't help it":* Merle Miller, *Plain Speaking: An Oral Biography of Harry S. Truman* (New York: Berkley Publishing Co., 1974).

p. 315 *"... doesn't sound like you, Harry":* Sharef, *Three Days*; and Truman, *Memoirs*.

p. 315 *"... going to use for a flag?":* Miller, *Plain Speaking*.

p. 315 *"... Arab territory that oil is found":* Confidential memorandum from Eliahu Epstein (Elath) to members of the Executive of the Jewish Agency for Palestine. Subject: "Position of the Oil Companies in the Palestine Question," March 17, 1948. Identified as "#15 Confidential," Foreign Office Papers, File 2513/2.

p. 316 *British behavior in the area?:* Confidential memorandum to members of the Jewish Agency for Palestine from Eliahu Epstein (Elath), March 19, 1948, on his conversation with Gen. Dwight D. Eisenhower on March 18, 1948. Identified as "#17 Confidential," Foreign Office Papers, File 2513/2. Remark quoted from intercepted phone conversation of May 24.

p. 316 *". . . until they get orders from London":* M. S. Comay, Report on "British Connection with Transjordan Arab Legion," for Eliahu Epstein (Elath), May 27, 1948. Papers, Foreign Office Papers, File 2513/2.

p. 316 *". . . much less sacrifice his life":* Epstein conversation with Eisenhower.

p. 316 *"It was horrible":* Ibid.

p. 316 *". . . Children of Israel and Isaiah":* Truman, *Memoirs.*

p. 316 *". . . Jews in Palestine who are gone":* Interview with Jeff Hodes.

p. 317 *". . . could talk like that":* Ibid.

p. 317 *". . . . that has to be done":* Interview with Dr. Melvin Urofsky, Hebrew University of Jerusalem, Institute of Contemporary Jewry, Department of Oral History, October 6, 1975.

p. 317 *". . . four or five million dollars":* Interview with Jeff Hodes, Shulamit Nardi, and Menachem Kaufman.

p. 318 *entire oil revenue of Saudi Arabia for 1947:* In David Ben-Gurion, *Israel, a Personal History,* trans. Nechemia Meyers and Uzi Nystar (New York: Funk and Wagnalls, 1971). Ben-Gurion has a diary entry on July 29, 1948: "Golda Meir has returned from America. Over $50 million was raised. We will receive 66 percent of $45 million."

p. 318 *. . . and fifty million cartridges:* Collins and La Pierre, *O Jerusalem!*

p. 318 *". . . made the state possible":* Syrkin, *Golda Meir.*

Chapter 17

p. 319 *". . . the same thing before nightfall":* Collins and La Pierre, *O Jerusalem!*

p. 319 *". . . our dead are piled up":* Ibid. Quote by poet Furmanim.

p. 320 *". . . hang onto Jerusalem by your teeth":* Ibid.

p. 320 *worked at the Jewish Agency:* Interview with Regina Hamburger Medzini.

p. 321 *". . . race down the streets":* Ibid.

p. 321 *". . . than Moslem holy places":* Israel and Mary Shenker, eds., *As Good as Golda* (New York: McCall Publishing Co., 1970).

p. 321 *". . . run a thousand miles":* Collins and La Pierre, *O Jerusalem!*

p. 322 *". . . wait all night for the explosion":* Lev-Ari interview with Golda.

p. 322 *". . . too fat to run":* Interview with Daniel Spicehandler, New York City.

p. 323 *subject to constant sniper fire:* Interview with Louise Spicehandler, New York City.

p. 323 *". . . more volatile than my father":* Interview with Aharon Remez.

p. 324 *". . . body without a head":* Interview with Moshe Kol.

p. 324 *". . . new machine guns":* Israel Galili, quoted in Lossin, *Pillar of Fire.*

p. 325 *"I pay cash!":* Collins and La Pierre, *O Jerusalem!*

p. 325   *". . . let my right hand wither":* Psalm 137.

p. 326   *". . . still vivid in my mind":* Private interview.

p. 326   *". . . graveyard for the Jews":* Hasan, *Enemy in the Promised Land.*

p. 326   *". . . and light it":* Collins and Lapierre, *O Jerusalem!*

p. 327   *". . . have nothing to fear":* Meir, *My Life.*

p. 327   *". . . just because they were Arabs":* Samuel interview with Golda, August 4, 1973.

p. 327   *". . . completely different":* Mann, *Golda.*

p. 328   *". . . would not listen":* Meir, *My Life.*

p. 328   *". . . a horrifying and fantastic sight":* Ben-Gurion, *Israel.*

p. 328   *". . . failed in my job":* Mann interview with Golda.

p. 328   *". . . deplorable act of appropriation":* Shabtai Teveth, *Moshe Dayan, the Soldier, the Man, the Legend* (Boston: Houghton Mifflin Co., 1973).

p. 329   *and the belt was still there:* Interview with Daniel Spicehandler.

p. 329   *". . . up against the wall and shot them":* Simha Flapan, *The Birth of Israel* (New York: Pantheon Books, 1987), quoting David K. Shipler, *The New York Times,* who cited Red Cross and British documents.

p. 329   *". . . mentally poisoned, in ecstasy":* David K. Shipler, *Arab and Jew: Wounded Spirits in a Promised Land* (New York: Times Books, 1986).

p. 329   *through the streets of Jerusalem:* Interview with Daniel Spicehandler.

p. 330   *". . . excommunicating the participants in the attack":* Collins and Lapierre, *O Jerusalem!*

p. 330   *". . . you have made history":* Eric Silver, *Begin, the Haunted Prophet* (New York: Random House, 1984).

p. 330   *". . . won't stop with the end of the war":* Flapan, *The Birth of Israel.*

p. 331   *". . . foul and defiling":* Ibid.

p. 331   *children died en route:* Shipler, *Arab and Jew.*

p. 331   *". . . simplification of the problem":* Flapan, *The Birth of Israel.*

p. 331   *". . . about the return of the Arabs":* Ben-Gurion, *Israel.*

p. 331   *". . . return must be prevented at all costs":* Flapan, *The Birth of Israel.*

p. 331   *". . . you Arab leaders":* Personal papers of Peggy Mann, New York City. *Falastin,* published in the Old City of Jerusalem, was quoted in Judith Elizur, *The Truth About Arab Refugees.*

p. 332   *would never be identified:* Collins and Lapierre, *O Jerusalem!*

p. 332   *". . . the century after":* Elie Wiesel, *Dawn* (New York: Hill & Wang, 1961).

p. 333   *a very quiet place:* Results of consultations regarding Golda Meyerson that took place April 12, 1948. Participants were Drs. Levenstein, Peled, Sheber, and Meyer. The report was signed by Dr. Y. Meir in the name of the Medical Committee, May 13, 1948, Kupat Cholim, Tel Aviv. Remez Papers.

p. 333   *"set up a mufti government":* Bar-Zohar, *Ben-Gurion.*

p. 334   *. . . "frightened and haggard":* Weizmann, *The Impossible Takes Longer.*

p. 334   *"Now I am one of five":* Meir, *My Life.*

p. 334   *in his parliament:* Syrkin, *Golda Meir.*

p. 334   *". . . sit on the throne of David":* Weizmann, *The Impossible Takes Longer.*

p. 334   *"Is that hurrying?":* Shenker, "Golda Meir, 80, Dies in Jerusalem."

p. 335   *". . . after there is a Jewish state":* Syrkin, *Golda Meir.*

p. 335   *"I knew we had to win":* Lossin, *Pillar of Fire.*

p. 335   *". . . extensive field artillery":* Sharef, *Three Days.*

p. 335   *". . . glad to meet you, Abraham":* Mann, *Golda.*

p. 335   *". . . who led you over the hills":* Syrkin, *Golda Meir.*

p. 335   *". . . but she never showed it":* Interview with Esther Herlitz, Tel Aviv.

p. 336   *". . . any help from us":* Derogy and Carmel, *The Untold History of Israel.*

p. 336   *". . . it will never be established":* Bar-Zohar, *Ben-Gurion.*

p. 337   *". . . fifty-fifty chance":* Ibid.

p. 337   *". . . on the Declaration of the State":* Samuel interview with Golda, August 4, 1974.

p. 338   *". . . of the expiring engine":* Sharef, *Three Days.*

p. 338   . . . *"as they surely would":* Collins and Lapierre, *O Jerusalem!*

p. 338   *". . . then who will stop the Egyptians?":* Ibid.

p. 338   . . . *"great sadness":* Sharef, *Three Days.*

p. 338   *". . . where we were going to meet":* Samuel interview with Golda, August 4, 1974.

p. 339   *". . . of course the place was packed":* Ibid.

p. 340   *". . . as it did that day":* Meir, *My Life.*

p. 340   *". . . of our own destiny":* Shenker, "Golda Meir, 80, Dies in Jerusalem."

p. 340   *". . . wept almost beyond control":* Wolf, *The Passion of Israel.*

p. 341   *". . . servitude of other nations":* Sharef, *Three Days.*

p. 341   *". . . meeting has ended":* Ibid.

p. 341   *". . . among the dancers':* Derogy and Carmel, *The Untold History of Israel.*

p. 341   *". . . in store for us":* "Panorama" interview.

p. 341   *Somebody got up and turned it off:* Yitzhak Rabin, *The Rabin Memoirs* (Boston: Little, Brown & Co., 1979).

p. 341   *"Truman had recognized us":* Meir, *My Life.*

p. 342   *". . . we will be in Tel Aviv":* Egyptian minister of war, quoted in Lossin, *Pillar of Fire.*

p. 342   *". . . massacres and the Crusades":* Mann, *Golda,* quoting Azzam Pasha.

p. 342   *"The price is worth it":* Ibid.

p. 343   *". . . is not a realist":* Comment made to the author in Tel Aviv, March 1949.

p. 343   *"No alternative":* Speech to the Sixth Conference of the Histadrut in Palestine, reprinted in *The Pioneer Woman,* November 1945.

p. 343   *". . . with a stone in his hand":* Speech by Golda to Council of Jewish Federations, Chicago, January 21, 1948.

Bibliography

This is only a selected bibliography of the most relevant books. Other archival material—documents, unpublished memoirs, letters, reports, articles, speeches, pamphlets—are all referred to elsewhere in end notes, footnotes, and acknowledgments.

Adelman, Maurice. *The Story of Ben-Gurion* (New York: G. P. Putnam's Sons, 1964).

Agress, Eliahu. *Golda Meir: Portrait of a Prime Minister* (New York: Sabra Books, 1969).

Aleichem, Sholem. *The Adventures of Menahem-Mendl* (New York: G. P. Putnam's Sons, 1969).

Antin, Mary. *From Plotzk to Boston* (Boston: W. B. Clarke Co., 1899).

Avishai, Bernard. *The Tragedy of Zionism: Revolution and Democracy in the Land of Israel* (New York: Farrar, Straus & Giroux, 1985).

Badt-Strauss, Bertha. *White Fire: The Life and Works of Jessie Sampter* (New York: Reconstructionist Press, 1956).

Bar-Zohar, Michael. *Ben-Gurion: The Armed Prophet* (Englewood Cliffs, N.J.: Prentice-Hall, 1968).

———. *Ben-Gurion: A Biography* (New York: Delacorte Press, 1979).

Baron, Salo W. *The Russian Jew Under Tsars and Soviets* (New York: Macmillan, 1976).

Baum, Charlotte, Paula Hyman, and Sonya Michel. *The Jewish Woman in America* (New York: Dial Press, 1976).

Ben-Gurion, David. *Israel, a Personal History* (New York: Funk and Wagnalls, 1971).

Benvenisti, Meron. *Conflicts and Contradictions* (New York: Villard Books, 1986).

Berkow, Ira. *Maxwell Street: Survival in a Bazaar* (Garden City, N.Y.: Doubleday & Company, 1977).

Bethell, Nicholas William. *The Palestine Triangle: The Struggle Between the British, the Jews and the Arabs 1935–48* (London: André Deutsch Ltd., 1979).

Blasi, Joseph Raphael. *The Communal Experience of the Kibbutz* (New Brunswick, N.J.: Transaction Books, 1986).

———. *The Communal Future: The Kibbutz and the Utopian Dilemma* (Norwood, Pa.: Norwood Editions, 1980).

Blum, Jakub, and Vera Rich. *The Image of the Jew in Soviet Literature: The Post-Stalin Period* (New York: Institute of Jewish Affairs/London: Ktav Publishing House, 1984).

Bowle, John. *Viscount Samuel: A Biography* (London: Victor Gollancz, Ltd., 1957).

Breck, Allen D. *The Centennial History of the Jews of Colorado 1859–1959* (Denver: Hirschfeld Press, 1960).

Bregstone, E. Philip. *Chicago and Its Jews: A Cultural History* (Chicago: Privately published, 1933).

Brownstone, David M., Irene M. Franck, and Douglass L. Brownstone. *Island of Hope, Island of Tears* (New York: Rawson Wade Publishers, 1979).

Burns, James MacGregor. *Roosevelt: The Soldier of Freedom, 1940–1945* (New York: Harcourt Brace Jovanovich, 1970).

Chafets, Ze'ev. *Heroes and Hustlers, Hard Hats and Holy Men* (New York: William Morrow, 1987).

Christman, Henry M. (ed.). *This Is Our Strength: Selected Papers of Golda Meir* (New York: Macmillan, 1962).

Cohen, Joseph J. *The House Stood Forlorn* (Paris: Imp. Les Éditions Polyglottes, 1954).

Cohen, Mitchell. *Zion and State: Nation, Class and the Shaping of Modern Israel* (Oxford and New York: Basil Blackwell, Ltd., 1987).

Collins, Larry, and Dominique Lapierre. *O Jerusalem!* (New York: Simon and Schuster, 1972).

Davitt, Michael. *Within the Pale* (Philadelphia: Jewish Publication Society of America, 1903).

Dawidowicz, Lucy. *The Jewish Presence* (San Diego: Harcourt Brace Jovanovich, 1978).

Dayan, Moshe. *Moshe Dayan: Story of My Life* (New York: William Morrow, 1976).

Dayan, Shmuel, and Yaël Dayan (eds.). *Pioneers in Israel* (Cleveland and New York: World, 1961).

Derogy, Jacques, and Hesi Carmel. *The Untold History of Israel* (New York: Grove Press, 1979).

Dubnow, Simon. *History of the Jews in Russia and Poland,* Vol. 3 (New York: Ktav Publishing House, 1975).

Eban, Abba. *Abba Eban: An Autobiography* (New York: Random House, 1977).

Eisenhower, Julie Nixon. *Special People* (New York: Simon and Schuster, 1977).

Elon, Amos. *The Israelis, Founders and Sons* (Tel Aviv: Adam Publishing Co., 1981).

Fallaci, Oriana. *Interview with History* (New York: Liveright & Co., 1976).

Fawcett, Millicent. *Easter in Palestine 1921–1922* (London: T. Fisher Unwin Ltd., 1926).

Flapan, Simha. *The Birth of Israel: Myths and Realities* (New York: Pantheon Books, 1987).

Frankfurter, Felix. *Felix Frankfurther Reminisces* (Garden City, N.Y.: Anchor Books, Doubleday & Company, 1962).

Garber-Talmon, Yonina. *Family and Community in the Kibbutz* (Cambridge: Harvard University Press, 1972).

Gilbert, Martin. *Exile and Return: The Struggle for a Jewish Homeland* (Philadelphia: J. B. Lippincott Company, 1978).

———. *Jerusalem: Illustrated History Atlas* (New York: Macmillan, 1977).

———. *Jewish History Atlas* (London: Weidenfeld & Nicolson, 1969).

———. *Russian History Atlas* (London: Weidenfeld & Nicolson, 1972).

———. *Sir Horace Rumbold: Portrait of a Diplomat, 1839–1941* (London: Heinemann, 1973).

Goell, Milton J. *Tramping Through Palestine: Impressions of an American Student in Israel-Land* (New York: Kensington Press, 1926).

Goitein, Solomon Dob. *Jews and Arabs: Their Contacts Through the Ages* (New York: Schocken Books, 1955).

Golan, Matti. *Shimon Peres: A Biography* (London: Weidenfeld & Nicolson, 1982).

Golden, Harry. *The Israelis: Portrait of a People* (New York: G. P. Putnam's Sons, 1971).

Goldstein, Israel. *My World as a Jew: The Memoirs of Israel Goldstein* (New York: Herzl Press, 1984).

Greenberg, Louis. *The Jews in Russia: The Struggle for Emancipation* (New York, Schocken Books, 1976).

Gunther, John. *Twelve Cities* (New York: Harper & Row, 1969).

Gvati, Haim. *A Hundred Years of Settlement: The Story of Jewish Settlement in the Land of Israel* (Jerusalem: Keter Publishing House, 1985).

Harkabi, Yehoshafat. *Palestinians & Israel* (New York: John Wiley & Sons, 1975).

Hasan, Sana. *Enemy in the Promised Land: An Egyptian Woman's Journey into Israel* (New York: Pantheon Books, 1986).

Hazleton, Lesley. *Israeli Women: The Reality Behind the Myth* (New York: Simon and Schuster, 1977).

———. *Jerusalem, Jerusalem* (Boston: Atlantic Monthly Press, 1986).

Holli, Melvin G., and Peter d'A. Jones. *Ethnic Chicago* (Grand Rapids, Mich.: William B. Eerdmans Publishing Company, 1984).

Horowitz, Dan, and Moshe Lissak. *Origins of the Israel Polity: Palestine Under the Mandate* (Chicago: University of Chicago Press, 1978).

Irwin, William. *Highlights of Manhattan* (New York and London: The Century Co., 1927).

Ish-Kishor, Sulamith. *Zalman Shazar: President of the People* (New York: Jewish National Youth and Education Dept. Fund, 1966).

Israel, Gerard. *The Jews in Russia* (New York: St. Martin's Press, 1975).

Johnson, Paul. *A History of the Jews* (London: Weidenfeld & Nicolson, 1987).

Jurman, Pinchas (ed.). *Moshe Dayan: A Portrait* (Tel Aviv: Massada, 1968).

Katzman, Jacob. *Commitment: The Labor Zionist Lifestyle in America: A Personal Memoir* (New York: Labor Zionist Letters, 1975).

Kollek, Teddy, with his son, Amos Kollek. *For Jerusalem: A Life* (Jerusalem/Tel Aviv/Haifa: Steimatzky's Agency, 1978).

Korngold, Shana. *Zichronot* (Memories) (Tel Aviv: Idpress, 1968), originally published in Yiddish and then translated into Hebrew. There is no official English translation.

Krimsky, Joseph. *Revisits and Revisions* (New York: Bloch Publishing Co., 1924).

Kurzman, Dan. *Ben-Gurion: Prophet of Fire* (New York: Simon and Schuster, 1983).

La Zebnik, Edith. *Such a Life* (New York: William Morrow, 1978).

Lash, Joseph P. *Eleanor: The Years Alone* (New York: W. W. Norton and Company, 1972).

Levitats, Isaac. *The Story of the Milwaukee Jewish Community* (Milwaukee: Bureau of Jewish Education, 1954).

Lieblich, Amia. *Kibbutz Makom* (New York: Pantheon Books, 1981).

Litvinoff, Barnet. *Weizmann: Last of the Patriarchs* (New York: G. P. Putnam's Sons, 1976).

Loeb, Sophie Irene. *Palestine Awake: The Rebirth of a Nation* (New York and London: The Century Co., 1926).

Lossin, Yigal. *Pillar of Fire* (Jerusalem: Shikmona Publishing Co., 1983).

Love, Kennett. *Suez: The Twice-Fought War: A History* (New York: McGraw-Hill, 1969).

Malkin, Carole. *The Journeys of David Toback: as Retold by his Granddaughter* (New York: Schocken Books, 1981).

Mann, Peggy. *Golda: The Life of Israel's Prime Minister* (New York: Coward-McCann, 1971).

Meir, Golda. *My Life* (New York: G. P. Putnam's Sons, 1975).

Meir, Menahem. *My Mother, Golda Meir: A Son's Evocation of Life with Golda Meir* (New York: Arbor House, 1983).

Meites, Hyman L. *The History of the Jews in Chicago* (Chicago: Jewish History Society of Illinois, 1924).

Miller, Merle. *Plain Speaking: An Oral Biography of Harry S. Truman* (New York: Berkley Publishing Company, 1974).

Netboy, Anthony E. *A Boy's Life in the Chicago Ghetto* (Jacksonville, Ore.: Privately printed, 1980).

O'Brien, Conor Cruise. *The Siege: The Saga of Israel and Zionism* (New York: Simon and Schuster, 1986).

Patai, Raphael. *The Seed of Abraham: Jews and Arabs in Contact and Conflict* (Salt Lake City: University of Utah Press, 1986).

Perlmutter, Amos. *Israel, the Partitioned State: A Political History Since 1900* (New York: Charles Scribner's Sons, 1985).

Pesotta, Rose. *Days of Our Lives* (Boston: Excelsior Publishers, 1958).

Peters, Joan. *From Time Immemorial: The Origins of the Arab-Jewish Conflict over Palestine* (New York: Harper & Row, 1984).

Prittie, Terence. *Eshkol, the Man and the Nation* (New York: Pitman Publishing, Inc., 1969).

Rabin, Yitzhak. *The Rabin Memoirs* (Boston: Little, Brown and Company, 1979).

Rabinowitsch, Wolf Zeev (ed.). *History of the Jews of Pinsk 1506–1941*, Vol. 1 (Tel Aviv: Haifa Association of the Jews of Pinsk in Israel, 1973); Yehoshua Gottlieb, "The Legend of Pinsk," pp. 110–12, abridged version of Hebrew text.

Rischin, Moses (ed.). *Grandma Never Lived in America: The New Journalism of Abraham Cahan* (Bloomington: Indiana University Press, 1985).

Roosevelt, Franklin D. *The Public Papers and Addresses of Franklin D. Roosevelt 1944–45* (New York: Harper & Brothers, 1950).

Rose, Norman. *Chaim Weizmann: A Biography* (London: Weidenfeld & Nicolson, 1987).

Roth, Cecil, and Geoffrey Wigoder (eds.). *Encyclopaedia Judaica,* 16 volumes (New York: Macmillan, 1971–72).

Sadat, Anwar L. *In Search of Identity: An Autobiography* (New York: Harper & Row, 1978).

Sadat, Camelia. *My Father and I* (New York: Macmillan, 1982).

Safran, Nadav. *Israel the Embattled Ally* (Cambridge, Mass.: Belknap Press, 1978).

St. John, Robert. *Eban* (Garden City, N.Y.: Doubleday & Company, 1972).

———. *Ben-Gurion: A Biography* (Garden City, N.Y.: Doubleday & Company, 1971).

Samuel, Rt. Hon. Herbert Viscount. *Memoirs* (London: Cresset Press, 1945).

Schiff, Ze'ev. *A History of the Israeli Army 1874 to the Present* (New York: Macmillan, 1985).

Segev, Tom. *1949 The First Israelis* (New York: Free Press; and London: Collier, 1986).

Segre, Dan Vittorio. *Memoirs of a Fortunate Jew: An Italian Story* (Bethesda, Md.: Adler & Adler, 1987).

Sharef, Zeev. *Three Days* (London: W. H. Allen and Co., 1962).

Shazar, Rachel Katznelson. *Plough Women: Records of the Pioneer Women of Palestine* (New York: Herzl Press in conjunction with Pioneer Women, 1975). Originally printed 1928, Council of Women Workers of Palestine.

Shazar, Zalman. *Morning Stars* (Philadelphia: Jewish Publication Society of America, 1967).

————. *Poems* (South Brunswick, N.J.: A. S. Barnes, 1974).

Shenker, Israel and Mary (eds.). *As Good as Golda: The Warmth and Wisdom of Israel's Prime Minister* (New York: McCall Publishing Co., 1970).

Sherwood, Robert E. *Roosevelt and Hopkins: An Intimate History* (New York: Harper & Brothers, 1948).

Shipler, David K. *Arab and Jew: Wounded Spirits in a Promised Land* (New York: Times Books, 1986).

Shulman, Abraham. *Coming Home to Zion: A Pictorial History of Pre-Israel Palestine* (Garden City, N.Y.: Doubleday & Company, 1979).

Silver, Eric. *Begin, the Haunted Prophet* (New York: Random House, 1984).

Slater, Leonard. *The Pledge* (New York: Simon and Schuster, 1970).

Slater, Robert. *Rabin of Israel: A Biography* (New York: Drake Publishers, 1978).

Spiro, Melford E. *Kibbutz: Venture into Utopia* (Cambridge: Harvard University Press, 1956).

Stern, Geraldine. *Israeli Women Speak Out* (Philadelphia: J. B. Lippincott Company, 1979).

Steven, Stewart. *The Spymasters of Israel* (New York: Macmillan, 1980).

Swichkow, Louis J. *Memoirs of a Milwaukee Labor Zionist* (Tel Aviv: Diaspora Research Institute, 1975).

Syrkin, Marie (ed.). *A Land of Our Own by Golda Meir* (New York: G. P. Putnam's Sons, 1973).

————. *Blessed Is the Match: The Story of the Jewish Resistance* (Philadelphia: The Jewish Publication Society of America, 1947).

————. *Golda Meir, Israel's Leader* (New York: G. P. Putnam's Sons, 1969).

————. *The State of the Jews* (Washington, D.C.: New Republic Books, 1980).

Tamir, Nachman. *Golda: Articles in Her Memory* (Tel Aviv: Am Oved, 1981).

Teveth, Shabtai. *Ben-Gurion: The Burning Ground, 1886–1948* (Boston: Houghton Mifflin Co., 1987).

————. *Moshe Dayan: The Soldier, the Man, the Legend* (Boston: Houghton Mifflin Co., 1973).

Tiger, Lionel, and Joseph Shepher. *Women in the Kibbutz* (New York: Harcourt Brace Jovanovich, 1975).

Truman, Harry S. *Memoirs: Years of Trial and Hope 1946–1952* Vol. 2 (Garden City, N.Y.: Doubleday & Company, 1956).

Tugwell, Rexford G. *To the Lesser Heights of Morningside: A Memoir* (Philadelphia: University of Pennsylvania Press, 1982).

Uchill, Ida Libert. *Pioneers, Peddlers and Tsadikim* (Denver: Sage Books, 1957).

Viorst, Milton. *Sands of Sorrow: Israel's Journey from Independence* (New York: Harper & Row, 1987).

Weingarten, Murray. *Life in a Kibbutz* (New York: Reconstructionist Press, 1955).

Weisgal, Meyer W., and Joel Carmichael. *Chaim Weizmann: A Biography* (New York: Atheneum Publishers, 1963).

Weizmann, Chaim (Barnet Litvinoff, ed.). *The Essential Chaim Weizmann: The Man, the Statesman, the Scientist* (New York: Holmes & Meier Publishers, 1982).

Weizmann, Vera. *The Impossible Takes Longer: The Memoirs of Vera Weizmann as Told to David Tutaev* (London: Hamish Hamilton, Ltd., 1967).

Wiberg, Ruth Eloise. *Rediscovering Northwest Denver* (Boulder, Colo.: Pruett Publishing Co., 1976).

Wiesel, Elie. *Dawn* (New York: Hill and Wang, 1961).

Wilson, Sir Harold. *The Chariot of Israel: Britain, America, and the State of Israel* (London: Weidenfeld & Nicolson, 1981).

Wolf, Leonard. *The Passion of Israel* (Boston: Little, Brown and Company, 1970).

Wright, Peter. *Spycatcher: The Candid Autobiography of a Senior Intelligence Officer* (New York: Viking, 1987).

Wyman, David S. *The Abandonment of the Jews: America and the Holocaust 1941–1945* (New York: Pantheon Books, 1984).

Acknowledgments

The richest resource for this biography was people, not paper. Golda's daughter, Sarah, was wonderfully cooperative with her time and memory, and so was her husband, Zecharia Rehabi. I am equally grateful to Golda's niece, Judy Bauman, whose recollections of Golda go back to Denver, Chicago, the early years in Palestine, the kibbutz at Merhavia. Her husband, Jack, had his own special stories, and I am thankful to both of them for making available their private family picture collection for my use. Their daughter, Alice Golembo, provided more pictures and more memories. Golda's nephew, Yona Kama, and his wife, Sarah, were similarly helpful, and so was Gideon Meir, Golda's grandson.

Of her small circle of closest friends, everyone helped. Regina Hamburger Medzini—who helped Golda run away from her Milwaukee home when she was fourteen, and who went with Golda to Palestine when they were both in their twenties—dug deep for me into her remarkable memory, made available her own unpublished memoir, gave me some of her select photographs. Marie Syrkin, Golda's most intimate friend who became her literary voice, and shared most of her private thoughts, gave me all the interview time I wanted, which was considerable, and provided me with a large amount of background material, articles, books, a look at some letters, photographs.

Lou Kaddar's help was invaluable. Lou was Golda's constant companion and associate. Nobody could have been more cooperative and she gave unstintingly of her time and her almost-photographic memory, made available a large file of letters, papers, articles, photographs, and other materials.

Rinna Samuel, the talented author of Golda's autobiography, not only told me much of what was not in her book, but alerted me to the long series of taped interviews with Golda—by herself as well as others—at the Lavon Institute for Labour Research in Tel Aviv. While Rinna Samuel had used much of it, there was much more that was fresh and most revealing. The Department of Golda Meir at Lavon Institute became a prime source of material for me, with an emphasis on Golda's work at the Histadrut. Lavon's director, Donna Bat 'Or, was completely cooperative, with Golda's daughter, Sarah, serving as a guide, interpreter, particularly with the large photo collection and the oral history.

No interviews could have been more important than the ones I had with Aharon Remez, son of David Remez, one of the two most important men in Golda's life. He made his father come completely alive to me and he gave me a view of Golda dating from his boyhood to the time he worked alongside Golda in vital international positions. The stories of Aharon Remez, and the keen perceptions of his wife, Betty, were invaluable. Even more so was the Remez-Golda correspondence they made available to me—the most revealing insight of a woman deeply in love.

Noted Israeli author and editor Nachman Tamir, who edited a memorial volume on Golda, and knew her well, told me many priceless stories, made available to me his collection of taped interviews, photographs, clippings, books. He not only suggested many contacts and helped arrange interviews, but even accompanied me as a translator with some key people. After I left Israel, Nachman did important follow-up research for me.

Some other interviewees who became dearest friends were Ariyeh and Miriam Gelblum. Much of what they told me will be more vital in a forthcoming volume, but Gelblum—who is surely one of Israel's most respected journalists and foreign correspondents—was a gold mine of suggested contacts. His insights were penetrating.

Another who became a warm, good friend was Nomi Zuckerman. Nomi's parents were among Golda's oldest friends. When Nomi was a young woman studying music, she lived with Golda and Morris at the time when their marriage was breaking up. Nomi's sensitive memories filled many gaps in my story, and she was so valuable in making contacts for me and arranging meetings.

The Harman family added more richness to my book. Avraham Harman and I knew each other as young men a long time ago, long before he became ambassador to the United States and now chancellor of Hebrew University. His wife, Zena, was a special protégée of Golda's, and she made her own reputation in the UN delegation and as a member of the Knesset. Their son David lived with Golda in Jerusalem for a long time while he was a student. All made important contributions.

The talented Sara Erez, who wrote a biography of David Remez, in Hebrew, helped make Remez come vividly alive to me. Shulamit Nardi, who worked so closely with Shazar for so many years, made him very vivid to me, too. And Eliezer Shmueli, Aranne's closest cohort for much of his working life, did the same for him. Yaacov Hazan, Golda's intimate friend, made me realize what their relationship must have been.

There were dozens of other people who helped fill out these portraits and these relationships. Golda had a small cluster of women who described themselves as "kitchen friends," women who shared tea and cookies and gossip and memories. They all added to the warmth of this book. Typical of them was Mosha Rabinowich, whose insights were among the most sensitive. Her son, Ben, now a prominent Histadrut official, also lived with Golda when he was a student, and his own recollections were most helpful.

Rivka Idelson's mother, Beba, was another *chavera* of Golda's, and the two reached the early rungs of power together, even lived together for a while. Beba branched out more into the feminist movement while Golda broke more into the man's world. Rivka's portrait of the two was clear and sharp. So was the picture painted by Judy Gottlieb, whose parents were also among Golda's earliest friends.

The bulk of my many interviews with Simcha Dinitz and Eli Mizrachi, who worked so closely with Golda for so long, concern my next volume of this biography, but much of what they told me also has bearing here. The same applies to Gershon Avner, Walter Eytan, Abba Eban, Chaim Herzog, Moshe Kol, Michael and Joan Comay, Mordechai Gazit, Amos Elon, David Breslau, Aharon Yariv, Esther Herlitz, Shlomo Hillel, Clinton Bailey, Dr. Yosef Burg, Zalman and Clara Chen, Leo and Sylvia Crown.

Beverly Mizrachi was marvelously helpful with memories, books, and contacts. She also did some follow-up research for me.

Michael Bar-Zohar, author of that excellent biography of Ben-Gurion, helped detail for me that relationship between Golda and Ben-Gurion. Robert Slater, who authored a pictorial biography of Golda, amplified some material not in his book. While Teddy Kollek wouldn't talk about Golda, he helped me in other ways.

More of those in Israel who helped much must be mentioned: Drora and Raanan Volcani, Yitzhak Eylam, Mrs. Bert Goldstein, Shulamit Aloni, Isser Harrel, Shmuel Toledano, Mike Arnon, Ariyeh Levavi, David and Aviva Passow, Esther Zackler, Yitzhak Navon, Batsheva Arianne, Yitzhak Ben-Aharon, Dr. Meron Medzini, Ariyeh Avner, Celia Stern, Faigel Berkenblitt, Dr. Yoram Beyth, Haim Gvati, Gad Jacoby, Dr. Israel Katz, Mimi Leightner, Marlin Levin, Dr. Arthur Levinson and Malka Rome, Nataniel Lorch, Shmuel Marachi, Yohanon Meroz, Uri Mertz, Yaacov Nitzan, Shoshana Pitelis, Prof. Eliezer Rachmilowitz, Berl Repetur, Shirley Shapira, Sonia Schelpark, Herbert Smith, Dr. Kalman Mann, Laky Kahn, Zmira Goodman, Haim Bar-Lev.

The historian at Merhavia kibbutz, Eliezer Reich, was most cooperative and produced all kinds of material and pictures. At the *Jerusalem Post*, Alexander Zvielli, director of the archive, and David Browner, in charge of photographs, were most generous in making everything available to us. Rebecca Hirsch, Sharon Meyer, and Rachel Yariv were similarly helpful at the office of the State of Israel Bonds in Jerusalem, as were Morris Dweck and Susan Morris at their New York office. We are grateful to Roger Dapiran for making available a taped speech by Golda. A personal note of thanks to Yossi Ofek and Geula Dagan for all their help.

Among the most important archives for this book, aside from Lavon Institute, were the State Archives of the Prime Minister's Office in Jerusalem and the Oral History Division of the Institute of Contemporary Jewry at the Hebrew University of Jerusalem. Lou Kaddar has been assembling the Golda Meir Archives at the State Archives, and Dr. Geoffrey Wigoder has been responsible for the Oral History Division. Both were most helpful on our project. At the State Archives, Dr. P. A. Alsberg and Gilad Livneh have been particularly helpful. Also important were Dr. Michael Heyman, Reuven Koffler, and the staff at the Central Zionist Archives, the helpful staff at the Israeli Government Press Office, and Uri Stern at the Center for Information on Russian Jewry.

For the American part of Golda's life, the research was more far-ranging:

In Milwaukee, Wisconsin, the most invaluable contributor was the remarkable Sadie Ottenstein with her prodigious memory of almost total recall. She amplified this with some valuable photographs and even more valuable suggestions and contacts. Special thanks to her grandson, David Ottenstein. Dorothy Weingrod, whose father, Isadore Tuchman, played such a key role in Golda's early career, provided insight into that relationship. Ruth Shapiro recalled stories from her days as Golda's student at the Folkshule and as her colleague at Milwaukee's public library. Hannah Glinker deserves special mention for her help, and so do Nathan Weinberg, Judith Kaplan, Rabbi Louis Swichkow, Dr. Lucy Glicklick, Mrs. Ateret Cohn, Eddie Magidson. Sara Leuchter, of the State Historical Society of Wisconsin, provided important tape recordings of many of Golda's friends, as well as key photographs and background material. Allan Kovan, archivist of the University of Wisconsin—Milwaukee, and his colleague, Stanley Mallach, made available other vital tapes and photos from their Golda Meir Library, and helped in many other ways. Very helpful was the staff of the *Wisconsin Jewish Chronicle*, Chuck Cooney of the Milwaukee County Historical Society, Robert Wills of the *Milwaukee Sentinel*, Richard Leonard of the *Milwaukee Journal*, and especially Jo Reitman of the News and Corporate Information Center of the *Milwaukee Journal-Sentinel*. My thanks, also, to Lois Simmons and Diane Smith of North Division High School and Roy Delarosa of Mayor Maier's office.

In Chicago, my special thanks to Joan Gold Lufrano, who contributed material for so many of my other books. Especially helpful, too, were Terry Fife of the Chicago Historical Society, Laura Linard and Cynthia Gordon of the Special Collections of the Chicago Public Library, archivist Dan Sharon of the Spertus College of Judaica Library, Nathan Kaplan, Sid Sorkin, Ben Sosewitz, Ann Barzel, Charles Bernstein, Faigel Unterman, Irving Cutler, John Anderson of the *Chicago Tribune*, and added thanks to Daniel and Clare Greenberg.

In Denver, my thanks, first of all, to John Livingston of the Rocky Mountain

Historical Society and his associate, Jeanne Abrahms. Polly Wilson Kemp, who has written extensively on Golda's Denver days for the *Denver Post*, was most generous in making available to us all of her notes and research. So did Ida Uchill, an author who has written considerably about the region. We are grateful to Lynn Taylor of the Western History Division of the Denver Public Library who gave us so much of her time, and to Dr. Beverly Chico, director of the Museum Outreach of the Mizel Museum of Judaica, for providing us with so much key background material. Roy Raney, historian and photographer of Denver's Jewish community and assistant director of communications at the National Jewish Hospital, was most helpful in re-creating the scene for us. Our thanks also to Bill Hosakawa, Chris Leppig of the *Inter-Mountain Jewish News*, Esther Cohen, Mike Zellinger. A special mention to Sarah Dubois, for all her help, and to Irene Morgan, for her vivid memories of Golda as a next-door neighbor.

In California, John and Harriett Weaver, as always, have been a steady source of information and support. Also helpful were Marilyn Hall, Paul Spindler, Ted Sandler, Len Slater, Sally Fleg, Aline Harris, Michael Litvak. Dr. Max Vorspan, vice president of the University of Judaism, and librarian Dr. Lou Shrub were also most helpful. A special note of thanks to Angela and Hunter Brashier and to Jack Smith, Tom Lutgen, and Marilyn Kelker of the *Los Angeles Times*.

In Washington, D.C., in addition to those already named, I would like to thank the staff at the National Archives, who were most helpful. Chana Weinberg gave me an insight into Golda and her son, Menachem—Chana's first husband—which I did not have. David Ginsburg had some most revealing moments in Golda's life after World War II. My dear friends Edgar and Phoebe Berman had some marvelous stories. Former Supreme Court Justice Arthur Goldberg told me of their early meetings in Chicago. Martin Peretz was most helpful and so was Robert Nathan. Max Kampelman, Joseph Sisco, Arnaud de Borchgrave, Eugene Rostow, Harold Saunders, Sheldon Cohen, Meir Rosenne, Philip Stoddard, Herman Edelsberg, Rabbi Stanley Rabinowitz, I. L. Kenen, Allen Lesser, Albert Lakeland, and Leonard Garment all gave important information for a later volume, but some of what they said had pertinence here, too. A personal note of thanks to Bob Levey for all his kind help.

In Boston, our gratitude, as always, to Dr. Howard Gottlieb, director of special collections at Boston University Library. Our thanks also to Victor Beach of the Special Collections Branch of Brandeis University, Michael Desmond for all his help at John Fitzgerald Kennedy Library. A more personal thanks to Dr. Herman and Doris Epstein, Dr. Leonard and Dorothy Gottlieb, Dr. Maurice Martin and Susan Miller Martin, Pearl and Lionel Bernier.

In Connecticut, a prime source was Aviva Cohen, not only for her own memories of Golda and her children, but particularly for her friendship with Golda's sister Clara. Aviva made Clara come alive. Also, Aviva's husband, Hanania, was a great help. Aviva gave me names of many others in Bridgeport who knew Clara and her family very well. One of them was Beatrice Berger, who gave us a marvelous taped interview she had done with Clara. Selma Rosenblatt, who worked closely with Clara, added much to this, and so did Dr. Abe Knepler. I appreciate the cooperation of David W. Palmquist, head of Historical Collections at the Bridgeport Public Library, the staff of the Westport Public Library, who found so many of my required books, and its research staff, including Stephen Armitage, who found answers to so many of my questions.

In New York, Dr. Jacob Katzman filled in much important information about Golda in New York in 1932, when he worked closely with her. Judy Sokoloff of Pioneer Women was invaluable as a source for contacts and archival material. Frume Mohrer, associate archivist at Yivo Institute for Jewish Research, and Dr. Lucjan Dobroszycki and his associate, Judith Helfand, were most helpful in our research of Pinsk photographs, but Dr. Mark Mirsky, who is writing a comprehensive work on the subject, was even more important. Additional thanks to Samuel Norich, Dina Abramowicz, Marek Web, Stanley Bergman, and Gloria Golan, all from Yivo. The staff of the Jewish Division of the New York Public Library—Nadine Werner, Alexander Gerwitz, Ruth Yarden, Judy Fixler —helped above and beyond the call of their duty. Andy Yale, archivist at the United Jewish Appeal, was very helpful. The one person in New York who seems to have more Jewish facts in her head, and at hand, than anyone I've met is Esther Togman, head of the Zionist Archives. Her willingness to help was outstanding, and her ability even more so. Also, her assistant, Judy Wallach, was most helpful. Esther Brumberg of The Museum of Jewish Heritage was important for our photography research.

Among important interviews in New York were those with Harry Beale, who traveled with Golda on many of her fund-raising tours and knew her intimately. Beale provided us also with background material and photographs. Julian Venezky, one of Golda's Three Musketeers, on her earliest American tours, enlightened us on that whole period. Another of the Musketeers, Sam Rothberg, whom I interviewed at length in Israel, helped me enormously with all kinds of suggestions, contacts, always adding his enthusiasm to mine. Rothberg was a man Golda trusted completely and he became, in effect, almost a godfather to her children. Rebecca Shulman was another of Golda's closest friends. Golda stayed at her home, a Connecticut country retreat, whenever she could. Ms. Shulman helped me a great deal. Our special thanks to Peggy Mann, who wrote her own book on Golda and made available to us all her notes and interviews.

My thanks to my dear friend Herbert Mitgang for all his advice and good counsel, his Israeli contacts, and the stream of books and articles he has sent me. My old friend Dr. Murray Krim, a noted psychologist, has given me his analyses of many of the relationships of my main characters. Another dear friend, Ruth Gruber, who has written extensively about Israel both as a prominent foreign correspondent and as an author, gave me the full benefit of her wisdom, memories, and her library.

Some more people who must be mentioned: Ed Plaut, Gordon Manning, Walter Bernstein, Alaine Krim, Fred Wasserman, Edie Frankel, Nava Schreiber,

Harry Louis Selden, Dr. Richard Eisenstein, James Eisenstein, Prof. Salo Baron at Columbia University, and Elias and Betty Kaplan.

A personal note of thanks to my dear friends Andrew A. Rooney, Ernest Leiser, and Jack Raymond, and to Jane Bradford. Olga Barbi again helped in some important research, and so did my dear daughter Elizabeth Martin. Meyer Steinglass enriched my perceptions of his former boss, Henry Montor. Judith Goodman Lautt, with whose family Golda and her children lived in Brooklyn, gave great details of that time. My thanks, too, to Sonia Lehr, Zelda Lemburger, and Walter Potaznick, O.D.

In Cairo, Carrie Rosefsky not only researched some important archival material, but also translated it. We are grateful to the staff of the al-Ahran Center for Strategic Studies in Cairo, as well as Gihed Auda, who was in charge of the Israel Research Section at the consulate there.

In London, I appreciate the help of Kenneth Harris, who did one of the best interviews with Golda for *The Observer* (London). He was so kind in opening *The Observer* files for me, and I am especially thankful to Jeffrey Care at *The Observer* Library. I am also grateful to Jane Estell of the BBC. My thanks also to Penina Stone for her research help, particularly at the Public Record Office and at the *Jewish Chronicle*. My special gratitude to Dr. S. Z. Levenberg of the Jewish Agency for his wealth of personal memories about Golda.

Most of the photographs used in this book are from private collections: Judy Bauman, Alice Golembo, Sadie Ottenstein, David Ottenstein, Judy Gottlieb, Aharon Remez, David and Aviva Passow, Regina Hamburger Medzini, and Sonia Schelpark. Others come from photo collections of the Central Zionist Archives in Jerusalem, the Yivo Institute for Jewish Research, the Milwaukee Public Museum, Israel Bonds, the Department of Golda Meir at the Lavon Institute for Labour Research in Tel Aviv, the Picture Collection of the New York Public Library, the Picture Collection of the Israeli Press Office in Jerusalem, and the Zionist Archives in New York.

Perhaps I've used the word "invaluable" too liberally in these acknowledgments, although many people were. But there is one person who was absolutely indispensable—my daughter Tina. She not only researched all the archival material in Milwaukee, Denver, Chicago, Los Angeles, Boston, and New York, but she also did all the interviewing there, and found those marvelous people who knew Golda and who are in this book. Tina also joined me in Israel, doing most of the archival research there and again joining me in the interviews. Her interviews were not only as good as mine, but sometimes better. The marvel was how well we worked together. She has a superb sense of pictures as well. And she not only organized all our vast material, but joined my wife, Marjorie, in the final editing, making vital and sensitive suggestions that have greatly enriched this book.

My wife, Marjorie, as always, is the first to read every draft of my work, and her editorial comment is always highly perceptive, tough, professional, and immensely rewarding. She is truly an excellent editor.

I am grateful to that noted historian Martin Gilbert, who read my manuscript so carefully and thoroughly and made superb suggestions. I am similarly grateful to Donny and Louise Spicehandler, who were part of the War of Independence in Israel, and who also read my manuscript, making their own valuable comments.

There has been considerable translation involved for this book. I am most grateful to Richard Kroll for his translations of material from Russian to English. Richard also lent us some important books from his library and provided some excellent background material. Doris Cramer and Robert Crawford translated material from French to English. Donny Spicehandler and Dorothea Shefer-Vanson translated some important articles from Hebrew.

Andrea Epter, Jackie Rudolph, and Yaron Benvenisti all did important research and translations. Jackie Rudolph had a particularly important translation and did it beautifully. They were all extremely helpful in following up on needed material after we left Israel. Jackie also arranged many of my appointments for me and found people I couldn't find. Benvenisti also researched the Hebrew files of David Ben-Gurion in Sde Boker.

My dear old friend Paul S. Green, who has helped me in so many ways on so many of my books, did so again. He interviewed many important people for me in Washington, D.C., sent me a continuous stream of articles and books and excellent suggestions, translated material from Yiddish, and arrived for the final proofreading of the page proofs. Other old friends, Ruth and Larry Hall, once again were also here for the proofreading—they always come from wherever they are. It has become a tradition of friendship. My daughter Elizabeth has joined us in this.

Aside from all the photographs in private collections, and those already mentioned from various archives, I am grateful to Shirley Green (who knows more about picture sources in Washington, D.C., than anyone) for helping search for some key pictures from the Library of Congress and the National Archives.

Our headquarters in Israel was the Mishkenot Sha'ananim in Jerusalem, the perfect place with the perfect staff and the perfect director. Director Karin Moses, with her complete awareness of the country, the people, and the history, made excellent suggestions and steered me between shoals.

This book, as all my books, would have been difficult without the great and constant help of my dear friend Mari Walker, who somehow manages to transcribe all my taped interviews—despite the great variety of almost indecipherable accents. She also converts all my scribbled notes into the cleanest typed copy. She is a marvel.

I must thank Hillel Black and Arlene Friedman, who were my early editorial supporters on this book, along with my agent, Sterling Lord. And my editor and publisher Robert Stewart, who made some excellent and important suggestions and has transmitted his excitement about it to everybody else. My thanks also to David Frost and Barbara Greenberg, who made the production seem so easy, Ruth Kolbert, Nancy Sugihara, and Heather Saunders, for their fine design contributions, and to my copy editors, Ann Bartunek, Sarajane Herman, and Lorraine V. Steurer, whose comments were highly professional.

There are many, many people I should mention with gratitude, but that would take another book. I hope they will forgive me. It takes thousands of pieces of mosaic to shape a biography, and it was my pleasure to put it together, but it would not have been possible without the minds and memories of hundreds of people.

Index

Abdullah ibn Hussein (king of
Transjordan), 290, 330, 332,
333–35, 336, 337, 342
Golda's secret visit to, 333–35
Adler, Victor, 171
al-Azm, Khaled, 331
Aleichem, Sholem, 5–6, 7
Allen, Mrs. (N.Y.C. teacher), 179
Altman, Dr. Ariah, 275
American Jewish Congress, 86–87
Anti-Semitism:
blood libel, 6
Dreyfus affair, 4–5
in Kiev, 3
Polish pogroms (1917), 67–68
in Russia, 6, 14–15
Russian Revolution and, 94–95
in World War I, 56–57
See also Nazi Germany
Aranne, Zalman, 227–30, 244, 256,
261, 271
biographical sketch of, 228–29

romance with Golda, 227–30
Avner, Gershon, 278

Balfour, Arthur James, 79, 80
Balfour Declaration (1917), 79, 112,
138, 219
Barash (Tel Aviv hotel owner), 108
Baratz, Yosef, 131
Baron, Salo, 177
Baskal, Abraham, 335
Begin, Menachem, 248, 272, 275, 330
on Deir Yassin massacre, 330
as leader of Irgun, 248
Beilinson, Moshe, 205–06
Golda's reaction to death of,
205–06
Ben-Gurion, David, 71–72, 110–11,
132, 138, 157, 160, 162, 169–71,
191, 200, 210, 212, 220, 221–22,
226, 227, 235, 246, 247, 248,
249, 250, 262, 263, 266, 267,
268, 270, 272–73, 278–79, 280,

Ben-Gurion, David *(cont.)*
 281–82, 283, 290, 293, 295, 296,
 299–302, 318, 320, 321, 324,
 330, 331, 332–33, 336, 339, 341
 arms for Jerusalem and, 299–302
 death of Berl Katznelson and, 246
 in England with Golda (1930),
 169–71
 "unhappy" decisions by, 331
 on working for homeland, 71
Ben-Gurion, Paula, 267
Ben-Zvi, Rachel, 107–08
Ben-Zvi, Yitzhak, 71, 107–08, 132,
 133, 157, 200
Berger, John, 98
Berkenblitt, Faigel, 143
Berlin, Irving, 11
Bevin, Ernest, 250, 259, 263, 265,
 266, 274, 279, 283, 285, 286–87,
 320
 Bevin commission (1945–46),
 258–61
 Black Saturday and, 265
 refusal to accept commission
 verdict, 263
Beyth, Hans, 296–97
 death in bus convoy, 296–97
Bialik, Chaim Nachman, 14, 181, 250
 poem on Kishinev pogrom, 14
Biarritz (Goedsche), 94n
Biskin, Leah, 186–87, 194, 196, 214,
 254
 friendship with Golda, 186–87
 moves in with Golda, 214
Black Hundreds, 15
Black Saturday (June 29, 1946),
 265–72
Blood libel, 6
Bloomgarden, Solomon, 68
 poem by, 68

Bluwstein, Rachel, 61n
Bols, Maj. Gen. Sir Louis J., 113
Born, Louise G., 65
Boyar, Lou, 308–09
Brandeis, Louis D., 63
 on Zionism, 63
Breslau, David, 188
 on impression of Golda, 188

Cahan, Abraham, 16, 205
Caruso, Pinchas, 90
Chemerow, Harry, 69
Chicago, Jewish population in, 77
Churchill, Randolph, 250
Churchill, Winston, 122, 236, 247,
 248–49, 258–59, 266, 273
 on bombing of King David Hotel,
 273
 on Jewish homeland, 236
 on Jewish terrorist groups, 248–49
Cohen, Benzion, 329
Cohen, Rachel, 339n
Committee of Thirteen, 300
Cranborne, Viscount, 236
Cunningham, Sir Alan, 253, 267,
 268–69, 274, 275, 276, 320, 338
 departure from Palestine, 338
 relationship with Golda, 276
Cyprus displaced persons camp,
 277–78

Dagan, Geula, 283–84
 news about British pullout,
 283–84
Danin, Ezra, 331, 333, 335
Dante, Alighieri, 82
Dashewski, Pinhas, 15
Daughters of the American
 Revolution (DAR), 195
Davar (*The Word*), 154, 159, 216,
 239

"Dawn" (Wiesel), 332
Dayan, Moshe, 216, 328
Degania Aleph (first kibbutz), 118
de Gaulle, Charles, 258
Deir Yassin massacre, 329–31
Denver, Jewish population in 1913, 42–43
Dialogue aux Enfers Entre Machiavelli et Montesquieu dans XIXème Siècle, Un, 94n
Disraeli, Benjamin, 108
Dreyfus, Capt. Alfred, 4
Dubinsky, David, 311
Dubinsky, Joe, 81
Dubinsky, Meyer, 81

Eban, Abba, 285
Eisenhower, Dwight D., 315–16
  interest in new state of Israel, 315–16
el-Husseini, Haj Amin-, 168, 209
Elath, Eliahu, 315–16
Ellis Island, 10
Eshkol, Levi, 271–72
Exodus Europe 1947, 285–87

Faisal (king of Greater Syria), 112
  on Zionists in Palestine, 112
Fallaci, Oriana, 288
Feder, Sarah, 39, 61
First Aliyah (1882–1903), 111
Fishman-Maimon, Rabbi, 340
"Flag Is Born, A" (Hecht), 287
Ford, Henry, 94
  anti-Semitism of, 94
Fourth Aliyah, 135
Frumkin, Heshel, 166–67

Galili, Israel, 336–37
Gelblum, Ariyah, 285

Ginsburg, David, 280, 287
  on Golda in 1947, 287
Goedsche, Herman, 94n
Goethe, Johann Wolfgang von, 282
  quoted, 282
Goodman, Benny, 78
Goodman, Fanny, 91, 179
Goodman, Jacob "Moshe," 91, 179
Goodman, Judith, 178, 179, 187, 192
Goodstein (family's choice for Golda's husband), 38
Golani, Yona, 296
Goldberg, Arthur, 78, 167, 237
Goldstein, Bertha "Bert," 161
Goldstein, Rabbi Israel, 161, 247, 311–12
Golomb, Eliyahu, 240–41, 261n
Gordon, A. D., 118
Green, Mike, 131
Green, Paul S., 285
Grossman, Capt. Noam, 328–29
Gurney, Henry, 276–77
Gusta (mistress of David Remez), 176, 202, 207

Hacohen, David, 228, 246
Hadari family, 109
Haganah, 234
Halifax, Lord, 263
Hamburger, Regina, 24, 26, 31, 34, 35, 37, 39–40, 46, 47, 51, 53, 55, 56, 57, 63, 66, 73, 75, 87, 89–90, 92, 93, 98, 99, 100, 101, 103, 109, 119, 139, 144, 163, 197, 320, 321
  relationship with Golda, 89
  on Shana Korngold, 47
Hamid, Jamil, 326
Hamlin, Isaac, 100
Harding, Warren G., 122
Hay, John, 14

Hazan, Yaacov, 256–57, 330
romance with Golda, 256–57
Hazanowitz, Mirka, 125–26
Heart, The (D'Amicis), 148
Hecht, Ben, 287
Heller, Sophie, 118
Herlitz, Esther, 333, 335
Herzl, Theodor, 4–5, 22, 45–46, 198,
339
the Dreyfus affair and, 4–5
Zionism and, 45–46
Herzog, Chaim, 295, 297
He-Yedid, 234n
Hillel, 72
Hirshberg, Rabbi Samuel, 63
on Zionism and American Jews, 63
Histadrut, 151–52
Hitler, Adolf, 208, 218, 220, 222, 251,
258
Ho Chi Minh, 278
Hopkins, Harry, 247
Hos, Dov, 240–41
Hussein (king of Jordan), 332
Husseini, Abdu Kader, 297

Ibn Saud (king of Saudi Arabia),
246–47, 342
on Jews in Palestine, 246–47
Idelson, Beba, 156, 198, 205
Idelson, Rivka, 156, 161, 163, 198,
204, 205, 228–29
International Conference on
Refugees, 217–18
Irgun (Irgun Zvai Leuni), 247–48, 253,
272–73, 274–76, 329–31, 332
bombing of King David Hotel by,
272–73
Deir Yassin massacre and, 329–31
Israel:
partition plan for, 250–51, 289–91
proclamation of statehood, 336–42

Jacobson, Eddie, 314–15
plea to Harry Truman by, 314–15
Jaffe, Harry, 325
Jerusalem, 137–38, 293–301, 319–28
besieged by Arabs (1947–48),
293–301, 319–28
history and description of, 137–38
Joly, Maurice, 94n
Joseph, Dov, 298, 320, 321, 325
Jaurès, Jean, 152

Kader, Rose, 87
Kaplan, Abe, 100
Kaplan, Diana, 100
Kaplan, Eliezer, 301, 305
Kastel, battle at, 324–25
Katzman, Jacob, 91, 181–82, 183
on Golda in New York (1930), 183
Katznelson, Berl, 132, 157, 159–60,
162, 177, 201, 210, 212, 226,
240, 245–46
death of, 245–46
influence upon Golda, 159–60
Kennedy, John F., 194
Kibbutzim, 118–19, 124–25
history of, 118–19
relationship between sexes on,
124–25
King David Hotel, bombing of,
272–73
Kishinev pogrom, 13–14
Kol, Moshe, 249
Korngold, Chaim (nephew), 97
Korngold, Judy (niece), 36, 41, 49,
97, 99, 107, 124, 129–30, 137,
139, 143, 148, 215, 299, 303
on Aunt Golda as "haven," 143
birth of, 36
kibbutz memories of, 129–30
Korngold, Sam (Shamai) (brother-in-
law), 12–14, 16, 30–31, 34, 35–

36, 38–39, 41, 44, 76–77, 96–97,
101, 137, 143, 169, 211–12, 241
arrival in Milwaukee, 30–31
marriage to Golda's sister Shana,
35–36
Korngold, Shana Mabovitch (sister),
3, 4, 8, 11–14, 15, 16, 17, 19, 21,
22, 23–24, 29–30, 31–32, 33, 34,
38–39, 41–48, 52, 57, 60, 76–77,
87, 95, 96–97, 100–01, 103, 108,
109–10, 114, 115, 119, 129, 137,
143, 164–65, 168–69, 190, 211–
12, 215, 245, 299, 302, 303, 312,
316–17
admiration as adult for Golda, 215
critical of Golda's neglect of
children, 164–65
decision to go to Palestine, 96–97
in Denver sanitarium for
tuberculosis, 31–32
influence upon Golda, 13, 30
joins revolutionary group in Kiev,
11–13
marriage to Sam Korngold, 12–13,
16
on parents and sisters, 29–30
relationship with Golda in Denver
house, 47–48
to U.S. to study nutrition, 168–69
Korngold, Yona (nephew), 159, 165,
169, 299
Kristallnacht, 219
Kuppat Holim, 203

Levashoff, General (governor of
Kiev), 3
Levi, Gershon, 181
on Shazar Rubashov, 181
Levin, Shmarya, 167n
Lichtenstein, Chia Weizmann, 12
Lirah, defined, 139n

Lohamei Herut Israel (Fighters for
the Freedom of Israel). *See*
Sternists
Lubetkin, Zivia, 238

MacDonald, Ramsay, 170
Mabovitch, Bluma (mother), 2–5, 8–
11, 12, 13, 14–18, 22–25, 26, 29,
30, 32, 37–39, 58–59, 61, 62,
81–82, 158–59, 215
family move to Kiev, 3–16
grocery store in Milwaukee, 23–25
opens Golda's letter from Morris
Meyerson, 58–59
in Palestine, 158–59
relationship with Golda, 24
Mabovitch, Morris (Moshe) (father),
2–5, 8–11, 15–16, 22, 23, 36–
37, 57, 58, 81, 158–59, 255
death of, 255
emigrates to America before
family, 9–11
family move to Kiev, 3–16
on the *goldena medina*, 9
in Milwaukee, 22, 36–37
in Palestine, 158–59
Mabovitch, Sarele (sister), 3
Mabovitch, Tzipka (grandmother), 2,
4, 5
"Mabowehz" name change, 23
Magidim, 167n
Manson family, 90, 93
Mapai party, 245, 246, 256
Mapam party and, 256
Marshall, George, 336
Meir, Golda:
accepts partition proposal, 250–
51, 289–91; admiration for Berl
Katznelson, 132, 159–60, 245–
46; in Alexandria, 104–05; on
America, 98; America's Great

Meir, Golda *(cont.)*
    Depression and, 183; appointed
    to Poale Zion Executive
    Committee, 64; Arab riots of
    1929, 168–69; Arab riots of
    1947–48, 293–301, 319–28;
    arrival in Tel Aviv (1921), 106,
    107–15; attitude toward Arabs,
    223, 327–28; bad health of,
    254–56, 332–33; Baruch
    Zuckerman and 92–93;
    becomes member of Vaad
    Hapoel (1934), 203; beginning
    of break from parents, 37–38;
    in Berlin (1928), 164; Bevin
    commission (1945–46) and,
    258–61; birth in Kiev, 4; birth of
    daughter, Sarah, 142; birth of
    son, Menachem, 140; Black
    Saturday (June 29, 1946) and,
    265–72; breakup of marriage,
    211–12; British refusal to help
    Jews immigrate to Palestine,
    217–19, 219–20, 236–37,
    249–50, 251–52, 258–63; British
    white paper on immigration
    (1939), 219–20; in Canada
    for Poale Zion, 84–85; as
    chain-smoker, 235, 255, 256; in
    Chicago for Poale Zion, 72–73,
    75–80; childhood protest of
    anti-Semitism, 35; Cyprus DP
    camp and, 277–78; daughter
    Sarah's kidney disease, 166,
    174–80; death of Berl
    Katznelson and, 245–46; death
    of father, 255; death of Moshe
    Beilinson and, 205–06; decides
    on kibbutz life in Palestine, 67,
    69, 78; decides to become a
    teacher, 37–39; decision-making
    and, 269; defends public life to
    sister Shana, 165; in Denver
    (1913–16), 41–53; deterioration
    of marriage, 133–34, 136,
    144–45, 163, 197, 198–99,
    211–12; differences with Morris
    Meyerson over Zionism, 63, 68,
    72; discussions with husband,
    Morris, on having children,
    130–31, divorce and, 163, 197;
    drawing of Dante and Beatrice
    and, 82; as "dynamic," 280–81;
    early courtship with Morris
    Meyerson, 48–53; early letters
    to Shana (1908), 32; early
    marriage relationship, 83–84,
    85–86; early memories of
    Milwaukee, 22; effect on
    Pioneer Women, 184–86;
    Eleanor Roosevelt and, 313;
    emigration to Palestine (1920–
    21), 88, 89–106; emotionalism
    of, 161, 191; enrolls at
    Milwaukee Normal School for
    Teachers, 65–67; escorts Mrs.
    Snowden on Palestine tour
    (1925), 132–33; *Exodus Europe
    1947* and, 285–87; failure to
    stop Arabs from leaving Haifa
    (1948), 327–28; family farewells
    before emigration to Palestine
    (1920), 95–97; fear in early
    childhood of, 6; feminism and,
    156–58, 231; first visit to
    England about Arab riots
    (1930), 169–71; first interest in
    Zionist ideas, 45; at first kibbutz
    convention (1922), 131–32; first
    "outdoor" speech for Poale
    Zion, 65; first visit to Wailing
    Wall, 113–14; first years in

Jerusalem, 137–41; Friday night Sabbath memory, 11; friendship with Leah Biskin, 186–87; friendship with Marie Syrkin, 193–95, 253–55; friendship with Masha Rabinovich, 230–31; fund-raising trip to United States (1948), 301–18; gossip about affairs of, 162–63, 207; guilt and, 83–84; Hebrew language and, 114–15, 131, 179, 203–04; high school graduation of, 64–65; at the Histadrut, 151–52, 156–73; hunger in early childhood, 5–6; hunger strike against British (1946), 261–63; International Conference of Refugees, lesson of, 217–18; joins Poale Zion, 59–65; journey from Kiev to America (1906), 15–19; kibbutz life ended by husband's malaria, 133–34; leaves parents' home for Denver, 38–40; leaves sister Shana's Denver house, 47–48; letter from Remez indicating jealousy of Shazar, 171–73; letter to Sam Korngold on Tel Aviv (1921), 110; life on Merhavia kibbutz, 118–34; Lithuanian Jews aboard *Pocahontas* and, 104; loneliness and, 48; loyalty and, 216–17; marriage to Morris Meyerson, 80–82; massive migration of Arabs and, 327–28, 331; migraine headaches of, 77, 166, 204, 254; Milwaukee neighborhood life, 27–29; missions abroad with Remez, 206–08; most dreaded childhood memory, 7–8; motherhood and, 148–51, 164–65, 187, 199–200, 225–26, 235, 288; in Naples, 102–03; in New York prior to Palestine journey, 89–95; in New York for treatment of daughter's kidney disease (1932), 176–80; at North Side High School (Denver), 44–45; number 2 bus convoy, Arab attacks upon, 295–97; organizes fund-raiser for schoolbooks at age eleven, 32–33; organizes march protesting Polish pogroms (1917), 67–68; Peel Commission (1937) and, 209–11; as Pioneer Women secretary in U.S., (1932–34) 176–77, 183–96; Poale Zion and AJC conventions in Philadelphia (1918), 86–87; in Ponta Delgada, 101–02; as private person, 226; preparation for emigration to Palestine, 97–99; promotions within Histadrut, 160–62, 203; proposal for *mifdeh* after Arab riots, 212–13; physical beauty of, 26, 66; relationship with Henry Montor, 306–12; relationship with mother, 24; return to Tel Aviv after kibbutz life (1924), 135–37; return to U.S. (1929), 167–69; return to Jerusalem after second kibbutz experience, 142–45; return to Merhavia kibbutz with two-year-old son, 141–42; return to parents' home from Denver (1916), 54, 55–73; reunited with Morris Meyerson in Milwaukee,

Meir, Golda *(cont.)*
  70–73; romance with David
  Remez, 136, 162–63, 200–03,
  207–08, 213–14, 225–27;
  romance with Shazar Rubashov,
  152–56, 163–64, 180–82, 197–
  98; romance with Yaacov Hazan,
  256–57; romance with Zalman
  Aranne, 227–30 244; as
  secretary of Moetzet Hapoalot,
  145, 151–52; secret visit to King
  Abdullah (1948), 333–35; on
  sex and affairs, 162–63; signs
  Declaration of Independence,
  337–38; singing and, 60, 66,
  101; Sir Alan Cunningham and,
  276; sister Shana's influence
  upon, 13, 30; speech at U.N.
  (1948), 307–08; as a speaker,
  33, 65–66, 87, 185–86, 193–94,
  303–05; statehood for Israel;
  proclamation of, 336–42;
  struggles as leading Jewish
  representative during British
  occupation, 222–24, 233–34,
  240–42; as student at Fourth
  Street Elementary School, 24–
  25, 37; on the S.S. *Pocahontas*
  (1921), 99–104; suffers mild
  heart attack, 332–33; on survival
  of the Jewish people, 298–99;
  teaches at Miss Kallen's school
  (Jerusalem), 144; teaches at
  Poale Zion Folkshule, 60; on
  terrorist groups, 253, 264, 275;
  text of speech at Chicago
  Athletic Club (1948), 303–05;
  traveling for Pioneer Women,
  188–93; travels to raise funds
  for Poale Zion newspaper, 83–
  85; trial of two Palestinian Jews

  for stealing British arms (1943),
  243–44; UNSCOP and, 289–91;
  as voracious reader, 56; Warsaw
  ghetto (1942) and, 237–39; on
  "working mothers," 150; works
  as librarian, 68–69; writing and,
  193; Zionist vision of self-
  reliance, 118
Merhavia kibbutz, 117, 118–34
Meyerson, Bertha (sister-in-law), 95
Meir, Gideon (grandson), 114
Meyerson, Menachem (son), 140,
  143, 147, 148–50, 165, 166,
  179–80, 183, 199–200, 206–07,
  211, 216, 225, 235, 254, 257–58,
  262, 271, 299, 302, 303, 338
birth of, 140
as child on N.Y. visit, 179–80
relationship with mother, 166,
  187, 199–200, 216, 225, 235
Meyerson, Morris (husband), 48–53,
  56, 58–59, 63, 65, 66, 70–73, 75,
  77, 80–82, 83, 84, 85–86, 87, 88,
  89–90, 92, 94, 99, 100, 102, 109,
  113, 114, 115, 117, 121–23,
  130–31, 133–34, 136, 137, 138,
  139, 140, 141, 142, 143, 144–45,
  147, 148, 153, 154–55, 163, 165,
  166, 171, 173, 177, 179, 190,
  196, 197, 198–99, 204, 211–12,
  214–15, 218–19
breakup of marriage, 211–12,
  218–19
debate with Golda over Zionist
  ideas, 63, 68, 72
deterioration of marriage, 133–34,
  136, 144–45, 163, 197, 198–99,
  211–12
early courtship of Golda, 48–53
early marriage relationship,
  83–84, 85–86

life following marriage breakup, 214–15, 218–19, 225

malaria ends kibbutz life, 133–34

marriage to Golda, 80–82

reaction to kibbutz life, 130–31

reunited with Golda in Milwaukee, 70–73

Meyerson, Rae (sister-in-law), 95

Meyerson, Sarah (daughter), 142, 148–50, 165, 166, 174–80, 183, 187, 198, 199–200, 207, 210, 212, 216, 220, 225–26, 235, 245, 258, 271, 287–88

birth of, 142

as kibbutz pioneer, 245

in New York recovering from kidney disease, 166, 174–80

relationship with mother, 166, 187, 199–200, 225–26, 235, 258

Meyerson, Sarah (sister-in-law), 49, 95

Milwaukee, 21–22, 26–29

immigration of Jews to, 21–22, 26–27

neighborhood life in, 27–29

Mindel (immigration official), 104

Montor, Henry, 300, 301–02, 306–12, 317

biographical sketch of, 306–07

relationship with Golda, 306–12

Morgenthau, Henry, 313

Morrison, Herbert, 259

Moyne, Lord, 248

Nachson project, 205, 324–25

buying of ships, 205

Israeli force to protect Jerusalem, 324–25

Naiditch, Golda (great-grandmother), 2, 3, 4

Naiditch, Menachem (grandfather), 2

Nardi, Shulamit, 161

Nazi Germany, 208–09, 217–18, 219, 220, 236

concentration camps, 236, 239–40, 250

invasion of Poland by, 220

Kristallnacht, 219

Nuremberg Laws, 208–09

Warsaw ghetto and, 237–39

Notrim, 234

Oblava, 6–7

Operation Broadside, 265

Oppenheimer, Franz, 119

Ottenstein, Aviva, 61

Ottenstein, Sadie, 55, 58, 61, 64, 66, 70, 71, 81, 83, 85, 88, 96

Pa'il, Meir, 329

Palmach, 234

Palmer, A. Mitchell, 94

Peel Commission (1937), 209–11

Perchonok, Louis, 66, 86

Pincus, David, 340

Pioneer Women, 132n, 176–77, 183–96

Golda's effect upon, 184–86

traveling and fund-raising by Golda for, 188–93

"Plan D," 328

Ploughwoman, The, 155, 207

Poale Zion, 59–65

"Pogrom," defined, 6

Ponta Delgada, 101–02

"Protocols of Zion," 94

Rabin, Yitzhak, 341

Rabinovich, Masha, 228, 230–31

friendship with Golda, 230–31

Rachel of Kinneret, 61–62, 118, 154

affair with Shazar Rubashov, 154

Golda's admiration for, 61–62

Ratcliffe, Sir John, 94n
Red Sunday, 15
Remez, Aharon, 201, 213–14, 224,
    251, 269–70, 323, 324
  as courier between father and
    Golda, 269–70
  on romance between father and
    Golda, 213–14
Remez, David, 132, 136, 145, 148,
    157, 160, 162–63, 171–73, 175–
    76, 190, 200–01, 202–03, 204–
    05, 207–08, 212, 213, 232, 241–
    42, 244, 255, 256, 261, 262, 266,
    269, 271, 281–82, 286, 288, 300,
    312–13, 323–26, 341
  biographical sketch of, 200–01
  as inspiration for Golda, 202–03
  during Jerusalem siege (1948),
    323–26
  letter indicating jealousy of
    Shazar, 171–73
  missions abroad with Golda,
    206–08
  pregnancy of mistress Gusta,
    175–76
  rekindling of romance with Golda,
    200–03
  romance with Golda, 136, 162–63,
    171–73, 200–03, 207–08,
    225–27
  rumors about affair with Golda,
    162–63, 207
Remez, Luba, 207
Repetur, Berl, 253
Rickover, Adm. Hyman, 78
Rilke, Rainer Maria, 237
Roosevelt, Eleanor, 249, 313
  relationship with Golda, 313
Roosevelt, Franklin D., 189, 217,
    246–47, 258, 313, 314
Rothberg, Sam, 308–09

Rubashov, Shneur Zalman "Shazar,"
    132, 152–56, 157, 160, 171, 176,
    177, 180–82, 190, 191–92, 194,
    195, 197–98, 202–03, 204, 207,
    212, 216, 261, 262, 271
  affair with Rachel of Kinneret, 154
  biographical sketch of, 152–53
  as influence on Golda, 181
  romance with Golda, 152–56,
    163–64, 180–82, 191–92,
    197–98
  visits Golda in New York (1930),
    180–82
  wife of, 155, 207
Rumbold, Sir Horace, 209–10

Sabelinsky, Louis, 36
Salk, Lee, 10
Samuel, Sir Herbert, 108, 112–13,
    119, 123
  on Palestine of 1914–22, 112–13
Sand, Nathan, 28
San Simon monastery, battle for, 322
Schamasaizer, Rabbi Tobias, 78
Scheinfeld, Rabbi Solomon, 81
Schreiber, Israel, 298
Senesh, Hannah, 237
Sereni, Enzio, 237
Sezon, 249, 253
Shcoenkerman, Boris, 27
Shamir, Yitzhak, 248
Shapiro, Ben, 72–73, 75–76, 87
  recruits Golda for Chicago Poale
    Zion, 72–73
Shapiro, Judy, 73, 75–76, 77, 79, 93,
    212
Shapiro, Raziel, 93, 212
Shapiro, Ruth, 68–69
Shapiro, Tehilah, 226
Sharett, Moshe, 170, 240, 266, 268,
    269, 282, 290, 314, 336, 340–41

Shaw, John, 276
Shazar, Rachel, 207
Shenkman, Malka, 192–93
Sherf, Zeev, 296
Shertok. *See* Moshe Sharett
Shragai, Shlomo Zalman, 323–24
Sigismund III (king of Poland), 3
Silver, Abba Hillel, 314
Simchoni, Yehudit, 207, 226
Singer, I. B., 86
  on Zionism, 86
Sneh, Moshe, 266
Snowden, Mrs. Philip, 132–33
  escorted by Golda on tour of
    Palestine, 132–33
Solel, Boneh, 136
Spencer, Albert, 288
  on Golda's competence, 288
Spicehandler, Abraham, 322
Spicehandler, David, 322, 328–29
Spicehandler, Ezra, 322
Spicehandler, Louise, 322–23
Spiegel, Arthur, 81
S.S. *Pocahontas*, 95
Stalin, Joseph, 246
Steinglass, Meyer, 192, 309
Stern, Avraham, 248
  verse by, 248
Stern, Clara (Tzipka) Mabovitch
    (sister), 8, 13, 17, 23, 25–26, 27,
    29–30, 32, 33, 38, 39, 57–59, 62,
    85, 95, 96, 148–49, 151, 168,
    180, 299, 312, 316–17
  on parents and sisters, 29–30
  relationship with Golda as adult,
    168
  renamed "Clara" in Milwaukee,
    25–26
  reunion with Golda (1948),
    302–03
  youthful resentment of Golda, 58

Stern, Fred (brother-in-law), 168,
    312
Stern, Robert, 298
Sternists, 248, 253, 274–76, 329–31
  Deir Yassin massacre and, 329–31
Sternman, Esther, 124
Stevenson, Adlai, 194
Strezin, Morris, 69
Struma, sinking of, 224
Sunshine, Max, 52
Syrkin, Marie, 85, 151, 193–94, 226,
    253–55, 267, 277–78
  friendship with Golda, 193–95,
    253–55
Syrkin, Nachman, 62, 193

Tel Aviv, 107–08, 115, 136–37
  in 1921, 107–08, 115
  in 1925, 136–37
Third Aliyah (1919–23), 111
Tropin, Ruth, 259
Truman, Harry S., 258, 313–16
  Eddie Jacobson and, 314–15
Tuchman, Isadore, 59–60, 65, 87
  influences Golda to join Poale Zion,
    59–60
Tuchman, Mrs. Isadore, 60, 70

Uncle Tom's Cabin (play), 35
Union of the Russian People, 14
United Nations Special Committee
    on Palestine (UNSCOP), 284,
    288–91
  Chaim Weizmann and, 288–89
  partition plan vote (Nov. 29,
    1947), 289–90

Vaad Hapoel, 203
Venezky, Julian, 308–09
Volcani, Dora, 149
Von Plehve (Russian police
    minister), 6

Wailing Wall, 113–14, 155, 321
Warsaw ghetto, 237–39
Weingrod, Dorothy, 81
Weizmann, Chaim, 79–80, 86, 112,
    170, 210, 219, 221, 235, 236,
    247, 249–50, 271–72, 279–80,
    288–89, 290, 314, 315, 331, 336
    disagreements with Golda on
        British, 271–72
    exchange with Balfour on
        homeland, 79–80
    proposals for nonviolence, 271–72
    UNSCOP and, 288–29
Weizmann, Moshe, 15
Wiesel, Elie, 332
Willems, Minnie, 46
Wingate, Orde, 234
Wise, Stephen, 210, 317
World War II, 220, 221–42, 243–58
    description of Palestine during,
        232–33
    See also Nazi Germany

Yadin, Yigael, 336
Yisraeli, Rivka, 297
Yosselevska, Rivka, 238–39
    horror story of Pinsk Jews and SS,
        238–39

Zackler, Esther, 76
Zalman, Schneur, 182
Zeit, Die, 85, 91, 92
Zionism, 4–5, 45
    history of, 4–5
Ziperstein, Dorothy, 190
Zola, Émile, 4
Zuckerman, Baruch, 73, 92–93
Zuckerman, Nina, 92
Zuckerman, Nomi, 92, 202, 211, 214,
    218–19
    on breakup of Meyerson marriage,
        211–12
    on Golda and Remez, 202